# MAUD GONNE

## Lucky Eyes and a High Heart

# MAUD GONNE

by
Nancy Cardozo

NEW AMSTERDAM
*New York*

First paperback edition published in 1990 by
NEW AMSTERDAM BOOKS
171 Madison Avenue
New York, NY 10010

*Library of Congress Cataloging-in-Publication Data*

Cardozo, Nancy.
Maud Gonne/Nancy Cardozo.
p.  cm.
Reprint. Originally published: Indianapolis : Bobbs - Merrill, ©1978.
Originally published under title: Lucky eyes and a high heart.
ISBN 0-941533-95-6 (alk. paper)
1. MacBride, Maud Gonne.
2. Revolutionists—Ireland—Biography.
3. Politicians—Ireland—Biography.
4. Feminists—Ireland—Biography.
I. Cardozo, Nancy.
II. Title.
[DA958.M25C37   1990]
941.5082'1'092—dc20
90-5977
CIP

*This book is printed on acid-free paper.*

Printed in the United States of America.

*For Nick and Jan*

# Acknowledgments

On the journey in quest of Maud Gonne MacBride, I received inestimable help along the way.

I wish to express my special gratitude to her son, Sean MacBride, and his late wife, Catalina MacBride, for gracious help and information and the use of documents and photographs. Thanks also are due to Anna MacBride White, Tiernan MacBride, Francis Stuart, Ian Stuart, and Imogene Stuart.

Senator Michael Yeats gave me generous access to the journals and works of his father, William Butler Yeats. Mrs. Michael Yeats and Anne Butler Yeats were hospitable and informative.

Laura and James Johnson Sweeney provided indispensable introductions to friends and contemporaries of Maud and Yeats. Patricia MacManus allowed the use of letters and manuscripts of her father, Seumas MacManus.

Bairbre MacDonagh Redmond and Liam Redmond were most kind in sharing memories of Maud's later years and introducing me to members of her circle. Lucile Redmond's devoted research in Ireland was invaluable. Simonne Gauthier Finnbogason secured important documentation in France.

Richard Ellmann, the incomparable biographer of Yeats

and Joyce, shared important insights. Victor Gollancz Ltd. allowed me the use of their files. Sir Isaiah Berlin, Tania Alexander, Maire Comerford, Sean Cronin, Arthur Davey, Norman Jeffares, F. S. L. Lyons, Patricia MacManus, Roger McHugh, Liam Miller, Michael Murphy, Nora Connolly O'Brien, Leon O Broin, Paul O'Dwyer, Niall O'Rahilly, Helen Roeloffs, Michael Scott, Mary Shore, P. L. Travers, Glenway Westcott, and Terence de Vere White contributed to my understanding of Maud and her Ireland.

Maeve Slavin was a knowledgeable guide and photographer in Ireland. Desmond Barrington photographed places. Finian Czira was helpful in making photographic reproductions. J. P. Brooke-Little, Richmond Herald of Arms, provided essential genealogical material.

I want to thank the New York Society Library for their kind cooperation. My thanks also to May Reis for dedicated research and secretarial assistance; to Molly Jordan for efficient, meticulous checking of quotations and sources, especially for the notes that begin on page 412; and to Ellen Moore for expert typing.

My loving gratitude to my friends and family, and in particular my husband, Russell Cowles, for their boundless enthusiasm and support. I am deeply appreciative of the generous help of John K. M. McCaffery and the scholarly advice of Eric Havelock and the late Matthew Josephson.

I am greatly indebted to the sensitive editing of Mary Heathcote, and to Anna Van and Gladys Moore.

The patient faith, encouragement, and guidance of my editor and publisher, Eugene Rachlis, sustained me in the writing of this book.

# Contents

*Illustrations follow pages 228*

She could have called over the rim of the world
Whatever woman's lover had hit her fancy,
And yet had been great-bodied and great-limbed,
Fashioned to be the mother of strong children;
And she'd had lucky eyes and a high heart,
And wisdom that caught fire like the dried flax,
At need, and made her beautiful and fierce,
Sudden and laughing.

—W. B. Yeats, 1903

# CHAPTER ONE

# An Overpowering Tumult

In January 1889 Maud Gonne was in London on her way from France to Ireland. At twenty-two she had already seen much of Europe, and her unconventional opinions had created a stir in government circles from Dublin to St. Petersburg. Her beauty and charm claimed many admirers. Heavy red-gold hair and large dark eyes set off her luminous complexion. Nearly six feet tall, she carried her height with graceful pride. Confident, vital, dedicated to a single purpose—Ireland's freedom from English rule—Maud Gonne was an irresistible force. In a society where women faced many obstacles in public life, she was beginning to make a place for herself in the nationalist movement.

Maud's reputation for glamorous patriotism preceded her when she went to call on John Butler Yeats, the well-known Irish portrait painter who was living with his wife and children in a London suburb. His son, William Butler Yeats, wrote of her visit: "I was twenty-three years old when the troubling of my life began. I had heard from time to time . . . of a beautiful girl who had left the society of the Viceregal Court for Dublin nationalism. In after years I persuaded myself that I felt premonitory excitement at the first reading of her name. Presently she drove up to our house in Bedford Park with an introduction from John O'Leary to my father."

Maud knew O'Leary, the great Fenian leader, from the Contemporary Club in Dublin. Influenced by his obsession with Irish literature, she had read the first small book of poems by W. B. Yeats, O'Leary's "most hopeful recruit." Now as she stepped out of her hansom cab in front of Number 3 Blenheim Road, she found herself in a neighborhood unlike the proper enclaves in which she had stayed as a girl with her upper-class London relatives. Bedford Park, a cluster of brick villas west of Hammersmith, had been designed by Norman Shaw in 1870 for pre-Raphaelite artists. Now, after twenty years, their ornate peacock-blue and gold rooms had faded and had been refurbished in the style of William Morris, with hand-hewn trestle tables, drab earth colors, and leafy patterns on the walls. Nearby, at Brook Green Lodgings, Yeats's friend the actress Florence Farr Emery lived among her Egyptian wall hangings in the casually exotic style of the artistic community.

Maud was acquainted with princes and rebels, generals and conspirators, and with the intellectuals of Continental salons. In Dublin she moved among Home Rulers, separatists, and Trinity students. Bedford Park was her first introduction to London's bohemia. As a friend of J. B. Yeats described it, "Many artists, writers and teachers lived there; few of them were well off and some were poor; but there was no lack of good-looking children, perhaps imprudently begotten, to be seen about the roads. There was a talking society called the 'Calumet,' much favored by Yeats . . . where all things were discussed in a free spirit. His own house was a great rallying-point—a transplanted slip of Old Ireland."

Except for Mrs. Yeats, who had recently suffered a stroke, all the family were gathered in the sitting room to greet Maud: the painter and his children, Willie; Susan Mary, known as Lily; Elizabeth, called Lolly; and sixteen-year-old Jack. The youthful Yeatses, who were enduring London for the sake of their father's work, welcomed her as a compatriot. Homesick for the hills of Sligo and Dublin talk, Willie was ready to see in O'Leary's messenger the embodiment of the country of his birth. Longing for one perfect love, an ideal instilled by the Romantic poets, he was pierced by Maud's beauty. She brought with her "a sound as of a Burmese gong, an overpowering tumult that had yet many pleasant second-ary notes."

Passionate minds have a calendar of their own. What Yeats remembered as a moment of exaltation had less signifi-cance for Maud. She always insisted that their first meeting occurred several years earlier, in Rathmines, outside Dublin, where O'Leary lived with his sister Ellen. "The room was filled with book-cases, carefully arranged and dusted. . . . After tea, Mr. O'Leary selected a number of books, chiefly Young Ireland literature, which Willie Yeats helped me to carry home." It was only natural that she should place her earliest recollection of Ireland's greatest poet in the presence of one of its greatest heroes: "A tall, lanky boy with deep-set dark eyes behind glasses, over which a lock of dark hair was constantly falling, to be pushed back impatiently by long sensitive fingers, often stained with paint—dressed in shabby clothes that none noticed (except himself, as he confessed long after)—a tall girl with masses of gold-brown hair and a beauty which made her Paris clothes equally unnoticeable, sat figura-tively and sometimes literally at the feet of a thin elderly man, with eagle eyes, whose unbroken will had turned the outrage of long convict imprisonment into immense dignity. He never spoke of that imprisonment. . . . John O'Leary, the master, and his two favorite disciples, William Butler Yeats and Maud Gonne."

There is no doubt, however, that on January 30, 1889, Maud entered the Yeats parlor with its Adam mantelpiece and a window that framed a leafless horse chestnut tree. The poet's younger sister, Lolly, wrote in her diary, "Miss Gonne, the Dublin beauty (who is marching on to glory over the hearts of the Dublin youths), called today on Willie, of course, but also apparently on Papa. She is immensely tall and very stylish and well dressed in a careless way. She came in a hansom cab all the way from Belgravia and kept the hansom waiting while she was here. Lily noticed that she was in her slippers. She has a rich complexion and hazel eyes and is, I think, decidedly handsome. I could not see her well as her face was turned from me . . ."

The young Yeats on whom Maud centered her attention could not stop gazing at her. "I had never thought to see in a living woman so great beauty. It belonged to famous pictures, to poetry, to some legendary past. A complexion like the blossom of apples, and yet face and body had the beauty of lineaments which Blake calls the highest beauty because it changes least from youth to age, and a stature so great that she seemed of a divine race."

Willie's brother and his two sisters looked up at Maud as if she were indeed a visitor from some other world. William Morris's wife and daughter, who gave them lessons in French and taught the girls embroidery, trailed about in flowing gowns like medieval princesses and were considered the height of feminine beauty. Maud Gonne's beauty was of another kind, a different femininity. The latest Paris fashion, elegantly fitted, showed off her small waist, and the oversight of her slippers did not keep her from looking regal. Her voice, seductive yet imperious too, had a note of the stage, a foreign intonation. Yet there was something warm and appealing about this outspoken young woman. The younger Yeatses listened in polite silence to her conversation. In a household noted for good talk, they had not heard its like before.

Her mind was alive with Irish problems—political prisoners, her work with the Land League, the forged Parnell letters, Gladstone's reform bills, and Home Rule. Willie Yeats, like both his mentor O'Leary and his high-minded father, distrusted agrarian agitation and political "transactions," but he was too shy to argue with her. Overwhelmed, he scarcely followed what she said, except when she praised war—which vexed his father—and told him that she loved his poems. She too was interested in mysticism and myth, and his musical nostalgia for the far away and long ago matched her own romantic yearning.

Younger than the poet, Maud had a much wider experience of the world and the self-confidence of an independent woman. His own "lack of self-possession and easy courtesy" plagued Yeats. Too well fathered by the domineering portrait painter, he was uncertain where his loyalties lay and suffered from the incurable provincialism of a writer whose country was not yet born. Only in the world of his imagination was he truly at home. His formal education had ended when he left high school to study art, and learning was now an endless pursuit. Mythologies fed his hungry mind. Blake had shown the way, and in London, drawn to the new religious cults and mystical orders influenced by Eastern religions, he came under the influence of Madame Blavatsky, the Theosophist, and the cabalist magician MacGregor Mathers.

Maud had no real schooling. She respected intellectual achievement and discipline and was eager to learn, but lack of scholarship did not diminish her self-regard. Exposed at an early age to a society that worshiped appearances, she was pleasantly familiar with her public image and had a gift for costume and gesture which served her well. Intuition and compassion directed her in public life. Impulsive, willful, with the blind faith of a visionary, she believed in destiny—Ireland's and her own.

By the time Yeats fell in love with her, Maud had taken on the form of the woman she was to become. Although accustomed to adulation, she was by no means impervious to his feeling for her. It differed from the infatuation of other more importunate and perhaps more virile suitors; his sensibility, poetic and intense, gave her a deep sense of herself. She invited him to dine, and the next evening Yeats called at her rooms in Ebury Street.

On February 1, Yeats was praising Maud to John O'Leary: "I dined with her . . . last night. She is not only very handsome but very clever, though her politics in European matters be a little sensational—she was fully persuaded that Bismarck had poisoned or got murdered the Austrian King or prince or what was it? who died the other day. It was pleasant, however, to hear her attacking a young military man from India who was there, on English rule in India. She is very Irish, a kind of 'Diana of the Crossways.' Her pet monkey was making, much of the time, little melancholy cries on the hearthrug—the monkeys are degenerate men, not man's ancestors; hence their sadness and look of boredom and old age—there were also two young pigeons in a cage, whom I mistook for sparrows—it was you, was it not, who converted Miss Gonne to her Irish opinions? She herself will make many converts."

Willie's evening with Maud was the first of many amiable interludes between her life in Ireland and in France. Her sister, Kathleen—beautiful too, but in a gentler way—and her lively cousin May Gonne were sometimes with them. More often, scorning convention, she had only her caged birds and monkeys to chaperone their innocent tête-à-têtes. Dense winter darkened the city outside; but, enclosed in the warmth of her room, they made their own country, imagining the caged birds were birds of spring; a vase of flowers in the firelight became blossoming apple trees. Beloved books lay close at hand: Victor Hugo, Swinburne, a copy of *The Wanderings of Oisin*, a draft of Yeats's latest poem:

> Come and dream of kings and kingdoms,
> Cooking chestnuts on the bars;
> Round us the white roads are endless,
> Mournful under mournful stars.
>
> Whisper or we too may sadden—
> Round us herds of shadows steal;
> Care not if beyond the shadows
> Passes Fortune's flying wheel.

At ease with her new friend, Maud found herself confiding in him: the painful loss of mother and father, the sorrows and joys of childhood in Ireland and England, her travels on the Continent, reckless escapades on "Fortune's flying wheel." But there were aspects of her current life which she could not share with him.

They had grown up in such different circumstances: Maud in high society and army circles, Yeats in a struggling artist's household. Ireland was the one strong bond between them, and their love of the land and the people went back to their childhood. Both had lived at one time on Howth, and their happiest memories were of that rugged promontory north of Dublin Bay where sea and sky met wind-swept moors of gorse and heather.

In 1872, when Maud was five, she had played with the cottagers' barefoot children on the cliffs and waded in the tide pools where eight years later Willie, who at fourteen had just read Darwin, knelt to study the colors of sea anemones. She knew the very cave, named for MacCrom, an evicted tenant who had once taken shelter there, which became Willie's secret hideout. The folk tales of the people who lived close to earth and sea had been embodied in their childhood games.

Since that time Ireland's troubled history, the trials of rebels and outcasts, the famines and the evictions had become a reality to Maud. A favored daughter of a British colonel, she had abandoned the butterfly life of garrison and castle to devote herself to helping the victims of cruel and despotic oppression. Even as a child she had compared the impoverished lives of her playmates at Howth with her own well-fed comfort. Later, riding with her father in County Kildare, Maud saw evictions for the first time. Families huddled in front of their roofless hovels while the landlord's agents made off with their few miserable possessions. She had seen grown-ups weep before, at her mother's deathbed, and now the sight of weeping people driven from their homes awoke anguished memories in the vulnerable little girl. "When I grow up," she vowed, "I'm going to change all that."

After her debut, dressed by Worth and splendid in her mother's pearls, Maud spent weekends in the great country houses that ruled Ireland. She saw landlord and tenant engaged in an age-old conflict, bitter and violent. The contrasts that had perplexed her as a child were no longer incomprehensible. The sides were clearly drawn between the rich and powerful, the destitute and weak.

Nationalist movements were worldwide in the late nineteenth century. In Great Britain and on the Continent patriots and liberationists were resurrecting the myths of their ancient forebears. When Maud and Willie sat by the fire, talking of their dreams of Ireland past and Ireland present, the legends that had thrilled them when they were children took on new significance. Maud remembered the round island floating just beyond Howth Harbor—"Ireland's Eye," once the Innisfallen of Oisin the Wanderer. Like Willie, she had once climbed over the great stone hidden among the rhododendrons of Howth Castle, the cromlech where Diarmuid and Grania, the legendary lovers, rested on their flight from Finn MacCool, the High King. Druidic gods and goddesses, Bronze Age warriors, Cuchulain and Queen Maeve—their traces were everywhere, in stones and cairns and half-remembered stories.

Yeats's ambition, he told Maud, was to recreate the myths in his poetry and to make Ireland one with its Celtic heritage. Great art must spring, as O'Leary preached, from the roots of a nation's culture. No revolution could succeed unless backed by a cultural revival, and Ireland's distinct and venerable tradition was in itself a reason for political separation from England. The youthful disciple had learned his lesson well. "From O'Leary's conversation," Yeats wrote, "and from the books he lent or gave me has come all I have set my hand to since."

When Maud insisted again and again that Ireland must be freed, by physical force if necessary, she was repeating an old Fenian refrain, but when she assured Yeats that his poetry would serve the Irish cause, she seduced his indolent brooding genius out of its shell of dreams. Having been involved in nationalist organizations in Dublin some time before Maud's arrival on the scene, the poet had made the gestures expected of a Young Irelander, but he had never seen himself as an active participant. Now, with her fervor, Maud set ablaze the spark O'Leary had lit.

She told Yeats she would like to act in a play suitable for Dublin audiences, and he offered to write one for her based on a folk tale about the Countess Cathleen O'Shea, who sold her soul to the devil for the sake of her peasants.

"When I told her I wished to become an Irish Victor Hugo, was I wholly sincere?—for though a volume of bad verse translations from Hugo had been my companion at school, I had begun to simplify myself with great toil. I had seen upon her table *Tristram of Lyonesse* and *Les Contemplations,* and besides it was natural to commend myself by claiming a very public talent, for her beauty as I saw it in those days seemed incompatible with private, intimate life. . . . We were seeking different things: she, some memorable action for her final consecration of her youth, and I after all but to discover and communicate a state of being."

"It was years," Yeats admitted in his autobiography, "before I could see into the mind that lay hidden under so much beauty and so much energy." If he ever did—for although he understood her nature better than anyone else, ambiguities of his own distorted her image in his mind and in his poems.

Maud Gonne led a separate life which he could not enter. Perhaps she revealed as much of her real self to him during those evenings by the fire in London as she did later when she confessed her secrets and their friendship was clouded by the ironies of history. "I felt in the presence of a great generosity and courage, and of a mind without peace . . ."

When he left her after dinner, Willie, who had no shillings for cab fare, walked all the way home from Belgravia. Maud's ardent spirits warmed him, so that he did not feel the damp or the grim danger of the greasy tenement rows. Her strange golden eyes and her "red lips, with all their mournful pride," stayed with him. "I was in love but had not spoken of love, and never meant to speak, and as the months passed I grew master of myself again. 'What wife could she make,' I thought; 'what share could she have in the life of a student?' "

Only an insatiable romantic would have even dreamed of such a marriage. Still a virgin, shy of sex though not of women, Yeats sought the ideal in life as in art, and continued to long for Maud Gonne partly because she was unattainable. She gave no indication that she was in love with another, but she made it quite clear to the poet that she was not in love with him. To forestall inevitable rejection, he attempted to belittle his overpowering involvement in a letter to a young woman writer in Dublin:

> Dear Miss Tynan . . . Who told you that I am "taken up with Miss Gonne"? I think she is very good-looking, and that is all I think about her. What you say of her fondness for sensation is probably true. I sympathise with her love of the national idea rather than any secondary land movement, but care not much for the kind of Red Indian feathers in which she has trapped out that idea. . . . I must wind up this letter presently and get to work on the "Countess O'Shea" that my mind may be full of it when I go for my walk an hour hence. It is a wild windy night, the sky full of ravelled clouds and [?] greeny blue—the sort of night that stimulates thought, and I must out.

The play for Maud was many years in the writing, but Yeats's notebooks were soon filled with poems that expressed his feeling for her, intense and melancholy, imbued with the particular tenderness that drew her affection even while she laughed at his concern for her safety.

> A pity beyond all telling
> Is hid in the heart of love:
> The folk who are buying and selling,
> The clouds on their journey above,
> The cold wet winds ever blowing,
> And the shadowy hazel grove
> Where mouse-grey waters are flowing,
> Threaten the head that I love.

On the brink of violent events, agitating on behalf of the tenants, reporting the conditions of Irish political prisoners, Maud had little time for herself. The hours she gave to Willie had a special meaning. Other women too, particularly the red-haired Katherine Tynan, found "his dark face, its vivid colouring, the night-black hair" appealing. The unruly lock that fell across his brow gave him a waiflike look. (Oscar Wilde, thinking him a penniless stray, once invited him for Christmas dinner with his family.) The young writer's Byronic pose, his flowing tie and short beard did not conceal his immaturity. But much as Maud enjoyed her power over him, they met as equals, quarreled sometimes and made up again, and one visit led easily to the next. "I saw her always when she passed to and fro between Dublin and Paris," Yeats wrote, "surrounded, no matter how rapid her journey and how brief her stay at either end of it, by cages full of birds, canaries, finches of all kinds, dogs, a parrot, and once a full-grown hawk from Donegal. Once when I saw her to her railway carriage I noticed how the cages obstructed wraps and cushions and wondered what her fellow-travellers would say but the carriage remained empty."

When Maud said goodbye to Willie under the great steel arches of Victoria Station, other travelers turned to stare at the striking young couple. Her slender height, the swinging beaver cloak, the glinting hair swathed in the veil she wore on her journeys, commanded attention. A theatrical presence, a little larger than life, made her beauty outrageous and anachronistic, as if a classic statue come alive moved through the confusion of passengers, the din of iron locomotives and steam.

Maud, unlike Yeats, did not suffer at their partings. It was always sad to say goodbye, but she looked forward to whatever might lie in wait at the journey's end. Alone in her compartment, she would lean back on the green plush, lift her veil and light a cigarette. Once again she was on her way: to Dublin, where she was finding her life's work; to Paris, the city of her secret life. The boat train rushing through the fog was carrying her into the unknown future which becomes the past. Irish rebel and Boulangist conspirator, Maud Gonne had traveled far from the country and the Victorian family into which she had been born.

# CHAPTER TWO

# The Air
# of Freedom

On December 21, 1866, Edith Cook Gonne gave birth to her first child in Surrey, England, near Aldershot, where her husband, Captain Thomas Gonne, was stationed with the Seventeenth Lancers. The baby was baptized Edith Maud at the village church in Tongham. Shortly afterward Captain Gonne was transferred to the Curragh, England's largest military base in Ireland, and his family followed him across the Irish Sea early in 1867.

Maud liked to say that she was two months old before she breathed the air of freedom. Her earliest recollections were set in a spacious house with formal gardens on the outskirts of Dublin—the Gonnes' first residence in Ireland. She rarely indulged in nostalgia except about Ireland, and a sensitive and fertile imagination kept her memories alive.

She walks beside her tall father through white plumes that swirl like smoke from a genie's lamp before her eyes, a little girl in her first snowfall. Snow, rare in Dublin even when it glazes the distant mountains, has added hardship to an unusually bitter winter, plaguing the ill-equipped Fenians in hiding on frozen hillsides and the British soldiers drilling in the Curragh. The snow is a magician's scarf, transforming the familiar shrubbery and brick walls of the garden in Donnybrook into vistas of fairyland. Wrapped in her big red Connemara cloak, Maud explores the wintry world with her father. She calls him Tommy rather than Papa, and all the excitement of her childhood is associated with him, this ruddy-faced officer with his straight military bearing. While her own footprints hardly break the frozen crust on the path, his heavy cavalry boots sink down to the spurs. Maud finds a broken holly branch with crystal jewels in its glossy green and runs back into the house with her treasure. Her mother, thinking it a gift, takes it from her hand. The little girl, unaware of her ability to hurt, snatches it away. "It isn't for you. Tommy says it will melt at the fire. I want to see." She was never able to forget the wounded look in her mother's eyes. Momentous or trivial, childhood experiences reiterated in the imagination formed a pattern, emerged as verities.

The larger pattern surrounding the child in Dublin in 1867 was the Fenian disturbances. Captain Thomas Gonne's transfer to Ireland was due to a massive garrisoning of the colony to prevent a new rebellion. Fenian had long been a dreaded word to the rulers of the depressed island, and once again Dublin Castle, seat of the British colonial government, was demanding increased armed protection. Besieged by angry tenants, landlords were fleeing their estates to the safety of their London houses, leaving their agents to deal with the marauders and the starving peasants; Anglo-Irish gentry were shipping their jewels and plate back to the Bank of England. The rebel leaders met in secret; their small bands of followers were on the move, and under cover of darkness and conspiracy armed men prowled the countryside.

> . . . Pay them back woe for woe,
> Give them back blow for blow.
> Out and make way for the brave Fenian men.

Since the early sixteenth century, Irish history had been a continual struggle against English domination, a series of aborted conspiracies, rebellions, and agitations crushed by the colonial rulers. In 1798 a rising inspired by the French Revolution and led by Wolfe Tone was put down by the English and was followed by the Act of Union which abolished the Irish Parliament. In 1848, when another revolutionary tide swept Europe, the Young Ireland insurrectionists were quickly defeated. Ten years later, inevitably, the movement for an independent Ireland rose again. In 1858 a secret revolutionary society organized by Irish exiles in France and America, under the leadership of the Young Irelander James Stephens, became known as the Irish Republican Brotherhood. In the British Isles and in America its members were called Fenians, after the legendary Finn MacCool and his legions, the Fianna.

Irish-American societies in the United States sent money and arms across the Atlantic to outfit an underground army. Emigrants and their sons who had served in the American Civil War returned to Ireland from the slums of Boston, New York, and Chicago to find the sod still fresh on the graves of their relatives and friends, victims of famine and rebellion. Trained in the bloodiest civil war the Western world had yet witnessed, Irish-American boys came home to join a movement that could make good use of their experience with rifle and bayonet.

In the 1860s there were some eighty thousand Fenians in Ireland and Great Britain; perhaps twice that number in America. The IRB had infiltrated the British Army: fifteen thousand Irish soldiers in its ranks were Fenians. The British government took precautionary steps: suspension of the Habeas Corpus Act in Ireland, suppression of the press, arrests of "traitors." John O'Leary, editor of the IRB's *Irish Press,* was one of the first convicted under the Treason-Felony Act, which denied him the rights of political prisoners. He was sentenced to twenty years' penal servitude.

O'Leary's speech from the dock expressed the separatists' credo: "I have been found guilty of treason—or treason-felony. Treason is a foul crime. The poet Dante places traitors in the ninth circle of his hell—I believe, the lowest circle. But what kind of traitors are these? Traitors against kin, country, friends and benefactors. England is not my country; I have betrayed no friend, no benefactor."

John O'Leary was shipped to England in 1865 to be held with other Treason-Felony prisoners in Portland Jail, on the bleak lime-rock coast of Dorset. Like ordinary convicts in the public works penitentiary, they were put to forced labor in the quarries, breaking stones, dragging the heavy loads like beasts of burden. The brutality of their punishment and their long sacrifice remained year after year a reminder of foreign tyranny, and England's coercive legislation actually strengthened the nationalists. Even the disapproval of the Catholic hierarchy could not prevent the spread of Fenian influence.

The specter of revolution haunted the age into which Maud was born. In the spring of 1867, in expectation of an armed insurrection, Captain Thomas Gonne was drilling redcoats in the Curragh. The family was living not far away in an enclave of Empire in the green suburbs of Dublin, where prosperous citizens and their servants spoke of rebels with a disdain that did little to mask their fear. "Fenian": with the name itself English nannies frightened children into good behavior. Tales of daring raids, rumors of atrocities were intensified by anti-Catholic bias. Alice Milligan, who grew up to become Maud's friend and colleague, wrote of her Ulster childhood:

> An army of Papists grim
> With a green flag o'er them,
> Red-coats and black police
> Flying before them.
> But God (who our nurse declared
> Guards British dominions)
> Sent down a deep fall of snow
> And scattered the Fenians.

The Gonnes' house, Floraville, was in a middle-class neighborhood of Anglo-Irish families. "Anglo-Irish," a literary term used to distinguish Irish works written in English from those written in Gaelic, has only recently been applied to a social class now almost extinct: the Protestant Ascendancy and their descendants. When Maud was a girl, they owned the country; they made its rules and its fortunes, as they had for three hundred years. The center and symbol of their power was Dublin Castle.

The Palladian façades were approached by graveled drives separated by tall hedges from the mud hovels of the tenant farmers who worked the vast estates. In town the Georgian houses, with their curved stairways, delicate fan-lights, and baroque plaster work, were an inheritance from eighteenth-century colonialists. Cultivated, leisured, the An-glo-Irish occasionally produced rebels as well as rulers. Lord Edward Fitzgerald, Wolfe Tone, Robert Emmet—the United Irishmen of 1798—were of that breed; a hundred years later Charles Stewart Parnell, Roger Casement, Erskine Childers were among the upper-class non-Catholic rebels who in-cluded Maud herself. The Anglo-Irish literary genius flow-ered in Burke, Swift, and Sheridan. Oscar Wilde, George Bernard Shaw, and William Butler Yeats carried on the tradi-tion.

Maud's first childhood friend was Anglo-Irish. Ida Jame-son, the youngest daughter of a prosperous whisky distiller, lived next door at Airfield. Superstitious servant girls fed the children's imaginations with tales of the supernatural, and the two little girls were avid believers in ghosts and fairies. A huge black dog with eyes of flame haunted the Donnybrook Road. Ida had seen it. Maud had her own visitors from the spirit world—a dark-eyed woman veiled in gray haunted her dreams—and the heroes and heroines from her storybooks mingled with rumors of real battles being fought in the dis-tant hills.

By 1868 the Fenians had been routed, but Captain Gonne remained with his regiment in Ireland. Edith Gonne gave birth to another daughter, who was named Kathleen Mary and baptized at the Curragh. Maud and her little sister played with their dolls and pets in the security of Floraville. Over the marble mantel hung Maud's favorite pictures of two golden angels, copied from Fra Angelico by Edith during her honey-moon in Florence. Oval frames held two portraits by the Irish painter William Wall: Maud, a cherub with a halo of blond curls, and her mother, smooth-haired, serene. "Mama was tall like a lily and very beautiful. She wore white and blue like the sky and all her jewels were pearls and turquoises." And like the lily Edith Gonne was delicate. Ill with tuberculosis, she was on her way to Italy with her husband and children in search of sunlight and health when she was fatally stricken. They were forced to stay on in London with friends in

Gloucester Terrace. There, on June 21, 1871, Edith Gonne died. She was only twenty-seven. Maud was four years old, Kathleen two.

The house in London was filled with strangers, a bewildering hush. Wanting her mother, Maud opened the door of the forbidden sickroom. Before the nurse could snatch her away, she saw Tommy kneeling at the bedside between lighted candles. He was crying. Men in black came to carry her mother away. Tommy lifted her in his arms to say goodbye to the silent white-gowned figure in the coffin and said in a strangled voice, "You must never be afraid of anything, even of death."

Edith Cook Gonne had lost her own mother when she was two years old and had been brought up by her paternal aunts. In her eleventh year her father died, and she was sent away to a rigid boarding school. Determined that Maud and Kathleen should not suffer a similar fate if she succumbed to the disease that had taken her mother, father, and two sisters, Edith had made her husband promise to bring up their daughters himself. Now that his wife lay under a white stone cross in Tongham Churchyard Tommy was faithful to his word. He took Maud and Kathleen back to Ireland.

The big house in Donnybrook held too many memories of happier days. Tommy took a cottage in Kildare, nearer the Curragh. Here was a new world of gentle fields and woodlands for Maud to explore. Her father showed her how to grow seeds and cuttings in the potting shed. Roaming the meadows behind the kitchen garden, she learned the ways of wild creatures. She was allowed to run free with her pets. There was a donkey for Maud and Kathleen to ride, strapped in panniers on either side of his plump back. When he lay down to rest, Maud would curl up in the curve of his neck, resting her cheek on his hide, which smelled as sweet as crushed clover. After her father, she loved best her animals and her little sister, with a fierce and equal possessiveness.

Maud had always been her father's girl. Now motherless daughter and bereaved husband grew still closer. An untypical Victorian papa, Tommy treated her with the affectionate camaraderie, both challenging and protective, that he might have given a younger brother. The little girl idolized him and tried to meet his standards. She tried to convince herself that if she was unafraid, nothing could harm her; she suppressed the fears and feelings which her gentle mother would have allowed her to express.

Because both her parents were almost eccentrically romantic, Maud escaped many of the rigid limitations imposed on English girls in the Victorian era. Perhaps something adventurous in the blood of both the Gonnes and the Cooks—Scottish, Irish, French: the Celtic strain mixed with the Anglo-Saxon—started her on her own romantic way. From her mother she inherited beauty and a flair for art. Her father instilled in her a soldier's valor and a spirit of high adventure.

Young Captain Gonne's record showed unusual accomplishments at a time when gentleman officers were frequently uneducable ne'er-do-wells. In accordance with the custom for younger sons with no taste for trade or government service, Tommy had purchased a commission in the Second Dragoons when he was twenty, and two years later, in 1857, he passed through Staff College as a lieutenant in the Seventeenth Lancers. He served in India during the Mutiny of 1858–59 and saw action at Terapore for which he received the Indian Mutiny Medal. Having mastered Hindustani (as well as Portuguese, French, Italian, and German), Captain Gonne was interpreter and staff officer to the Cavalry Flying Column in Central India. From 1868 to 1873 the dashing soldier of the Queen was brigade major of the Cavalry in Ireland.

Quick intelligence and eagerness for knowledge enabled Maud's father to profit from all his experiences, but he found Ireland a most congenial country, as did many Englishmen of means whose ambivalent attitude toward their Irish peers resembled the feeling of affection and condescension of a legitimate son toward an attractive bastard brother. The horse-raising country, the hunt, the relaxed social and garrison life appealed to Thomas Gonne. He was resolved to make in Ireland as much of a home for himself and his daughters as a widower could.

When Tommy was away on duty his little girls were entrusted largely to the care of their English nurse, Mary Anne. When he was at home, life was exciting, and he was at home more now than he had been when Maud was a baby because the tension in Ireland had decreased. The Fenians, inadequately organized, pathetically underarmed, failed in every show of strength, but the 1867 uprising had far-reaching consequences. Their campaign of violence in England—the rescue of prisoners by force in Manchester, the dynamiting of a wall of Clerkenwell Jail which killed a number of innocent people—reinforced the angry conviction of those who insisted that Ireland required a strongly punitive government. But at the same time the terrorist tactics moved others to examine the conditions which had led to such desperate acts and to consider the wisdom of reform in place of repression. Gladstone, Prime Minister after the Liberal Party's return in the 1868 election, was persuaded that the Irish problem was a "malaise" to be cured rather than punished. Parnell, son of an American mother and an Anglo-Irish father, was a student at Cambridge when he learned his first political lesson from the promise and failure of Fenianism, and he began to consider alternative methods to achieve independence for Ireland. It seemed clear that the use of physical force by a minority required political backing.

Home Rule was beginning to dominate the political friction between England and Ireland and to become the key to the rise and fall of the Liberal and Conservative parties. At Christmas 1870, pressured by the reformers, Gladstone announced the release of most of the Treason-Felony prisoners. Clemency was qualified by exile. None was permitted to reside in England or Ireland until the termination of his sentence. John O'Leary went to Paris, the convenient refuge for Irish rebels, where as a young medical student among artists and anarchists he shared lodgings with Swinburne, Whistler, and du Maurier. In 1871 the city he had loved during the Second Empire was in a state of shock from the German siege and the horror of the Commune's defeat. O'Leary went on to America to work with an old comrade, John Devoy, in the Clan na Gael, the American section of the IRB.

While Maud was exploring the natural world in County Kildare, new forces for social change were developing. Gladstone's Parliament enlarged the franchise, disestablished the Church, and passed Land Reform acts. These measures combined with seasons of better crops to maintain an uneasy peace in which the men and women who would be the leaders in storms to come could grow up.

At the end of a year in the lush pasturelands of Kildare, Maud came down with a severe bronchial attack. Tommy was alarmed, and when the doctors recommended sea air, he moved his little family to Howth, the peninsula that stretched like the arm of a sleeping giant north of Dublin Bay. An ugly little house opposite the Bailey Light became Maud's new home. Every weekend that Tommy was off duty she and Kathleen were wedged securely into the seats that hung over the wheels of a cart called an outside car and driven down to pick up their father and his parcels of sweets and toys at the Sutton railway station.

Nanny, a sociable soul, visited the Howth cottagers, and Maud, tagging along, quickly made friends with their children. In their cabins she saw for the first time chromos of the Virgin and the Sacred Heart. The colored pictures torn out of books and journals were tacked up on the smoke-smudged walls, and there too were black-and-white engravings of handsome men in old-fashioned costumes. When Nanny was not around to listen with her "English ears," the old people would explain to Maud that these graybeards and gallant youths were Ireland's greatest men—the leaders of the '98 rising, the Manchester Martyrs, heroes whose sacrifice for their country was equated with the selflessness of saints. The old people were guarded in their speech, for Maud was a child of the enemy, but she remembered all they said while her friends made room for her by the turf fire and let her share their griddlecake and potatoes. Sure-footed as mountain goats, Maud's ragged little companions led her along the steep bluffs of Howth Head and gathered sea-gull eggs for her from the perilous cliff face where ghosts from the battles of the Fianna howled in the incessant wind, and old dreams of a French fleet come to rescue Ireland hung on the horizon.

"No place has ever seemed to me quite so lovely as Howth . . ." Maud wrote seventy years later. "Sometimes the sea was as blue as Mama's turquoises, more strikingly blue even than the Mediterranean, because so often grey mists made it invisible and mysterious. . . . We were never allowed to go near the cliffs alone, but on the other side of the house, far up the heather-covered hill to Granny's cabin, we were free to wander and play as we pleased." Maud's body could still recapture the sensual pleasure of the child who felt the earth beat with her own heartbeat. She had heard the earth sing, and throughout her life she returned to it, Antaeus-like, for regeneration.

By the time Maud was six and an untamed tomboy, Thomas Gonne realized that something must be done. Girls might not require too much learning, but it was essential that they be domesticated. Even the cottagers' children were learning to read and write in the village schoolhouse, while his daughters could hardly spell and were quite undisciplined. The wives of his fellow officers accused Tommy of neglecting his parental responsibility. At a garden party given by Lord Howth a pretty croquet partner gave him some sound advice. Maud and Kathleen, in black velvet dresses, pink silk stockings, and huge straw hats with curled ostrich feathers, squatted in the kitchen garden of Howth Castle gorging on gooseberries, unaware of the momentous change being planned for them.

Soon afterward a governess arrived from England to take the girls in hand, but life in Ireland proved too rigorous for the poor clergyman's daughter, who could not keep up with the two wild little creatures on their own terrain. Tommy decided that the supervision of growing girls was impossible for a widower with an army career and that he must break his promise to his dead wife. He sent Maud and Kathleen with their nurse and the English governess to live in London with Edith Cook Gonne's old aunts.

The Cooks were prosperous London drapers. Maud's grandfather, William Cook of Roydon Hall, was heir to the fortune of Cook, Son and Company. He had married Margaretta Cockayne Frith in Paris in 1840, and Edith was their only child to survive infancy. When William Cook died at the age of forty-two, his collection of old masters inherited from his father, a distinguished patron of the arts, passed to a younger brother, Francis Cook of Doughty House, Richmond, Maud's Great-uncle Frank. Another brother, Edwin

Adolphus, and three sisters were still living, all born during the reign of George IV. The sisters were the formidable Victorian ladies who had made Edith's orphaned childhood so unhappy. Great-aunt Augusta Tarlton, the childless widow of a clergyman, reigned over the gloomy family residence at 24 Hyde Park Gardens.

Uprooted from the countryside and separated from her father, Maud, who had long been alternately spoiled and bereft, was subjected now to rejection. Banished to an unsympathetic alien atmosphere, she was angry and bewildered. Great-aunt Augusta, who took the two little sisters into her home with a certain reluctance, lived in the huge house in Hyde Park Gardens all alone except for her servants. The old lady's limited affection was entirely spent on a fat, incontinent lap dog. Despite her means she was thrifty to the point of miserliness, and Maud, remembering the open-handed generosity of the poor people of Howth, was perplexed by skimpy meals served on magnificent plate, and offended by the tight-lipped airs of the servants. The routine of the household was strict and boring: household prayers every morning at eight, lessons in the nursery, piano practice, supervised walks in the park, obligatory drives with Great-aunt Augusta.

In the name of discipline and industry Victorians oppressed their offspring, particularly their daughters. By 1873 John Stuart Mill and his wife had already published a work on the subjection of women, but the subjection of children still passed unnoticed as the liberal attitudes of the Enlightenment toward child rearing were superseded by an industrial society that required a firm family structure. Although life with their well-to-do relatives imposed no physical hardships, the two motherless sisters were deprived of warmth and understanding except from their nurse and the young Gonne cousins whom they saw once in a while. Missing her father, restrained and bored, Maud wilted like a caged wild bird.

Eventually Great-aunt Augusta turned the children over to her brother, Francis Cook, in Richmond Park. The regimen was much the same, but Doughty House had its fascinations. The winter garden boasted tropical palms and bamboo three stories high. Two long picture galleries housed the

Cook art collection: the famous Van Eyck, the Velásquez, and other paintings by lesser Spanish masters. The music room had a fine organ, and a Steinway grand for musical soirées. Great-uncle Frank had the gusto for high living that characterized the circle around the Prince of Wales. Lavishing his riches in the right places, he was later made a baronet for paying some royal gambling debts. He also entertained royalty at Montserrate, his fabulous *paláçio* in Portugal. Years before, Lord Byron, and even earlier the notorious rake William Beckford, had visited its fantastic fountains and marble terraces bedecked with rare orchids, peacocks, and swans.

Francis Cook had purchased Monserrate in 1856 for his wife, Emily Lucas, the daughter of a rich Lisbon merchant. By the time Maud met her, Great-aunt Emily had faded. A neglected ghost in rusty black silks and lace mantillas, she too was a prisoner in Doughty House. When she could manage to steal a pound or two from the housekeeping account, which Great-uncle Frank checked every week, she would sneak up to London in a hired fly to buy dolls for her nieces. Sometimes she played the harp in the music room, and Maud, listening to the melancholy tinkle, pitied her great-aunt. Among the Cooks, women did not seem to count for much.

But Emily Cook, who had also been kind to Maud's mother, managed to rescue Maud herself from the tyranny of the family. Dissatisfied with the girls' progress under the tutelage of the clergyman's daughter—their French was weak; their deportment could well be improved—she persuaded Captain Gonne that they should be educated in France. As if to further the plan, Maud had another attack of bronchitis; the dreaded cough returned. Again a change of climate was prescribed, and this time her father decided on Europe. Hearing that she and Kathleen were to leave for France, Maud wrote her first poem: "Hooray, hooray, hooray! To-day we are going away."

Maud never saw her benefactor again. After Great-aunt Emily died in 1884, Sir Francis Cook married Tennessee Claflin, an American woman of a very different style. She and her sister, Virginia Woodhull, were the first women brokers in Wall Street and, no less extraordinary, outspoken advocates of free love and equal rights for women. When Sir Francis died in 1901, a month after Edward VII became king, the exuberant Tennessee took over Doughty House. In what Maud considered just retribution to Great-uncle Frank, his widow's weeds floated across the rotogravure pages of society papers like a flag, outraging righteous respectability.

# CHAPTER THREE

# Mademoiselle

Maud left London when she was ten, and her next six years were spent on the Continent—the south of France or Italy in the winter, Switzerland in the summertime. Moving from rented villa to grand hotel, from one country to another, she learned to welcome change. Travel gave her a view of the great world and taught her to be adaptable, at ease with strangers; but she paid a price. Although Maud adored her little sister, she was deprived of sustained and sustaining affections and rivalries with friends her own age. Her education was left entirely in the hands of governesses; no schoolmates reappeared at their appointed desks to greet her each year. The Gonne cousins would join her for brief holidays at some watering place, but the friends she made among the youngsters who flitted through hotel lounges and across croquet lawns, picnic grounds, and beaches came and went with the seasons.

She was often lonely, and to compensate for the lack of normal companionship, Maud depended on Tommy and clung to the fantasies that peopled her childhood world. Imaginary playmates, they obeyed her summons and never deserted her. Maud endowed these extensions of herself with magic powers to protect her against hostile authority. Seem-

ingly so self-possessed, she was exceptionally vulnerable to
loss and loneliness. The menagerie of pets that traveled with
her from country to country in the days before quarantine
restrictions were a surrogate family which she possessed completely, and she became a surrogate parent to her younger
sister.

Tommy was away on military duties for extended periods. Stationed in Vienna as military attaché, he was sent to
Herzegovina during the Turko-Russian War; he served with
the Rumanian Army at Plevna and with the Austrians in
Bosnia. Maud and Kathleen were often left with their old
nurse and their new governess in the small villa he had rented
between Cannes and Grasse. Shaded by feathery mimosa and
longleafed pepper trees, the Villa Fleurie was surrounded by
orange orchards and fields of Parma violets, the scents of the
parfumeries of Grasse. In the garden a fountain tinkled into
a marble basin, and tiny emerald frogs sat on its rim at night,
croaking insistent love songs. Maud was happy in the sun-
burned hills of Provence, and more than fortunate in the
Frenchwoman Tommy had engaged as governess.

"I owe to her most of the little education I possess," she
wrote. Limited it was except in literature and languages, but
it included what was essential for the growth of an independent spirit. "Mademoiselle was a strong Republican and the
most efficient French woman I have ever met, and that is
saying a great deal, for all French women seem to me so
efficient. She succeeded in making us love our lessons and find
them exciting as play; she taught us history, some would say
with a republican bias, but it was human history, and she
taught us to love human beings. . . ."

In her memoirs Maud neglected to mention the name of
the first woman to influence her mind. Mademoiselle, like so
many in her profession—part teacher, part servant—remains
anonymous, although she gave her pupil the means to make
her way out of obscurity. Through her the sisters acquired
the attitudes of a society that cultivated women's sensibilities
as well as their morals and valued art and intellect as enhance-
ments of life for both sexes. The country house Mademoiselle
was building with her savings, the neat rows of vegetables she
tended herself, the pretty drawing room lined with her own

books—all were a lesson in themselves. Daughter of the Republic, granddaughter of the Revolution, Maud's governess passed on to her the traditions of eighteenth-century women, the power of the salon, the egalitarian rules of the land. Aristocratic and agricultural France had not yet been transformed by the manufacturing economy which in England had employed and enfranchised men, while women were relegated to subordinate domestic roles. Mademoiselle encouraged in Maud aspirations that the great-aunts in London would have considered quite inappropriate. "Independence, *ma chérie*," she said, "is the most precious of all things, and everyone can be independent."

Courage alone was not enough. One must be practical and self-reliant as well. Yet as Maud learned and matured, she did not entirely relinquish the fantasies of a lonely child. She dramatized her life to fill its empty moments; and, with her father away, she romanticized him, anticipating those glorious holidays when he was on leave.

In 1879 Colonel Gonne came back from India, where his regiment had been guarding the far-flung outposts of Victoria, Empress of India, against the raids of the Moguls of Afghanistan, who feared the encroachment of British dominion. Returning to France after a prolonged absence, Tommy was struck by the change in his older daughter. The little girl who had ridden her pony beside his high-stepping cavalry horse in the Curragh, the tomboy he had taught to handle guns and animals, had become a young woman. She was proud of her height, five feet ten, extraordinary for a woman at that time, and showed none of the self-consciousness that makes tall girls seem gawky. Eager to be grown up, she made Nanny twist the red-gold hair, so heavy that it was almost unmanageable, into a knot at the nape of her neck. Her father's approval delighted her.

He took great pleasure in showing her off. A bon vivant, Tommy enjoyed the arts, especially music and the theater, and Maud was a charming and appreciative companion. He took her with him to Paris. The debacle of the early seventies forgotten in a flood of prosperity, the city was again the center of the art world. In the academic salons, Bouguereau, Carolus Duran, and Meissonier glorified the sentiments and heroic battles of French history; in the studios and cafés of Montparnasse, young artists were talking about new forms. Courbet and Monet had already startled the bourgeoisie, who had begun to purchase their frank nudes and naturalistic landscapes, only to be shocked anew by the dazzling light of the Impressionists. Maud and her father visited the Louvre, the shops and the cafés, and spent their evenings at the theater and the opera: Sarah Bernhardt playing melodramas by Sardou, Eleonora Duse in her debut, new plays by Ibsen. Only Wagner was barred from the capital of a country still imbued with the anti-German chauvinism engendered by the Franco-Prussian War. They went to Bayreuth to hear the *Ring*. On Wagner's fantastic stage Maud watched giants and dragons subdued by heroes and heroines. The Teutonic myths and the emotional music made an enduring impression.

Kathleen was considered too young for these excursions, but Tommy treated Maud as if she were his contemporary. Even as a child she had been his confidante, and now she listened to his pronouncements with the rapt attention of a girl in love. Once in Rome they watched Pickman, the conjurer, hypnotize volunteers from a crowd gathered in the Piazza Navona. Tommy spoke of his faith in the Will, "a strange incalculable force": if he had willed to be Pope, he told Maud, he would have been. She believed him. Perhaps will power would provide a magic formula to banish all fears and allow her to control her own life.

Tommy encouraged Maud's stubborn determination, as indulgent with her as if she were a demanding mistress. Since he had not remarried, Maud naturally saw herself as the central love of his life. His time for her was limited, but no wife or visible rival stood between them. On their sightseeing tours together she and her youthful, handsome father were often taken for a honeymoon couple, and both played up to the misconception. The pretense, which the Colonel found amusing, had more serious consequences for Maud.

She could be flirtatious with her father at no risk; used to charming him with impunity, she remained singularly oblivious to her physical attraction for other men. To give in order to win love, to subdue in order to be won—such bargains were not part of her experience. She looked on men as she looked on her father, as equals and comrades. Maud's deep involvement with her father circumvented sexuality, and her passionate desires sought release in some ideal fulfillment identified with him. When she was in Vienna with her father, her first proposal arrived, correctly addressed to Tommy, who disposed of the matter with alacrity. She knew nothing about it until her would-be fiancé, an Austrian officer, suddenly dropped out of her circle of acquaintances. Every opportunity was available, but the career of a society belle hunting husband or lover held no appeal for Maud.

Thomas Gonne had one female relative who had escaped the restrictions of the family long before. Great-aunt Mary had been a noted beauty in her time and, at seventy, having buried two husbands, was living in Paris with her latest lover. Her hobby was launching lovely young women into society. The moment she laid eyes on Maud, the Countess de Sizeranne saw the radiant complexion powdered and veiled, and the luxuriant gold-brown hair tamed and curled. Maud's willowy figure, her regal bearing needed only a touch of *haute couture* to become a masterpiece.

Maud was intrigued by her father's aunt and the apartment in the Place Vendôme—hung with red damask, scented with potpourri—which was so unlike the Gonnes' musty houses filled with London fog and stale cigar smoke. The Countess always wore black velvet, not for mourning but because it set off her pale, skillfully preserved skin. In the fashion still prevalent among the aging mistresses of the salons, she had her snow-white hair coiffed à la Marie Antoinette. Her domestic staff consisted of her French maid and her English secretary, a pretty young man who to Maud's surprise was called Figlio. Great-aunt Mary wanted to keep Maud with her in Paris and make a professional beauty of her. Tommy was firmly opposed. Fearful of dangerous liaisons, he allowed her only one day with his aunt.

In the morning they visited the beautician. Powder and rouge simply dimmed the glow, and Maud left Guerlain with her face scrubbed clean again and a gift of L'Heure Bleue; then on to the modiste's, where a brimmed hat veiled with black lace was pinned to the brilliant coils of her hair. At the proper hour she and Great-aunt Mary set out in a carriage for the Bois to see and be seen in the fashionable promenade of French society, Russian nobles, English aristocrats, American tourists.

While Maud is being viewed by *le tout Paris*, in a different arrondissement, home of students and the poor, John O'Leary climbs the steep stairs to his garret in the Hôtel Corneille. In Paris again for the IRB, he lives surrounded by the dusty books he collects on the quais. In the same neighborhood his old leader, James Stephens, also still in exile, lives on the charity of sympathetic French syndicalists. Paris, the lure of artists and tourists, is once more, in 1881, a haven for political refugees, Nihilists from Russia, anarchists from Italy, German socialists, Irish separatists. There is room for all while wealth and frivolity ride in the Bois, parade along the boulevards. But the Republic of Grévy and Gambetta is far from secure. The bourgeoisie is uneasy, and in the Faubourg St. Germain the shutters on the ancient mansions of *"le gratin"* are locked. Conflicts and conspiracy are spawned in the streets of Paris, which have seen so much of change and violence.

Maud rides through the Bois de Boulogne seated next to the Countess. Powdered curls piled in the style of the *ancien régime* slip from their pins as the old lady nods and dozes. Maud's wide eyes, shaded by the black lace brim of her hat, look out at the passing scene, returning stare for curious stare, smile for smile, while the landau carries her toward the end of her day in Paris with Great-aunt Mary. The Belle Epoque, which the English call the Fin de Siècle, will be the beginning of an era that will see the fall of empires, the birth of nations.

# CHAPTER FOUR

# The Making of a Rebel

In 1882 tension was rising again in Ireland, the country garrisoned by more British forces than were used to hold the subcontinent of India. Thomas Gonne was sent back as Assistant Adjutant-General at Dublin Castle. Maud and Kathleen remained on the Continent to continue their education. In Rome they stayed with old friends of their mother's. The Beresfords, Irish Unionists loyal to Britain, moved in Vatican circles, and at a reception in their *palazzo* Maud was introduced to a Mr. George Errington, recently come from England on a secret mission to the Pope. It was common knowledge that many of the Catholic clergy in Ireland, among them even the Archbishops of Dublin and Cashel, were supporting the Land League in its effort to secure rights for the tenants. The English hoped that Errington could persuade the Vatican to publish a rescript against Land League agitation. The diplomatic maneuvers between Government and Church meant nothing to Maud. Afterward she realized the significance for Ireland of Errington's mission, but at the moment she was interested only in the ceremony at St. Peter's, for which he had provided the tickets. Her first view of the Pope from the red velvet box was unforgettable: the mass of worshipers, the majestic splendor of Leo XIII, "like a white flame against the crimson background of hanging damasks, carried on his Golden Sedia through kneeling throngs." Spectacles weighted with history, religious and national ceremonies, ruins of temples and fortresses were magnificent backgrounds for the world of Maud's imagination.

It was intended that Maud should study abroad for another year before her debut. She gave every impression of being a well brought up young lady, but Roman society was not like Mademoiselle's Provence, and at sixteen her adventurous spirit, unrestrained by firm parental guidance, was bound to lead her into trouble. Not quite a young barbarian like Henry James's Daisy Miller, Maud was still remarkably innocent, for all her gracious manner. Tall and fair, she was a target for masculine attention, particularly in Italy, and her candor attracted adventurers who were quick to mistake enthusiasm for invitation.

With the stubborn independence Thomas Gonne had once encouraged, Maud devised all sorts of stratagems to elude her chaperones; a parasol left behind in a shop on the Corso or a Baedeker dropped in the glory of the sunset on the Pincio provided the excuse for a brief taste of freedom. A clandestine rendezvous in the Colosseum with a young Italian had unforeseen repercussions. She was no more in love with him than with any of the other young men who flocked around her, but the escapade itself excited her senses. In the moonlit arena of echoing stone arches, it was easy for her to entertain the romantic notion that they were destined for each other, and she accepted his proposal of marriage.

When Thomas Gonne was informed of Maud's engagement, he cabled his daughters to come to Dublin at once. The summons released Maud from a commitment made on a moment's impulse, and although she promised her heartbroken fiancé to be faithful, the engagement was soon broken.

Overjoyed to be reunited with Tommy after so many separations, Maud was home at last, content to shed some of her romantic aspirations and live in the present. In the spring of 1882 there was much going on in Dublin to occupy her interest. The dominant issue was Home Rule, which under Parnell's parliamentary leadership had united conservative and radical nationalists in the Irish Parliamentary Party. The dominant reality in Ireland was the Land War. The failure of the potato crop in 1879, though not so severe as that in 1848, had coincided with a general agricultural depression in Great Britain to cause acute hardship. Landlords turned their acres into pasture—cattle were more remunerative than the tillers of the soil. By the following year ten thousand impoverished tenants had been driven from their homes or had their houses battered down over their heads. General Gordon, the defender of Empire in the Sudan, was shocked by conditions in the west of Ireland: ". . . the state of our fellow countrymen in the parts I have named is worse than that of any people in the world, let alone Europe. I believe that these people are made as we are, that they are patient beyond belief, loyal, but at the same time, broken spirited and desperate, living on the verge of starvation in places in which we would not even keep our cattle."

The tenants' desperation, outweighing their loyalty, erupted in more than two thousand violent acts against the landlords—crop burnings, cattle maiming, death threats. Shortly before Errington was sent on his mission to influence Leo XIII, the Pope whom Maud had seen in all his magnificence, the Vatican's official position had favored the struggling tenants: ". . . in consequence of the unsupportable state of the Irish peasantry the people must shake off their oppression. The crimes committed in Ireland are not attributable to the Land League . . ."

In 1879 Michael Davitt, a Fenian leader released after seven years in Dartmoor Prison, had founded the Land League to organize tenants for self-protection against exploitation and evictions. His goal, ownership of the land by the people, was to lead eventually to nationhood. The League's program, which combined land agitation with parliamentary steps toward Home Rule, was supported by Parnell, who became its president. Parnell's sisters, Anna and Fanny, headed the women's division, the first militant women in Irish politics.

By the time Maud returned to the scene of her early childhood, the landlords' power was being weakened by Davitt's no-rent program and Parnell's political manipulations as M.P. from Meath and later from Cork. Gladstone pushed a Land Reform bill through Parliament by accompanying it with a strict Coercion Act for Ireland, and the long process of concession and repression continued. In 1881 Parnell, along with Davitt and John Dillon, was arrested for land agitation and held in Kilmainham Jail in England. Under Anna Parnell's leadership the Land League protested with a general strike. The next year, swinging toward appeasement, Gladstone released Parnell and his colleagues under the so-called Kilmainham Treaty. The Prime Minister agreed to pass a more effective Land Act, Parnell to curb Land League extremism.

The compromise alienated Davitt and even Anna Parnell, who felt that her brother had sold out the Land League which had worked so effectively for his release. At the same time Unionists were indignant at Gladstone's pardon of Parnell and his Fenian colleagues; the Viceroy and his chief secretary resigned in protest. Lord Cowper and William Forster were replaced by more liberal representatives of the Crown: Earl Spencer, Viceroy for the second time; and a new chief secretary, Lord Frederick Cavendish. Home Rulers, nationalists, and Unionists hoped for a peaceful resolution of the devastating agrarian conflict.

The provincial capital was in a holiday mood in the spring of 1882 when Colonel Gonne's daughters arrived just in time to see the state entry of the new Lord Lieutenant. Tommy reserved seats for them at the Kildare Street Club, and on May 6, a Saturday, Maud and Kathleen rested their kid-gloved arms on the window sill and looked down on the parade of dignitaries. Lady Spencer, in her coach drawn by four black horses, looked much too old and fat to be a "Faerie Queene," but Earl Spencer, "Old Foxy," cut an elegant figure with his pointed red beard. Tommy, of course, seemed the most dashing of all the cavalrymen who passed by between the ranks of red-coated troops and Royal Irish Constabulary in full regalia who lined the streets. The police were out in full force to keep order among the excited crowds. Not all the spectators had gathered to cheer. In the club the officers' wives spoke nervously of possible disturbances. Before his resignation Chief Secretary Forster, known to the people as

"Buckshot" because of his literal interpretation of the Coercion Act, had received nineteen threats of assassination.

That very night two murders took place in Phoenix Park. Lord Cavendish, the young chief secretary on whom the Irish liberals—those who, regardless of party affiliation, wanted peaceful change—pinned their hopes, and his undersecretary, T. H. Burke, were on the way to their homes in the great park in the heart of Dublin when they were set upon by terrorists, members of an extremist Fenian group that called itself the Invincibles. Burke's throat was cut; and Cavendish, who tried to defend him with his umbrella, was stabbed to death.

Parnell and Davitt, just released from Kilmainham, were at the Westminster Palace Hotel when they heard the news on Sunday morning. Parnell, close to hysteria, was ready to resign from Parliament. Davitt, no less disturbed but less volatile, managed with Gladstone's reassurances to dissuade him.

"I think the most anti-English of us had a sick sense of guilt in those first hours," wrote Katherine Tynan.

> We felt the blood was on our hands. . . . I must have returned to the house white-faced, for a sympathetic peasant woman said to me: "Don't take it so much to heart, avourneen. Sure it isn't the dead that's most to be pitied, God help them! God help the Irish in England!" We said that to each other often in the days that followed when the air seemed full of blood and the brotherliness and sympathy were changed to sullenness and hatred and desire for revenge. For once again Ireland was thrown back into the melting pot; there was to be another more drastic Crimes Act, and the atmosphere was charged with pessimism and despair.

The Kilmainham Treaty and the Phoenix Park incident cast shadows over Parnell's meteoric career, but his popularity continued to grow among Home Rulers and nationalists. Maud, however, was sequestered among loyal Unionists who looked on Parnell as a traitor to his class; she was still far removed from independent and creative Irishwomen. Katherine Tynan, daughter of a wealthy Catholic farmer, and the Parnell sisters might attend meetings of the Ladies' Land League and frequent the artistic and literary circles where the two young art students, the "opal hush poets," Willie Yeats and his friend George Russell, part of the "hermetic crowd," were writing verse and dabbling in clairvoyance. For the present, Maud's life was restricted to Dublin Castle and the military enclave in Phoenix Park.

As a colonial court Dublin Castle's purpose was to impress as well as administer. Succeeding Lord Lieutenants vied with each other to spellbind a populace almost always on the verge of open rebellion. Jennie Churchill had enjoyed the display when her father-in-law, the Duke of Marlborough, was Viceroy. His predecessor, the Duke of Abercorn, "old magnificent," had insisted that the ladies of his family wear long flowing veils that streamed behind as they drove in procession for his state entry. He would have the presentations in the Drawing Room stopped while he combed and scented his beard, disarranged by the chaste salutes of the debutantes. The pretty ones were asked to the dais twice.

"Sometimes the Lord Lieutenant, representing his King at the Castle of Dublin, almost outkinged the King," Lady Fingall, a contemporary of Maud's, wrote of Earl Spencer's reign. "I have been told that for magnificence and brilliance only the Indian Viceregal Court, with its mingling colours of East and West, could compare with it." While the children of the poor starved in ditches and begged in the slums, the Crown still claimed fealty. Impoverished Dubliners would crowd the gates of the Castle to watch the royal show. "They shivered on the pavement in their thin, ragged clothes, waiting for hours sometimes, so that they might see the ladies in their silks and satins and furs step from their carriages into the warmth and light and gaiety that received them," the Countess remembered. "Even then I was dimly aware of that appalling contrast between their lives and ours."

Maud celebrated her seventeenth birthday in Dublin, and at Christmas 1885 was being groomed for her formal entry into that world of light and gaiety. The Season opened right after Christmas and continued through the Levee, the Ladies' Drawing Room, and a round of Castle parties, to reach a

climax at the great ball in St. Patrick's Hall on March 17.
Colonel Gonne's daughter, with her glamorous European
background, was the center of attention among the Colonel's
army friends. The officers' wives envied her striking looks,
her Paris clothes; and although the obligatory social round
could become tedious, Maud quite enjoyed the swath she cut.
She used her theatrical talents to good effect and impressed
the ladies of Dublin Castle with a frock of pale gray poplin,
embroidered to Tommy's approval with silver shamrocks.
How charming! How Irish! When Maud met Oscar Wilde at
a party at Dublin Castle, he thought her "positively charming." She wore green velvet with white flowers, and Wilde
wrote, "I saw you and you looked like a water lily."

For her debut at the viceregal court, Maud has designed
a gown of thick white satin sprayed with iridescent beads,
gauze petals appliquéd on the train to spread like water lilies
about her feet. Like every other debutante, she must undergo
endless fittings at Mrs. Sims's. Having traveled to London to
outfit Princess Alexandra, the Dublin dressmaker is the
Worth of Ireland. Her pier glass holds Maud's reflection,
slender, six feet tall in her dancing slippers. She hears the
older belles waiting their turn in the gilt chairs along the wall
describe how the Lord Lieutenant will kiss each debutante as
she is presented. Declaring that the *droit du seigneur* is an
outmoded relic of feudalism, Maud will have none of it. The
seamstress drops the pins from her pursed lips; the ladies click
their tongues. From what French abomination has this young
woman acquired her unconventional attitude?

Mademoiselle would have been relieved to know that
when Maud was presented at the viceregal court she was
spared the indignity of being bussed and brushed by Earl
Spencer's beard. The Prince of Wales was in Dublin on a visit
intended to pacify a disaffected populace. (Some unruly
demonstrators had held up the royal train temporarily at
Mallow Station, but on the whole his reception had been
satisfactory.) His rotund figure filled the throne as the line of
debutantes, white plumes trembling nervously over piled-up
chignons, approached the dais to be introduced. In the royal
presence Lord Spencer must restrain himself from kissing
rosy unrouged cheeks, and Queen Victoria's un-Victorian

son, only a representative of the Crown, may not exercise his favorite prerogative.

Maud thought many of her contemporaries were far more beautiful then she. It was her complexion, the result of a healthy diet, that accounted for her particular radiance. In St. Patrick's great hall a bevy of well-nurtured beauties gathered that evening. "The Marchionesses were most admired," observed Augusta Gregory. "Lady Kildare, who I refuse to believe is rouged, and Lady Ormond as pretty as Millais has painted her, and Lady Congynham in the stolen Crown Jewels." Lady Gregory, demure young wife of the elderly Unionist Sir William, wrote her English friend Wilfred Blunt, nationalist sympathizer and "*enfant terrible* of politics," that she had manifested her loyalty to the Crown by attending the ball. The Prince, she noted, "looked very fat, the Princess very pretty . . . in her white dress and diamonds. I took a seat in a commanding position and felt as if the dancing and display of beauty and diamonds were all done for my benefit. . . . I have seen a crystallization of the pomps and vanities of this wicked world enough to last for a long time. As an antidote, I spent today in visiting some of our own poor people."

Under the Waterford chandeliers, candlelit crystals, Maud danced with the Duke of Clarence and felt no discomfort, but only "respect due to royalty" restrained her from crying out when he clumsily trod on her toes and the paste buckles on her shoes cut into her insteps. Adding insult to injury, the Duke, who "had the vacant look of an idiot," said, " 'I was told that Dublin was celebrated for its pretty girls. I have not seen one since my arrival.' He was suddenly and most unceremoniously pushed aside by his royal father, who had overheard his remark: 'Get out, you young fool, saying such a thing to a beautiful woman!' And the Prince of Wales led me on to the Royal dais." She had received the supreme accolade.

Later rumor had it that Maud sang the rebel song "The Wearing o' the Green" to the royal ear. There was a tradition of bold, outspoken Irishwomen. Bertha Lampart from County Meath, maid of honor to Victoria, was said to have been offered a royal gift for having pleased Her Majesty by dancing an Irish jig. When asked what she would like, she answered: "The head of Mr. Gladstone on a dish, ma'am." Maud had a mischievous turn of mind, but she had not yet come to scorn the rulers of Ireland. When the Duke stepped on her thin dancing slippers, she might have quoted Parnell: "We shall never gain anything from England unless we tread on her toes," but at seventeen she accepted the royal discomfort along with royal attention and was proud to be the belle of the viceregal season. When her debutante pictures appeared in the society pages, she joined the company of Lily Langtry and Lady Churchill as one of society's professional beauties.

As a reward for her triumph Great-aunt Mary sent her a diamond pendant and invited her to Homburg in August. After stopping at the Hôtel Continental in Paris to visit the couturiers, Aunt Mary paraded her niece around the fashionable spa, the casino, the theater, the dance floor. So much public display began to get on Maud's nerves. Strangers pestered her for autographs. The Prince of Wales arrived to take the waters. One day the aging playboy known to his familiars as Bertie or Teddie stopped to address the girl he had danced with in St. Patrick's Hall. On such casual encounters are legends made and reputations lost. Colonel Gonne, concerned about a scandal in high places, hurried to Homburg in time to prevent an invitation from his Royal Commander which could not be refused. To Aunt Mary's disappointment he rescued his daughter from a potentially glorious danger by whisking her off to Bayreuth. Maud was delighted to leave the risqué ambience of the *haute monde* for Tommy's indulgent protection; it was more amusing to travel abroad with him and have strangers take her to be his mistress or his bride. In a life that seemed to require her to act many parts, Maud most enjoyed the ones she played with Tommy.

And she excelled at acting. Her abundant talent took many forms because it lacked direction: no prime ambition, no consuming purpose, no strong affection except for her father and her sister. Her energetic will, her self-dramatization disguised an as-yet-unformed identity.

Daughter of the Garrison, a role more demanding than heroic, was certainly not enough. As Colonel Gonne's official hostess, she was fully occupied but bored to distraction by the officers and their wives, who seemed provincial even by the standards of their provincial station. Dublin social climbers, no less tiresome, infuriated her by fawning on the British, who made no attempt to conceal their contempt. The officers' wives seemed either pretentious or pathetically victimized by trivial domestic problems. The men at least expressed an interest in the affairs of the world. To liven things up, Maud invited some of the generals to tea. They turned out to be widely traveled and well informed. Captivated by the Colonel's daughter, the elderly military officers made Maud's afternoons a regular institution.

As if she were mistress of a salon, she attempted—with some success—to propagate her father's opinion that the military should not be used for police duty in Ireland. But she often tired of the social chores and, turning the housekeeping over to Nurse Mary Anne, escaped to the country and the less onerous responsibility of being a houseguest. Her sister, who had not yet come out, was still tied to Nanny's apron strings and was not included in the round of house parties and hunt balls to which Colonel Gonne's friends invited Maud.

In County Meath or County Cavan she would ride old Yellow Jack for miles across rolling fields, past willow-circled lakes, the walls of crumbling monasteries and watchtowers. In a landscape haunted by centuries of conquest and rebellion, she saw the "other Ireland" for the first time with adult eyes. Here were the ruins of the present which the living had been forced to abandon when the land agents' battering rams destroyed their homes. Maud rode her horse past little heaps of rubble that bordered the pasturelands owned by absentee landlords, the Lords of Cavan or the old Marquis of Clanricarde, infamous for cruelty during the Great Famine. She saw men, women, and children walking the roads on their way to the workhouse or an emigration port.

"The evictions!" Forty years later Maud Gonne told an interviewer that it was the evictions that transformed the viceregal belle into an Irish rebel. "The big change came when I was nineteen. . . . I went down to the country to a hunt ball which was being held in the Midlands, and while I was there I heard that some families were being evicted by the man whose guest I was. I saw the plight of the poor people. They were clinging to their bits of furniture. They wandered about looking for a place to spend the night. I could not bear it."

Maud's host, whose identity was not revealed in her memoirs, may have been Lord Headfort or Lord Farnham. "Mr. R," as she called him, was a hard-drinking man who came in to dinner cursing the Land League for laying waste the countryside and interfering with the hunt. On his way home that evening he had come across the family of one of his troublesome tenants huddled on the roadside. The wife was dying. "Let her die . . . ," he said. "These people must be taught a lesson."

Early next morning Maud left for Dublin. Her father, who had been slow to see the plight of the Irish peasants as more than a local problem of native sloth and mismanagement, surprised her by forgiving her for her abrupt departure. He seemed to understand, and shortly after the unpleasant incident Tommy demonstrated a shift in his sympathies by confining the troops to barracks when a Land League procession led by Michael Davitt marched through Phoenix Park. Later that fall, to Maud's great joy, he decided to resign his commission and stand for Parliament as a Home Rule candidate.

It took an unusually open mind and an extraordinary degree of moral courage for an English officer to sacrifice a brilliant career and in effect turn against the Empire he had served loyally for more than half his fifty years. His apostasy was no simple capitulation to the wiles of a beloved daughter. Thomas Gonne was willing to gamble on the future. There was at least a chance of success for the "Union of Hearts," as the movement for Home Rule was sentimentally known to liberals in Ireland and England.

Parnell was the great manipulator. In accordance with his pact with Gladstone, he had founded the National League, a moderate organization with goals of agricultural and constitutional reform. His obstructionist tactics in Parliament won concessions for the Irish peasant. But Gladstone's Home Rule Bill was opposed by a coalition of Conservatives, Whigs, and Radical-Liberals led by Joseph Chamberlain and by Lord

Randolph Churchill, who considered it "a conspiracy against the honor of Britain" and invented the slogan "Ulster will fight and Ulster will be right!" which became the Unionists' war cry. In June 1886 Gladstone's bill for a moderate form of Home Rule was defeated and his Liberal government fell. Lord Salisbury became Prime Minister. With the Conservatives in power, it was even more urgent to support the Home Rulers, and Maud was thrilled to read the draft of Tommy's planned campaign speech.

Sworn to silence until the resignation of his commission became official, she went off with her sister for a holiday at St. Wolestons, the country estate of Claude and Eva Cane. Eva Cane was from Malta—a ravishing beauty with hair as heavy as Maud's; when loose it fell in ripples of gold to the floor. Claude was an attractive young officer, and Maud adopted the young couple as her best friends. Their European style appealed to her, and they shared her interest in the spiritualism that was prevalent among a generation increasingly alienated from Victorian morality and materialist values. Freemasonry and Eastern mysticism replaced orthodox religions; ouija boards, fortune telling, and astrology were popular parlor games. Reading the stars and the tarot cards, Maud saw herself beside Tommy in a glorious crusade for Ireland's freedom.

That dream was to remain unfulfilled. Maud was not destined like Kitty O'Shea to be the "power" behind a great leader. While Maud and Kathleen were enjoying the autumn days with the Canes at St. Wolestons, Thomas Gonne came down with a fever. They hurried back to Dublin. Even before the doctor diagnosed typhoid, Maud's nights were tormented with a prescient nightmare: a great procession was passing the barracks where she had stood with her father to watch the Land League parade through Phoenix Park. This dark throng moved slowly in the opposite direction, and she followed it toward the shore, where a coffin was being lifted from a gun carriage and hoisted onto a boat at the North Wall.

Thomas Gonne died November 30, 1886. Ten days after her nightmare, Maud stood with Kathleen on the pier while a band played the Dead March and their father's body in the flag-draped coffin was sent on its final crossing to England. In

Tongham Churchyard a marble cross was waiting for him beside his wife's grave.

When her old nurse helped her into her black crepe dress and veil, Maud was putting on widow's weeds. She would never cease to grieve for the loss of her father. Tommy's voice spoke to her from beyond the grave. Whatever guilt she felt at continuing to live she assuaged by adding to her own his ambitions and his hopes for Ireland's freedom. Maud had planned to devote herself to Tommy's career as a parliamentary reformer. His death made her orphan, exile, and outlaw. In his will, made in 1883, Thomas Gonne had named his elder brother, William, as guardian for his daughters. Maud was banished again to an England which she now considered the hateful oppressor of the Irish people. As a woman not yet of age, with no resources of her own, she was at the mercy of her relatives, a prisoner in the enemy's camp. Against such a fate she could only rebel.

# CHAPTER FIVE

# Banishment

The London to which Maud returned in 1887 was besieged by demonstrating trade unionists and unemployed workers. Trafalgar Square, no longer a serene monument to Empire, was a forum for union organizers and anarchists. Expressly forbidden by her great-uncle, William Gonne, to be out in the streets at all that day, Maud was determined to hear the speeches. Under leaden skies shot through with silver, she saw the dark hordes marching toward Nelson's fragile pillar. Allowing herself to be caught in their ranks, she was carried into the square by the tumultuous press of determined men and women.

A stranger reached down from the speakers' platform, and two burly arms swung her up to safety. Pausing to catch her breath, Maud leaned on one of the stone lions, and her slim black-garbed figure attracted the attention of Tom Mann. The union organizer approached her. Was she with the labor movement? Maud informed him she had come from Ireland, where oppressed people were also fighting for their rights. When he suggested that she speak to the crowd, she refused, feeling quite unprepared for the occasion. But later, sensing the response to Mann's fiery speech, the intent silence, the roar of applause, she was thrilled by the powerful current that ran from the orator through the audience.

And then it was cut off. A small band of baton-swinging police marched into the Square. The audience deserted, streaming down every side street. Some of the speakers followed them. A man with a Russian accent who remained with Maud on the platform commented that English crowds had no courage. Unlike the Irish, these cowed working people would never dare a revolution.

During the eighties London was a temporary home for many revolutionaries fleeing the Czar's police and for the secret agents who shadowed their flight. Conservatives like Maud's relatives feared the exiles, even while they condemned the Czar's despotism and his forays into British territory. Her uncles and aunts suspected all Russians of carrying bombs. They forbade her to see a girl she had met in Europe whose parents were attached to the Russian Embassy. When she brought a copy of Madame Blavatsky's *Isis Unveiled* into William Gonne's house, her uncle confiscated it because he was convinced that the author had been in India as a spy for Russia. Uncle William banned all newspapers except the *Morning Post*. Arthur Balfour, the new chief secretary for Ireland, was said never to read the papers at all. The *Pall Mall Gazette* was barred from the Gonnes' reading table, not because it was the scandal sheet of the day but because W. T. Stead, its crusading pro-Irish editor, was supposed to have fallen into the hands of wily Madame Olga Kireev Novikov, a Russian aristocrat who wrote under the pseudonym "O.K." and was known as the "M.P. for Russia," since she had some influence with Gladstone.

Maud was fascinated by anarchists and revolutionaries; like the Fenians, they had the courage to risk everything for liberty and justice. It was impossible not to be aware of the squalid lives in the slums that surrounded the elegant homes of Mayfair and Belgravia. Willie Yeats, transplanted from Dublin to London that year, called the city a "black hole" and observed the women of the tenements, so unlike the old women of Dublin, "who, though mad with drink and gaunt with poverty, carried themselves erect, belonging to romance."

The poor in London were more destitute and desperate than the peasants in rural Ireland. "And in London it was always winter," wrote Ford Madox Ford. "Above the darkness brooded the Hard Times.. . . . It is difficult to think how people lived then. In cold, in darkness, lacking sufficient clothes or sufficient food. With the aid of gin perhaps, or beer when you cadge a pint. . . . ninety percent of the population of London in those days depended for its *menus plaisirs*—its glimpses of light, of pleasure, its beanfeasts, its pints at the pubs—on windfalls. . . . You lived in slums in Seven Dials, Whitechapel, Notting Dale. You burned the stair rails and banisters, the door jambs, the window frames for fuel."

George Bernard Shaw, who had arrived in London from Dublin with vague anarchist principles, was now a committed socialist. The Fabian Society attracted middle-class intellectuals who saw with Tennyson an age of chaos, "crammed with menace." The first woman's suffrage committee had already been organized in the industrial city of Manchester. Emmeline Pankhurst's daughters, Christabel and Sylvia, perched on the stairs above the parlor to eavesdrop on the conversation of their parents' guests: the flamboyant reformer Annie Besant; Keir Hardie, the Scottish union leader; the German socialist Wilhelm Liebknecht; Eleanor Marx.

Maud's relatives did everything to discourage her participation in liberal movements. Tommy had had a sense of adventure, but all the romance of the Gonne family seemed to have died with him. Maud was curious about her Gonne forebears. It was believed that they had owned land in County Mayo in the early eighteenth century, and there was a story about an ancestor who had acquired some Church property by unscrupulous means. The local priest placed a curse on his house: no daughter of the Gonnes would ever be happy in marriage. The accursed Gonne later disinherited his son, Tommy's grandfather, who returned to England to establish a wine importing business in the City of London. Since that time the lands in Ireland had been sold off, and sherries from Spain, port and madeira from Portugal provided wealth for the Gonnes, almost as much as cloth from India brought to the drapers of Cook and Sons Ltd. Now Tommy's eldest brother headed the Company. Another brother, Charles, had been in the Bombay Civil Service. Maud's Uncle William, the wine merchant, believed that women belonged at home and did his best to keep them there. Kathleen could amuse herself with books and paint box or writing love letters to a young officer back in the Dublin garrison. But Maud could find no way to carry out her commitment to Ireland. Ever since Tommy's death her willful spirit had languished in repressed rebellion. The high hopes they had shared were shattered. Parnell's party still had some strength in Parliament, but a move to destroy him was under way. Early in 1887 the London *Times* published letters bought from an impoverished Irish journalist which implicated Parnell in the Invincible assassinations. To Maud, Ireland's independence, like her own, seemed a lost cause.

She thought of joining her father in death; she lost weight and got pneumonia. Her sympathetic cousins May and Chotie, the lively daughters of Tommy's brother Charlie, forestalled her half-conscious intention by persuading their parents to invite Maud and Kathleen to live with them at Ascot. But Uncle William held the purse strings, allotting two shillings sixpence weekly to his wards. In a last-minute effort to keep control of them and their inheritance, he lied about their father's estate. It had been so poorly managed, he told them, that their share would be negligible, and they would be compelled to accept Great-aunt Augusta's generous offer to adopt them.

Maud's response to this threat was to look for a job. The practical alternative to being a perpetual prisoner was to be self-supporting. She had no intention of becoming the conventional "lady's companion," no matter what Uncle William said. Cousin May Gonne was going to study nursing, but Maud was unable to qualify for a certificate at the Charing Cross Nursing Institute because of "weak lungs." Kathleen and Cousin Chotie could study painting at the Slade and look for husbands if they chose; Maud made a different plan.

She had often played in amateur theatricals in Dublin and, aspiring to be another Bernhardt, had studied with the old Dublin actor Granby and taken elocution lessons from Chancellor Tisdale, a Protestant divine who loved the stage. Hermann Vezin, an American actor transplanted to England, had admired her in a benefit show for Dublin's Royal Hospital and offered his services if ever she should decide to go on the stage. Prudently chaperoned by Nanny, Maud went to see Vezin backstage in the Strand. He was as good as his word. Lily Langtry had just made a successful debut; Oscar Wilde's "discovery," the Jersey Lily who became a mistress of the Prince of Wales, was no more talented and no more beautiful than Maud. "Will is a strange incalculable force": Tommy's daughter had begun to take charge of her own life.

Four months later Uncle William was aghast to read "Maud Gonne" in red letters on a garish poster announcing her as leading lady in *Heartsease*. Although Ellen Terry had helped to raise the social status of actresses in England, the older Gonnes still considered the theater close to prostitution. Maud refused to take a stage name to preserve the family honor. Her own was to honor as she chose, and its two short syllables had a pleasing theatrical ring. *Heartsease* was a translation from a French drama of the boulevards by Eugène Scribe. Based on the tragic liaison between the eighteenth-century actress and the Comte Maurice de Saxe, *Adrienne Lecouvreur* provided Maud with a role that suited her.

The story of Maud's early years reminded Yeats of Victorian novels about maidens victimized in a world of deception. Maud never thought of herself as a victim, and was determined never to be one. She was still a captive in her Victorian family, trying to break free, when she came face to face with a woman wronged by events close to home, too close for comfort. The scene, which Maud could never forget, might have been played in some music-hall melodrama.

She is having tea with Uncle William. A pale, rather beautiful young woman in black appears unannounced in the drawing room. She has come to ask for financial assistance, "enough to keep the child." She claims that her daughter is Thomas Gonne's, born while he lay dying in Dublin. Maud, who has been pouring tea, bursts into tears, remembering that on his deathbed her father had asked her to make out a draft for some money to be sent to a "Mrs. Robbins." Distraught with grief at that terrible moment, she had not questioned him. Now the memory of her father's last request gives credence to the story "Mrs. Robbins" is telling. The child must be cared for. Maud manages to persuade Uncle William that discretion, if not human decency, would be served by a sizable check.

Tommy's hidden "infidelity" was a betrayal, but it was still secondary to the ultimate betrayal of his death, and it was a reality she could cope with. She immediately assumed the responsibilities her father had bequeathed: she provided care and clothing for the baby girl and paid frequent visits to the run-down lodgings on the Edgeware Road where "Mrs. Robbins" lived. A son from an early marriage had gone off to sea. In time Maud came to admire the lonely fortitude of the woman who had been Tommy's mistress, and the older woman began to trust Maud's loving interest in her little half-sister. Maud felt that "Daphne" belonged to her too. From then on she took care of the little girl, whose real name was Eileen, and helped "Mrs. Robbins," a woman of Irish birth named Margaret Wilson, in any way she could.

This new responsibility was an added incentive for Maud to earn money of her own. The little traveling troupe she had joined at least provided a small income, a chance for fame. With her looks and voice Maud seemed born for the stage, but she found it difficult to submerge her strong personality in illusory parts and submit to direction. Although she could be highly disciplined, her ambition to succeed as an actress was not compelling enough to enable her to endure the exhausting drudgery of rehearsals in drafty halls. The dust, the cold, the rigorous work on voice production strained her vocal cords, and she began to cough again; still she refused to give up her first job. But on the day the company was to start its tour, Maud collapsed with severe hemorrhaging of the lungs. Terrified of being ill and dependent on Uncle William again, her contract broken, her career failed, she appealed to Great-aunt Mary for help. The Countess, who had exchanged her plush apartment in the Place Vendôme for a similar nest in Chelsea, took Maud and Kathleen in and tried to restore their spirits and Maud's health.

Uncle William was relieved to be able to place his difficult wards in someone else's care, but in relinquishing the administration of their allowance he was forced to reveal the truth about their inheritance. Under Thomas Gonne's will, when she came of age Maud would receive her half of a trust set up in 1865, along with a share of the family diamonds, real estate, and residual income. In a year's time she would have the means to lead her own life; her dream of freedom would come true.

By spring Maud was beginning to recover. Kathleen and Chotie amused her with tales of the girls studying art at the Slade. Restricted to the Antique Rooms, they sketched from casts of half-draped figures. Once, on a visit, Great-aunt Augusta happened to glimpse a live nude model and fled without ever finding a niece among the sexless Roman statues. Ironically, women who were expected to care for wounded soldiers under the most unaesthetic conditions were forbidden to draw from life, and when May, a rosy Florence Nightingale, visited Maud, they laughed at the hypocrisy of the world they faced.

That summer the doctor advised a cure abroad, and Maud and Kathleen were on their way to France again. Great-aunt Mary could show off her two beautiful nieces at a fashionable spa in the Auvergne. Kathleen was safely engaged to her Captain Pilcher, and Maud could endure another season in society knowing that in a short time she would be twenty-one and would have an income of her own. Tommy had willed it so, and France was a stone's throw from Ireland, where she would carry on alone the work she had planned to share with him.

# CHAPTER SIX

# The Bold Boulangiste

The convalescent gazed through the shimmering heat waves of July at the thunderheads that menaced the little spa at Royat with the clamor of armies in battle. The Puy de Dôme loomed above the other mountains of the Auvergne. On those ranges of Byzantine outcroppings, turrets and cupolas where Vercingetorix had led his tribes against Caesar's legions, Celtic bagpipes still wailed from high sheep pastures. Since Roman times the thermal springs had lured aristocratic invalids to Vichy and Mont Dore, and to Royat, Great-aunt Mary's favorite health resort, where the *beau monde* and the *demimonde* gambled for money and love. Flanked by her two ravishing companions, the Countess de Sizeranne strolled the graveled paths among tilted parasols flirting with straw boaters and gold-braided caps. When it was too hot for the promenade, they would sit in the shady square and listen to the town band play military music.

Maud was bored, idle, and frivolous. One afternoon she looked up over the scalloped rim of her black lace fan into the eyes of a tall Frenchman who was being introduced. M. Lucien Millevoye: his melancholy dark eyes showed a definite interest. The long, saturnine face, the concupiscent mouth not entirely concealed by handlebar mustache and beard, seemed mysteriously familiar. She was convinced that they had met before, or perhaps in some other time and place she had experienced a similar agitation, the tension of a gathering storm. Maud was falling in love for the first time. Lucien Millevoye was already smitten.

Millevoye came from a family of steadfast Bonapartists in Picardy distinguished for jurists and government officials and for the poet Charles Millevoye, Lucien's grandfather, known in the early nineteenth century for his sentimental verses, *La Chute des Feuilles*. Lucien himself had already served as magistrate in Paris and at thirty-two was contributing editor on foreign affairs for *La Presse*. As a journalist he proselytized for the Boulangists and was a prominent member of General Georges Boulanger's National Party. His fervent French nationalism was part of his appeal for Maud. Having pledged herself to the freedom of Ireland, she had every reason to approve of his dedication to the glory of France, Ireland's historic ally.

The Third Republic, rife with corruption and economic upheaval, in 1887 faced grave opposition from both the right and the left. Millevoye, ambitious in his politics, was allied with Royalists and Bonapartists, the Catholic clergy, the old aristocrats and the nouveaux riches. Believing that too much democracy was weakening France, they feared a repetition of the terror of the Commune and wanted a strong central government to guard against the anarchists within and the threat of German imperialism from without. Boulanger, *"le brave Général,"* was their man of the hour; *"revanche"* their battle cry. Lucien Millevoye and his close friend Paul Déroulède, the founder of the Ligue des Patriotes, were staunch lieutenants of General Boulanger.

Like Maud, Lucien suffered from pulmonary disease and was in Royat ostensibly for a "cure." But she soon realized that the primary purpose of his stay was to be near his idol. Removed from his position as Minister of War because of his jingoistic attitude against Germany, the General had recently been banished to a post in Clermont-Ferrand. Georges Clemenceau, socialist and Germanophobe, at one time a supporter of Boulanger, now mistrusted his drive toward war over the lost provinces Alsace and Lorraine. President Grévy was wary of Boulanger's political ambitions. The handsome General on his white horse attracted society ladies and midinettes, and his Napoleonic pose captured the imagination of a people still smarting from the 1870 defeat by the Germans. *"Il reviendra!"* When Maud met Millevoye in the Auvergne, he was plotting to restore the General to power.

She found his ardent patriotism as attractive as his ardor for her, if not more so. If at first she shied away from his physical advances, she flung herself with no hesitation and with all the passion of youthful love into a deep emotional involvement. She discovered in Lucien a lover with whom she would find a place for herself in public life. They would help each other: the hopes she had once had for herself and her father were coming true.

As Maud regained her strength and was able to accompany him on excursions into the foothills of the Puy de Dôme, there was ample opportunity for their liaison to develop. Lucien persuaded her that she would be wasting her talents on the stage; an actress, even another Bernhardt—never. He had much higher ambitions for her. She would become an Irish Jeanne d'Arc. He would publicize Ireland's cause in the French press; the infamous English were France's hereditary enemies and therefore as much his as hers. In return Maud would work with him to regain Alsace and Lorraine. This was no ordinary love affair. She saw it as an "alliance."

Lucien played his part well. He introduced Maud to Boulanger at a dinner arranged for the purpose in a country inn housed in an old mill between Clermont-Ferrand and Vichy, where *"la belle meunière"* served her celebrated fresh trout. La Boulange, as his followers were called by their opponents, used the inn as an appropriate rendezvous, and the General frequently stayed there with his mistress, Madame Bonnemain.

Earlier that year Lady Randolph Churchill had met Boulanger in Paris at a dinner party. The General in his tight-fitting uniform struck Jennie as comically banal. The man on whom the attention of France, and indeed of all Europe, was focused "seemed unable to rise above his middle-class origin." Less sophisticated and much less snobbish than Lord Randolph Churchill's American wife, Maud was intrigued by

Boulanger's good looks, gray eyes, light beard, and surprising mildness of manner. She wondered, Marguerite Bonnemain being absent, if the woman he loved was ruthless enough to be the power behind the man in the manner of Kitty O'Shea, who was rumored to be Parnell's mistress.

Already Maud could envision her life as Millevoye's mistress and accomplice, a dangerous life dedicated to noble ideals. The prospect of adventures far removed from humdrum society blinded her to the discrepancy between the Boulangists' counterrevolutionary nationalism and the revolutionary nationalist movement of Ireland. Like many impermanent treaties, Maud and Lucien's "alliance," as she called it, was based on a common enemy rather than a common cause. She had much to learn, and her lover, practiced in political intrigue, could give her lessons in the art of influencing public opinion through rhetorical oratory and propagandistic journalism.

Great-aunt Mary thought her protégée should have attracted a more aristocratic or more famous protector and did her utmost to discourage the misalliance. Maud had to connive again to escape the vigilance of her chaperone. How confusing moral conventions and unconventional morality were. Having been exposed to such a variety of standards, Maud resolved the confusions by acting on the dictates of her own preference. She had witnessed the cautionary fate of her own father's mistress, with its punishing loss, as well as the painless peccadilloes of royalty. She knew something about the sexual intrigues of politicians and the discreet affairs of aristocrats, and had met Great-aunt Mary's implausible secretary. On the other hand, she was all too familiar with the raised eyebrows of her Victorian relatives; she had observed their unhappy marriages and her sister Kathleen's long, frustrating engagement. Her own romantic life must somehow be different, and her solution to the problem was, of course, romantic.

Unhappily married, Lucien was separated from his wife, Adrienne, and their son, Henri, as much as a good Catholic and man of good family could be in France. It was clear to Maud from the outset that he would never be her husband. But she had no desire to be married. That Lucien was known to be a philanderer did not trouble her either. They were in love, and more than love was at stake in their alliance.

After the fashion of Pope's lady, "with a rage to live/ With too much spirit to be e'er at ease;/ With too much Quickness ever to be taught;/ With too much thinking to have common thought," Maud Gonne embarked on her first love affair. Despite her passion, Maud challenged her infatuated lover with a puzzling resistance, a reluctance to submit to his will. *"Elle etait amante et ne savait pas être maitresse."* Juliette Adam, editor of the *Nouvelle Revue,* who had made the observation about George Sand, might well have detected the same characteristic in Maud when, later on, Lucien introduced Maud to Madame's salon in Paris. No one meeting *"la belle Irlandaise"* could fail to recognize that she would be her own mistress.

In the fall, the cure accomplished, their new life launched, Maud and Lucien parted for the time being. She was on her way to Constantinople. As a child in France she had become acquainted with the family of Sir William White, now British Ambassador to Turkey. His daughter, Lilla, hearing of Maud's illness, had invited her to spend a month at the embassy on the Bosporus. Before she sailed Maud managed to elude her chaperones for a last day alone with Millevoye. He had been electioneering for Boulanger in the southern provinces and met her in Marseilles. They dined in the Vieux Port, where Lucien bought her a small ivory-handled revolver, a suitable parting gift. From one of the shops displaying sailors' booty, Maud purchased a little marmoset with moist sad eyes, a mascot captured on tropical shores, who perched on her shoulder as she boarded her ship. Having won permission at last to travel by herself, she called him Chaperone.

The marmoset, accustomed to a sailor's life, was at home on shipboard, but Maud, prey to seasickness, suffered throughout the rough six-day voyage. At the first landfall, in the Cyclades, the captain's warning of brigands and worse dangers for ladies traveling alone could not deter her from hiring a Greek tradesman to row her ashore. While the ship was being coaled she had a few hours to walk the steep streets in search of Turkish sweets and cigarettes. When she started back to the ship at dusk with her Greek oarsman, Maud realized he was rowing her in the wrong direction. Her angry protests had no effect, but when she took Lucien's gift out of her reticule, her would-be kidnaper turned about. Until they reached the ship she sat holding the revolver on him, a Byronic figurehead, her traveling veil blowing in the breeze off Hermopolis.

Lucien had wisely made her promise never to be without a gun. Tommy, who had taught her to shoot in Rigby's gallery in Dublin, had told her never to be afraid, but Maud knew she could never pull the trigger to kill. For the remainder of the voyage she obeyed the captain's orders, passing her time on deck with her most interesting fellow passengers, the wives of an old Turk, sipping innumerable lemon sherbets as they reclined under a billowing canopy on cushions of purple silk.

In Constantinople the British Embassy restricted Maud just as the Turk had held his wives in their improvised seraglio on shipboard. She and Lilla were always accompanied in the streets by a huge guard in uniform. His fierce manner embarrassed Maud so much that with all her ingenuity she failed to penetrate the barriers between West and East. Hoping to feel less of an outsider, she sometimes walked about the embassy grounds with Lilla, both girls dressed up in veils like Turkish princesses, a masquerade they enjoyed until it was rumored that the British Ambassador was keeping a harem. Sir William put an end to the fun with that "terrible roar" of his, which according to Sir Charles Dilke, the radical M.P. who was a visitor in Turkey at the time, was "almost necessary to go with his appearance . . . 'old White,' a polar bear, if I ever saw one, always ready to hug his enemies or his friends . . . a great Ambassador."

In December 1887, after Maud had left Constantinople, she celebrated her twenty-first birthday. She had come of age and into her inheritance at last. She could afford to live on her own. Millevoye summoned her to Paris and she went at once, to plunge into a Boulangist conspiracy exciting and dangerous enough to satisfy her craving for adventure. Millevoye had connections in St. Petersburg and had already used the good offices of the journalist Mikhail Katkov, a rabid Slavophile and an adviser to Alexander III, in a shrewd move to

win Russian support. If Boulanger was to succeed in over-
throwing the Third Republic, he would require help from
abroad, and the Russian Bear would be a mighty ally in Eastern Europe against France's enemies, Germany and England.
Maud was commissioned to carry a secret document to Russia
for the Boulangists.

A novice in the world of undercover diplomacy, she was
well aware that a Franco-Russian pact would weaken the
British Empire and work to Ireland's advantage. Millevoye
sent her to Juliette Adam. Once Gambetta's mistress and still
an advocate of *revanche*, the grande dame of the Republic had
no sympathy for Boulanger; but, intensely patriotic, eager for
a Franco-Russian alliance that would restore France to its
rightful glory, she was willing to assist Millevoye's intrepid
courier. England and Germany were also trying to chain the
Bear; it was necessary to move swiftly. Without questioning
too deeply, Juliette Adam entrusted Maud with confidential
papers and an introduction to Princess Catherine Radziwill,
an influential friend in St. Petersburg.

The Polish princess, who wrote under the pen name
Count Vasili, told in *My Recollections* how documents concerning Bulgaria which Bismarck, Chancellor of Germany, later
pronounced forgeries,

> originated from the circle of immediate friends and
> supporters of General Boulanger . . . these people,
> in order to counteract the effect of the repudiations
> of Prince Bismarck, sent another batch of papers to
> the Russian Court . . . by a young lady whose name
> has often been mentioned since, Miss Maud Gonne,
> who arrived in St. Petersburg in the spring of that
> year 1888, and spent some weeks at the Hôtel de
> l'Europe, where I was staying too. Through an in-
> troduction which I procured for her, the documents
> were handed over to M. Pobedonostev, the Procura-
> tor of the Holy Synod, and by him put under the
> eyes of Alexander III.

In exchange for the Czar's backing, Millevoye offered Boulanger's assurances of a defensive alliance against Germany

and French support for Russia's domination of the Bosporus. But the Russian Foreign Office was strongly pro-German, and "the Tsar was far too shrewd a man to allow himself to be drawn into an adventure which, besides everything else, had against it a shade of ridicule." Millevoye, as Princess Radziwill realized later, had made a grave error when under false pretenses he enlisted Juliette Adam's aid for Boulanger's foreign intrigue.

Maud set off across Europe by train with Chaperone and Lucien's little revolver to guard her, the secret documents sewn into the skirt of her dark traveling dress. The possibility of spies and counterplots only enhanced her relish for the assignment. She spotted a German who was never without his attaché case walking up and down the corridor outside her compartment and guessed he must be the envoy to the Czar from Berlin. On arriving at Wierballen, near the border between Germany and Russian-controlled Lithuania, Maud was told her papers were not in order. The young German was only too happy to arrange things for her with the customs officials, who also obliged him with a private carriage in which he and Maud could travel for the last night of the journey. She decided it would not be diplomatic to ward off his amorous advances with her revolver. Instead, as a naïve Irish girl, she appealed to his sense of honor, and the outcome, according to her memoirs, was that two secret agents spent the rest of the journey holding hands and chatting about Russia and Ireland.

Maud preferred to live dangerously, although, when possible, in a certain style. Along a sandy track from Germany and ever north along the coast, through a land of isolated farms strangely reminiscent of Ireland, her luxurious carriage was pulled by a wood-burning locomotive; the inexhaustible forests of Russia stoked the engines. Tempting platters of cold meats, fish, and caviar lined the buffet in the dining car, and the passengers' glasses were filled with dark gold tea from hissing brass samovars. "Travelling in Russia is the most luxurious in Europe," W. T. Stead of the *Pall Mall Gazette* was told when, like Maud, he went to court the Czar in the spring of 1888.

The crusading inventor of yellow journalism recognized the importance of Russia's increasing might, its armies drawn from a population as inexhaustible as its forests. England could not afford such an enemy. Influenced by Olga Novikov's attempts to promote friendship between the two countries, the journalist was on his way to interview Alexander III, and, a self-appointed ambassador of good will, he was hoping to effect a rapprochement. On his way to St. Petersburg he had stopped in Paris to interview General Boulanger, "by no means a man for a coup d'état." When Maud arrived in St. Petersburg, Stead had already had his first audience with the Czar in the Winter Palace and was recording it for his book to be published that fall, *The Truth About Russia.*

With the help of Princess Radziwill, who greeted her with open arms as a friend of Juliette Adam, Maud managed to deliver her messages to the Czar ahead of the counterproposals from Germany. She saw them turned over to Pobedonostev, the Czar's old tutor, a grim, bigoted tyrant. "No one . . . could have known that I, without a passport, had carried to Russia the draft of a treaty which, a few years later, was to change the whole of European diplomacy and alliances in an opposite direction from that desired by England."

Her mission accomplished, Maud relaxed for a fortnight in St. Petersburg, cold, stately, and squalid. Driving in the Princess's troika along the Nevski Prospekt, she saw the city of stone and water illuminated by the Czar's newfangled electric street lamps.

W. T. Stead, who also stayed on in Russia to write his articles, was enchanted to discover Maud Gonne at Princess Radziwill's soirées in the Hôtel de l'Europe, where his Russian Egeria, Madame Novikov, sometimes joined them. Stead's obvious interest in Maud made Olga Novikov exceedingly jealous, but diplomacy on every side averted an international scandal and they remained friends. Stead had a weakness for strong, independent women. He also championed their "fallen sisters," and his sensational crusades against the white slave trade combined moral outrage and prurient curiosity in a manner that was common among his fellow Victorians. They led to a brief imprisonment in Holloway prison, and also boosted the circulation of the *Pall Mall Gazette.* "He was a man with puritanical beliefs constantly warring with a sensual temperament, which induced in him a sex obsession," wrote Maud, who was repelled by this aspect of his nature. "He could talk of nothing else and introduced it in every conversation on whatever subject."

Although Stead was working for England in Russia, his support of Home Rule for Ireland was in his favor. Maud was pleased to hear him praise the Land League and her hero, Michael Davitt. Greater than Parnell, he told her, Davitt was the man she must meet, and the Land League was the proper place for her to work for Irish freedom. She remembered Stead's advice, and he never forgot how in St. Petersburg he had met

> one of the most beautiful women of the world, born protestant, who became a buddhist with theories of pre-existence but who in all her pilgrimages from shrine to shrine, has never ceased to cherish a passionate devotion to the cause of Irish Independence. She is for the Irish Republic and total separation, peacefully if possible, but if necessary by the sword, that of France and Russia not excepted. . . . Everywhere her beauty and her enthusiasm naturally makes an impression and although she is hardly likely to be successful where Wolfe Tone failed, her pilgrimage of passion is at least a picturesque incident that relieves the gloom of the political situation.

# CHAPTER SEVEN

# Looking for a Revolution

The mail boat out of Holyhead rose and fell in the Irish Channel. Maud stood at the rail to see Dublin Bay, a pale crescent at dawn, and, half-imagined in the mist, the blue mountains beyond Bray. As the little ship steamed past the Head of Howth she felt its wild magic spell again, the Ireland she had loved as a girl. There was the Martello Tower on Sandycove Point, the flags, the masts clustered in Kingstown Harbor. She was coming home, but this time Tommy would not be waiting to meet her on the quay.

So much had happened in the two years since she left the North Wall with her father's coffin that even he might not have recognized the idealistic rebel looking for a way to serve her adopted country. Sarah Purser painted her soon after she returned, but left her spirit out. The portrait shows a pretty young woman wearing flowered silk tied at the waist with a satin bow. Her pearl and pink complexion under the beribboned straw hat is repeated in the rhododendron blossoms in the foreground. Maud's arm, resting so gracefully on a pedestal, holds a little gray monkey; not Chaperone, who perished in the cold wind of St. Petersburg, but a successor, whose round eyes stare out of his wizened face. Maud disliked the portrait; "sweet one and twenty" she called it. Yeats found it vulgar: "The diary of a certain Marie Bashkirtseff had just been made popular by the commendation of Gladstone. It was the thoughts of a girl full of egotism, sensationalism, and not very interesting talent. Miss Purser's portrait, in pose and in expression, was an unconscious imitation of the frontispiece of that book." The witty Dublin painter who had studied with the young Russian émigré at Julien's atelier in Paris was "so clever a woman," wrote Yeats, "that people found it impossible to believe that she was a bad painter."

The first woman member of the Royal Hibernian Academy, Sarah Purser supported Irish artists whom she considered deserving and was among the first to recognize the talent of Jack Yeats, who was to become the most famous of her protégés. She also founded An Tur Gloine, the "Tower of Glass," a cooperative workshop in which artists trained in the dying craft of stained glass designed and made windows for churches and public buildings. The eccentric birdlike spinster failed to capture Maud's character in the saccharine painting and with her sharp tongue often criticized her Paris bonnets. Yet Maud, who was generous in her admiration for independent Irishwomen, kept up a friendship with her. Praising her talents, she introduced Miss Purser to a newspaperwoman in Paris: ". . . . *Elle n'a pas mes idées politiques mais cela n'importe pas que je l'aime beaucoup.*"

In her Harcourt Terrace studio with its faded French furnishings, the easel and draped model stand enameled by the green light from the canal, Sarah Purser held her afternoons for artists and writers. It was there that the young writer Stephen Gwynn met "for the first time the lady whose advent in Dublin made a great stir among us, for Maud Gonne did not frequent the ordinary dance-giving society, but lived entirely among the literary and political young men, as enfranchised young women would do quite naturally today. But forty years ago," as Gwynn remarked in his memoirs,

> her way of life would have excited some comment, even had she been plain and poor. Since she was by our standards rich and immensely tall, and of the most surpassing beauty, there was a buzz of gossip,

through which she moved, amused rather than indifferent. There was a tale of her inviting all her friends to meet the chaperone who was arriving from Paris, and then walking in with a small gray monkey on her arm. At all events, I can swear to the sensation she made when she walked the streets with a wolfhound beside her.

Maud went everywhere with her dog, which despite varying descriptions was a Great Dane named Dagda after the Celtic sun god, and an awesome chaperone. "We were still timidly conventional in Dublin of that day. . . ." Katherine Tynan wrote.

No woman who was not very emancipated drove on an outside car unaccompanied by a male escort. Miss Gonne drove on a car quite alone, with only her bulldog for escort. . . . He followed her once majestically into the dining room of the Westminster Palace Hotel, where she sat at a table at which were a couple of Irish patriots. She was absorbed in conversation when a waiter came and stood respectfully waiting to speak. At last she looked up. Some people in the dining-room had objected to the presence of Madam's bulldog. . . . "Remove him," said Miss Gonne, with the slightest pause in the conversation. The waiter looked at the bulldog and like a prudent man departed. Presently came the manager. "Would Madam be good enough to remove her dog? It was entirely against the rules," etc. etc. "Remove him," said Miss Gonne, proceeding with the conversation. In the result the bulldog stayed.

Maud's appearance in provincial, gossip-ridden Dublin elicited more curiosity about her European adventures than respect for her purposes. Dublin Castle had accepted her as Colonel Gonne's daughter while her father was still alive. Now, having no use for the tedious respectability of government society, she deliberately flouted it. But it was less easy to gain acceptance in the other Dublin of intellectuals and politicians. Even among the so-called bohemians she was unconventional, and nationalists were suspicious of her upperclass English connections. The greatest obstacle in her path was her sex. In a city where membership in political organizations, literary societies, and social clubs was limited to men, Maud faced the barriers of an old tradition in which women were meant to serve other purposes. It was far easier to enter politics holding a man's arm, but even that protection did not guarantee success. Anna Parnell had her brother's blessing when she founded the Ladies' Land League; when he withdrew his support after the Kilmainham agreement she was forced into retirement. Maud could enter public life with Millevoye, but she was on her own in Dublin, which she discovered was a man's city, its streets named after battles, its monuments to heroes of lost causes. Daniel O'Connell, William Smith O'Brien on their pedestals, and the victorious Nelson, Joyce's "one handled adulterer," high on his pillar, lorded it over Sackville Street, where men walked to work or to their pubs. With no father, husband, or brother to sponsor her, how could Maud expect to succeed?

At first she stayed at Airfield, in Donnybrook, with her former neighbors. The older Jamesons were hidebound Unionists, but Ida had been converted to Home Rule. Maud's bond with the friend of her childhood had survived their long separation. Reunited, they exchanged gold rings inscribed "Eire," which like superstitious schoolgirls they swore to wear forever. To launch Maud in intellectual circles Ida invited Charles Hubert Oldham, a Trinity College Home Ruler, to tea. Editor of the *Dublin University Review*, he had published W. B. Yeats's earliest lyrics, and he was popular among the nationalists. Maud found Oldham agreeable company and handsome as a prince, although he tended to be oversensitive. (Yeats compared him to a toad, "so timid that if you frown at it for a quarter of an hour it will die.") The young student of politics and economics was easy with his hostesses, and as one of the men in Dublin who believed that women had a duty as well as a right to share in public life, he did not condescend to their lack of historical information. He invited Maud to the next meeting of the Contemporary

Club, the discussion group he had founded three years earlier which met every Saturday night in his lodgings at 116 Grafton Street. Maud had found a sponsor and a friend.

The Contemporary Club was typical of Dublin's talking societies, where debates continued through the night, till the birds in College Green awoke and the milk cart rattled past. The club had no specific political affiliation; the members, however, were predominantly for Home Rule and independence, and entirely male—John O'Leary, back from exile; J. B. Yeats, who had brought his older son along in 1885 to read his first attempts at verse to a distinguished gathering; Stephen Gwynn; Dr. George Sigerson, the neurologist, who had studied with Charcot; the Gaelic scholar Douglas Hyde; the visionary art student George Russell. T. W. Rolleston, the scholar-poet with the Greek profile, and the barrister J. F. Taylor, full of courteous diction and with an irascible temper, were favorites of the veteran O'Leary. Oldham was recording secretary for the talkers, who were an extraordinary group even by Dublin standards.

When he introduced Maud, the only woman in the smoky room overlooking the gray walls of Trinity, twelve men stopped talking and rose to their feet. "Maud Gonne wants to meet John O'Leary; I thought you would all like to meet Maud Gonne." In the early hours of the morning J. F. Taylor and O'Leary saw her home. She had conquered the first barrier, and her instruction in Fenian politics was under way.

Read, O'Leary told her. Study Irish literature and history and then go out and lecture. He saw in Maud the potential of a great propagandist for Fenianism, with her looks, voice, and great enthusiasm, and he was eager to put her to work among her society acquaintances, for the conversion of upper-class Anglo-Irish Unionists had become the hobby of his later years. Not yet sixty, O'Leary showed the toll taken by twenty years of prison and exile. With his long gray beard and eyes like a caged eagle, Maud thought him ancient and wise. She was aware of his moral force, a purity she had not known of in other public leaders. His stoicism and eloquence won her allegiance as it had won that of an earlier generation of nationalists who had known him as the editor of the *Irish People*.

> Because you suffered for the cause;
> Because you strove with voice and pen
> To serve the law above the laws
> That purifies the hearts of men . . .

T. W. Rolleston wrote the dedication to O'Leary in *Poems and Ballads of Young Ireland*, published that year. This first offering of the Irish Revival included works by Yeats and Hyde and by women too—Katherine Tynan, Rose Kavanagh, and Ellen O'Leary. Women were still barred from membership in literary societies but were allowed to attend lectures on ladies' night, to publish, and to read aloud. As the newly elected president of the Young Ireland Society, O'Leary invited Maud to attend. In this literary circle imbued with Fenian theories, Maud was inspired by patriotic Irish literature. The early-nineteenth-century revolutionists, the first Young Irelanders, had produced a body of work by Thomas Davis and Clarence Mangan, the *Nation* poets; by the novelist Charles Kickham; and by Sir Samuel Ferguson, translator of Gaelic lore—O'Leary's bibles. His house in Rathmines became Maud's church and library.

Ellen O'Leary, who now devoted her life to caring for her brother and his books, had been an organizer for the first Fenians in the 1860s. Discovering that she was a poet, Maud encouraged the proud but retiring sister of the great man to assemble her work for publication.

Maud read O'Leary's books; she absorbed the pure flame of his spirit and listened to his views. Yet she remained a perplexed disciple. She wondered at his contempt for William O'Brien, the Land Leaguer who had stayed naked in Tullamore Jail rather than suffer the indignity of a political prisoner forced to wear convict's stripes. O'Leary, though he belonged to the secret Fenian society, the IRB, denigrated its violent element, believing terrorism to be the last hideous resort of men who had, like Dostoevsky's "Possessed," abandoned all principles. "There are things a man must not do to

save a Nation." An aristocrat of revolution, a separatist opposed to Home Rule, he also scorned the political tactics of
the National League and the Parliamentary Party.

O'Leary loved Ireland, yet it seemed to Maud that when
he castigated the Land League for diverting revolutionary
momentum from separatism to agrarian reform, he showed
little concern for the physical welfare of the Irish people. She
saw the dusty books in his study, piled on the tables, overflowing onto the shabby carpets, and thought how remote all
those printed words were from the illiterate, the poor, who
had never yet held a book in their hands. Yeats, in this room
before her, had pulled the same volumes down from the
shelves and been convinced when O'Leary preached: "there
is no fine literature without nationality"; without a cultural
revolution Ireland could have no national revolution.

Maud felt far removed from revolution, although as one
tea party led to another, the doorways she entered diminished
in elegance. The upholstery in parlors grew shabbier, while
the talk became more stimulating than the strong Irish tea.
With O'Leary, Taylor, and Oldham behind her, she was beginning to make an impact on nationalist circles. At a recital
in Oldham's rooms Ida Jameson sang "Let Erin Remember"
instead of the obligatory "God Save the Queen." In their
all-Irish program Maud read poetry and, like a towering
young Druidess, moved the audience to tears with "Roisin
Dubh," the patriotic song translated by Clarence Mangan as
"Dark Rosaleen."

> The earth shall rock beneath our tread,
> And flames wrap hill and wood,
> And gun peal and slogan cry
> Wake many a glen serene,
> Ere you shall fade, ere you shall die,
> My dark Rosaleen! . . .

Her first public performance was a small triumph. Indignant letters in the press protesting the omission of the
national anthem at a public gathering enhanced the young
convert's reputation among Irish rebels, and workmen's clubs

and fraternal organizations invited her to read for them. The Jamesons forbade their daughter to participate in such activity, and Ida's dangerous friend decided it would be expedient to leave the chilled hospitality of Airfield.

Maud moved into the Gresham Hotel in the center of Dublin. The lounges were crowded with hard-drinking, loud-voiced men, and after a few days during which she began to suspect that the obsequious waiters were government spies, she found more congenial quarters. An apartment above Morrow's Bookshop in Nassau Street became her home in Dublin: "big sparsely furnished rooms with peacefully faded carpets, and not too comfortable armchairs; but when I had induced the landlord to remove from the walls various pictures of British battle-scenes and added a low couch and many coloured cushions and a few tall vases for green branches, they were pleasant enough and convenient to a pleasant place indeed for reading and writing, the National Library." At closing time Maud's new friends, many of them scholars and writers, would drop in for tea. Their gatherings soon became an institution, and later on she took pride in recalling that "Many now famous poems and plays had their first reading in those rooms in Nassau Street, and many plots were hatched in them, plots for plays and plots for real life."

One of the first callers, Douglas Hyde, a vehement young Fenian from County Roscommon, was reading law at Trinity. A student of languages, he had picked up Gaelic from the country people around Frenchpark, Lord Freyne's estate, where his father was the Protestant rector. When Maud met him he was twenty-eight and beginning his life work of rescuing the language and folklore of Connaught from oblivion. On Sunday, December 16, 1888, Hyde wrote in his diary: "To Sigersons in the evening where I saw the most dazzling woman I have ever seen: Miss Gonne who drew every male in the room around her . . . We stayed talking until 1:30 A.M. My head was spinning with her beauty!!" Two days later, when she invited him to Nassau Street with Ellen O'Leary and Rose Kavanagh, he made a great impression: a gentleman-scholar with an old-fashioned snuffbox and the vigor of the country about him. He recited some of his translations for the ladies:

Your fair thin forehead, the wide world's wonder,
Your tresses that hang in a golden sheaf,
Have torn the strings of my heart asunder,
And covered my heart with a cloud of grief. . . .

Hyde was able to transpose the rhythms and the flavor
of Irish speech into English; translating Gaelic folk tales and
songs with the fine ear of a lover, he opened a rich vein for
his contemporaries involved with the revival of the nation's
heritage. Reading Hyde's first collection, *Beside the Fire,* Yeats
recognized the importance of the folk poets: ". . . in them the
Irish poets of the future will in all likelihood find a good
portion of their subject matter. From that great candle of the
past we must all light our little tapers."

Maud asked Douglas Hyde to teach her Gaelic. Her decision to learn the language of the people was largely motivated
by the fact that the government tried to prohibit its use. In
districts where Gaelic was still spoken, shopkeepers were not
allowed to write it on their signposts; "x" became the Irish
signature. Children beaten for speaking their parents' language at school mocked their elders at home, ashamed of the
*shanachies*—storytellers—of their own culture and the Irish
prayers inherited from the time of St. Patrick. For centuries
England had silenced the people's tongue, so that laws and
regulations in English, incomprehensible to the uneducated,
kept most people ignorant of their rights and wrongs. Inspired by Hyde's enthusiasm for reviving the language, Maud
began her lessons with him.

> 4 February 1889. I went to Miss Gonne at 11 A.M. to
> give her her first lesson in Irish. She received me
> graciously. I stayed for lunch with her and we
> toasted cheese together by the fire. We talked about
> all sorts of things: le brave général, the state of Ire-
> land, etc. We did not do much Irish. She is viva-
> cious, talks well and has traveled a lot.

There were morning lessons in the rooms above Morrow's Bookshop throughout February and March. Frances
Crofton, a young singer, was Hyde's sweetheart at the time

but he was often available to escort Maud Gonne or Ida Jameson or Rose Kavanagh to a musicale or a theosophical lecture and home through the cold, gas-lit streets to talk the sun up while they cooked omelets over the fire.

> 18 February. To Miss Gonne in the morning to give her a lesson. I stayed for a couple of hours but we did not do much Irish. . . .
> 13 March. To F. C. in the morning and went for a walk with her. Afterwards I visited Miss Gonne and talked with her for two hours. She was very cordial and made me a present of her portrait.

Maud found it difficult to acquire a new language except by hearing it constantly. Too impatient to learn by rote, she was satisfied to be able to say a few phrases in Gaelic; the outlawed tongue always drew a sympathetic response from the nationalists in her audiences. She discontinued the lessons after a few months and took a course in nursing, which she thought might be more useful. "So Douglas Hyde never succeeded in making me an Irish speaker," she wrote, "any more than I succeeded in making him a revolutionist."

O'Leary's book list read, she was more familiar with Irish history now. The brutal record of invasion and resistance, subjection and rebellion, persecution and conspiracy, the facts and figures of colonial exploitation and devastation composed a truth more significant to Maud than folklore. She could understand the roots of what was taking place in Ireland as it entered the final decade of the nineteenth century. The age-old policy of divide and rule still held the colony for England by repressing the Catholic majority. Its corollary was still the technique of balancing repression with concession to prevent a unified rebellion. Now Lord Salisbury's Conservative government was instigating land reform. It set up Congested District Boards to resettle overcrowded areas, passed a Land Purchase Act, and provided some relief for unemployed laborers in public projects for road construction and sorely needed railways. At the same time, to pacify Unionists fearful of Home Rule and rebellion by a growing nationalist movement, "Bloody" Balfour's "Perpetual Coercion Act" empowered the Lord Lieutenant to impose censorship, declare any Irish association illegal, and inflict heavy penalties for demonstrations of disaffection. Trial by jury could be dismissed, and local magistrates allowed broad leeway to sentence and commit. In three years after passage of the Crimes Act of 1887, five thousand people were charged with offenses against the Crown.

The Irish Parliamentary Party was under a cloud. The publication in the *Times* of letters purporting to be from Parnell and implicating him in the Phoenix Park murders had weakened his power. A libel suit against the *Times* by an ambitious IRB member, Frank Hugh O'Donnell, only increased suspicions about Parnell's link with the Invincibles. Just when passage of Home Rule seemed imminent, Unionists and Conservatives had set out to destroy the "Uncrowned King of Ireland," and the commission set up to determine whether the Parnell letters were forgeries remained silent.

Maud saw the patterns of ancient tyrannies repeated in the present, but at heart she was moved by her own experience, what she had witnessed with her own eyes, the brutal evictions, the unjust imprisonment of some of her friends. While her lovely and far more placid sister was in London waiting to marry her English fiancé, Captain Thomas Pilcher, Maud disowned the country of her birth and turned violently against England.

How does one join a revolution? In Dublin she had gained some small reputation as a nationalist, but Millevoye's Irish Jeanne d'Arc could scarcely boast of her accomplishments: studying Gaelic and nursing, lecturing and reciting in private parlors and clubrooms. While her French ally and lover was campaigning for a glorious victory for General Boulanger, Maud was a woman in a man's country, where men enjoyed talk as in other countries they enjoyed making war or love. Weary of the debates that seemed to occupy most of the time and energy of Dublin's nationalists, she longed for action. At times she even wondered if there was any revolution for a woman to join.

Michael Davitt had been crushingly unreceptive when she called on him in London, just after her mission to St. Petersburg. Fired with W. T. Stead's enthusiasm for the founder of the Land League, she had been too outspoken. She wanted to devote her life to the Irish cause, she told him, and could take advantage of anti-British connections in Russia and France. Parnell's working-class colleague, eager to reestablish the Parliamentary Party's reputation at home and abroad, welcomed her and her connections in high places. But a shade of suspicion crossed Davitt's face when Maud expressed her opinion that violence by the Irish was merely just retaliation for violent subjugation by the Crown and should not be considered criminal. What game was she up to, this beautiful upper-class girl with her theatrical voice and manner and elegant dress? Home Rule hung in the balance, and Davitt, an experienced Fenian and politician, knew how delicate the situation was. Terrorism could be too easily used by the English to turn the masses of the British Isles against the "Union of Hearts" and alienate them from the nationalist movement.

Michael Davitt's family had been evicted from County Mayo after the Great Famine of '48, and as a child he had been sent to work in the mills of Lancashire. At the age of eleven he had lost his arm in a factory accident. From his earliest years he had felt close to the working people of England and believed that they would back the Irish people's struggle. Returned to his homeland, the young Fenian had been arrested under the Treason-Felony laws for his alleged part in an assassination plot. In 1870 he was sentenced to fifteen years, of which he served nine in Portland Jail. Because he had only one arm, he was harnessed like a dray horse to the carts pulling stone from the quarries. Davitt's *Leaves from a Prison Diary,* published in 1885, was one of the first and most affecting appeals for prison reform based on personal experience. On his release, unvanquished, he had founded the revolutionary Land League. Now a member of the Parliamentary Party, he maintained his faith in the English labor movement and still hoped for an alliance between Irish nationalism and British democracy.

He heard the aristocratic young Englishwoman sitting beside him at Westminster recite the creed of a dynamiter. Was she an *agent provocateur,* a spy sent to entrap him? He ended the interview abruptly by giving her a pass to the

Ladies' Gallery. Humiliated, Maud sat among the M.P.s' wives and lady friends. Women's skirts and whispers rustled around her; below, on the floor of the House of Commons, men were engaged in the business of government.

She was more successful when she went to see Tim Harrington, secretary of the National League, at his office in Sackville Street. By the fall of 1888 news of her growing reputation among the nationalist groups in Dublin had already influenced him in her favor. Unlike the sensitive, class-conscious Davitt, Harrington was willing to accept her credentials, although she was informed that, like all other Irish political associations, the National League barred women from membership. However, Tim Harrington had a job for Maud Gonne. Like John O'Leary he realized what a stunning propagandist she would make, and his organization was sorely in need of one who also happened to have the means to travel.

When the Land League's no-rent policy and agitation were replaced by the constitutional compromises of the National League, Parnell's more militant colleagues, William O'Brien, Dillon, and Harrington, had conceived the Plan of Campaign, a system of collective bargaining and boycott in which tenants offered reduced rents; the sums, if refused by their landlords, were to be withheld entirely and placed in an emergency fund to help the evicted. "Land grabbers" trying to buy out their farms under the Land Purchase Act of 1888 were ostracized and harassed. After more than two years of struggle to meet the demands of agricultural depression, the Plan of Campaign was in a state of emergency, and the National League was hard-pressed to provide extra funds. Harrington wanted Maud to investigate and publicize conditions in the west of Ireland, as always the scene of the most violent reprisals. Her mere appearance there would give heart to the tenants. Harrington provided her with introductions to organizers in the field and to sympathetic clergymen, the fighting priests who supported the Plan of Campaign in secret.

Maud had triumphed. The barriers which had seemed insurmountable no longer stood between her and her work for Ireland, and she could leave the talkers and dusty libraries.

"Being young and hasty, I secretly felt action not books was needed; I did not then realize how the written word may lead to action and I drifted off to speak at other meetings held on wild hillsides, where resistance to evictions was being organized."

# CHAPTER EIGHT

# The Wild Hillside— the Woman of the Sidhe

Maud invited her venturesome cousin, May Gonne, to go with her to Donegal. Dagda the Great Dane escorted them on the long journey that took them almost two hundred miles northwest of Dublin. They rode on horseback in the county of hidden loughs and treacherous bogs, a storm-swept, infertile land where people struggled with primitive tools to wrest a living from earth and sea. At Letterkenny, the cathedral town of the diocese of Raphoe, the two young heretics dined with the Most Reverend Dr. O'Donnell, the youngest bishop in Ireland and surely the most handsome. Ten clerics who had gathered for a diocesan conference joined them at table. Maud's dinner companions were courteous but guarded. In April of 1888 the Vatican had issued a rescript against the Plan of Campaign. The great liberal Pope whom Maud had seen in all his magnificence with Mr. Errington—now a baronet for his intrigues with Rome—had finally condemned the tenant action against landlords in exchange for England's promise that there would be a Catholic university in Ireland. Many Catholics were bitter, clergy and laymen alike.

Maud's host, however, disapproved of his fighting priests. Father Kelly of Dunfanghy was a troublemaker who encouraged tenants to resist eviction with every weapon at hand—sticks and stones and boiling water. Father MacFadden had read the Pope's denunciation of the Plan of Campaign to his parishioners in Latin so that none of them could understand it. A district inspector who tried to arrest Father MacFadden in Falcarragh Church one Sunday was attacked by the congregation and killed. The priest had been held in jail until he was acquitted after a sensational murder trial. Maud was disappointed in the Bishop of Raphoe for not living up to his renowned ancestor, Red Hugh O'Donnell, who had fought back against the English in the sixteenth century.

The next morning she and her cousin set out for Falcarragh with a groom to guide them. Dagda followed along the narrow roads or bounded across the bogs after hare and grouse. The Great Dane's feet were so badly cut by stone and thorn that Maud had two pairs of leather boots made to protect him on future journeys. The group crossed the sandhills of Dunfanghy, where Muckish, the hulking shape of a pig, dominated the cloudy sky, and a piercing wind from the ocean, bitter with rain and salt, blew down on them through the mountain passes. The little party was an incongruity in the vast bleak landscape, yet the sight of two ladies in elegant habits riding out in the bad weather did not seem odd to the country people, accustomed to the eccentricities of English horsewomen, Lady Bountifuls on their rounds to the poor. They could not guess that Maud was another type, one not seen here since the days of the Land Wars.

In Falcarragh, where the police, the courts, the town itself were the property of Colonel Olpherts, the situation was hopeless enough to discourage any Land Leaguer. Maud saw children sent to prison for want of a fine because they had cut turf high on the landlord's mountain to warm their hovels or had gathered seaweed for manure on the seashore that was also his. The magistrate's questions were in English, which few of the culprits understood; only their sentences were translated into Gaelic.

Olpherts' agents had served a hundred and fifty eviction notices, and the Tenants' Fund was too small to care for the thousand people made homeless. Maud watched battering rams at work as tenants were routed from their hovels by the bailiff and his Emergency Men. An old woman carried out of her doorway on a mattress blinked in the cold daylight which she had not seen for years and clutched a rosary in her claw-like hands; a young woman, too weak to walk down the road, sank in the ditch with her day-old infant. Following the crude machine of destruction on its cart across Colonel Olpherts' estates, Maud saw six families made homeless in a single day. Many died of exposure that winter in Donegal.

In the Land Wars' second phase the savagery and the weapons were now on the landlord's side. The sniper's bullet, the wooden pike, arson and midnight raids were discouraged by the National League. Parnell could not afford the political embarrassment, and, lacking his full-hearted support, the Plan of Campaign never became a mass movement. An expensive operation involving only 116 estates in four years, its greatest contribution lay in teaching tenants to cooperate in self-help.

Maud began to realize that she was only a "free-lance," working as best she could in the bloody aftermath of a great agrarian movement. But she gave herself completely to the work and with her seemingly inexhaustible energy went back and forth from Dublin to Donegal, reporting to Harrington, writing letters to the press, raising funds, recruiting tenants for the Plan of Campaign, and doing all she could to alleviate misery on the spot. Her little hotel room in Falcarragh often sheltered the homeless from cold and hunger; she nursed the ill and the dying.

She persuaded Pat O'Brien, known as "little Pat the builder" because of the Land League huts he had helped build, to come to Donegal. The huts "were at least better than the workhouse. Some of them were better than the miserable cabins from which the people had been driven. They were the cooperative effort of the whole countryside; boys and girls vied with each other collecting stones for the walls, strong farmers supplied the straw for the thatch, skilled thatchers and masons worked enthusiastically and for love—no one asked pay. When the houses were finished a barrel of porter and home-made cakes and a local fiddler and blazing turf torches celebrated the house warmings."

In Donegal Maud discovered her métier—working with people. Her capacity for organization was inspiring, and effective too, and as the huts were built and the hungry fed at her communal soup kitchens, the country people who worked with her endowed Maud with legendary powers. They called her "the Woman of the Sidhe," one of the fairy people, after the mythical goddess who rode through Donegal on her white horse surrounded by birds of good omen.

O'Leary disapproved. He had no use for agrarian reform and the campaigns of William O'Brien and John Dillon, hating "those two politicians above others. . . . 'They want to influence English opinion at the moment, and they think a Home Rule Bill will come before they are found out. They are gambling with other people's lives.'" A year later, when Maud visited the new town built for the tenants of Tipperary who were fighting the landlord, O'Leary, always free to criticize, told Yeats, "She is no disciple of mine; she went there to show off her new bonnets." O'Leary owned land in the old town, but his disapproval was based on principle. Maud, who had her own principles, was too independent to be a consistently loyal disciple, and as a woman she was open to criticism as either vain or fanatical. Emotional commitment was often seen as hysterical in women but accepted as a necessity, an asset, for men involved with the nationalist movement. John Dillon, M.P., a tall, strikingly handsome avenging angel with dark eyes flashing in his thin pale face, could have been speaking for Maud when he said, "I learned to hate [the landlords] because I saw that they had this country by the throat. I learned to hate them because I saw that throughout all the long time since they were planted here by William and by Cromwell, they never showed the faintest interest in the welfare of the country. . . . I learned to hate them because I read and saw with my own eyes that every effort in favour of Irish nationality was stamped and crushed out with all the savage brutality of a class who knew that they were hated by the people, and who knew that that hatred was just."

Maud Gonne's friends and colleagues were concerned about her zeal, but they did not hesitate to exploit it. She had exceeded Harrington's expectations, and he asked her to campaign with him in England for the Irish Parliamentary Party. Barrow-in-Furness, in Lancashire, was such a Conservative stronghold that the Liberals did not enter a candidate in the by-election. Maud approved of an Irish candidate's running on his own with no support from English Liberals and no cant about the "Union of Hearts," and although she was reluctant to leave her work in Donegal, she agreed to go.

Confronted with her first large audience—more than a thousand people turned out—Maud discovered that stage fright combined with intense emotion could work to good advantage. Describing the devastation she had seen in Donegal, she burst into tears and sat down with her face in her handkerchief. The crowd stood up and applauded wildly. After that, addressing five meetings a day seemed easy, and canvassing door-to-door became routine. Duncan, the Irish Party's man, won comfortably.

Maud Gonne had scored another personal success, but again she had broken the code of her mentor, O'Leary. In fact one more Irish seat in Parliament meant little to Maud. She could hardly take pride in breaking a path for women in England; Jennie Churchill and the Primrose League had made political campaigning respectable. Still without the right to vote, women were nevertheless useful to their male representatives, and especially so if they were attractive and socially prominent.

To belittle the Irish victory in Lancashire by attributing it to a woman's charm, the Tory press made much of Maud's electioneering. Her name appeared in headlines over society photographs taken at the time of her debut. The Gonnes were impressed; Great-aunt Mary highly approved. London hostesses with Liberal connections showered Maud with invitations. She was seated next to members of Parliament at dinner parties, entertained at tea on the terrace of the House of Commons. Everywhere she was received she continued to use her influence for Ireland's cause, and she did not hesitate to approach susceptible men in powerful positions. An elderly baronet whom she referred to only as "Sir John" envisioned Maud as the perfect wife and hostess for a politician's salon. To woo her, the Liberal M.P. expressed sympathy for the much harassed Irish M.P.s—William O'Brien, John Dillon, and David Sheehy were under constant threat of arrest and in and out of Tullamore, Galway, and Dundalk jails. But Sir John drew the line at amnesty for the Treason-Felony men serving their long sentences in Portland and the "Dynami-tards" convicted for conspiring to blow up the House of Com-mons and London Bridge, and these were the cases that were closest to Maud. In Donegal she had seen the tragic lives of women whose sons and husbands were imprisoned during the Land Wars, and she felt that amnesty for political prison-ers was an important cause. John Morton, a young Liberal barrister who had fallen in love with her, offered more than Sir John in this matter, and promised to work for her as soon as he became secretary to Sir John Morley, Gladstone's Cabi-net Secretary for Ireland.

At last work, love, and ideals combined into a way of life for her. At the end of January 1889, when Maud went to call on the Yeatses in Bedford Park, her spirits were high. The poet would always remember how radiant she was: "Her complexion was luminous like that of apple blossoms through which the light falls . . ." and how she stood "that first day by a great heap of such blossoms in the window" and vexed his father "by praise of war, war for its own sake, not as the creator of certain virtues, but as if there were some virtue in excitement itself." Willie found himself defending her at once, because "a man young as I could not have differed from a woman so beautiful and so young."

Over the years the belief spread that it was Maud who first led the young poet into public life, and sometimes she encouraged it. "My real use to Willie was, I kept him in close touch with the people. Willie and I fought very hard in the struggle for Ireland," she said in a radio interview when she was eighty. "He went on all those committees really to help me more than anything else; he was wonderful at a committee meeting and used to be able to carry things very often. He could be very much on the spot." Yeats too reinforced the legend that his political activities had been for a woman's sake. Ambivalent about his involvement, the poet later tended to overlook the fact that he "had been drawn into politics before he ever heard of Maud Gonne."

While the Colonel's daughter was riding in Phoenix Park and dancing at the Castle, young Yeats was already a joiner of clubs and secret societies. He had learned *Robert's Rules of Order* long before Maud attended her first public meeting, and as O'Leary's disciple he had joined the IRB in 1886. He was active in literary matters in the Young Ireland Society and, excited by new versions of ancient philosophies, he and two school friends, George Russell and Charles Johnston, founded the Dublin Theosophical Lodge. Before he left Ireland in 1887 the dreamy poet had demonstrated a flair for fellowship and organization. In London the following year he joined the Esoteric Section of the Theosophical Society, where Madame Blavatsky, that "nice old bag of tricks," presided. Yeats admired her for being, like William Morris, "unforeseen, illogical, incomprehensible." Fascinated by mystics, he fell under the spell of the cabalist MacGregor Mathers and became an initiate in his Hermetic Society.

The poet Maud met at Bedford Park was a committed Irish nationalist and a committee man, even while his "antithetical self" was seeking some spiritual revelation. Maud came into his life when he was hoping to unite his personality, ready to fall in love. He began to write poems to her when he was lecturing to the Southwark Literary Society, a group of Irish clerks and shopgirls in one of the poorer London districts, and Maud had a part in his decision to transform the circle of "giggling youths" into a serious organization with a nationalist purpose. Two years later, when it became the Irish Literary Society and a center for Irish authors and journalists in London, Willie experienced "the happiness that Shelley found when he tied a pamphlet to a fire balloon," and Maud's approval made it even more exciting. For her part, though she did not return his romantic love, she was profoundly influenced by his persistent wooing.

He took her to a meeting of the Theosophical Society in Kensington and introduced her to Madame Blavatsky, now nearing the end of her long life—no one knew how many years or reincarnations it had held. Maud saw the enigmatic Russian, with pale eyes in a large yellow face, playing patience at a baize-covered table. Her followers seated around the long room looked drab to Maud, who described the evening with amusement: "The room was lit by a gas chandelier and there was evidently water or air in the pipes for it flickered badly. 'Spooks in the room,' said Madame Blavatsky, and in a lower tone to me: 'They are all looking for a miracle.' " The gas flickered and went out, and she whispered that now the members thought they had seen one. "Flapdoodles," she called them.

Maud was already a member of the Dublin Theosophical Lodge, one of the few groups in that city which admitted women. She told Madame Blavatsky that Unionist members had objected on principle to her Land League work. "They must be flapdoodles in that Dublin Branch," was the response. "Of course you can do what you like in politics. That has nothing to do with Theosophy." Shrewd, energetic, full of ancient wisdom, Elena Petrovna Blavatsky had established herself as a priestess. Maud was not looking for a new religion or a miracle; she wanted to discover how to use her own power.

Yeats had friends in London, people of influence. Maud was eager to meet them, and on one occasion he took her to a meeting of the London Amnesty Association in Chancery Lane. The chairman, Dr. Mark Ryan, a member of the IRB and a trusting, benevolent man, welcomed Maud's interest in political prisoners. Men from Ireland, Scotland, and America had been held for years in Portland and Dartmoor jails. Among those serving the longest sentences were Thomas J. Clarke and Dr. Thomas Gallagher, arrested in 1883 under the Treason-Felony Act. James Egan, arrested a year later for illegal possession of nitroglycerin, had been sentenced to twenty years, and his partner, John Daly, to life. "Doomed to a Living Death" ran the headline on August 16, 1884, in the *Irish Nation,* the paper published by John Devoy in America. Prison regulations allowed only one twenty-minute visit every four months, and since the prisoners' impoverished families lived far away, most of the men had seen no one from the outside world for years.

Maud wanted to visit Portland Jail, and Dr. Ryan suggested that she take a companion along, so that by talking with each other they could give the prisoners, who were not allowed to ask questions, some information about the current political situation. She obtained permission for her visit by writing a letter to the Home Secretary on Uncle William's engraved stationery. Signing it with her middle name, Edith, she described herself as a benevolent lady with messages from the families of eight of the prisoners.

Maud and the journalist-illustrator who accompanied her to Portland were shown into a cubicle containing two chairs, "exactly like the cage of wild animals at the zoo, with iron bars in front giving onto a passage about four feet wide." Facing them was a similar cage into which presently, with a great clanging of metal and keys, the warder brought a man dressed in a yellow garment striped with black arrows. The warder sat in the passage between them, holding a gun. Maud tried to find out from the prisoner what had happened to his cellmate, Dr. Gallagher, who was said to have gone insane, but the poor man, having almost lost the power of speech, could tell her nothing.

Maud's first encounter with prison life was a nightmare that she knew was an insufferable reality for the eight men who took their turns in the cage. From that day on she devoted herself to the welfare and release of all political prisoners. Yeats wrote:

> They had brought to light the woman in her, for instead of "Mother Ireland with the crown of stars upon her head" she had these seven and twenty prisoners to brood over. I noticed an increased simplicity, a surrender of self; if she hated England, and I do not think it was as yet a bitter hatred, her charity was greater than her hate. Her visits to any prisoner moved her deeply. Once, pity seems to have given her a very precise pre-vision. She told me the tale at the time . . . she had seen three or four [prisoners], and then came a man who had lost one eye, and now the other was going. . . . The convict was in great pain and tried to tell her how he had lost his eye. The warder said this was forbidden, and that if he spoke of it he would be taken back to his cell, but, clinging to the bars, the man began his story. . . . Maud Gonne said suddenly, not knowing why she spoke, "Do not say anything: I know how your eye was injured, but (do) not trouble (yourself), you will be released in six months."

Coming away the artist said, "I am sure you did it out of kindness, but you have done a very cruel thing. You told those men they would all be released, and you told each man how soon, and they are all life-sentences." She answered, "I hardly remember anything, but I know it will all come true." He then told her after what periods—one year, two years, six months, or whatever might be—she had told each man he would be free. Every prophecy was fulfilled and, she tells me, to the letter.

Maud worked to make her predictions come true. She lectured, she organized committees. At times her correspondence about amnesty for prisoners occupied eight hours of her day. Effective work and miracles are sometimes confused in the public imagination, and the tale of Maud Gonne's amazing prophecy became part of her legendary power as the Woman of the Sidhe among the dispossessed and powerless people of Ireland who had lost faith in everything except miracles.

# CHAPTER NINE

# A Double Life

Maud's energy increased with each success, and every victory lent wings to her feet—hut building in Donegal, committee meetings in Dublin and London, trysts with Willie, and a love affair in Paris, where she kept a small apartment at 61 Avenue Wagram. Douglas Hyde, on a holiday abroad with his sweetheart, wrote in his diary:

> 27 June 1889. We went to lunch with Miss Gonne at midday. There was a little Serb there who was in Paris for an agrarian congress. He spoke no English and we all had to speak whatever much or little French we had. Miss Gonne speaks like a Parisienne. I caught only a little of what they said. We had a very good lunch with black coffee and liqueur and cigarettes. F. C. and Annette said that Miss Gonne was the most beautiful woman they had ever laid eyes on. I had a long talk with the Serb who told me about the hunting of wolves and bears in his country.

But it was to be with Millevoye that she came to Paris, and he had every reason to be pleased with his Irish ally. Maud had proved herself an able organizer in the field and an effective public speaker; she was also learning the fundamentals of political work. For his own part, Lucien had suffered a great disappointment.

As expected, the popularity of *"revanche"* had given General Boulanger an overwhelming victory in the Paris by-election of January 1889. His triumphant followers carried him off to a celebration at the Café Durand. Cries of *"Vive Boulanger!"* rising from the crowds in the Rue Royale outside the restaurant were echoed by thousands along the boulevards. Paul Déroulède's Patriotes, backed by the restless students of Paris, were ready to march behind their hero to the Elysée Palace. Millevoye and his friend were among the faithful who urged the General to seize the moment for a coup d'état, although others, like the journalist Henri de Rochefort, remembered the fate of Napoleon III and thought it wiser to wait for the outcome of the general election; Paris might well be the center of the civilized world, but Paris was not France. Boulanger chose to be cautious and refused to march against President Carnot. After the cheers and the grandiloquent speeches, like some middle-class gentleman leaving a family reception he drove off with his mistress, Madame Bonnemain, who had been waiting for him in a private room upstairs at the café.

Threatened with arrest by Jean Constans, Minister of the Interior and a friend of Juliette Adam, the General fled the country. After a brief whirl of being lionized in London, he retired to Brussels, Marguerite Bonnemain's home. With the decline of Boulangism a French court tried its leader in absentia, condemned him to exile, and outlawed Paul Déroulède's Ligue des Patriotes. The Eiffel Tower straddled the Champs de Mars, a new symbol of bourgeois prosperity, and, like fires in a live volcano, antirepublicanism and archnationalism subsided temporarily.

Although the romantic aura of Boulangism vanished along with the General and his mistress, Maud, following her lover, continued to support the reactionary movement in France. Millevoye remained loyal to his fallen idol and was able to find enough sympathizers to win a seat as deputy from Amiens in the election that fall. In the Chamber of Deputies he could do more for Ireland than before. The alliance flourished.

Maud had seen the weakness in Boulanger and the pathetic Madame Bonnemain. Now Parnell's love affair with Kitty O'Shea was beginning to cast an ominous shadow on the nationalist cause, and, in December 1889, what had not been secret became a public scandal when Captain William O'Shea sued his wife for divorce. That month, just before her twenty-third birthday, Maud went to London for Kathleen's wedding. She had never liked Captain Pilcher, a conservative army man ten years older than Kathleen, and she thought somberly of the old curse on the Gonne women's marriages. A scandal is a romance no longer secret, as one of the Prince of Wales's mistresses had said, and Maud was determined to keep her own love affair hidden. A scandal in France would jeopardize her reputation as an Irish heroine; in Ireland it would make her work impossible. It was necessary that she lead a double life, and her sense of privacy and independence demanded it.

In the summer of 1890 she was back in Donegal. News of the return of the Woman of the Sidhe spread from outlying farm to farm like the great wind that blew from the sea, and people flocked to Falcarragh and Gweedore to see Maud Gonne.

It was said that Parliament was trying to kill the land movement with kindness; the Land Acts passed between 1881 and 1888 had encouraged the sale and purchase of holdings on the great estates. But coercion and eviction continued to be more effective. Most of the land on Colonel Olpherts' estates had been bought up, and there was little space left for building huts. Established tenants, fearing prosecution, would not shelter the evicted. The area was losing the only people who could restore it to economic health.

The crisis brought unusual visitors to Donegal: newspaper reporters, European agriculturists, and curious reformers. At night the hotel hallway was lined with the muddy serviceable boots of Englishwomen, Liberals and social workers who assured Maud that when their party was back in power England would right all the wrongs in Ireland. "By clearing out of Ireland, I hope!" she replied.

Maud's elderly suitor, Sir John, came from London to prove his interest in the Irish problem and persuade her that she could accomplish much more for the tenants as the wife of a Liberal M.P. Following her to the shabby farmhouse she was visiting, he presented her with a diamond pendant. Without a second thought she handed it to the farmer's wife. It would pay the rent and far more. Sir John left in a fury but returned soon after and bought the jewel back for the price of the rent. The fame of the Woman of the Sidhe grew.

Involved with her life in Ireland, she was none too pleased when Millevoye upset their pattern by coming to Ireland for the first time. She knew nothing of his plan until she received a message that he had fallen ill while riding north from Derry. She found him burning with fever at the primitive hotel in Dunfanghy. She spent a week nursing her lover back to health and quarreling with him. He thought she should be propagandizing for Ireland in France, that she was wasting time on a handful of peasants. He told her she was ruining her health in a cold, doomed country and wanted her to leave with him. Maud disliked being told what to do even by the man she loved, and Lucien went back to France alone.

He had only repeated what John O'Leary and others had already told her. Maud would not admit her own doubts. She too knew she was ill. The wind pierced her through the sealskin cape she had kept from the time of her viceregal debut; her thin-soled shoes were soaked from the bogs. At night she coughed, and her handkerchief was spotted with blood in the morning. But she had committed herself to find homes for the tenants of Gweedore, and the Woman of the Sidhe could not fail them.

When Maud visited Dublin that winter she found her friends perturbed about Parnell and Kitty O'Shea. Parnell was cleared of complicity in the Phoenix Park murders when the *Times* Commission found that the journalist Richard Piggot had forged the published letters, only to be caught in the ugliness of a divorce on grounds of adultery. Parnell did not contest the charges, and Captain O'Shea won his suit. Gladstone commanded Parnell to resign; his Home Rule Bill and the future of the Liberal Party hung in the balance. Parnell's refusal to step down aggravated the tension in the Parliamentary Party.

Maud, who had criticized Parnell for not giving enough support to the Land League and to the Treason-Felony prisoners, now saw him as the victim of an English plot to destroy Home Rule. She admired his adamant refusal to accept Gladstone's demand, his self-mastery in the face of bitter accusation by friends and foes. Cold and passionate, Parnell won many hearts but split his party. Michael Davitt, John Dillon, William O'Brien, Tim Healy, and the majority of the Irish M.P.s, led by Justin McCarthy, turned against him; a small group around John Redmond remained loyal. Eight months later Lady Gregory was writing her friend Wilfred Blunt, "All our country is for Parnell . . . but they will probably vote with the priests."

While Maud was in Dublin she arranged for the publication of the collected poems of Ellen O'Leary, who had died the year before. Dr. Sigerson, with whom she was working on the book, became alarmed about her health and urged her not to go back to Donegal but to start a treatment of injections which he believed could cure consumption. She refused and went back to hut building in Gweedore.

Maud gave up her work for the tenants only when Pat O'Brien came to tell her that a warrant was out for her arrest. He made the necessary arrangements to get her out of the country and drove her to a remote place on the moors where the night train, passing on its way to Stranolar, was flagged down at dusk. Maud escaped on the well-traveled route that so many had taken—to the boat at Larne, to England, to France and exile. But for her France was another home, where her lover waited.

# CHAPTER TEN

# The New "Speranza"

In Dublin, Yeats would mention Maud Gonne at every opportunity for the pleasure of speaking her name, and although many people praised her work for the National League, what he heard was not always pleasing. A Unionist landlord had seen her, at a meeting of his tenants, clapping her hands when someone shouted, "Shoot him!" Sarah Purser, with her customary malice, gave him the current gossip: " 'So Maud Gonne is dying in the south of France . . .' and went on to tell how she had lunched with Maud Gonne in Paris and there was a tall Frenchman there . . . and a doctor, and the doctor had said to her, 'They will both be dead in six months.' "

San Raphael offered few worldly distractions—just two sleepy hotels, a marketplace with stalls of vegetables and fruits, glossy aubergines and grapes, a harbor of fishing boats. Maud and Lucien spent their days among the pines high above the Mediterranean. Maud took her watercolors and sketched in the woods, or searched among the fallen needles for mushrooms. When evening chilled the slopes of the Esterel, she worked on her embroidery while Lucien read beside the fire.

Into this calm retreat came an agitated letter from Willie.

It contained a strange poem he had written for her, "A Dream of Death":

> I dreamed that one had died in a strange place
> Near no accustomed hand;
> And they had nailed the boards above her face,
> The peasants of that land,
> And, wondering, planted by her solitude
> A cypress and a yew:
> I came and wrote upon a cross of wood,
> Man had no more to do:
> "She was more beautiful than thy first love,
> This lady by the trees":
> And gazed upon the mournful stars above,
> And heard the mournful breeze.

Maud was both touched and amused. Her thoughts began to turn to the world beyond the peaks of the Esterel. She knew that when she grew strong enough to climb the nearest blue slope she would be ready to take up her work again. She started to write about Ireland, the evictions and the prisoners. Millevoye edited her articles and sent them to publishers he knew in Paris. When *"Un Peuple Opprimé"* appeared in *La Revue Internationale,* edited by Madame Rattazzi, Napoleon's great-niece, Maud received several invitations to lecture to French Catholic societies. The world was beginning to invade the lovers' idyll, and later that spring a snake arrived in paradise—Paul Déroulède, Lucien's best friend.

Edmond and Jules de Goncourt described Déroulède when he was in his twenties, already a successful playwright, pretentiously enfolded in a silver-embroidered coat, a cross on his breast and a part in the middle of hair glued to his temples. Now in his thirties, campaigning to revive his Ligue des Patriotes, Boulanger's former lieutenant stopped on his way from Nice to Paris to confer with Lucien.

In the woods, while the two friends reminisced over past exploits after the grilled trout, roast pheasant, and wine of their *déjeuner sur l'herbe,* Maud saw how much influence Déroulède had over her lover and resented his intrusion all the more. Though like Millevoye he claimed to favor a republic *plébiscitaire*, she suspected Déroulède would support any party that believed in *revanche*. In the Chamber of Deputies he was already denouncing Jews for trying to "dechristian-ize" and weaken France, but it was not his anti-Semitism that concerned Maud. She had grown up in a society that regarded Jews with suspicion. What disturbed her was Déroulède's hatred for Germany and all things German. She was afraid that in his extreme nationalism he would accept even England as an ally, and would take Millevoye with him into the camp of those who had killed Joan of Arc.

Maud held her peace until Déroulède left them. Then she quarreled with Lucien about his friend. She was homesick for Ireland and tired of being idle. One morning, without telling her lover, she set out to climb the blue mountain. Dagda, having learned to hunt from Millevoye's hounds, flushed an occasional partridge as he leaped over the thin crust of snow that melted away as the sun rose higher. She was herself again, and the holiday was over.

On St. Patrick's Day 1891, Maud gave her first after-dinner speech at the annual banquet of l'Association du Saint Patrice. Vefour, the fashionable restaurant in the Palais Royal, served a suitable menu, from potage Shamrock to glacé Killarney. The place cards made clear the Irish origin of the titled guests: le Comte O'Neill de Tyrone, le Comte d'Alton O'Shea, Capitaine Patrice Mahon. They were descendants of the "Wild Geese," the Irish earls who took flight to France in the sixteenth century; their forebears had led Irish brigades in the French armies ever since. In the 1870s O'Leary and J. P. Leonard, a Young Irelander and professor of English at the Sorbonne, had inspired this enclave of nostalgic noble-men in Paris to form an association, but through the years it had become more genealogical than political. The members, naturally anti-English, were equally anti-Republican and often invited royal pretenders to sit on the gilt throne set up at their receptions. Maud found their pomp and ceremony absurd and their spiritual pretensions hilarious. The white-haired Comte de Crémont, convinced that he had been a tiger in a previous incarnation, recognized Maud Gonne as his tigress mother.

Attending the exclusive *diners de Saint Patrice* was much

like going to a fancy-dress ball, but sometimes Maud had the opportunity of sitting next to Comte d'Arbois de Joubain-ville, a serious scholar of Celtic literature, or Comte d'Abba-die d'Araste, the distinguished philologist. Although the asso-ciation allowed no women members, Ireland's Joan of Arc was welcome to speak from the red-velvet-draped dais. The captains and the counts adored her, but she received more generous contributions for starving tenants and families of Fenian prisoners from the Irish servant girls who went to mass at Notre Dame des Victoires.

Some members of the Irish-French community were genuinely interested in the struggle for freedom, and Maud sought them out. In an article for *United Ireland* Yeats re-ported that she had organized l'Association Irlandaise

> to keep France informed of the true state of the Irish Question. She began to work by presiding at a dinner given by French sympathizers . . . and made a great stir by her eloquent statement of the case for Ireland. . . . "Gentlemen, the tyranny of England towards Ireland for many centuries has been a crime against God and whole of humanity. . . . Your great poet, Victor Hugo, has called hunger 'a public crime,' and that crime England has carried out against Ireland by cold premeditation and cal-culation. . . . Do you ask what we are seeking for? I will tell you. We are three things—a race, a coun-try, and a democracy—and we wish to make of these three a nation."

In early 1891 Maud had her first child, a son whom she and Millevoye named Georges. What would have been impos-sible as a way of life for her in conventional Dublin was manageable in Paris, with a little discretion and a great deal of influence. Millevoye, a married man, had his family's repu-tation as well as his political career to protect; but he provided every care and protection for Maud and the baby they both doted on.

In the spring she took a larger apartment in the Avenue de la Grande Armée. Her ménage now consisted of a French-

Irish secretary, a French maid, and an Irish nanny for little Georges. In Paris as at Nassau Street, Maud presided over an informal salon. Gregarious and generous, she had a wide circle of friends—people as disparate as Jules Bois, who wrote of the occult, and the dashing Italian socialist Amilcare Cipriani, who flaunted red shirt and cape and had been one of the founders of the International Working Men's Association and a leader in the Paris Commune. When O'Leary visited he would find Stephen MacKenna, the translator of Plotinus; Augusta Holmes, the French-Irish composer; and Comte Bonaparte Wyse, brother of the editor Madame Rattazzi and a member of the Association du Saint Patrice—all having tea with Maud, while her pet canary pecked at the sugar bowl.

Courtesans and cocottes were the feminine symbols of the Belle Epoque. The fabulous entertainments of Paris, the music-hall posters, the elegant costumes, feathered hats and veils did not entirely obscure the fact that many women were beginning to earn money in jobs and professions formerly restricted to men. They were also becoming increasingly active in movements for social change.

Among such women Maud began to find the camaraderie she had looked for unsuccessfully in the company of men. Her closest friend was Madame Avril de Ste. Croix, who assisted in Maud's first publishing venture, *L'Irlande Libre,* a press service that gave news of Irish affairs. The Dutch writer Louise Stratenus invited Maud to lecture in Amsterdam and Groningen. In the Salle Humbert de Romains, Maud saw Augusta Holmes conduct her own symphony, *L'Irlande,* "a strange-looking figure in a white shirt-front, short-tailed coat and black skirt." They became acquainted, and soon the extraordinary musician who had studied with César Franck was visiting Maud and playing Irish tunes on her piano to annoy the English neighbors.

French was Maud's second tongue, and she developed an oratorical style remarkable even in a country famous for its rhetoric. At the Catholic University of the Luxembourg she described the Great Famine:

Men and women ate the dogs, the rats, and the grass
of the field, and some even, when all the food was

gone, ate the dead bodies. . . . Whole families, when they had eaten their last crust, and understood that they had to die, looked once upon the sun and then closed up the doors of their cabins with stones, that no one might look upon their last agony. Weeks afterwards men would find their skeletons gathered around the extinguished hearth. I do not exaggerate, gentlemen. I have added nothing to the mournful reality. If you come to my country, every stone will repeat to you this tragic history. It was only fifty years ago. It still lives in thousands of memories. I have been told it by women who had heard the last sigh of their children without being able to lessen their agony with one drop of milk. It has seemed to me at evening on those mountains of Ireland, so full of savage majesty when the wind sighed over the pits of the famine where the thousands of dead enrich the harvests of the future, it has seemed to me that I heard an avenging voice calling down on our oppressors the execration of men and the justice of God.

She wrung tears from cynical politicians and sous from the pockets of students who adopted the eloquent young beauty and carried her off to speak to Republican and Catholic societies in the provinces. In drab lecture rooms and city halls audiences were as fascinated by her as by the magic lantern she used to show her "documents," slides of battering ram and homeless peasants. "While speaking, the Celtic Druidess looked at no one, her great black eyes full of flame." A thousand people gave her a standing ovation in Bordeaux. At La Rochelle her fervor inspired the crowd to demonstrate outside the British Consulate.

"What a singular scene—" Yeats wrote in *United Ireland* in January 1892. "This young girl of twenty-five addressing that audience of politicians, and moving them more than all their famous speakers although she spoke in a language not her own." He went on to compare her with Oscar Wilde's mother, who wrote on Irish folklore under the pen name Speranza. "What does it mean for Ireland? Surely, that here is the new 'Speranza' who shall do with the voice all, or more than all, the old 'Speranza' did with her pen."

Maud Gonne succeeded in breaking what the Fenian John Mitchel called "the wall of silence" England had built around Ireland. Millevoye had insisted that propaganda work was her métier, and it turned out to be her triumph. With her press service and her speeches she managed to get some two thousand items a year into the French press. The internationally influential *Figaro* published a front-page story based on her speeches, *"Les Atrocités dans les Bagnes Anglais."* She was quoted by papers in Russia and Germany and countries as remote as Egypt. There was growing evidence that disapproval from abroad was troubling the English Home Office and Foreign Ministry.

She had been warned by the Paris correspondent of the *New York Daily News* that money was the only thing that affected the French press. "I proved her wrong," Maud wrote. "France is a country of great ideas and enthusiasms. Because I represented a great cause of human liberty everyone was kind. . . . I told myself all this success was luck, destiny, the will of the Gods."

Her liaison with Millevoye was serving her well in France. She depended on his connections with the press and government officials to advance the Irish cause, and she put to use all that the ambitious politician taught her. Unfortunately, her lover's opportunism began to extend even into their private life, and Maud was appalled when he suggested that her sexual favors could help their cause. Disparate values, divergent goals led to increasing friction between them. She was often troubled and unhappy, but she still believed in their political alliance, and she could not bring herself to leave the father of her child.

# CHAPTER ELEVEN

# Life out of Death

"She did not seem to have any beauty, her face was wasted, the form of the bones showing, and there was no life in her manner." More than a year had gone by since Maud fled Ireland, and she and Yeats did not see each other until she returned in July 1891. Willie came at once to her rooms in Nassau Street and was "overwhelmed with emotion, an intoxication of pity," at the change he saw in her; ". . . she hinted at some unhappiness, some disillusionment. The old hard resonance had gone and she had become gentle and indolent."

The following day he left as planned to visit his theosophical friend Charles Johnston in Ballykilbeg. They explored the old castles of County Down, made tissue-paper fire balloons which they chased across the hills. Willie tried to forget his concern for Maud.

During her absence in France he had remained faithful to his love. Johnston had broken Madame Blavatsky's rule of celibacy by marrying. MacGregor Mathers, Yeats's newest mentor, was about to marry Moina Bergson, sister of the French philosopher. At twenty-six Willie was still a virgin. The writers he knew in London were deliberate "decadents," given to every form of dissipation. When they boasted

in detail about their sexual exploits he would leave the room.
"I had never since childhood kissed a woman's lips." Maud
had become his rationale for inhibition, and he avoided temptation by telling himself, "No, I love the most beautiful
woman in the world."

While Yeats was in Ballykilbeg, Maud had a strange
dream, and on waking she wrote him about her vision of a
past life when they were brother and sister, sold into slavery
in the Arabian desert and traveling together across endless
sands. Her letter brought him back to Dublin. A few moments after he arrived at the Nassau Hotel he asked her to
marry him. He hardly looked at her but sat "holding her hand
and speaking vehemently." After a moment she drew her
hand away. She told him she could not marry him, but asked
for his friendship. Her request, which he considered unconventional, was not meant to be cruel or capricious. Maud
depended on him for understanding and sympathy, the close-
ness she had once known with Tommy. Yeats was exceptionally intuitive about women's feelings, and she felt as easy with
him as if he had been a brother. Still, she did not dare tell him
about her life in Paris, her troubles with Millevoye, her delight in her little son. Willie could not be trusted to keep a
secret, and fear of grave damage to her reputation, as well
as her need for his friendship, kept her from telling him
the truth. She told him only that she would never marry, and
she was relieved that he did not press her to become his mistress.

The next day she went out to Howth with Willie, and
some of her old gaiety returned as they revisited the hidden
coves, the wind-swept headlands each had loved in childhood.
Lying side by side on the springing heather, they watched the
gulls drifting overhead, and Maud told Willie that "if she
were to have the choice of being any bird she would choose
to be a sea gull above all." He transformed her passing
thought into "The White Birds."

> I would that we were, my beloved, white birds
>    on the foam of the sea!
> We tire of the flame of the meteor, before it can
>    fade and flee;

And the flame of the blue star of twilight, hung
    low on the rim of the sky,
Has awaked in our hearts, my beloved, a sadness
    that may not die.

That evening Maud took Willie to the little cottage near the Bailey Light where her nanny had retired. The old woman asked her unrestrainable charge, the little girl who had run so wild and gone so far, if she and Yeats were engaged to be married. Their nostalgic expedition to Howth cost ten shillings, a great sum for Willie, but when O'Leary, who had been asked to lend a few pounds, scolded him for extravagance, Willie informed him: "She does not let me pay the whole fare but stipulated a good while ago that she should pay her own share."

Maud spent many days with Yeats that summer. The passage of the Land Purchase Act in August and the imprisonment of William O'Brien and Dillon had brought the Plan of Campaign to a standstill; and fear of arrest kept Maud from political work. She had time to listen to Willie read aloud the play he was writing for her. *The Countess Cathleen*, he told her, was a "symbol of all souls who lose their peace, or their fineness, or any beauty of the spirit in political service, but chiefly of her soul that had seemed so incapable of rest," and in her unaccustomed and uneasy idleness Maud responded to the lines: "There is a kind of joy in casting hope away,/in losing joy,/in ceasing all resistance."

The interlude was shattered by an urgent message from Millevoye. Their child was ill. Maud gave Willie to believe that the Boulangists demanded her presence and that, although she considered most of them self-serving adventurers, she could not refuse. When she left, Yeats went to Sligo to finish his play, finding some anodyne for his distress in writing and in the company of his uncle, George Pollexfen, with whom he had a psychic bond.

For Maud there was no solace. Her baby was dying of meningitis. Brought up by servants herself, she had thought nothing of leaving little Georges with nursemaids in Paris while she traveled to England and Ireland. She had abandoned him; now he was being taken from her forever. Incoherent with grief and consumed by guilt, she forgot discretion enough to write Willie about "a child she had adopted" and "the death bird that had pecked at the nursery window the day when it was taken ill, and how at sight of the bird she had brought doctor after doctor."

When her son died, Maud temporarily lost her ability to speak French; she took chloroform in order to sleep and soon became addicted. She and Millevoye had the little body embalmed and ordered a memorial chapel to be built for it. A sense that she had been responsible for Georges's death bound her more than ever to her lover. The loss of the child opened the scars of earlier bereavements.

Fall 1891 was a season of death. On September 30, in Brussels, Boulanger committed suicide on the grave of his mistress. Clemenceau, hearing of it, remarked that inside the "Man on Horseback" was only "the soul of a second lieutenant." In Brighton, on the sixth of October, Parnell suffered a heart attack and died in the arms of his wife, the former Kitty O'Shea. Boulanger's death was an anticlimax to a failed cause, Parnell's a tragedy for the Irish.

Maud had met Parnell for the first time not long before, at the home of his friend and doctor, Dr. Joseph Kenny, while he was on his last campaign, wooing the "hillside men" with promises to revive the land movement and, as when a young man, espousing physical force. Like many others, Maud believed that on the verge of a triumphant return to power Parnell had been murdered by the English. She suspected them of using a weapon more deadly than calumny and disgrace when the authorities refused to allow his friends Captain O'Kelly and Pat O'Brien to see him in his coffin.

Grieving for her child, Maud left France in October. By chance she returned to Ireland on the mail boat that was carrying Parnell's body home. The little steamer tossed through heavy seas under a sky that showed no light at dawn. A dark canopy of wet umbrellas covered the crowd waiting in silence on the pier at Kingstown. Yeats was there to meet her.

They breakfasted in the dining room of the Nassau Hotel. The other guests thought Maud too theatrical for wearing deep mourning for Parnell. Yeats alone knew why she was in black. Over and over she repeated the details of Georges's death, and in her frenzy she insisted on going to Parnell's burial at Glasnevin Cemetery. Yeats, hating crowds, refused to accompany her.

Friends and enemies, Parliamentarians and Fenians, marched side by side in the largest funeral procession ever to pass through Dublin.

> Over a sea of tossing heads, falling, rising, and sinking again, polished by the falling rain, silent, the coffin went on, in the midst of the rolling drumbeat of the Dead March. Ireland's uncrowned King is gone. And a wail came from a voice in the crowd, keening. . . . No damask, silk or brocade threw beauty into the moving, silent throng; . . . no bishops, posing as sorrow and salvation, in purple and gold vestments, marched with the mourning people; many green banners, shrouded with crepe, flapped clumsily in the wet wind, touched tenderly here and there, with the flag of the United States and the flag of France, floated over the heads of the stricken host, retreating with its dead to the place that would now be his home forever.

Maud stood in the thick mud of Glasnevin and saw the star falling in lurid daylight over Parnell's grave. "It was witnessed by thousands. While his followers were committing Charles Parnell's remains to the earth, the sky was bright with strange lights and flames." Mourning her own loss among the vast crowd mourning for Parnell, Maud became strangely exhilarated at the thought that the Irish Party and Parliamentarianism were being interred with the corpse of their leader. "Dusk was coming on. As the thud of the earth sounded on the coffin, a rift in the leaden sky parted the clouds and a bright falling star was seen. Life out of death, life out of death eternally."

Yeats's philosophy of recurrent life cycles took on a new meaning. Maud often visited Willie in Ely Place, where he was staying with George Russell and some young Theosophists who experimented with meditation, hashish, hypnosis, and a vegetarian diet. Willie's school friend, the poet and painter now known as AE, made his living as a bookkeeper at Pim's the clothier, but his life was devoted to visions. His eyes that could see supernatural beings in ordinary places shone deep gray behind thick glasses. An irresistible gentleness emanated from the bearded mystic in his shabby clothes.

Maud asked AE how soon after its death a child might be reborn, and was told that it might be reborn to the same parents. The concept of reincarnation gave her hope again, and she ignored Willie's halfhearted effort to change her literal interpretation of a doctrine he considered hypothetical and symbolic. Her grief and remorse compelled her to seek relief in Yeats's spiritual philosophy.

Using cabalistic rituals he had learned in the Golden Dawn, they tried again to evoke and exorcise the gray-veiled figure which still haunted her. Yeats received only a vague impression, but Maud had a vivid encounter. She had been a priestess in ancient Egypt and had given false oracles for money under the influence of a priest who was her lover. Because of this wrongdoing the persona of her past life remained a shadowy spirit seeking reunion. Theosophical theories corroborated the result of the experiment, and AE received a similar vision of her in Egypt, and so did MacGregor Mathers's wife.

Maud did not question her own clairvoyance, but she feared her veiled persona might be a force for evil. The woman in gray had described herself as a murderess of children. Deep feelings of guilt were not easily exorcised. "She had come [to] have need of me," Yeats wrote, ". . . and I had no doubt that need would become love. I had even as I watched her a sense of cruelty, as though I were a hunter taking captive some beautiful wild creature."

In November she went with him to London, and on the sixteenth she was initiated into the Order of the Golden Dawn. After passing four initiation proceedings, she became an "outer member," with the grade of 4-7. Her motto was "Per Ignum Ad Lucem. Constatina." Yeats had advanced to grade 5-6, a Lord of the Portal, and was known in the Order as "Demon est Deus Inversus." The mumbo-jumbo in the

Golden Dawn reminded her of the fancy-dress frivolities of the Association du Saint Patrice, and for all their exotic trappings, her fratri and sorores in the Golden Dawn disappointed Maud by being as ordinary as Madame Blavatsky's "flapdoodles." She met three outstanding exceptions: Moina Mathers, the glamorous "Vestigia"; Florence Farr, the exquisite actress, "Sapientia Sapientia dono Data"; and Miss Annie Horniman, "Fortier et Recte," the daughter of a wealthy Manchester merchant, wearing high-necked puce and magenta silks.

At an initiation ceremony in the Masons' Hall in Euston Street, Maud became suspicious of the Golden Dawn's affiliation. Yeats insisted its symbolic rituals were Rosicrucian, but Maud's old army friend Claude Cane, himself a Mason, informed her that one of the passwords was used in his order. Freemasonry was too closely identified with British institutions to allow her to feel entirely comfortable with MacGregor Mathers's cabalistic rites. Although she believed in the spirit world and was impressed by Mathers's sorcery, she could not accept it all with the Order's high seriousness.

Maud had her own belief in the power of the will, inspired by Tommy when she was a girl, and she knew it was her own power on which she must rely. For some time she had been convinced that by an effort of will alone she could project her self out of her body. Some of her close friends, Ida Jameson, Charles Oldham, and J. F. Taylor, were also convinced; each had been aware of her presence in Dublin when she was in fact across the Channel. She herself paid a visit on the "astral level" to her friend Amilcare Cipriani, and when he challenged her she was able to describe just how he sat at his desk that particular night, a piece of red flannel tied around his neck for a sore throat. She could list the contents of his room in the Rue Legendre which she had not seen at any other time. While her physical body was in bed in Paris, Maud's astral being had watched her sister Kathleen nurse her sick son, Toby, in an unfamiliar house in Howth and had felt the maternal anguish which she knew all too well.

Intense concentration could produce desirable results. She was able to break her addiction to sleeping drugs and hashish. But Maud was wary of the temptation to escape from active life in psychic games. "Though will is all-powerful," she wrote, "I think each human being has only a limited amount to draw on and achieves little if he fritters it on many things, and I realized that was the danger against which I had always to guard."

Maud was recovering from the shock of her child's death. Like a pendulum set in motion, her spirit swung toward life. Yeats, who now desired to make her his lover, dreaded losing her again. Knowing she would approve of occult studies if they could be used in some practical way for Ireland, he discussed with her a plan that would use her psychic power and the mystic rituals of the Golden Dawn to revive the Celtic myths. Mathers had lost his job in Horniman *père's* museum in Forest Hill, and he and Moina were living in Paris on a stipend from the merchant's daughter Annie. At one time O'Leary had thought Mathers might be useful, but he had come to distrust the power-seeking Magus. He worried even more about Yeats's magical experiments than about his extravagant courtship of the wayward disciple.

Yeats's letters to O'Leary were full of her as always: "We had a 'Rhymers' meeting at Ellis's for Miss Gonne who has now departed for Paris where she stays for a week or ten days more, probably, and then returns here for a few days and so back to Dublin." Maud had been introduced to Yeats's literary friends who frequented the Cheshire Cheese in London: Ernest Dowson, whose religion was love— "desolate and sick of an old passion"; Lionel Johnson, the crippled religious idealist; and her favorite among them, Arthur Symons, translator, poet, critic, publicist for French Symbolism. They were rebels in their art, opposed to Victorian morality, striving for sensibility rather than conscience, in love with beauty for its own sake. Taken to meet the "Rhymers" by a proud Willie Yeats, Maud created a sensation as the physical incarnation of a heroine Burne-Jones might have painted. She was almost too vital for them. Lionel Johnson, although pro-Irish, had been prepared to dislike Maud Gonne for being too worldly and practical, but at a public dinner he changed his mind: "I had thought she did her work, perhaps, from love of notoriety, but it is a sense of duty. I saw while she was speaking that her hand was trembling. I think she has to force herself to speak."

Maud enjoyed Willie's Rhymers but found them feckless, and Yeats himself soon decided they were doomed by their English traditions. The great Victorians—Arnold, Tennyson, Swinburne—whom they wished to supplant, the rigid society they despised, forced them into self-destructive patterns of rebellion, and the creation of an art too rarefied for all its skill. Yeats named the English poets "the Tragic Generation." He was Irish: schooled by O'Leary, inspired by Maud, the young poet who had thought himself too provincial had begun a body of work dedicated in all its interwoven themes to a nation that would be reborn.

He published *The Countess Cathleen and Various Legends and Lyrics* that year with a dedication to her, and he copied his "Rose" poems expressly for her in a vellum-covered manuscript book she had given him. "When You Are Old," a testament of Yeats's love, was a rendition of Ronsard's sonnet to his mistress, Hélène de Surgères,

> *Quand vous serez bien vieille, au soir, à la chandelle,*
> *Assise auprez du feu, devidant et filant,*
> *Direz, chantant mes vers, en vous esmerveillant . . .*

Of all the poems in the collection, Maud preferred "The Two Trees," with its exaltation of mystical love. And the Countess Cathleen spoke lines she might have written for herself:

> I have heard
> A sound of wailing in unnumbered hovels,
> And I must go down, down, I know not where . . .

# CHAPTER TWELVE

# Revival and Discord

In January 1892 Maud went back to Paris and her work, lecturing and raising money for Irish prisoners. That spring, when she delivered the contributions she had received to the London Amnesty Committee, she was greeted with good news. Peter O'Callaghan, whose pitiful condition in Portland Jail had wrung her heart, was now in hospital for the removal of his injured eye. The cases of John Daly and James Egan had been reopened. In an unexpected reversal the chief of police in Birmingham had admitted that their supposed cache of nitroglycerin was planted in Egan's backyard by a double agent. Once the evidence was made public, John Redmond, the Parnellite M.P. who had previously avoided action for the Treason-Felony men, put pressure on the Home Office.

Now that the Liberals were campaigning to get back in power, Maud used her connections with M.P.s on behalf of the prisoners. Her ever hopeful suitor, John Morton, boasted that as Sir John Morley's secretary he had influenced the statesman to write a pamphlet in favor of amnesty. However, Morley did not include the Treason-Felony convicts in his plea, and Maud told Morton that the Irish would defeat his employer in the next election. To prove her point she refused to promise to campaign for Morton himself in a by-election that summer.

Spence Watson, the Quaker treasurer of the Liberal Party, insisting that Portland was a paradise compared to the Czar's prisons, urged Maud to join his Free Russia Association. Her own countrymen came first, she told him. When the Russian Embassy invited her to visit prisons in Russia so that she might describe their superiority, she declined, knowing they would allow her to see only the Czar's model institutions. She could never speak well of any prison. She turned down the opportunity to prove that the English, with all their pretensions to equal justice, were as brutal as the most infamous despot in Europe. Instead she continued her work for amnesty, lecturing in Manchester, Liverpool, Newcastle, Edinburgh, and Glasgow.

"I came to hate her politics," wrote Yeats. "My one visible rival." One day she stayed away from a political caucus to play with the tamed hawk someone had sent her from Donegal. Her candidate lost by a few votes and she blamed Yeats; "but for you," she said, "he would have been returned." O'Leary went on belittling Maud's politicking: "a beautiful woman seeking excitement"; and Sarah Purser chaffed Yeats: "Maud Gonne talks politics in Paris, and literature to you, and at the Horse Show she would talk of a clinking brood mare." He defended her by extolling the very force of spirit which took her away from him. He had urged O'Leary, "Help her to work on the Young Ireland League, for what she needs is some work of that kind in which she could lose herself, and she is, so far, enthusiastic about the League. Oldham who does not believe in it will probably try to damp her ardour. She could help by getting people together at her rooms and persuading them to lecture." Hoping to keep Maud close to him by involving her in his new plans, Yeats begged AE to go and see her whenever she arrived in Dublin, to "keep her from forgetting me and occultism."

In May 1892 Yeats and Rolleston established the Dublin branch of the Irish Literary Society, which was taken over by the veteran Fenian editor Sir Charles Gavan Duffy, recently returned from years of exile. The National Literary Society, as it was called in Ireland, was affiliated with Young Ireland groups throughout the country. By publishing books of Irish literature and distributing them to libraries set up in cities and towns throughout Ireland, Yeats hoped to foster a new school of Irish writers and create a new audience; a national identity would arise from a truly national culture. Maud agreed to serve on the founding committee, which represented a wide range of political opinion, from the Unionist Sir Horace Plunkett, founder of a cooperative farmers' association, to the separatist O'Leary; from the traditionalist Duffy to the young scholar Douglas Hyde. Dublin could do without another literary society, thought Maud, but Yeats's innovative project might serve the Irish people.

To Yeats's delight she gave up her rooms in Paris and immersed herself in work for his society. In June she shared the rostrum with Yeats and Dr. Sigerson at the first big meeting of the National Literary Society. In August she was arranging for a concert by William Ledwidge, the Irish singer called Ludwig, at the inaugural ceremony.

In the fall Maud had a sentimental reunion with Millevoye in the Auvergne, at the inn of *la belle meunière*, and then went to Paris to raise money for Yeats's libraries. At the same time she promoted a scheme of her own to develop cottage industries for Donegal weavers by selling Irish tweed to French modistes.

Back in Ireland again that winter, Maud distributed Irish books and lectured in country towns. Still questioning the importance of spreading culture ahead of food, she persevered and established three of the seven libraries set up by the National Literary Society. Yeats's plan to send out a traveling theater in the wake of the book carts did not materialize, and Maud Gonne was the only player to go on tour. But her appearance in those remote villages meant more than the books she brought with her.

Writing about Maud's work in the confused period after Parnell, when the nationalist forces needed to be united by some new direction, Yeats said, ". . . a mastery over a popular feeling, abandoned by the members of Parliament through a quarrel that was to last for nine years, was about to pass into her hands." Yeats himself was making a bid for that mastery, but his crusade for a new national literature was plagued by dissension from the outset. Personal rivalries, conflicts between political, religious, and intellectual factions reflected the currents of nationalism in the Irish Renaissance.

While Maud was raising money in Paris, Douglas Hyde, president of the National Literary Society, addressed a meeting in Leinster Hall on November 25, 1892. His speech, "On the Necessity for De-Anglicising the Irish People," challenged the Irish to be Irish, to end the ignominious anomaly of aping the English and hating them at the same time. Hyde struck a popular chord, and a few months later Eoin MacNeil, a young civil servant in County Antrim, took up the challenge and founded the Gaelic League, of which Hyde also became president. His organization was nonpolitical, but Hyde's former pupil supported his belief in the importance of a separate language for a separate nation. Yeats, for whom the substance of Gaelic legend was more important than the tongue, criticized Hyde for capitulating to the popular taste of the traditionalists, "the Harps and Pepperpots."

Few of his colleagues understood Yeats's desire to create a new literature free of the patriotic rhetoric that had become banal. Historians and scholars who wanted to promulgate their dry theses outvoted him. Attacking the works of the Young Irelanders of '48, Yeats outraged old Duffy, who had published the Young Irelanders in the *Nation* fifty years earlier, by calling the traditional verses outworn war cries. Except for AE and O'Leary, who stood by him, his founding committee sided with the traditionalists. Oldham and J. F. Taylor, Maud's good friends, deserted him, and Maud herself saw no harm in republishing the old-fashioned rhymes and war songs which still stirred Irish patriots.

> Did they dare, did they dare to slay Owen Roe
>     O'Neill?
> Yes, they slew with poison him they feared to
>     meet with steel.
> May God wither up their hearts! May their blood
>     cease to flow!
> May they walk in living death who poisoned
>     Owen Roe!

Unable to believe that the future of Ireland was at stake in her friends' dispute, she tried to keep out of it and disappointed Yeats with her lack of support. She warned him against the intellectual snobbery which offended popular sentiment. When Archbishop Walsh denounced the unorthodox religious element in *Countess Cathleen,* Yeats's opponents had another weapon, and when even the young intellectuals turned against him, O'Leary felt forced to tell Yeats he could accomplish no more in Dublin.

Despairing over public defeat, Yeats began again to urge Maud to marry him; he decided he needed a "hostess more than a society." More concerned with work than personal matters, she again retreated from his "perplexed wooing." Her ability to overlook intellectual differences for the sake of friendship or common political goals tormented Yeats, who saw her surrounded and loved by his enemies. J. F. Taylor's apparent influence exacerbated his jealousy, and at one meeting the infuriated young poet and the proud master of rhetoric came to blows in her presence. Unhappy, Willie grew defensive and inarticulate. Maud accused him of arrogance, and to punish him she neglected him for the company of more active men and women.

Willie Rooney, an aspiring young poet of nineteen, and his comrade, the brilliant, taciturn, and equally young printer Arthur Griffith, both came from working-class Catholic families. They were interested not only in the dissemination of Irish culture but in independent political action to unite Parnellites and anti-Parnellites. Rooney had organized the Celtic Literary Society to serve the working people of Dublin. Maud, with her total disregard of class, had the highest admiration for its democratic principles and liked its journal, *An Seanachie,* which encouraged contributions from "backwoodsmen," a welcome antidote to Yeats's erudite literary goals.

In Dublin's slums, in the Catholic townships of the South, and in the industrial centers of the Protestant North, a new generation of disaffected youth was growing up. In England too, where Irish nationalism claimed attention from Keir Hardie's Independent Labour Party, young trade unionists, along with Socialists like James Connolly, were joining

the struggle for independence. The leadership of the nationalist movement was passing out of the hands of Anglo-Irish
idealists and upper-class politicians. New voices spoke out at
committee meetings, and as the drive for women's rights
gathered momentum, some of the most outspoken were
women. Anna Johnston, the delicate poet who wrote under
the pen name Ethna Carberry, and Alice Milligan were planning to publish a nationalist journal in Belfast, to be called the
*Shan Van Vocht*, the "Poor Old Woman." At "headquarters"
on Nassau Street, Maud introduced her new friends to the
older Fenians. Arthur Griffith and Willie Rooney came with
their sisters and the young women from Belfast to meet John
O'Leary, Dr. Sigerson, and J. F. Taylor. Douglas Hyde, AE,
and doddering Sir Charles climbed the steep stairs to her
rooms. The talk that went on over countless cups of tea and
innumerable cigarettes was more of politics than books, rang-
ing from Horace Plunkett's plans for Irish agriculture to Willie Rooney's revolutionary Fenianism. Maud was drawn to
every rebellious spirit. "It was my philosophy of life applied
to art and politics. I never willingly discouraged either a
Dynamiter or a constitutionalist, a realist or a lyrical writer.
My chief preoccupation was how their work could help forward the Irish Separatist movement."

Yeats would join the gatherings at Nassau Street and
suffer the tedium of political discussions simply to be near
Maud. She seemed to him an easy prey for the unscrupulous
who took advantage of her generosity, and, seeing her surrounded by admirers, he criticized her lack of discrimination.
She accused him of being an insufferable snob. She deplored
his tendency to withdraw from life; he feared her incautious
involvement. Both were stubborn: Maud with the self-confidence of conviction, Willie with the inflamed ego of self-doubt.
Their arguments about Irish art versus patriotic propaganda,
an Irish elite opposed to a popular mass movement, struck a
fundamental discord. Early in the summer the tension between them exploded in a violent quarrel—and behind it
loomed the sexual impasse, his unrequited desire, her refusal
to marry.

As if to raise a stronger barrier between herself and
Willie, Maud fell ill. Her cold developed into severe lung

congestion. Yeats's literary opponent, Dr. Sigerson, refused to let her have visitors. An old Fenian whom she had befriended sneaked up to her rooms and, letting himself in, knelt by her couch to beg her not to die, vowing that if she did, Dublin would hold its biggest funeral ever. A pathetic woman, one of Maud's many protégés, came to nurse her and turned out to be a troublemaker, hinting at some unpleasant mystery behind the drawn curtains at Nassau Street. Willie found the woman morbidly offensive but, beside himself with anxiety, arranged to meet her by night in a public garden to try to keep informed about Maud's health. She told him he would never see Maud Gonne again. "She loved another, indeed perhaps two others, for ill as she was she had decided to hurry back to France to be present at a duel between them . . . had even forbidden them to fight before her arrival." He could no longer endure the hideous lies circulated by his enemies in Dublin: "I had been Maud Gonne's lover, and there had been an illegal operation and I had been present during the operation." Yeats fled to Sligo and sought consolation in the shimmering mountain lakes, the Innisfree of his boyhood.

Maud and Yeats, both still in their twenties, had become controversial figures. Their Dublin, contentious and traditional, was too small to grant them privacy. Both of them tended to dramatize themselves, and as their paths diverged their private quarrel became a public drama. Maud thought he chose the more difficult way, "a road of outer peace and inner confusion." For her there were no alternatives. She plunged ahead, single-minded. She did not bother to refute the slanders of enemies and envious colleagues, but, ill and unhappy, desired only to escape. Her cousin May came over from London to take charge and, ignoring Dr. Sigerson's protests, made arrangements for Maud to leave for France. She was so weak she had to be carried to the train.

# CHAPTER THIRTEEN

# La Sale
# Epoque

After Boulanger's suicide and the death of the little boy named with such loving expectation for the *brave Général*, Millevoye had severe spells of melancholia. Distressed by her own illness, Maud arrived in Paris to find a defeated man waiting for her. Millevoye and Déroulède had been forced to resign from the Chamber early in 1893, when graft and bribery exposed in the failure of De Lesseps' canal venture in Panama ousted more than a hundred deputies. Even Clemenceau was implicated in the scandal through funds received for his paper, *La Justice*, from Cornelius Herz, a Jewish financier involved in De Lesseps' company.

The virulence stirred up by the Panama Affair exploded in the crack of dueling pistols behind empty grandstands at Auteuil and Longchamps. Edouard Drumont, editor of *La Libre Parole*, the most rabid anti-Semitic journal, challenged a Jewish army officer. Déroulède, whose "Patriots" were multiplying in the racist Ligue de la Patrie, challenged Clemenceau, and news of their duel may have prompted the rumor in Dublin about two Frenchmen fighting over Maud Gonne.

In June 1894 an Italian workingman assassinated President Carnot, crying, *"Vive la révolution, vive l'anarchie!"* Corruption, anti-Semitism, and violence were climaxed by the arrest of Captain Dreyfus on charges of giving secret information to Germany. La Belle Epoque degenerated into La Sale Epoque, and "through the center of it, turning to make a front now here, now there, and beating down opponents with his mace, Clemenceau long strode, reckless, aggressive and triumphant."

"*L'homme sinistre,*" as he was called by the reactionaries, escaped the smears of the Panama Affair only to fall into a trap laid by Millevoye's colleagues. Forged documents, purportedly stolen by a Mr. Norton from the British Foreign Office, were used to prove that Clemenceau, now a leader of the pro-English parties, was in the pay of England. His constituents turned against him, taunting, "Spik Ingleesh, A-oh yes!" and he lost the next election. But the forgeries were soon exposed, and Millevoye, who had publicized the Norton papers as bona fide, was discredited. His letters to the press claiming he had been deceived by M. Develle, Minister of Foreign Affairs, in a scheme worthy of "the Venetian Republic," were in vain. As journalist and as politician he was ruined, and many of his former allies, including his friend Henri de Rochefort, the volatile editor of *L'Intransigeant,* deserted him. Paralyzed by the fear that he was too old to begin again, Millevoye turned to Maud for help.

Knowing how action could restore her own energy, she urged him to fight back. The editorship of *La Patrie,* a newspaper owned by Jules Jaluzot, director of the department store Les Printemps, was available, and she persuaded Lucien to take the job. Her prescription resulted in more than a cure; success restored Millevoye's influence, and he began to publish Maud's anti-English propaganda again. She learned that Clemenceau was displeased: "We must break the friendship of Millevoye and Miss Gonne, or break them one through the other." The enmity of the pro-English forces in France was a measure of her accomplishment, but Maud became alarmed when a prefecture official whom she met in Madame Rattazzi's crowded salon whispered that she harbored a spy in her own household.

She was accustomed to the antics of the "G men," the Castle sleuths in Dublin who followed her even into the inner sanctum of ladies' garments in Switzers department store, and she was fully aware that the British Secret Service was trailing her around Paris. But she always trusted people close to her, and she found it unthinkable that anyone employed in her home would betray her. Compelled to investigate, she realized that her mail was being delayed, and a camera hidden in a servant's room on the top floor of the apartment house convinced her against her will that Maria, the French maid who had cared for her for three years, must be the traitor.

Shaken, Maud went off for a day at Fontainebleau to think things out. With Dagda to protect her she wandered through the forest of birch and oak where posted signs warned: "Those who leave the beaten paths should beware of adders." Snakes underfoot or brigands among the trees were no menace compared to the plot at home. That evening she dined alone at the restaurant near Les Gorges de Franchard and, smoking one cigarette after another over her wine, recalled the time when a French doctor had ordered her to have an operation to cure a minor illness, and Maria, obviously acquainted with him, had infuriated him by impulsively begging Maud not to follow his advice. The incident, puzzling at the time, was clearly part of an ominous pattern.

She accused the maid of intercepting her mail for the English, only to learn from the distraught woman that it was not the British Secret Service but Clemenceau who was paying Maria's son for photographs of Maud's letters. They were to be used for blackmail to prevent Millevoye from publicizing Clemenceau's financial involvement with Cornelius Herz.

Maud dismissed Maria and, refusing to be bullied, insisted that Millevoye publish his incriminating information about Clemenceau. However, the purloined letters continued to worry her. By chance she spotted the editor of one of Paris's scandal sheets in a shooting gallery on the Champs Elysées. On a hunch, she went in and challenged him to a match. Tommy's early target practice served her well, and Maud Gonne was declared the winner by the assembled journalists and duelists: *"Mais elle est terrible, la belle Irlandaise."* She heard no more about her letters.

Maud had become entangled in the vicious charges and countercharges which split French society at the time of the

Dreyfus case. The Boulangists she had met through Millevoye seven years earlier, when she was young and much more
innocent, had become anti-Semites and counterrevolutionar-
ies. The heroic dream that had united Maud and Lucien was
dissolving in an ugly Götterdämmerung. Yet Paris was still
the capital of the world for artists, its studios and theaters
alive with the Symbolists' experimental dramas, the post-
Impressionists' fluid color; the revealing scarves of the dancer
Loie Fuller expressing a new freedom. Mallarmé wrote: "The
whole age is full of the trembling of the veil of the temple," and Yeats copied the phrase in his journal. He came to
Paris for the first time in February 1894, with an introduction
from Arthur Symons to Paul Verlaine. He climbed the rotted
stairway in the Rue St. Jacques and met the old master of
Symbolism and the homely woman who was servant and
mistress in their den cluttered with papers and rags, drawings
and absinthe bottles.

In Paris, Yeats stayed on the Left Bank with the Magus
of the Golden Dawn and his wife at 1 Avenue Duquesne in
the Champ-de-Mars. Despite her doubts about Mathers,
Maud was fond of his wife and intrigued by their performances. Moina, an enchantress in white chiffon, hair flowing
loose and crowned by a paper lotus, practiced the rites of Isis,
while her husband, wearing long robes and a leopard skin
with spots symbolizing the zodiac flung over one shoulder,
invoked the goddess. His brother-in-law, Henri Bergson, was
obviously unimpressed, and his fine clothes and discreet manners seemed out of place when he visited the bizarre household.

Maud's new apartment, more spacious and elegant than
any she had occupied before, was on the Right Bank, on the
Avenue d'Eylau. She had not fully recovered from her illness
and, as Yeats noticed when he came to call, still climbed the
stairs slowly and with difficulty. Careful to conceal Millevoye's part in her life, Maud kept Willie at a distance, but she
was happy to show him the Paris she had known and loved
for so long: the tree-lined boulevards open to the sky, the little
streets under the wings of Gothic angels, the magnificence of
the Opéra and the French Academy. Willie too preferred the

chimeras and demon lovers painted in sumptuous color by Gustave Moreau to the subjects of his pupils, Monet and Rouault. At her Téâtre de la Renaissance, Sarah Bernhardt in Rostand's *La Princesse Lointaine* was playing a part Yeats might have imagined for Maud.

She went with him to the opening of *Axel,* by Villiers de l'Isle-Adam. With her beside him to translate, they sat listening to interminable flowery passages: "I am the most mournful of virgins. . . . Alas, flowers and children have died in my shadow. Give way to my love. I will teach you the marvellous words which intoxicate like the wine of the East. . . . Oh, to veil you with my hair, where you will breathe the spirit of dead roses." For five long hours they watched Count Axel of Auersburg and Sara, a young French noblewoman, madly in love, persuade themselves if not the audience that they must renounce their passion and die together to find a greater fulfillment.

"One fat old critic who sat near me," Willie wrote in his review of *Axel* for the London *Bookman,* "so soon as the Magician of the Rosy-Cross, who is the chief person of the third act, began to denounce the life of pleasure and to utter the ancient doctrine of the spirit, turned round with his back to the stage and looked at the pretty girls through his opera glass . . ."

Maud could not accept Villiers' philosophy, "As for living, our servants will do that for us . . ." which had great appeal for Yeats. She would always plead for life, just as, in the play, Sara resisted the poisoned goblet in Axel's castle and begged the Count to remember the fight for justice and the freedom of the human race. Yet the lovers' renunciation affected Maud, for she had conflicting feelings about physical love. She no longer had any physical desire for Lucien, and at the same time she wanted to have another child. She clung to the idea that the spirit of little Georges might be reborn to them, and Lucien shared her fantasy. For that wild hope she resumed intimate relations with her lover, and on one occasion they made love in the vault of their son's memorial. When their second child, a girl whom they named Iseult, was born early in 1895, Maud cherished the belief that she had been conceived in that sacred place.

She was fiercely possessive of her infant and hated to leave Iseult in the care of servants. Her beautiful little daughter, loved from the first as a person in her own right, reawakened Maud's powerful maternal feelings, and that most rewarding responsibility made it difficult for her to resume work for Ireland. But as always she believed that commitments must be carried out, and the Irish cause took precedence over her personal affairs. She gradually began to write and lecture again, and in the summer of 1895 she went to England to work directly for the release of the political prisoners.

# CHAPTER FOURTEEN

# "In Dreams Begins Responsibility"

Maud had vowed that she would see John Morley, Gladstone's Chief Secretary for Ireland, defeated in the next election for ignoring the cases of the Treason-Felony prisoners. The Liberal M.P. who had refused to speak out for their release was campaigning in Newcastle-on-Tyne, and Maud hurried there to persuade the Irish Party leaders to support Keir Hardie's Labour Party candidate. Her electioneering helped split the Liberal vote, and Morley lost to his Conservative opponent.

Her personal triumph was a hollow victory. The Irish Parliamentary Party, leaderless and divided, no longer held the balance in Parliament. The rise of the Independent Labour Party in England gave the Conservatives a large majority in the general election of 1895. Lord Salisbury was back as Prime Minister, and the imperialists were in control, with Joseph Chamberlain heading the Colonial Office. The race for the gold of South Africa got under way with the ill-fated Jameson Raid. British garrisons were in action from the Sudan to Bengal. The Irish nationalist movement was at a standstill, the Plan of Campaign dissolved, the representation at Westminster powerless. It was time to find different weapons.

The Amnesty Association, with two hundred thousand

members in the British Isles alone, could exert considerable pressure on the government. Disapproval from abroad had even more influence on an imperialist government which tried to retain the myth of benign colonialism. The propaganda Maud circulated in the French press was extremely effective in opening prison gates. One by one the long sentences were lifted, releasing men who had aged beyond their years: some to exile; others, less fortunate, to hospitals and insane asylums. After serving ten years of a life sentence for the bombing of the Tower of London, young Jimmy Cunningham got a new start in the healing hands of Maud's old nurse in Howth. Her interest in each of the Treason-Felony men from Portland was personal, and she continued to look after them and their families; as Oscar Wilde, now in Reading Gaol, had said about George Sand, "For the aristocracy of the intellect she had always the deepest veneration, but the democracy of the suffering touched her more."

To keep up her work in two countries, she crossed the Channel many times. She rarely spent more than a month in one place, and chance more than deliberation kept her from meeting Willie. While she was in London he was invited to visit Sir Henry Gore-Booth and his family in their great house in Sligo. He had parted from Maud in Paris rejected and hopeless, and in the aristocratic ambience of Lissadell, Willie was much taken by the daughters of the great house: Constance, whose voice reminded him of Maud's, and the sympathetic Eva, to whom he gave his heartbroken confidences. Maud, having lectured in Scotland, was on her way back to Paris when Willie returned to London.

He left his father's house in Bedford Park and took rooms at Fountain Court, in the Temple, with Arthur Symons. Thirty, and determined at last to shake his obsession for Maud in the pursuit of another love, he was attracted by the distinguished dark beauty and cameo profile of Olivia Shakespear. Lionel Johnson's intellectual cousin flirted with him at a London dinner party and gave the impression that in her unhappy life with an older husband she had many extramarital adventures. Yeats soon discovered during their carefully public trysts in picture galleries and railway carriages that Mrs. Shakespear was almost as inexperienced as he. In a desperate attempt to establish intimacy, he invited her to Fountain Court in Symons's absence. Distracted by thoughts of his old love, he forgot his door key when he went out to buy cakes for tea and was forced to let himself back in through an attic window. The tête-à-tête did not lead to the hoped for consummation, and Willie kept the sympathetic Symons, who never lacked a mistress, awake all night listening to his talk about Maud Gonne.

On the day of the fiasco, Maud saw an apparition. She was talking with some friends in her hotel in Dublin when Willie appeared before her eyes. She asked his spirit to return to her later, and that evening he came again to stand beside her bed. All that night their spirits wandered together over the cliffs of Howth, and the next morning she wrote him about it: "It was very sad and all the sea gulls were asleep." Her letter put an end to Willie's ambivalent courtship of the unhappily married woman. "All my old love had now come back to me," he wrote, and as in the swans' courting dance—one advancing, the other retreating—Maud drew closer to him again. Willie's infatuations for other women— Florence Farr or Olivia Shakespear—gave Maud no cause for concern. Her impulse to write him, and her hallucination too, sprang from her unhappiness about Millevoye and a deep need for the understanding and sense of identity Willie alone could give her.

Her unconventional way of life, her controversial politics kept her in the public eye, and public acclaim demanded a continuing performance which sometimes exhausted her inner resources. "She hated her own beauty," wrote Yeats; "not its effect upon others, but its image in the mirror." And she belittled her physical attractiveness as if it were a gift from the gods that was a burden rather than a blessing. Maud's remarkable looks won superficial attention, but she missed the reassurance of being recognized for herself.

"Women who have poets for friends have no idea how lucky they are." Maud Gonne needed her poet who held the miraculous mirror in which she saw herself reflected noble and complete. She sensed that if she should draw too close, her reflection would become distorted. "My outer nature was passive," wrote Yeats; "but for her I should never perhaps have left my desk—but I knew that my spiritual nature was passionate, even violent. In her all this was reversed, for it was her spirit only that was gentle and passive and full of charming fantasy, as though it touched the world only with the point of its finger. . . . I, who could not influence her actions, could dominate her inner being."

Or so he believed, and he continued to seek some spiritual project for Ireland in which he might direct Maud's energies. His ideas about a Celtic revival had taken a new form when he visited Douglas Hyde at Frenchpark in Roscommon, the heartland of Ireland rolling and green over the burial mounds of Iron Age tribes, the realm of Maeve, the Warrior Queen of Connaught. In Lough Key, where he and Hyde went fishing, there was a castle on a wooded, rocky island where Druids must have walked. Abandoned but habitable, it was for rent, and from that day on, Yeats thought of Castle Rock as a temple where he and Maud would be priest and priestess. Together they would create mystic rites and disciplines for a new cult, similar to the Order of the Golden Dawn but associated directly with Irish culture. The finest young men and women in the country would come to Lough Key to be initiated into the mysteries and, fortified with supernatural power, set out from Ireland's modern Eleusis to work for national independence.

Yeats's dream of a Castle of the Heroes revived Maud's enthusiasm for what they might accomplish together. "The land of Ireland, we both felt, was powerfully alive and invisibly peopled, and whenever we grew despondent over the weakness of the national movement, we went to it for comfort. If only we could make contact with the hidden forces of the land, it would give us strength for the freeing of Ireland. Most of our talk centred round this and it led us both into strange places."

When Willie returned to Paris that winter it was to work with Maud on rituals for the Castle of the Heroes. She introduced him to the Celtic studies of John Rhys and D'Arbois de Jubainville, her friend from the Association du Saint Patrice. They read the sacred books of the cabala and studied the symbols of the tarot, the sword, stone, spear, and cauldron corresponding to the four talismans of the ancient Celtic people. Enthralled by magic, Maud neglected her lectures and deadlines; her past disagreements with Willie disappeared like the pale smoke of incense in their midnight séances. "Politics were merely a means of meeting," he wrote, "but this was a link so perfect that [it] would restore at once, even [after] a quarrel, the sense of intimacy."

Kindred spirits were enlisted to help in the establishment of their mystical Irish order. George Pollexfen in Sligo was called on for his extraordinary psychic visions, and Lady Gregory in Galway, whom Yeats had met for the first time that summer, contributed her knowledge of Irish folklore. AE sent messages from Dublin. In Paris they worked with Mathers and the Scottish poet William Sharp, whose mysterious alter ego, Fiona Macleod, offered her services to the Castle of the Heroes. All were sworn to secrecy. They met in bustling cafés and hushed drawing rooms and talked of the spirit world.

Maud and Willie took hashish to heighten their fantasies and recorded them in a notebook filled with sacred symbols. They found they could evoke the pagan gods, Willie transforming the visions Maud saw in her trances into images of Druidic lore. "There would be, as it were, a spiritual birth from the soul of a man and a woman. I knew that the incomprehensible life could select from our memories and, I believed, from the memory of the race itself."

Maud could not enjoy sedentary work in a hothouse atmosphere indefinitely. Deciding to combine spiritualism with practicality, she urged Willie to help her organize a branch of the Young Ireland Society in Paris. L'Association Irlandaise, inaugurated on New Year's Day 1897, had for its first members Stephen MacKenna, the classicist; Richard Best, the Celtic scholar; Arthur Lynch, Paris correspondent for the *Daily Mail*; and Miss Barry O'Delaney, secretary of *L'Irlande Libre*.

In the Hôtel Corneille, where he was staying, Yeats met John Millington Synge, a student of languages who was reading Marx, Thoreau, and Racine and writing morbid verse in a little garret under the gabled roof. Yeats tried to dispel the young Irishman's melancholy with talk of Ireland. Synge was interested in the Irish literary revival, and was soon taken to see Maud Gonne in her apartment on the Avenue d'Eylau. She had already captivated his closest friend, Stephen Mac-Kenna, who was struggling to make a living as a free-lance journalist on the Rue d'Assas. "Synge lives on what Mac-Kenna lends him, and MacKenna lives on what Synge pays him back."

Maud introduced Synge to the critic Augustin Homan, who had translated Shaw's plays and arranged for him to work with D'Arbois de Jubainville, whose lectures on Celtic literature at the College of France he found of "inestimable value." A solitary man, not a joiner, Synge allowed himself to be lured into Maud's Association Irlandaise with serious reservations. Believing that Ireland could come into its own only when socialist ideas took hold in England, he was strongly opposed to the use of physical force in the struggle for freedom. His sympathies were nationalist, but he loathed political movements and their propaganda. According to MacKenna, who held Maud in high esteem, Synge "flamed or rather turned a filthy yellow with rage over them," and "gently hated Miss Gonne for those she launched or tolerated." Once when she was giving a lecture on Queen Victoria's complicity in the Irish Famine, a French member of the audience asked Synge if her statements were true. He shrugged his shoulders and replied, *"Je ne sais pas."* Early in the year he withdrew as an active member of her Association:

> Dear Miss Gonne, I am sorry to trouble you again so soon, but I have something to say which it seems better to say by letter than in one of our meetings, as there French members might misconstrue our difference of opinion. You already know how widely my theory of regeneration for Ireland differs from yours . . . I wish to work in my own way for the cause of Ireland, and I shall never be able to do so if I get mixed up with a revolutionary and semi-military movement. . . . If you think well I shall be glad to attend your meetings in a purely non-official capacity. . . . As a member I should have henceforth to contend every point raised in reference to the journal . . . but as a spectator I can still help you

where and whenever it is in my power and for the
rest keep an uncompromising silence.

Maud expressed her hope that he would continue to
come to the meetings, and for months afterward the handsome young writer was present, tactful and silent.

At the end of January 1897 the Hôtel Corneille, which
harbored so many artists and scholarly refugees at the rate of
one pound weekly, became too expensive for Yeats. He had
to leave Maud and abandon their work, though not their
dreams, for the Castle of the Heroes. With only a dozen members, the Association Irlandaise became primarily a talking
society that sent messages of support to nationalist organizations in Britain and America, where intensive preparations
were beginning for the Wolfe Tone Centenary the following
year. Maud saw an opportunity to be useful.

She decided to go to America to raise funds for the '98
commemorative committees as well as the Amnesty Association's prisoner relief work. Much to her surprise, the Dublin
Wolfe Tone Committee refused to give her authorization.
Furious at being turned down, she followed Yeats to London
to ask him to use on her behalf his influence as a member of
the London committee. He was more than willing to help,
and the spirit of '98 carried him with her back into active
public life. He allowed himself to be elected president of the
Centenary Association for Great Britain and France, thinking he could prevent any swing toward the extreme Fenianism he feared. To keep Ireland from violence—and Maud and
Ireland were now almost synonymous in his mind—Yeats
constructed another grand scheme. Representing all nationalist factions, the Wolfe Tone Committees should form a council which would send delegates to Westminster as Ireland's
only parliamentary representatives. There was a chance that
their united front would make the English give way, so that
force would not be necessary to achieve separation.

Maud, who had been among the first after Parnell's
death to urge publicly that all Irish members of Parliament
should withdraw from Westminster, thought Willie was
whistling up the wind. She suggested to him that "eighty
ragged and drunken Dublin beggars or eighty pugilists be

sent to Parliament 'to be paid by results.' " He felt wronged by her mockery, considering all the difficulties he had put up with for her sake. But Maud always spoke her mind to Willie, and in her youthful spontaneity "never admitted the difficulty in doing anything."

In April, shortly after the outbreak of the war between Greece and Turkey, she returned to Paris. In a city seething with partisans, her associates were all strongly pro-Greek. She was meeting with them one evening on the terrace of the Café Harcourt to "conspire" against the Turks when a mob of students with similar sympathies ran down the Boulevard Saint Michel pursued by baton-swinging police. To escape the mêlée, her little party climbed up on chairs and tables and were crushed against the plate-glass window of the café. Synge, already suffering from Hodgkin's disease, received a heavy blow on the head and was in bed for weeks. The incident was decisive for MacKenna, who left soon after to fight in Greece, where the dashing Italian anarchist Cipriani had already gone. A month later Maud saw her friends return, Cipriani on crutches, MacKenna disappointed by the ugliness of modern Greeks. Maud scolded them for their Byronic little war. Killing was justifiable only for one's own country.

# CHAPTER FIFTEEN

# Jubilees and Conspiracies

Jubilee 1897—the sixtieth year of Victoria's reign. While Maud was in London, Keir Hardie asked her to help organize anti-Jubilee protests in the "heart of the Empire." She called at his office, where the Independent Labour Party published its newspaper, to explain that her work was with and for the Irish people. Her words carried a note of contempt. She still remembered how the huge crowd of workers in Trafalgar Square had melted away before a few unarmed police. Ever since, she had considered all English people, Liberals and Conservatives alike, cowards. Hardie's forces had no chance of achieving power in the near future, she thought. Uninterested in long-term ideologies, Maud put her faith in popular movements and leaders who were strong and pragmatic.

James Connolly was such a man. Irish, he happened also to be a Socialist. When Maud met him in 1897 he had begun to form the Irish Socialist Republican Party, an amalgamation of the handful of Socialist groups in Ireland. Born of Irish parents in Edinburgh in the dank slum of Cowgate, he had gone to work at eleven as a baker, become a printer, then served as a soldier in the British Army. The stocky, square-jawed youth emerged from his rough apprenticeship a Marxist and a dedicated Socialist. At twenty-eight he had come to

Dublin with his wife and children to work for a free republic. Only five feet six, Connolly more than balanced his lack of physical stature with the bravery, brilliance, and sense of humor that made him a popular leader among men. Women liked him too; they saw in him one of the rare leaders who treated them as equals.

Maud loved and admired him, "the bravest man I knew," and she printed excerpts from his speeches in *L'Irlande Libre*. She was no Marxist, but she appreciated Connolly's sympathy for working people and felt instinctively that he would put Ireland's freedom ahead of international revolution. Anna Johnston and Alice Milligan published his articles in their *Shan Van Vocht* with an editorial disclaimer for his Marxism which was less inflammatory than they feared, but prophetic.

> If you remove the English Army tomorrow and hoist the green flag over Dublin Castle, unless you set about the organization of the socialist republic, your efforts would be in vain. England would still rule you. She would rule you through her capitalists, through her landlords, through her financiers, through the whole array of commercial and industrial institutions she has planted in the country and watered with the tears of our mothers and the blood of our martyrs. England would still rule you to your ruin, even while your lips offered hypocritical homage at the shrine of the Freedom whose cause you betrayed.

Barred from participation in the Wolfe Tone Committee demonstrations, the Irish Socialist Republican Party decided to hold an independent anti-Jubilee protest. Without hesitation Maud accepted Connolly's invitation, but when she saw her name billed as the principal speaker at a Socialist meeting she balked. The close link with Socialists could harm her influence elsewhere.

Yeats, in Dublin to meet with the Wolfe Tone Centenary Executive Council, happened to be with Maud the morning she told Connolly she had changed her mind, and saw the party leader leave Nassau Street downcast at losing Maud's eloquence and popular appeal. His followers would doubt that he had ever had her support. Willie "softened her heart" on the young Socialist's behalf, and that same afternoon she went to see him in the tenement district near the Liffey. Charlemont Street—the stench and filth of blackened hallways, derelicts sprawled on the landings, families of six in one dim-lit room. Nothing she had encountered in the hovels of Donegal was so ugly or demeaning as the life of the poor in the Dublin tenement where Connolly and his wife Lillie and their four children lived.

She stood in the doorway with Dagda at her side, and Nora Connolly, aged six, looked up at the tall, beautiful figure which seemed to fill the room with light. Mrs. Connolly was bathing her youngest child, Agna, in the tin tub. The great beast lunged forward to lick the cake of soap, and the baby screamed as her mother clutched her. "His name is Dagda," said Maud. "Don't be afraid." Wherever poverty existed, women and children suffered most. For the sake of Connolly's family Maud changed her mind again.

On June 20, the eve of Victoria's Jubilee, Maud stood on a chair in College Green addressing Connolly's Socialists. Yeats listened with the crowd below as she told how she had gone the day before to St. Michan's to decorate the graves of Irish martyrs, only to be turned away because of the Queen's holiday. Speaking slowly in a low voice that yet seemed to go through the crowd, she asked, "Must the graves of our dead go undecorated because Victoria has her Jubilee?"

Connolly and Maud shared a penchant for showmanship, madcap and reckless. For the anti-Jubilee demonstration on June 21, Maud arranged for the use of a window in the National Club in Parnell Square to project lantern slides of eviction scenes and pictures of Irish martyrs imprisoned or executed during Victoria's reign. Sympathetic workmen in the Dublin Corporation would cut the city's electric power to extinguish the festive lights displayed in Unionist store fronts. Maud embroidered black flags in white with facts and figures about the death toll of the famines, and Connolly saw to the construction of a large black coffin inscribed "The

British Empire," to be carried in a mock funeral procession.

The night of June 21, Maud and Yeats with some of the other delegates to the Centenary Executive Council left their meeting in City Hall and joined Connolly's parade. The Irish Socialist Republicans marched up Dame Street bearing the coffin she had designed, draped with her flags on a rickety handcart. Maud strode through the dark streets, head thrown back in exultation. "With a joyous face, she had taken all those people into her heart . . . ," wrote Yeats. "Then I too resigned myself and felt the excitement of the moment, that joyous responsibility and sense of power." Bystanders joined the procession; windows were smashed, Unionist shops looted. Mounted police were rushed from Dublin Castle. Connolly saved the coffin of the British Empire from capture by telling the pallbearers to throw it into the Liffey. The crowd roared wild approval. Police and horses charged. Connolly was knocked down and arrested. More than two hundred were wounded that night, and one woman was killed.

Next morning Maud went out to Bridewell Prison, where Connolly was being held, arranged to get him a lawyer, and found him some breakfast. She paid his fine herself, raised bail for the many others who had been arrested, and got Tim Harrington to defend them.

Connolly managed to put on more illegal demonstrations that summer, and Maud continued to admire his boldness, as she had after the first one: "Bravo! all my congratulations to you! You were right and I was wrong about this evening. You may have the satisfaction of knowing that you saved Dublin from the humiliation of an English jubilee without a public meeting of protestation. You were the only man who had the courage to organize a public meeting and to carry it through in spite of all discouragement—even from friends!"

Preparations for the Wolfe Tone Centennial in Irish enclaves all over the Empire were injecting a new and sorely needed spirit of unity into the nationalist movement. Maud's speeches for the Centenary Committee drew huge audiences. As Yeats noted, "She could still, even when pushing an abstract principle to what seemed to me an absurdity, keep her own mind free, and so when men and women did her bidding, they did it not only because she was beautiful, but because that beauty suggested joy and freedom."

Willie joined her on a lecture tour through the Midlands and Scotland, and during the long hours they spent together in railway carriages she took time from the organizational details that occupied her to talk about his concerns. He wrote Lady Gregory from Manchester:

> After the meeting this morning Miss Gonne and myself went to the picture gallery to see a Rossetti that is there. She is very kind and friendly, but whether more than that I cannot tell. I have been explaining the Celtic movement and she is enthusiastic over it in its more mystical development. . . . I have been chairman of a noisy meeting for three hours and am very done up. I have a speech to prepare for to-night. Everything went smoothly this morning in spite of anonymous letters warning us to keep a bodyguard at the door.

They were rebels together. Yeats had joined the Irish National Brotherhood, a splinter group of the IRB, two years before, and half as a lark Maud had persuaded Dr. Ryan, head of the INB in London, to swear her in as the first woman member. The IRB in England was split into two factions, which mirrored the split in the Clan na Gael in America between the "Triangle," the pro-terrorist followers of Alexander Sullivan, and the followers of John Devoy, who disapproved of "Dynamitards." The Dublin Committee supported Devoy. Maud's sponsor was a Sullivanite. The official IRB forces controlled the Wolfe Tone Centenary Committee. Maud's difficulty in obtaining authorization for the trip to America arose from the bitter factionalism of a secret society.

There were nests of vipers in secret societies. Intrigues, often the result of personal rivalries, were easily exploited by British spies and foreign agents. "Irish and Nihilists Plot to Assassinate the Czar . . ." Reading the headline in the morning paper, Maud saw a suspicious connection between the news and the so-called Ivory conspiracy case, which was stirring up international problems for Ireland. Late in 1896 Edward Bell, or Ivory, had been arrested in Scotland for having conspired with four others to cause unspecified explosions. P. J. Tynan, who claimed to be "No. 1" of the Invincibles, had been picked up in Boulogne by the English, who also found two more alleged conspirators in Rotterdam.

Maud was sure that the charges were rigged to discredit the Irish movement among the French people; the bomb scare in Paris was timed to interfere with ceremonies welcoming Czar Nicholas to celebrate the Franco-Russian Pact and thus cast suspicion on the anti-British parties in France. At last the alliance with Russia which she and Millevoye had sought for General Boulanger ten years ago was about to become effective; and England, in a last-ditch attempt to break it, was linking Irish terrorists with a plot to assassinate the Czar. John Devoy in America, also convinced that an *agent provocateur* was involved, printed a circular implying that Scotland Yard had infiltrated the violent wing of the Irish Brotherhood.

Maud went to work to foil the destructive plot herself. When Ivory's case came up for trial in 1897, she persuaded J. F. Taylor to handle Ivory's defense and paid a hundred pounds of her own toward the fee of the solicitor, Charles Russell, who had exposed the anti-Parnell forgeries in 1889. At the trial Taylor was able to bring evidence that a British agent, "Jones," had masterminded the alleged conspiracy, and immediately the Crown prosecutor dropped the case. The brilliant victory made Maud relentless in her determination to prevent England from getting Tynan extradited from France. She went to Paris to urge Millevoye to use his influence. After their months of separation she expected him to be irritated, but she was surprised at his reluctance to cooperate. French newspapers were filled with disparaging articles about unwanted Irish exiles and conspirators. Millevoye told Maud she was ruining her standing in France, not to mention his, by refusing to repudiate her mad countrymen. She stood her ground, "in the name of our alliance," and Tynan was not extradited.

No one in a clandestine oath-bound organization was safe from malicious betrayal. In a man's world, where loyalty was assumed to be a masculine attribute and women were mistrusted as undependable, Maud, stubbornly independent, was particularly vulnerable. English-born, her father a British colonel, a member of the ruling class, she was an easy target for suspicion. Yeats wrote O'Leary:

> Miss Gonne has sent me a letter of the Comte de Crémont's telling how Macarthy Tealing has gone to Paris and [is] representing himself in her presence and in the presence of another member of the committee of the Association of St. Patrick as deputed to denounce Miss Gonne as an English and German spy. . . . I wish you would write, as your word would of course carry more weight than anybody else's. . . . I have written telling of Tealing's expulsion from the Young Ireland Society some years ago for insolence to yourself. Tealing has for years been slandering Miss Gonne in the most ignoble and infamous way.

O'Leary came to her defense, and Tealing was also refuted by Michael Davitt, who had entirely changed his opinion of Maud Gonne. Soon after the episode she was able to return the favor by refuting slanders against Davitt circulated by the half-demented troublemaker F. H. O'Donnell. The "Mad Rogue," as Yeats called him, had been expelled from the Irish Party, having done great damage to Parnell by suing the London *Times* for libel in 1888. Suffering from a desperate megalomania, O'Donnell was trying to reenter political life by making unscrupulous use of the "new movement," as the INB called itself, to attack his former colleagues. Yeats and Maud succeeded in exposing his malicious work, and the "Mad Rogue" swore vengeance against them both.

In spite of Devoy's disapproval of the "new movement," Yeats finally won the Dublin Centenary's approval for Maud's lecture tour in America. Before leaving that fall, Maud went to Aix-les-Bains with her cousin May for a brief rest. She tried her luck at the gambling tables and won four hundred francs for an impoverished French countess. She believed that her luck worked best when she tried to do something for others. That night at the casino she went on to win more than enough to pay for the trials of all the Jubilee riot prisoners.

A few days later she said a worried goodbye to her little daughter in Paris. John Devoy's colleagues in the Clan na Gael were spreading unsavory rumors. O'Leary, a Devoy man himself, had been informed that many thought Maud Gonne must be a spy. In the Irish-American community damaging stories were circulating about machinations against Ireland by a nonexistent brother of Maud's. Shortly after Maud sailed from Queenstown, Yeats remarked to Lady Gregory, "I am afraid Miss Gonne will have a bad time in America."

It was essential to be always on guard, but on many occasions Maud simply trusted to luck. She trusted her instinct and sometimes, faced by an important decision, gave in to superstition. Once before a demonstration Yeats found her in the midst of "many caged larks and finches which she was about to set free for the luck's sake." When she embarked for America she took her canary with her.

# CHAPTER SIXTEEN

# The Land of the Clan

Autumnal storms and the machinations of the Cunard Steamship Company harassed Maud from the moment she embarked on her first Atlantic crossing. To discourage American tourist trade in Ireland, English ocean liners did not dock at Queenstown. Passengers with their steamer trunks and hatboxes, emigrants with their string-tied bundles were packed into a tender and delivered, wet and shivering, at the swaying ladder of the ship anchored out in Cork Harbor. Maud, who was a poor sailor even on her short trips across the Channel, retired at once to her cabin.

When she watched from the safety of the cliff top on Howth as great waves broke on the rocks, Maud found the wildness of the sea exhilarating, but she could not abide the sensation of being tossed about in the grip of an uncontrollable force. Anticipating nine days of agony, she intended to stay below decks fortified with sedatives. She let Twee-Twee fly about in the stuffy little cabin, and his life was threatened by a big brown rat. She rescued the bird, but in her misery she thought briefly that death might be welcome for herself. Maud was rescued from total despair and a diet of chloral by Fridtjof Nansen, the Arctic explorer, who had spotted her on the tender, looking pale and dramatic in black cloak and veil.

Her *mal de mer* was assuaged by her curiosity about the famous Norwegian scientist and humanitarian, and, wrapped in rugs on a deck chair, she listened with fascination to his tales of skiing across Greenland and drifting north on an ice floe toward the Pole.

She and Nansen tried to investigate conditions in the hold, but the captain refused to relax the ship's rule against crossing class boundaries, and even Nansen was forbidden to explore the emigrants' quarters. No outsider was allowed to see how Irish peasants were exploited by a government which forced them to give English shipping lines their life savings to carry them to industrial ports overseas. Maud planned to suggest that the Compagnie Transatlantique compete with Cunard for the refugee traffic and promised herself she would never sail again on an English ship.

In New York Harbor at last, the liner was piloted through the Narrows and past the Statue of Liberty. The city shone in the cold light of morning while excited men and women huddled at the rail searching for familiar faces, friends or relatives waiting for them on the pier. Maud and Nansen, who was also going on a lecture tour, parted, and a group of Clan na Gael dignitaries whisked her through customs and carried her off to the Waldorf Hotel on Fifth Avenue at Thirty-third Street.

Her expensive accommodations struck Maud as a waste of money sorely needed for more worthwhile purposes, but William Lyman, the head of the Clan's welcoming committee, explained that in America, "if you don't appear to have lots of money, you won't get money." Maud agreed to stay in her suite long enough to be interviewed by the press.

Two reporters arrived just as she was about to let Twee-Twee stretch his wings, and, startled, she slipped his cage under her chair. In the middle of her interview, while she was expressing her hope that the indignation of Americans would procure the release of Dr. Gallagher, who though an American citizen was still held in Portland Jail, Twee-Twee joined in, "ecstatically singing his unearthly little Hartz Mountain song." The situation might have been used to make her appear ridiculous, and when a reporter looked around and remarked, "Sounds like a bird," Maud asked innocently, "What is that delicious music? Is it some wonderful new American invention of making invisible music?" One of the reporters said, "It must be a musical box in the room below. Sounds mount," and the interview went on.

> Maud Gonne, last Sunday night recited anew the story of the wrongs of Ireland. It was at the Grand Opera House, in Eighth Avenue, New York, that this gifted daughter of Erin made her first appearance on the lecture platform in the United States. She was greeted by a vast gathering of compatriots. The greeting was warm, enthusiastic. Men rose in their seats and cheered this young queen of Irish womanhood. Ex-Secretary of the Navy, William McAdoo, who presided, introduced her as the Joan of Arc of Ireland.

On October 27, Maud stood on the stage of the opera house and faced two thousand people. In her low-cut gown, her hair an amber halo around her proudly held head, she was as regal as any prima donna. Satin dresses, feathered hats, binoculars in the boxes, a blur of pink faces under bonnets and caps in the balconies—Maud was the focus of all eyes in the vast gilded hall. Carried away by the wave of response from the audience, she overcame her stage fright and spoke in a voice that carried to the farthest listener. "When I left Ireland my friends told me I would not be a stranger in America. My reception in New York demonstrates this truth. I do not merit this praise that has been bestowed upon me. I am simply performing the duty that every Irishwoman owes to her country. . . . In spite of the demoralization of the last few years, the Irish are as determined as ever that their country shall be free. The Queen's Jubilee, that hideous mockery, was celebrated this year. Ireland will celebrate its jubilee next year. England's jubilee marked only sixty years of plunder, rapine and piracy. Ireland's jubilee will reflect the noblest struggle for independence the world has ever seen . . . next year she will honor the memory of the men of '98. In the last hundred years one million people have died from starvation in a country of plenty. At the beginning of this century

Ireland had eight million and a half of population. Today she has only four million and a half."

Almost two million of the people lost to Ireland were here in America. Survivors of the Great Hunger, their children and grandchildren were listening to Maud's speech. Each Irish family in America had left relatives and friends behind, struggling on the poor soil under oppressive conditions; many had friends who were in hiding or in prison. At a reception held after her speech at the Gaelic Society on Madison Avenue, the people who shook Maud's hand were eager for news from Ireland. They had prospered in America and were ready with contributions and countless personal messages for Maud to deliver back home. She personified their ideal, the antithesis of the cartoon image of an oppressed peasantry—Paddy with his pig and pint—the butt of English humor from which the Irish-Americans wanted to dissociate themselves. In the Great Democracy they loved Maud Gonne for being upper class.

Exile and enforced emigration had always been England's expedient method of reducing social and economic pressures in Ireland. Ironically, it was from the ranks of the "Great Clearances" in America that an organization arose with the leadership and wealth to achieve the revolution in Ireland. The IRB was directed in large part from America and was "maintained almost entirely by moral and material support from the Clan-na-Gael. Envoys from the IRB attended every convention of the Clan-na-Gael and went back to carry on the work," wrote John Devoy.

Maud asked James Egan, the former Treason-Felony convict, to accompany her on the lecture circuit. Having been sent into exile four years earlier, Egan was working in the Clan, trying to help his comrades still in English jails. The funds he had raised for the Amnesty Association were being held up by Devoy, whose territory Maud had invaded with her characteristic disregard for authority. Her letter of introduction from O'Leary was not delivered because Devoy refused to see her.

Determined to get the funds Egan had collected away from Devoy, Maud made little headway until she happened to recognize a man seated on the platform at one of her lectures as the *agent provocateur* in the Ivory case. She refused to speak until the chairman, William Lyman, had the informer removed. She used the incident to advantage by threatening to publicize it unless Lyman procured the sequestered Amnesty funds.

Devoy had ordered his followers to boycott her lectures, but outside New York James Egan was able to introduce Maud to members of both factions of the Clan. There was a Devoy man, Luke Dillon, who had been involved with the dynamite explosions in the House of Commons and Scotland Yard back in the eighties. There was Patrick Egan, a Sullivanite who had once been treasurer of the Land League. An active member of the Democratic Party and American Ambassador to Chile, Egan gave Maud introductions to congressmen. Dynamitards or politicians, it made no difference to her so long as they worked for Irish nationalism and were willing to contribute.

Maud had mastered a declamatory style that Michael Davitt called sunburstery, the verbal equivalent of flag waving, thought of as Irish but very much in the American grain. William Jennings Bryan was its prime practitioner, although the Sligo-born William Bourke Cockran, a prominent New York lawyer and politician, ran him a close second. A bon vivant like his fellow Irish-American, the lawyer and art patron John Quinn, Bourke Cockran belonged to the class of Irish in New York that had "arrived" and was one of the many well-to-do Irish-Americans who backed the Clan. He shared the podium with Maud on several occasions. She thought her sentences less "flowery and perfect" than his, but she was as much applauded even when she boldly stated that Irish freedom could be won in "the only way the freedom of any nation and of America herself had been attained."

Boston, Philadelphia, Washington, Chicago, Minneapolis, St. Louis, Denver. Riding west in swaying parlor cars full of green plush, Maud looked out at farm lands dotted with fat red and white barns and the great unsettled tracts of forest and prairie. It was heartwarming to be greeted at clean new railway stations by friendly Irish voices, but her adventure had its arduous side. On her one-night stopovers to speak in the big cities Maud experienced what Yeats, writing of his

American tour a few years later, described as the "feeling of the traveling actor, the homelessness, the weariness, the excitement, the alternate elation and depression, the dangers and comforts of the ego." At one whistle stop she ran into her shipmate, Nansen, who admitted that he could no longer stand the strain of constant lecturing to adoring ladies' clubs. The conqueror of Arctic wastelands gave up and went home to Norway. Maud went on to conquer the West.

By the time she and James Egan reached Colorado she too was worn out by the tea parties, the lines of well-wishers in Hibernian clubrooms decorated with potted palms and Irish, American and sometimes French flags. Like the bouquets in her overheated hotel rooms, she wilted. The snowy peaks of the Rockies hung like a mirage of peace in the vast sky west of Denver, and as if in answer to her need, a summons came from the mountains.

> We found ourselves with a free day in Denver and were both delighted, as the constant travelling and lectures were very tiresome and I was getting unbecomingly thin. As I was leaving the theatre, three boisterous lads pushed their way unceremoniously through the crowd who were seeing us into our carriage. "We have come to kidnap Miss Gonne; we are going to take her into the Rockies." They were miners from Victor and Cripple Creek. One of them had a strong Cork accent. . . .
>
> It ended in Egan and myself getting into the carriage they had waiting and away into the moonlit night up the mountains, a wonderful journey through gorges and roads edging dark precipices. We arrived in the early morning at Cripple Creek where, in a wooden frame house, an Irishwoman from Co. Mayo welcomed us with tea and bacon and eggs and then put me to bed in a bare little room and told me to sleep till the men called for me at twelve o'clock to take me down a gold mine where I was to give the men from two shifts the latest news from Ireland.

The next day she caught the train for St. Louis laden with bits of shining gold rock, three hundred dollars for the prisoners, and "messages innumerable for folk at home and promises that when the fight was on for Irish freedom the men would be back with us."

Maud returned to New York with a thousand pounds for the Wolfe Tone Celebration and the Amnesty Fund, which was gratifying, but it was the men and women she remembered afterward, and those who met Maud never forgot her. O'Donovan Rossa came to the boat to say goodbye when she set sail for Ireland. The big, gentle Dynamitard had undergone torture at the hands of the English in the 1860s. Because he protested his treatment as a political prisoner in Dartmoor, he was made to spend "thirty-five days with his hands manacled behind his back," and to lap his food and water like an animal from a bowl on the floor of his cell. "He had spent some of the time reading a copy of D'Aubigny's *History of the Reformation* by turning pages over with his teeth." In America, Maud had met heroes.

# CHAPTER SEVENTEEN

# The Spirit of '98

When Maud returned to Ireland and arrived in Ballina, County Mayo, for the Wolfe Tone celebration, banners above the railroad tracks proclaimed the message of the Irish insurrection:

> Who fears to speak of '98?
> Who blushes at the name?
> When cowards mock the patriot's fate
> Who hangs his head in shame?

The heroes of the eighteenth century who died in their attempt to free Ireland with the spirit of the French revolution and the assistance of French armies were invoked by self-styled patriots and school children, members of Parliament, archbishops and IRB leaders. Torchlight parades, brass bands, monuments and floral wreaths: the thousands of pounds raised by the '98 committees disappeared in clouds of oratory.

Early in the spring of 1898 Maud went to Tralee to speak at the laying of a stone for a Wolfe Tone memorial, and she was at Mt. Melick for the unveiling of a handsome Celtic cross. She preferred plain stone crosses or simple granite blocks inscribed with heroes' names to the elaborate statues that looked as if they had been torn from the plaster work of provincial churches to mock the Spirit of '98 in town squares. But when Yeats scolded her for encouraging bad taste with her memorial subscriptions she wondered, "How could it be otherwise with a School of Art which deprecated nude models for students?"

Maud's success at raising money for local monuments enhanced her popularity, and Ballina received her at the station with the welcome usually given a hero back from the wars or a victorious football player. "Mr. Malone's wagonette was waiting outside, and Miss Gonne and friend, Miss Nally Balla, a co-worker, being seated in it, the horse was withdrawn and the wagonette was drawn by willing hands to the residence of Mr. T. B. Kelly." The reporter for the *Ballina Herald* went on to rave over her appearance on St. Patrick's Day at the opera house: "Miss Gonne, in a green costume, and without any head dress, her abundant light hair covering her side face—tall and graceful in her person—was the observed of all observers while the hall rapidly filled. . . . Her sweet voice, clear enunciation, and graceful action were pleasing far beyond description, and when she made an appeal to the patriotism of the audience, in a subdued almost plaintive tone of voice, the effect was almost electrical."

Families of Mayo peasants had come on foot for miles over the flooded boglands to see Maud dedicate the Wolfe Tone monument. An old grandfather asked her, "Where are the French?" She pointed out her Paris friends on the platform, Madame de Ste. Croix among them. "No, no," he said. "I mean the French Army," and many poor people who had emptied their pockets for the Spirit of '98 were as disappointed as he to find platforms decorated with flowers and flowery speeches instead of armed men ready to march against the English.

Maud's public acclaim had never been higher. On the podium with James Stephens, the founding father of the IRB back from his long exile, she addressed a hundred thousand demonstrators in Manchester. She was the main speaker at St. Michan's in London: Yeats was in the chair and Cipriani gave a speech in French at Maud's request—had he not fought with

Garibaldi for Mazzini's dictum: "Without a country you are the bastards of humanity . . ."?

Delegates from Australia, New Zealand, and South Africa representing far-flung Irish communities, as well as sympathetic nationalists from the Continent, attended the culminating celebration in Dublin on August 15. Only the Irish-Americans failed to live up to Maud's expectations. The Clan had promised shiploads of republicans, but the outbreak of the Spanish-American War diverted them, and the ships they would have sailed in were used for troops. The few middle-class Irish who came on their own from America were primarily interested in nostalgia and relatives, and were conspicuously absent at the ceremonial laying of the foundation stone for Dublin's Wolfe Tone memorial.

Yeats, whom the IRB had asked to speak to offset the Parliamentarians John Redmond and John Dillon, sat on the platform next to the perennial presider, John O'Leary, and the veteran James Stephens. Maud was supposed to be there too, but at the last moment she rebelled against what she considered an empty and hypocritical show of unity and refused to be on a platform with Lord Mayor Thomas Pile, a Unionist and a Dublin Castle pawn. Instead she stood below in the crowds at the foot of Grafton Street, watching the workmen lower the foundation stone into the excavation —into its grave, as it turned out, for no statue of Wolfe Tone was ever erected in St. Stephen's Green.

There were loud cheers when Yeats stood up to speak, the lock of dark hair blowing across his forehead. " 'England had persuaded herself that Ireland, discredited by disunion, was about to submit—to accept a handful of alms. We have answered her today. She is no longer deceived. The people have made this movement.' Someone in the crowd cried: 'No, no, it is Maud Gonne that has made it.' " But she would not go to the platform.

Yeats, still seeking a united front for the nationalists as a safeguard against violent action, believed that the Wolfe Tone Celebration marked a turning point and was pleased. Undoubtedly the local Centenary Committees served as a catalyst in reuniting the Irish Party. But Maud was disappointed by the immediate results. Working with the committees, she had been angry at the money and forensic energy wasted in memory of the past and saw the continuing fissures beneath the show of unity. After all the speeches and the applause, she felt the letdown of some great opportunity lost. People had been roused to a fervent pitch of national feeling, and James Connolly, the one man who might have seized the situation and used it well, was not present at the Wolfe Tone ceremonies. Maud's Socialist friend and colleague was working for the people in the west of Ireland.

Blighted crops and ruinous debts in the counties along the Atlantic Coast, where famine was chronic, had brought about a situation ominously similar to the Great Hunger of fifty years earlier. Connolly was trying to organize the tenants in Kerry. His Socialist principles applied to the agrarian crisis turned out in practice to be simply an extension of the type of Land League work in which Maud was experienced, and Connolly called on her for help in the present crisis. It was necessary to rouse the people to help themselves, so that they would not perish, as their forebears had.

Maud and Connolly prepared a leaflet on "The Rights of Life and the Rights of Property" to be distributed in the stricken areas. In Kerry, the old home of Daniel O'Connell, the Catholic Emancipator of the early 1800s, where many priests risked excommunication for the sake of their suffering parishioners, the devout Connolly felt justified in quoting the Church Fathers for Socialist purposes, and the nominally Protestant Maud approved of using Holy Scriptures to encourage starving tenants to help themselves to the means of survival owned by the landlords. They buttressed their argument by quoting Pope Clement I, Pope Gregory the Great, and Cardinal Manning, and continued:

> Fellow Countrymen: At the present juncture when the shadow of famine is already blighting the lives of so many amongst us, when famine itself in all its grim horror has already begun to claim its victims . . . we desire to offer a few words of calm advice . . . to move you to action before it is too late and to point out to you your duty whether as fathers or sons, as husbands or as Irishmen.

In 1847 our people died by thousands of starvation though every ship leaving an Irish port was laden with food in abundance. The Irish people might have seized that food, cattle, corn . . . have prevented famine and saved their country from ruin, but did not do so, believing such action to be sinful and dreading to peril their souls to save their bodies. In this belief, we know now they were entirely mistaken. The very highest authorities on the Doctrine of the Church agree that no *human* law can stand between starving people and their RIGHT TO FOOD including the right to take that food whenever they find it openly or secretly with or without the owner's permission. His Holiness Pope Leo XIII has lately recommended the writing of St. Thomas Aquinas as the best statement of Catholic Doctrine on Faith and Morals. . . . "Is it lawful to steal on the plea of necessity?" "The institution of human law cannot abrogate from natural law or Divine law . . . therefore the division and appropriation of goods that proceed from human law cannot come in the way of man's needs relieved out of these goods . . . If however a need is so plain and pressing that clearly the urgent necessity has to be relieved . . . then the man may lawfully relieve his distress out of the property of another, taking it—either openly or secretly . . ."

Maud paid twenty-five pounds out of her Amnesty funds to have their manifesto printed, although had she been the sole author she would have addressed women too, the victimized mothers and wives who were often the prime movers in seeking redress. Connolly saw to the distribution in Kerry, and Maud went to Mayo carrying bundles of their subversive literature.

She stopped briefly for a Wolfe Tone memorial ceremony in Castlebar, where General Humbert's troops and the unarmed Irish had routed the English in the battle of '98 known for its swiftness as the "Races of Castlebar." On the battlefield John Daly, an activist again since his release from

Portland, presented her with an old French coin and a bullet. She had them made into a brooch, which she liked to wear as a token of the glorious day when Irish and French had fought side by side for a republican Ireland.

From Castlebar, where Michael Davitt had formally launched the Land League during the famine of 1879, Maud traveled north by mail car through the country where the blind poet Raftery had sung of Wolfe Tone's followers, the "boys of the heather who marshalled their bravest and best." County Mayo was devastated by starvation and pestilence. Between Ballycastle and Belderrig, Maud saw new graves in the little wind-swept churchyards. They were only half filled with fresh earth; people were too weak to bury their dead. Government doctors were signing countless certificates for death by "heart failure." If starvation was admitted, the authorities were liable for prosecution for not having ordered relief, and relief funds were running out. A man or woman, whichever happened to be head of a family, was employed at road building for sixpence a day. The average family consisted of twelve people, and where, as was frequently the case, the father was absent, the mother was forced to leave her infants at home to work on the roads while grown sons remained idle. The hungry had been forced to eat seed potatoes and there would be none left for sowing.

At Belderrig, Maud found lodgings above the general store. The proprietress apologized for the narrow bed and gutted candle on the table, a poor cold room, not fit for a lady —who, ignoring the apologies, simply asked for more candles. Wrapped in her old fur cloak, Maud sat up all night writing articles for the Dublin papers and an appeal for famine relief to be printed in the *New York Irish World*, whose publisher, Patrick Ford, she had met on her trip to America. At dawn she was out visiting the sick and dying. She bought oatmeal and condensed milk and organized a cadre of women to cook and distribute food and helped them nurse the sick. Apathetic from physical weakness, too browbeaten to even dream of stealing a sheep, the peasants found Maud's leaflet alarming when they could read it, but her efficiency and confidence did something to restore their courage. The men of the village agreed to meet with her when the fishing boats came in at night. They listened with interest when she proposed that they demand that relief funds be used to build a fish-curing station instead of useless roads.

Monsignor Hewson, the parish priest of Belmullet, helped Maud prepare for a mass demonstration, translating her speeches into Gaelic and consulting with her on a list of minimum demands to be presented to the Board of Governors. On the day of the demonstration Belmullet was overrun with families from every farm and village in the region.

Ten thousand ragged, barefoot people listened in silence while Maud, perched on the back of a wagonette, exhorted them to act for themselves. The demonstration had been timed to take place when the Board of Governors from Dublin Castle was meeting with local officials in the Belmullet courthouse. She told the crowd that if they endorsed her list of minimum demands she would present them to the government authorities. When she read the list they responded with a cheer that was not a cheer but a shrill crying, an insistent, chilling sound that echoed against the hillsides and would reverberate in Maud's memory for the rest of her life. "It occurred to me, as I looked upon those poor starving creatures, that I, who did not know what hunger was, I who had never suffered as they suffered, might become, as it were, the expression of their thought and of their will."

She went into the courthouse and put the demands for more relief, better use of it, and free seed potatoes before the representatives of the Congested Districts Board and the Magistrate. "I have seen enough die of hunger," she told the startled officials. "I will now say to the crowd—and they are ready to do whatever I advise—to begin at once by sacking this town, and to take all they want for themselves and for their families. I will myself accompany them. It will take you two days to bring your troops here. In two days these poor people will be dispersed among the mountains. I know you can arrest me then, and a certain number of these unfortunates as well, and may perhaps even shoot some of them. But you will gain a sorry renown for yourselves by shooting the starving."

Ghosts from the past stood with Maud in the courtroom, shades of Ribbonmen, Whiteboys, and rapparees who had marauded the great estates in the seventeenth, eighteenth, and early nineteenth centuries. The men seated at the conference table were all too aware of what was taking place outside, the marching sound of thousands of feet beating the bare ground, the ominous cries of anger. It took only five minutes' hurried consultation for them to decide to meet Maud's demands.

The good news spread through the throngs, and when Maud came out of the courthouse they pressed around her, laughing and crying, kissing her hands and clothing. In Donegal they had called her the Woman of the Sidhe, and in Mayo too, where folk tales were still repeated around the turf fires, Maud was given the name of a legend. Long ago a wise man, Brian Ruadh, had foretold that in a time of famine a woman would preach revolt and there would be fighting and in the end the English would be driven from the land. The peasants in Mayo who benefited from Maud's practical and direct action called her the Woman in Green.

Land Reform acts were breaking the feudal power of the landlords, but the root causes of agricultural poverty remained: maldistribution, too many people trying to scratch a living from too few acres, and the misuse of the land by its new purchasers, the sheep ranchers and cattlemen who could afford to buy up vast estates. "To look over the fence of the famine-stricken village and see the rich, green solitudes which might yield full and plenty spread out at the very doorsteps of the ragged peasants was to fill a stranger with a sacred rage."

Horace Plunkett had started a cooperative movement in the eighties and in ten years had set up over 876 creameries and co-op societies in his Irish Agricultural Organization. AE thought well enough of the IAOs to leave his draper's counter at Pim's and edit Plunkett's journal, the *Irish Homestead;* in 1897 the poet became a co-op organizer. Maud approved of his cooperative movement as having at least interim usefulness. She was less sanguine about the new project of one of her old heroes from the great days of the Land League, William O'Brien, now living in Mallow Cottage just outside Westport, under the shadow of Croagh Patrick.

O'Brien saw the present crisis as an opportunity to advance the Irish Party and himself. He had summoned John Dillon, Tim Harrington, and John Redmond to Westport in January 1898, and together they had established the United Irish League. They represented both sides of the Parnellite split and thus formed the nucleus of a reunited Irish Party. The new land movement relied more than ever on constitutional reform, "constructive unionism," a far cry from the revolutionary ideals of Michael Davitt and the Ladies' Land League of Anna and Fanny Parnell. Maud had grown up in the struggle under their influence: ". . . the agrarian and National struggle were inherently one," she wrote; "the land and the people, from whose union the national soul is born."

All over Ireland pockets of feudalism still survived. In Woodford in County Galway tenants had long been subject to desperate conditions and evictions under the Lords of Clanricarde, notorious even among the infamous landlords of the Great Famine. "What a wretch Clanricarde is," Lady Gregory wrote of him to Wilfred Blunt, "and can't you spare us a little pity for having him held up as a typical Irish landlord?"

In 1899, Maud agreed to address a tenants' meeting in Woodford that had been proscribed by government authorities. Arriving on the mail train, she found the little town garrisoned by police, and she was taken in secret a few miles out of town to a country crossroad. From a makeshift platform on the back of the chairman's cart Maud addressed a ragged group of men in frieze coats. Halfway through her speech she saw a band of Royal Irish Constabulary coming down the road. A hundred strong, they closed in on three sides of the little meeting around the cart. The officer in charge threatened to arrest her if she did not stop speaking. She ignored his warning. He gave an order to fire. She paused and, in the silence, heard the barrels click. Her ragged audience, wielding their ash plants and stones picked from the roadside, turned and faced the police. Maud stepped down from the platform. The police lowered their guns; the sticks and stones did not fly, though fists were clenched in yearning for a fight.

Maud had kept her head; her will power, controlling

every nerve in her body, had saved men's lives. Martyrs would have aroused great indignation and made the cause of evicted tenants a burning issue again, but she would not be responsible for the slaughter of unarmed people in an unequal battle.

Maud's efforts to help tenants in Mayo and Galway were as innovative as her work in Donegal, but conditions on the land were changing. She could not succeed on a large scale because a merchant class was beginning to gain control of Irish agriculture.

Three years later, in 1902, the last wave of evictions was taking place on Lord Freyne's estate. Maud went to report on the situation at Frenchpark, where Douglas Hyde had grown up, where Yeats had discovered their Castle of the Heroes dreaming in the lake. John Dillon, outraged by Lord Freyne's brutal reprisals against tenant agitation, urged "driving every landlord out of the country." At Frenchpark John Fitzgibbon, an old IRB man who had fought for the Land League, told Maud that homes of tenants who refused eviction orders were burned to the ground by the landlord's agent, who poured paraffin on the thatch and ignited it while families were still inside. Women and children were horribly burned. Maud addressed meetings, raised relief funds, wrote press releases. She wired Harrington for help, and John Redmond, the Parnellite M.P. who was making a strong bid for leadership of the reunited Irish Party, was sent to speak in Roscommon.

At the meeting, Redmond in top hat and frock coat insisted that Maud's Great Dane be removed from the platform. Maud had no use for the politically ambitious Redmond. Still, she needed help in prosecuting the agent responsible for the cruel fires. Ironically, there was a strong law against arson of dwelling houses which had been passed in the old days to protect landlords from reprisals, but in a further irony the agent was acquitted. His counsel was able to prove to the judge's satisfaction that hovels with no locks on the doors were not dwellings and therefore not protected under the law.

"I should have known," wrote Maud, "that British law in Ireland follows British policy, and British policy was supporting landlords and their agents. . . . During Victoria's reign alone, one million two hundred and twenty-five thousand people died of famine . . . four million one hundred and eighty-six thousand emigrated; three million six hundred and sixty-three thousand were evicted. . . . More and more I realized that Ireland could rely only on force, in some form or other, and that it was absurd to say that any Irishman, whatever he did, had committed a crime against England or against civilization."

# CHAPTER EIGHTEEN

# A Spiritual Marriage

Maud's way of life caused Yeats great anxiety. He saw her constantly menaced by conspiracies, betrayals, and enmities of clandestine activity, vulnerable to attack by the government authorities, and threatened by the anger of desperate men and women, the violence of the mob. Nothing Willie said, no plan of his, rational or fantastic, could stop her headlong drive along what he considered a most dangerous course. During the Centennial Year he had seen a great deal of Maud as they worked together in committees and demonstrations, and although she was certainly practical as well as idealistic, he deplored the "raging abstraction" of her views, the fury at injustice which drove her to act beyond the limits of her physical strength. At thirty Maud was more delicate than she liked to admit. Fatigue resulted in a recurrence of the lung ailment she had had since childhood. She would become pale and gaunt, and the shadows around her great eyes would deepen, the clear lines of her cheekbones and jaw grow hard. At such times she had a tragic look that gave Yeats every reason to feel concern.

Yet Maud did take time to rest more often than he or anyone realized. She was secretive about her vacations to preserve the public impression of inexhaustible energy, a woman always in motion. Sometimes she would stay in bed and read Balzac, Dumas *fils*, or a more frivolous novel. If that did not cure her, she would indulge herself at some health resort for a few days, and Lucien might join her at Royat or Aix. And she could always retreat from the pressures of the world at the Carmelite convent in Laval, where Iseult was cared for by the nuns during their increasingly long periods of separation. The reunions with her little daughter were a joy, and the chaplain of the convent was a friend from her early days with the Boulangists.

The Abbé Dissard, now a canon, had become her unofficial spiritual adviser. Convinced that Maud's restless spirit would eventually find its peace in the Church, he tried to persuade her that her belief in reincarnation was no more than a form of ancestor worship and wondered how it was possible for her to have anything to do with a religion that recognized Queen Victoria as its head. Maud replied that she had left the Church of England as soon as she became a free agent because she wished to remain free. She valued the Canon's friendship but would not like to confess her sins to him or to any man, and she found it impossible to believe in the infallibility of the Pope, because Leo XIII had succumbed to English pressure and denounced his followers in Ireland for fighting for the people's rights. As Maud talked to the Canon in the convent gardens, where painted plaster saints looked out from stone grottoes, the sisters dressed in simple brown robes passed by with heads bowed over their rosaries; they loved the enchanting dark-eyed Iseult and prayed, as nuns must pray, for her mother's conversion.

Maud believed in all the gods, Christian and pagan, as she believed in herself. Her instinct for self-preservation was her guardian angel, or as she sometimes phrased it, she was protected by the shield of the Celtic sun god Lug. Leaving her work on an impulse, she would make a pilgrimage into the Irish countryside. She would go to Howth to visit her old nurse. Since Maud had helped Eileen's mother find a governess's job in St. Petersburg, her half-sister had been living with Nanny. Seeing the twelve-year-old growing up among the country people, Maud felt her own youthful energy return. The sacred places of Ireland—Tara, the court of the

High Kings in prehistoric times, a Druid temple at New Grange—the land itself revived her.

"I knew a phoenix in my youth . . ." In middle age, Yeats, comparing Maud to other lovely women, was still awestruck by her resurgent strength. But when she returned from America in the winter of 1897–98, Maud was glad to take a brief vacation from fund raising and go on a mystical quest with Willie. He wrote AE from London in January that they were off "for a week or two perhaps to some country place in Ireland to get as you do the forms of gods and spirits and to get sacred earth for our evocation. . . . Maud Gonne has seen a vision of a little temple of the heroes which she proposes to build somewhere in Ireland when '98 is over and make the center of our mystical and literary movement." In a worried postscript Willie inquired, "How much could I live for in the country if I stayed a couple of weeks or so?"

On her modest income Maud could afford to come and go as she pleased, carrying pets and friends along. Willie, who was always hard up, was too proud to let her pay his way, but fortunately inexpensive lodgings could be found in Sligo. Maud's gift for drawing out the cottagers enabled them to find stone crosses tilted in ancient graveyards and haunted groves on Knocknerea. Their vivid imaginations could easily evoke warriors riding the wind at sunset over Queen Maeve's cairn; Aengus, the Queen's consort, soaring in the flight of a mountain lark. Maud had a waking vision of the Castle, small and terraced, where heroes and heroines would learn to be as brave as Cuchulain, as steadfast as Maeve.

Back in Dublin, in between '98 Committee meetings Maud met Willie to continue their mystical studies. They received a puzzling message for AE: "Number the people of God. . . . Is it an appeal to you to help in that systemization which you so dislike?" Yeats asked him in a letter. "Miss Gonne and myself both got a message for you, which seemed to be the same thing, but in different words. These messages at worst are messages from one's deeper self."

Maud went back to Paris in the spring for a brief visit and Willie followed her. "I have been out on a bicycle in the Bois de Boulogne and it was like a summer ride," he wrote Lady Gregory from "Aux soins de Monsieur MacGregor

Mathers, 87 Rue Mozart, Auteuil." "I am buried in Celtic mythology and shall be for a couple of weeks or so. Miss Gonne has been ill with bronchitis. One of her lungs is affected a little so that she has to rest. She is unable to do any politics for the time and looks ill and tired. She comes here to-morrow to see visions. Fiona Macleod (this is private as she is curiously secret about her movements) talks of coming here too, so we will have a great Celtic gathering."

There were mysteries in the Rue Mozart. The person who wrote rather mediocre Celtic verses under the name of Fiona Macleod never materialized, but the Scotch journalist Sharp was clever at hiding his dual nature, and MacGregor Mathers was a most persuasive Magus. He could dance a Highland fling and toss silver knives around his head, and Maud still took a childlike pleasure in his conjuring, but she was more suspicious than ever of his connection with Freemasonry: in France the Masons were pro-English. Yeats was also having his difficulties with Mathers and suspected that despite his saffron kilt the High Priest of the Golden Dawn was not at all interested in the Celtic revival but only in holding on to his position as leader. Rivalries divided the fratri and sorores: Florence Farr and Annie Horniman set against Mathers, Mathers against Yeats, and Aleister Crowley, notorious for black magic and orgiastic séances, was trying to gain control of the Golden Dawn.

It was clear to Maud that the cabalist had nothing constructive to offer, and she withdrew from the Order. Unable to make Willie understand that his involvement with such petty squabbles was a waste of time if not an actual betrayal of the Irish cause, she was determined to keep the Castle of the Heroes their private enterprise and devoted as much time as possible to working on it with Willie during the hectic summer and fall of 1898.

She visited him in London in the lodgings he had recently moved to in Bloomsbury. She entered a new world. The neighborhood, which was not unlike Bedford Park, had a seedy urban elegance. "There was a kind of blackguard beauty about Woburn Buildings at night. . . . The houses had come down in the world, and as it were, gone on the streets. They seemed to screen discreet vice . . ."

Maud, in evening dress, carrying one of her smaller dogs, the dachshund or the little terrier, would usually arrive after dinner to help "Yeaty," as his housekeeper called him, "far into the morning." A curving stairway led to the first landing and the entrance to Willie's brown-papered sitting room, shrouded in blue-green velvet draperies, the furnishings heavy and somber. There was an odor of violets, incense, and cigarettes. Over the mantelpiece hung an illustration by Willie's father of Blake's ballad, "I thought Love lived in the hot sunshine." Blake's first engraving for Dante, "The Whirlwind of Lovers," was hung next to a large photograph of Maud. Their notebooks and tarot cards, Willie's from France and Maud's from Italy, were spread out on the table with strict orders to Mrs. Old not to disturb them or the candlestick and tumbler of water.

They used the ancient method of "skrying" to enhance consciousness, concentrating intently on the water in the glass as Joseph in Egypt had looked into his divining cup and Jakob Böhme had gazed on his light-struck pewter plate. Maud learned many of Willie's tricks of meditation, and by "letting the will move of itself" she was able to enter another state of consciousness. Stretched out on Willie's green velours couch, she would quickly fall into a trance while he chanted cabalistic spells. The candle-lit room flickered like some Wagnerian underworld with figures from the past, the pagan images of *The Golden Bough*. Pagan or Christian, Maud and Willie viewed these evocations as significant for Ireland's spiritual rebirth.

In a black and gold notebook dated December 1898, Maud described how they received the Initiation of the Cauldron, a purification from the Druid of Murias (water), when they visited his sacred mountain in a dream and were told to "bathe in the green fire." She submitted to the "Initiation of the Stone" and Willie that of the "Wand," and having passed through these elemental initiations they were prepared for the ritual of the White Globe which was governed by the High Druid. In her trances Maud saw figures such as Blake might have drawn, archetypal images of "that age-long memoried self." Was she so suggestible, or was she so attuned to Willie that the images that floated through his mind were also hers? She knew he "loved symbols, to crystalise his thought, and he meditated much on them," and she allowed him to lead her through the Celtic twilight as if in a play he had written about doomed, immortal lovers.

Yet in the outside world Maud was uneasy about being seen with Yeats too often. She warned him, "I do not say that the crowds are in love with me, but they would hate anybody who was." She worried about her reputation, and yet she could not resist teasing Willie when, "fearing to compromise her," he would not stay at the same hotel in Dublin.

He worried about all the dangers that dogged Maud's footsteps, but she seemed impervious, moving through screaming mobs and police skirmishes unscathed. Only once during the busy summer of 1898 did her guardian angel abandon her, when the horse pulling her carriage slipped and fell in Sackville Street. She was thrown onto the pavement, her arm broken and her face severely bruised. Sarah Purser insisted on looking after her, and when Willie realized the accident was not serious he went to visit Lady Gregory, who had been waiting for him at Coole Park.

The tall-windowed house at Coole, the light of the past, old books and marble busts, the elegant life enchanted Yeats but did not relieve his unhappiness. He found little consolation at Coole Park, which his hostess thought "so radiant . . . the great white horse-chestnuts in bloom, the smaller red ones, the crimson and white hawthorn, lilac and laburnum, the leaves so fresh, the paths carpeted with the brown blossoms of the beech." In all that earthly beauty Yeats was miserable, "tortured by physical desire and disappointed love. Often as I walked in the woods at Coole it would have been a relief to have screamed aloud. When desire became an unendurable torture, I would masturbate, and that, no matter how moderate I was, would make me ill. It never occurred to me to seek another love. I would repeat to myself again and again the last confession of Lancelot, and indeed it was my greatest pride, 'I have loved a queen beyond measure and exceeding long.' "

Lady Gregory did her utmost to provide a sanctuary for the impoverished, unhappy young poet with whom she was more than a little in love. In her forties, she still had the eager inquiring spirit of the young Augusta Persse who rode to hounds over the rolling lands of her Protestant ancestors, the Lords of Roxborough. Daughter of a Galway landlord, a landlord herself, and widow of a successful diplomat and former governor of Ceylon, Augusta Gregory had once written a pamphlet attacking Home Rule as Rome Rule. But for her, life was "a series of enthusiasms," and when she met Yeats in 1897 his fervor for all things Irish sent her out among the Galway people to learn their Kiltartan dialect and collect their folk tales. She already had a proprietary interest in the Irish peasant, and because of Yeats she embraced Irish nationalism and dedicated herself to making his dream of an Irish theater a reality.

Maud heard all about the mistress of Coole from Willie. He had made a convert and gained a patroness whom he could call "mother, friend, sister and brother." It did not occur to Maud to consider the plump, graying woman, "rather like Queen Victoria," a rival; and she was astonished when, demure and dignified as always, Lady Gregory arrived at Nassau Street to question her intentions—and left with obvious relief. "It did not seem exactly her business," Maud wrote, "and I had answered rather shortly that we were neither of the marrying sort, having other things which interested us more . . ."

Maud was gracious to the older woman for Willie's sake, but they never became friends. Lady Gregory was a gifted, independent woman who was now, as she put it, seeking "to add dignity to Ireland," and Maud respected her for that. Her support of Yeats's Irish Literary Theatre was no mean contribution. Maud was more than willing to be one of its guarantors; she approved of it and wanted to have a say in it too.

It was Willie's own attitude that gave her cause for alarm. She knew how high society attracted him. "He found himself among the comfortable and well-fed, who style themselves the 'upper classes,' but whom Willie, shuddering at the words, and discriminating even among them, called 'Distinguished Persons'; and some of them undoubtedly deserved the title . . . but the attitude of the well-fed is often patronising to the Shan Van Vocht, not reverent." AE told Maud that he and his wife had been patronized at Coole and had sworn never to return. Arthur Symons, who had introduced Yeats to Lady Gregory, called her "La Strega." Maud did not see her as a witch, but she noticed that some visitors to Coole became "less passionately interested in the National struggle and more worried about their own lack of money." Not all the "Distinguished Persons" who carved their initials next to AE and WBY and JMS and DH on the trunk of the beech in Lady Gregory's garden deserved that much immortality. The novelist George Moore, for instance: Maud considered him pompous and egotistical; and even Willie, at first impressed by the self-styled priest of Aphrodite who had known Paris in its heyday, fell out with him.

Maud kept her distance from the charmed circle at Coole. And in spite of her interest in the new theater she refused to act in its first production, *The Countess Cathleen.* Yeats's play made the peasants appear ignorant and superstitious, and Maud disliked the role of the Countess. It was all right for May Whitty, the English actress, to play a wealthy woman who sold her soul to the devil to save her starving peasants, but not for Maud Gonne, the Irish nationalist. No matter how noble the motive, the act was blasphemous.

*The Countess Cathleen* was again condemned by the Church, and the "Mad Rogue," F. H. O'Donnell, seeing a fine opportunity for revenge on Yeats, attacked it in a popular pamphlet, "Souls for Gold." It was rumored that Arthur Griffith was bringing a group of men from the quays to applaud whatever the Church would not like, and Catholic students from University College circulated a petition against the play. James Joyce was one of the few students there who admired it. Yeats suffered the indignity of having to ask the Castle police to prevent possible rioting in the Ancient Concert Rooms on opening night, May 8, 1899.

Maud was well out of it. In preserving her own reputation, Maud was also beginning to formulate a position on the issue of art versus propaganda. She and Willie were on opposite sides.

When the Wolfe Tone celebrations were over, Maud watched Yeats become involved in theatrical matters to the exclusion of all else. She knew how he was torn:

He hated crowds, I loved them. His generous desire to help and share my work brought him into contact with crowds and with all sorts of people, men from the country and men from the towns, working for Ireland's freedom. I hardly realized then how important that contact was to him and sometimes felt guilty at taking so much of his time from his literary work. As we sat together through the boredom of conventions and long committee meetings, where his dominating personality and practical grasp of detail made him a powerful ally, it sometimes seemed like using a fine Toledo blade instead of a loy in the spade-work of political organisation; but I remember Willie's astonished pleasure when, after a meeting, some shy boy would come up and shake his hand because he had read his poems and loved them; I know that contact was good for him.

While he was still unrecognized by many of his Irish colleagues, Maud was writing to "dear Willie" at Coole Park:

All I want of you is not to build up an imaginary wall of duty or effort between you and life—for the rest the gods will arrange, for you are one of those they have chosen to do their work.

As for the possible changes or dangers which you speak of for me. I am under the great shield of Lug; the day I am no longer protected, if that day comes, my work for Ireland will be over—I should not need, *I could not accept* protection from anyone, though I fully realize and understand the generous and unselfish thoughts that are in your heart and I love you for them. . . .

I am glad you are in the country with Lady Gregory. I am sure it is good for you to be with her and you will do beautiful work. There is a peace and restful ease you need. I am in my whirlwind but in the midst of that whirlwind is dead quiet calm which is peace too.

Goodbye my friend. I cross tomorrow to England. I will be with my cousins, 28 Hyde Park Gate, S. W. till Wednesday the 11th when I go to France.

Always your friend,
Maud Gonne

Maud refused the commitment of becoming wife or mistress to a young poet who had freed himself from a powerful father but not from the need of maternal care which his sick mother had never been able to provide. The contradictions and responsibilities of their own lives separated them again and again far more than superficial arguments, yet neither found it possible to let the other go. Sometimes Willie was tormented beyond reason:

... You would come hither, and bend your head,
And I would lay my head on your breast;
And you would murmur tender words,
Forgiving me, because you were dead:
Nor would you rise and hasten away,
Though you have the will of the wild birds ...

There were other women in his life now. Katherine Tynan had married a lawyer, H. A. Hinkson, and was living in London, but her position as a patron and colleague was better filled by Lady Gregory, the middle-class farm at Clondalkin replaced by the great house at Coole. There was Florence Farr, who sat at Willie's feet in Bloomsbury, chanting his verses to the psaltery designed by Arnold Dolmetsch. Willie's sisters, Lily and Lolly, had once thought she would be his mistress, but the actress—who had many lovers, including Shaw—refused to be faithful to any, and her friendship with Willie remained platonic. There was Althea Gyles, the scatterbrained young artist who designed elaborate covers for two of his books. Yeats admired her work while he deplored her love affairs, not her immorality but her lack of discrimination. His relations with Olivia Shakespear had deteriorated even more unhappily, for her at least, when Maud came back into his life. Maud knew that she had only to raise a hand and he would forsake them all.

Yeats was in his midthirties, and the great love of his life remained unconsummated. George Moore, inquisitive by nature and himself a perennial bachelor, wanted to know why; and Yeats's literary friends, less prurient but no less envious of his growing reputation, speculated with all the rapacity of provincial gossips. Was he saving himself for his art? "Which produces the finer fruit, the gratified or the ungratified passion?" George Moore in his mordant memoir of his years in Ireland recalled breakfasting with Yeats on a train to Galway. "We talked of her whom he had loved always, the passionate ideal of his life, and why this ideal had never become a reality to him as Mathilde had become to Richard (Wagner). Was it really so? was my pressing question, and he answered me: 'I was very young at the time and was satisfied with . . .' The words I supply, 'the spirit of sense,' are merely conjectural."

If it occurred to Moore that Maud's feelings might have something to do with Willie's situation, he did not take that into consideration. Victorian women were not assumed to have passionate physical desires. George Moore had reason to be well aware that the "gentler sex" was no more docile than the male in desire. His English mistress, "Stella," had complained, "You don't make love to me often enough." Sara Purser summed him up: "Gentlemen kiss but never tell. Cads kiss and tell. George Moore doesn't kiss but he tells."

The independent spinster's quip delighted Maud and all her women friends, who laughed at the hypocrisy of the double standard imposed on them, knowing that in fact it was no laughing matter. Havelock Ellis, who had shared Arthur Symons's chambers in Fountain Court before Yeats moved there, published the first volume of his *Studies in the Psychology of Sex* in 1897. It was immediately suppressed even in England. In Ireland women were still considered possessions of men as daughters and wives. Shaw wrote that he was "born in Dublin in 1856 which may be taken as 1756 by London reckoning." If Ibsen's Nora had opened the door in Dublin she would have walked out of her marriage to find all other doors locked against her. Puritanical codes for women, reinforced by provincial Catholicism, demanded female chastity as the price for independence. Maud did not aspire to the free-spirited eroticism of Sarah Bernhardt or Isadora Duncan, but she did need to be respected in the society she had chosen.

One morning when Willie called for Maud at the Nassau Street Hotel she asked him if he too had dreamed a strange dream the night before. Willie told her that for the first time ever, in a dream, she had kissed him.

Maud made no comment, but that evening they dined alone in her rooms and she told him of her dream, which had been so intense she thought it must have been his too: "When I fell asleep last night I saw standing at my bedside a great spirit. He took me to a great throng of spirits, and you were among them. My hand was put into yours and I was told we were married. After that I remember nothing." Then she kissed him for the first time with "the bodily mouth."

When Willie came to see her the next day he found her sitting gloomily beside the fire. " 'I should not have spoken to you in that way,' she told him, 'for I can never be your wife in reality.' " When he asked her if she loved somebody else, she answered that there was no one else but she had to be a "moral nature for two." Still she did not speak of Lucien or their daughter.

"A little later," wrote Yeats, "how many days I do not remember, we were sitting together when she said, 'I hear a voice saying, "You are about to receive the initiation of the spear." ' We became silent; a double vision unfolded itself, neither speaking till all was finished. She thought herself a great stone statue through which passed flame, and I felt myself becoming flame and mounting up through and looking out of the eyes of a great stone Minerva." The emotion each of them felt was so charged, and the ambivalence in their situation so great, that the images were easily incorporated into a "spiritual marriage."

For Maud this unconsummated union was a practical compromise. For Willie it was both delight and anguish. "Were the beings which stand behind human life trying to unite us," he wondered, "or had we brought it by our own dreams? She was now always very emotional, and would kiss me very tenderly, but when I spoke of marriage on the eve of her leaving she said, 'No, it seems to me impossible.' And then, with clenched hands, 'I have a horror and terror of physical love.'"

Having gone so far, she could not turn back. Maud told Willie how she had fallen in love with Millevoye and in her youthful passion had bound herself to him in the "alliance" that drew her into Boulangist adventures and advanced her work for Irish nationalism in France. She admitted that she had become Lucien's mistress shortly after they met, and at her own insistence, she said. But the sexual act, for reasons she could not explain, became repellent. At last she told Willie the truth about her son, whose death had caused her so much grief. If little Georges had not died she would have broken with Lucien and lived entirely in Ireland, for he had failed her. In desperation she had even engaged herself briefly to another man. Then, believing the lost child might be reborn, she had gone back to Lucien, and now she had a beautiful little daughter. Maud gave Willie to understand that since Iseult's birth four years earlier she had not been intimate with her lover. "But she was necessary to him. 'She did not know what would happen to him if her influence was not there.'"

Incapable of keeping his anguish to himself, Yeats told everything to Lady Gregory. They agreed that Maud must be "appeasing a troubled conscience by performing to the last tittle every duty. . . . And in all that followed," he wrote, "I was careful to touch as one might a sister. If she was to come to me, it must be from no temporary passionate impulse, but with the approval of her conscience."

In their spiritual eroticism Maud and Willie were children of their time, still bound by traditional restraints but struggling to find new freedoms. At the turn of the century, sexual energies were often expressed indirectly. Free love brought the problems of illegitimate children. Spirituality was a safer outlet. Annie Besant lived in celibate affection with the freethinker Charles Bradlaugh. Shaw had a mystical betrothal with William Morris's beautiful daughter, May. Yeats himself praised spiritual marriage as the deepest union possible between man and woman and believed that the tragedy of physical love was its inability to destroy the virginity of the individual psyche.

Early in 1899 Maud left Willie again to return to Paris. He consulted tarot cards, and mediums in Dublin and London. He asked the visionary AE what course he should pursue in his wooing. The cards were ambiguous, as were the mediums, and AE told him to give up his mad pursuit. Lady Gregory received a plea for help and, returning from Venice at once, urged him to follow Maud. By February he was in Paris, writing from the Boulevard Raspail:

> My dear Lady Gregory . . . I don't know whether things are well or ill with me, in some ways ill, for she has been almost cold with me, though she has made it easy for me to see her. If you knew all . . . you would understand why this love has been so bitter a thing to me, and why things I have known lately have made it, in a certain sense, the bitterer and the harder. It may be that Russell is right. I have little to set against what he says except a few omens. I would not so much lament, but I am sure that if things remain as they are she will never leave this life of hatred which a vision I made her see years ago told her was her deepest hell, and contrasted with the life of labour from the divine love which was her highest heaven.

"MG talks of crossing over on Tuesday," Willie wrote Lady Gregory,

> but she seldom gets away the day she expects. We shall cross over together. I have had rather a depressing time here. During the last months, and most of all while I have been here, she has told the story of her life, telling gradually, in more detail, all except a few things which I can see are too painful for her to talk of and about which I do not ask her. I do not wonder that she shrinks from life. Hers has been in part the war of phantasy and of a blinded idealism against eternal law. I am probably more

depressed than I should be as I am emerging, with a headache, out of a cold of an astonishing violence . . . MG is quite convinced that it is the work of a certain rival mystic, or one of his attendant spirits. She points out that I went to see him without it and came back with it, which is circumstantial evidence at any rate . . . MG is going to Ireland to the evicted tenants.

# CHAPTER NINETEEN

# The Crowded Years

"People wondered at the scope of my activities," Maud wrote in one of her rare moments of introspection. "Unconsciously perhaps, I had redoubled work to avoid thought. . . . The lack of personal thought may have made me at times lose sense of proportion. Dimly, I think I always realised I had not the qualities of generalship. I would get so absorbed in a small corner of the battlefield that I would lose sight of the important spot; so I trusted blindly to the spiritual force of Ireland to supply the need and remained passively impulsive to do the work to hand."

She had seen the last Treason-Felony prisoner, Tom Clarke, freed from Portland Jail in August 1898 after serving fifteen years of a life sentence for his involvement with a dynamiting plot. In the spring of 1899, before he left to work with the Clan in America, Maud traveled with Clarke to Limerick, where another former prisoner, James Daly, recently elected mayor, presented them with the keys to the city. Clarke had turned gray during his ordeal in Portland, but, still in his forties, he retained the intransigent Fenian spirit of the man who ten years before had refused to turn state's evidence against Parnell, saying he would rather rot in prison than dishonor himself. James Daly, who had refused the same bribe, conferred the Freedom of Limerick on his old comrade and honored Maud for her relentless campaign to win freedom for all the Irish prisoners.

The outbreak of the Boer War in the fall of 1899, the first visible crack in the British Empire since 1776, encouraged England's imperial rivals. French rightists exploited their country's "500-year-old hate for England." Millevoye's editorials in *La Patrie* propounded a frenzied chauvinism with Maud's wholehearted approval. As England suffered defeat after defeat in the Transvaal from a poorly armed people fighting for independence, Maud presided with Millevoye at pro-Boer demonstrations in France. Lucien became a familiar figure to the Irish and French partisans who frequented her apartment in Passy.

Millevoye's political fortunes had improved and he had been reelected Deputy from Amiens. His grandiloquent phrases were heard in the Chamber again, defending the political agitations of his friend Déroulède. His tall, thin figure towered over those of other government and military officials in the Rue Royale when General Marchand returned from his abortive attempt to wrest Egypt from England at Fashoda. The newspaper venture Maud had encouraged had reestablished him as a spokesman for the anti-British forces. She could be proud of her lover again, and she kept a sharp eye on the paper for articles that would advance the Irish cause in Europe and supplied ideas for many of its editorials.

The Irish journalist Arthur Lynch, who was about to leave for the Transvaal to cover the war for *Collier's*, was present at a luncheon and saw Millevoye instruct Maud in the etiquette practiced by the *haute bourgeoisie*. "A discreet knock came to the door and a nun entered. Miss Gonne begged to be excused for a time, and then explained to the two or three of us who were at the table—one of them being Millevoye . . . that an offer of marriage had been brought to her. Millevoye took the matter quite gravely, and remarked that, according to French custom, the right and proper course had been taken, and that if she wished to refuse the offer, she must send back a correct and especially polite reply."

If she had accepted, Maud would have become a marquise in one of France's wealthiest families, according to Lynch, who had some misgivings about her judgment but praised her generosity and charm, "a manner, not altogether an affectation, of looking at visitors, each one in turn, as if he or she were the one person on earth whom Miss Gonne had been longing to see."

Back in Dublin, at the Contemporary Club, Maud met H. W. Nevinson, the liberal English journalist.

> At my first meeting with her she was lovely beyond compare. All night we would sit up waiting to see her arrive by the morning train. All night we would sit up conversing, if she were there, that we might see her home with the milk. . . . In my first note of her I say, "not overwhelmingly clever nor at all smart," and that description remains true, nor does anyone regret the absence of cleverness and smartness in that indignant and passionately sympathetic heart. . . . At the club she sat long silent, perhaps bored by the political conversation, perhaps thinking of Paris from which she had just arrived. But when the others began asking me questions about the Greek War and fighting, at once she roused herself and became eager, listening and asking questions with the rest. Then I saw the meaning of that strong and beautiful chin. I knew that her longing was for action in place of all the theorizing and talk, so general in Dublin; and then as though by some prophetic insight, I foresaw the kind of marriage she would certainly make. "The first man of action," I said to myself—"the first man of resolute action whom she meets will have her at his mercy."

Maud had not yet met him, although by the fall of 1899 she had heard of John MacBride. In 1896 he had left his home in Westport, County Mayo, and gone to Johannesburg to earn a living as an assayer in the Rand mines. MacBride had known Arthur Griffith in the IRB, and he persuaded the young unemployed printer to join him in South Africa, where jobs were plentiful. Griffith worked as a machine supervisor in the mines and helped MacBride organize for the

Fenians among the Irish émigrés and exiles. When hostilities between the English and the Boers came to a head that summer, MacBride issued an appeal "to Irishmen to remember England's manifold infamies against their own country, and on this account to volunteer the more readily to fight against a common enemy for the defense of Boer freedom." At midnight on October 11, the "Major" from Mayo and the Irish-American "Colonel" Blake led their Irish Brigade with the Boer commandos across the frontier of Natal in the first action of the war in South Africa.

"The end of an epoch . . ." For Maud's friend Nevinson the Boer rebellion meant that the "under-dogs" were on the march. Subjugated peoples saw hope for themselves as the little armies in the veldt began to destroy the illusion of an empire's invincibility.

For the first time in a century England's military expansion was condemned not only by her enemies abroad but by her own people at home. Liberals, pacifists, socialists opposed the government's war effort, and the jingoism that approached hysteria in British aggression against the tiny South African republics set off a wave of revulsion among men and women of good will. From London, a city of gloom where friends no longer friends passed one another on the street without speaking, J. B. Yeats wrote his son in Dublin: "I wish I knew a Pro-Boer somewhere. Here they are all against me." Sickened by the war fever, George Moore gave up his London life and went back to live in Ireland.

Opposition to the war united the Irish members of Parliament. Led by John Redmond, the Parnellite split healed at last, the Irish Party joined the Liberals against the government. John Dillon was the first to speak out in the House of Commons in fierce condemnation of the British effort to dominate South Africa: "We know from long and bitter experience what that means. Predominant race! that is what you are fighting for—to put the Dutch under your feet . . . but allow me to tell you, you will never succeed." Always a reluctant M.P., Michael Davitt protested by dramatically retiring from the House of Commons on October 25, 1899: "I would not purchase liberty for Ireland at the price of one vote against the liberty of the Republics of South Africa."

The pro-Boer speeches at Westminster reflected the hopes of men and women in every city and hamlet in Ireland. Crowds gathered in the streets of Dublin to cheer reports of each British setback. The Fenian cry for separatism which had been drowned in the double talk commemorating Wolfe Tone sounded again in the land. Maud heard the familiar clichés revived, but the context had changed, and as different voices with new themes spoke in nationalist meeting halls, the crisis carried her into the center of rebellious activity in Ireland during the Boer War. "England's Difficulty, Ireland's Opportunity."

There is a change coming, a big change,
And riches and store will be nothing worth,
He will rise up that was small-eyed
And he that was big will fall down.

The time will come and it's not far from us,
When strength won't be on the side of authority or law,
And the neck will bend that was not bent,
When that time comes it will come heavily . . .

Arthur Griffith was in Dublin again. After helping Mac-Bride organize '98 Centennial celebrations among the Irish in Johannesburg, he had become homesick for the intellectual ferment of Dublin politics and returned in the fall of 1898 at the insistence of his colleague Willie Rooney, who was convinced that the time was right for a new nationalist paper. The two fledgling publishers whom Maud had admired for their brilliance at the Celtic Literary Society were short on funds but full of optimism. They took over the subscription list of the *Shan Van Vocht*, which Alice Milligan and Anna Johnston had had to give up. On March 4, 1899, their first issue appeared, and although it bore the respected name of John Mitchel's 1848 newspaper, the *United Irishman*, its first editorial condemned the ideals of traditional nationalist organizations: "When they admit the supremacy and acknowledge the right of British law in Ireland, they cannot claim to be the national ideal, which, rightly interpreted, ought to mean an Irish state governed by Irishmen for the benefit of the Irish people." Advanced nationalists had a new spokesman in Ireland. John MacBride wrote to America urging the Clan na Gael to send funds to help the *United Irishman*, which was equal to a dozen organizers.

Maud had a new publisher in Dublin. Griffith reprinted her articles from *L'Irlande Libre* and asked her to write for his weekly. Yeats and AE, George Moore, W. K. Magee ("John Eglinton"), James Starkey ("Seumas O'Sullivan"), Oliver St. John Gogarty, Padraic Colum—all contributed articles, and the formidable array of talent made the eight-page penny weekly one of the best-written journals of the day. James Joyce, a seventeen-year-old intellectual in his second year at University College and already hypercritical of the Irish-Ireland movement, praised Griffith's paper as "the only newspaper of any pretensions in Ireland."

Griffith adopted a diversity of nationalist policies. A revolutionary thinker, he disagreed with the constitutionalists who hoped to achieve Home Rule at Westminster. Although a member of the IRB, he differed from the partisans of physical force in advocating passive resistance, nonviolent opposition to English rule and English law. His disapproval of violence did not spring from deep moral conviction; he simply thought it ill advised. Although Maud herself joined in the chorus of rhetoric glorifying the long line of failed insurrections in Ireland, she too saw the futility of inciting a poorly equipped people to attack a superior enemy. Griffith was practical after her own heart.

He and Willie Rooney wrote most of the editorial columns in the *United Irishman*. Griffith's byline, "Cuguan," Afrikaans for dove, had been his nickname in the Transvaal. His waddling gait, caused by a defective tendon, earned him the gentle epithet; his nature was touchy and taciturn. Five feet five, Griffith had the exaggerated pride of the small man, and his rigid principles prevented him from unbending except with close friends. But it was his austerity, which others found puritanical and forbidding, that attracted Maud; an unusual selflessness in the young man who sought greatness for his country first, himself second.

Griffith's newspaper office soon became one of Maud's favorite haunts. As one visitor described it, "There was just enough room for a desk and a couple of chairs, one window, very dusty, dust everywhere. But the visitor never saw those things at first. Sitting at that desk, on a chair that was most rickety, was a small man, modest in appearance and demeanour, unobtrusive, not remarkable until he looked full at you, and then you forgot everything save that powerful head, those hard, steadfast, balancing eyes."

Maud respected Griffith and trusted him, but there was no romantic love in their close association. James Connolly, the Socialist, valued Maud's aid despite her patrician background, and for Griffith, though he called her "Queen," she was far more than a figurehead or a go-between for an unknown journalist with Dublin's literary set.

The *United Irishman*'s circulation increased rapidly with the growing opposition to England's war in South Africa. In October Maud and Griffith formed an organization to send aid to the Boers. Yeats, Connolly, and John Redmond's brother William served on the executive board of the Irish Transvaal Committee. Convinced that the savagery of British militarism meant the imminent decline of the Empire, O'Leary accepted his usual post as presiding officer. John Dillon and Michael Davitt sent donations. Maud took the chair at the inaugural meeting on October 10 in the old rooms of the Celtic Literary Society. She called for a vote to congratulate Major MacBride, and it was resolved that a flag inscribed with the motto "Our Land—Our People—Our Language" be sent to the Irish Brigade.

Earlier that year James Connolly had put forth the Socialist position on the crisis in the Transvaal. "The modern state is but a committee of rich men administering affairs in the interest of the upper class. . . . There is no pretense that the war will benefit the English people." Griffith had little interest in Connolly's working-class ideology; middle-class mercantile interests were more pertinent to his nationalism. But Maud was in favor of as many anti-English demonstrations as possible, and on August 27 she had sent a message of support when Connolly addressed a meeting of the Irish Socialist Republican Party in the first public protest against the Boer War.

Maud's turn came next at an antiwar rally in Dublin

outside the Custom House, when she and Griffith spoke to twenty thousand noisy demonstrators. The stocky little journalist, with his blue gaze and bristling mustaches, stood beside her on the platform, "hunched close inside his thick dark Irish coat." Sean O'Casey saw him; a "dark-green velour hat on his head, a thick slice of leather nailed to his heels to lift him a little nearer the stars."

Griffith was not a good public speaker, but he carried conviction, and Maud's eloquence gave wings to his message. In November half the populace of Cork turned out to welcome them, and once again the horses were removed from the traces and the people pulled Maud's carriage through the streets. Wherever they spoke, jubilant throngs greeted them with cries of "Up the Boers!" In December, after England's "Black Week" at Magersfontein and Stormberg, good news came from Colenso. Major MacBride, thrown from his horse in battle but unharmed, had received the surrender of Colonel Bullock, while the English commander in chief, Sir Redvers Buller, retreated from the field. Each Boer victory increased the number of Irish sympathizers, and as the casualty lists mounted, the number of recruits for the British Army declined.

In an attempt to popularize "Joe's War," as Lord Salisbury called it in ironic tribute to the nonconformist Liberal turned imperialist, it was announced that Trinity College would confer a degree on Joseph Chamberlain. The Transvaal Committee decided to hold a simultaneous antigovernment demonstration. Just before Christmas, Dublin Castle plastered the city with posters proscribing the Transvaal Committee's meeting, and the police threatened Maud with arrest if she tried to speak.

The government ban added fire to her defiance. Willie Redmond, M.P., failed to appear on the appointed date. Davitt, who had gone to investigate conditions in the Transvaal, sent Pat O'Brien, M.P., in his place. Maud and the other speakers climbed into the wagon that was to serve as a platform and set off for Beresford Place.

As they turned out Abbey Street they were met by a cordon of police, who succeeded in halting them only long enough to haul the driver away. Connolly, who had deliberately seated himself in front, seized the reins. Ignoring the police, he drove the horses at a mad gallop through the barricades, and the crowd pressing into Beresford Place surged through the gap. John O'Leary stood up in the lurching wagon, still on the move, to open the meeting, and Maud gave a resolution to support the Boers, while the people gathering in their wake yelled approval. Mounted police managed to steer them all into the yard of the South Street police station, but the crowd was large and unruly, and the sergeant in command, having spotted an M.P. in their midst, let them go. On they streamed, waving flags Irish, South African, French, and American, across O'Connell Bridge past Trinity College. O'Casey watched their approach: ". . . a long car, benched on both sides, drawn by two frightened hearse horses. A stout, short, stocky man, whose face was hidden by a wide-awake hat, was driving them. Several other men, pale-faced and tight-lipped, sat on the seats, facing each other; and with them was a young woman with long lovely yellow hair, smiling happily, like a child out on her first excursion."

The bravest man Maud knew turned to her as they sped along Dame Street: "There are only two sentries at the gates. . . . Shall I drive in and seize the Castle?"

Within the grimy walls of Dublin's fortress armed men were ready to fire. Maud hesitated, and in that moment Connolly relinquished his boyish fantasy and drove on past Dublin Castle. The prize was not to be won by a mob of unarmed daredevils, who gradually dispersed down Parliament Street. But the Transvaal Committee had created a memorable disturbance during the staid ceremonies at Trinity.

Elated by the response in Ireland, Maud was ready to carry her pro-Boer campaign to America. She would ask the Clan na Gael to support the Transvaal Committee and also raise money to keep Griffith's newspaper afloat. Her second lecture tour was arranged by an IRB man from the West, "Rocky Mountain O'Brien," and as he was not involved with the Clan's factional arguments, she trusted that Devoy would be less hostile.

Before she left for America, Maud took her pro-Boer plans to the Boers themselves. She went to Brussels to arrange for sending an ambulance from Irish sympathizers to the Transvaal. Dr. W. J. Leyds, Ambassador Extraordinary of the South African Republic in Brussels, welcomed her offer, but the next plan she put before him made him rise from his chair in surprise. Bombs disguised as lumps of coal were to be placed in the holds of British troopships sailing for South Africa. Maud could not bear to kill a bird or see a child hungry, but in the belief that the explosions would halt Irish enlistments, she was willing to let men, many of them Irish, be blown to bits. She tried to convince the South African representative that his office should provide the necessary funds.

Dr. Leyds was speechless. Sitting opposite him in his copy office this elegant lady was asking him to sanction a crime that would make a mad anarchist blanch. Her French co-conspirators would design the explosives, Maud told him, and the IRB had contact with seamen who would place them in the bunkers. The plan was known to one other member of the IRB besides Dr. Ryan, who had given it his approval.

The Ambassador exclaimed that this was not a "recognized means of warfare." Maud countered that English evictions in Ireland and the infamous English concentration camps in the Transvaal caused the death of countless innocent civilians and were not recognized means of warfare either. Leyds protested that concealing bombs in troopships would have disastrous diplomatic repercussions and alienate the English Liberals who were defying their government by supporting the Boers. He could not take part in such an irresponsible plot. Maud accepted his decision but cautioned him against placing his faith in the Liberals.

The following day Dr. Leyds's secretary appeared in her drawing room on the Avenue d'Eylau. The Ambassador had reconsidered her request and was willing to put two thousand pounds at her disposal. Maud agreed to postpone leaving for Ireland for twenty-four hours so that the secretary could get the money. He was back the next day, but without the two thousand pounds. When he explained, Maud was horrified. A man who claimed to be in the IRB had called on the Ambassador to advise him that the operation was too risky for a woman. This unidentified Irishman had convinced Dr. Leyds that he had been sent to Brussels in Maud's place to procure the money.

An *"indiscreet karakter,"* Dr. Leyds said of Maud Gonne in his letter of January 21, 1900, to Montagu White, the Republic's former consul general in London. *"Haar indiscreet karakter blijkt meer en meer,"* he warned again a few days later. Maud thought Dr. Leyds was irresponsible, Mark Ryan a fool. In London Dr. Ryan assured her that he had sent no one to Brussels, and that of course the British Secret Service was to blame. He did not seem perturbed except by Dr. Leyds's indiscretion, but Arthur Griffith shared Maud's suspicion that it was the work of a traitor inside the IRB.

Maud was relieved that she was about to leave for America. She could not have chosen a more propitious moment. The Spanish-American War had spread from Cuba to the Philippines, and American forces had joined with the British to put down the Boxer Rebellion in China. A wave of military expansionism such as the world had never experienced before had given rise to a new phenomenon: a movement for international peace. Kipling might urge Americans to "Take up the White Man's burden" with his verses in *McClure's Magazine*, but radicals and reformers were outraged by the "earth hunger" that had begun to infect the Republic freed from the Empire a century earlier. In Boston's Faneuil Hall liberal Democrats and intellectuals including Jane Addams and Mark Twain met to form the Anti-Imperialist League. Workers in Chicago, among them a budding anarchist, Leon Czolgosz, listened to Emma Goldman denounce war. In New York the liberal editor and politician Carl Schurz was trying to form a third party to defeat President McKinley and his expansionist supporters. Imperialism had become a political issue in America, and the Irish-Americans who rejoiced at news of England's defeats in the Transvaal were now a significant political force. Maud's hopes were high when she set sail from Le Havre in January 1900.

This time her transatlantic crossing was calm, and the atmosphere on the French liner was congenial. On January 28, Maud stood at the rail of the *Normandie,* waving at the tiny figures far below in the steamer the Clan had chartered to escort her into New York Harbor.

Prepared now for extravagant display, the show and glitter of American publicity, she made no complaint about her suite at the Savoy. The Academy of Music, at Irving Place and Fourteenth Street, had been sold out some time before her arrival, and when she entered the vast auditorium on the night of February 4 she saw five hundred extra chairs placed on the platform to hold the overflowing audience.

The Academy of Music rang with "hisses and cheers," reported Patrick Ford's *Irish World*, "as Miss Gonne vehemently denounced the British conduct of war in the Transvaal" and praised the Irish Brigade: "The presence of that splendid body of our fellow-countrymen saves Ireland's honor . . . Freedom is never won without the sacrifice of blood. Our chance is coming. The end of the British Empire is at hand." In Providence, Chicago, Philadelphia she lifted her audience to a pitch of exaltation. A photograph of her taken in New York caught the dark glance of a conquering angel. When she learned of Luke Dillon's attempt to blow up the Welland Canal, between Lake Erie and Lake Ontario, to halt the flow of matériel to the British forces in Africa, she entertained the notion that she might have helped inspire the daring act for which he was to serve fourteen years in Canadian jails.

The Chicago Clan sent medical supplies and a group of the "finest looking" body of men, wrote Michael Davitt, that reached the Transvaal from abroad. Yet aside from a few newspaper correspondents who "had come to write and remained to fight," there were no more than forty American volunteers for the Boer cause.

Maud was bitterly disappointed at the Clan's failure to take advantage of the general antiimperialist climate. Irish influence in American politics was too diffuse. The President was reelected, Theodore Roosevelt was vice-president, and six months later, after McKinley's assassination, the Rough Rider of the Spanish-American War was in the White House, and America continued to sell military supplies to the British in the Transvaal.

Maud had expected too much, of others as of herself, but in her immediate purpose, fund raising, her second American tour was successful. She had the satisfaction of bringing back a thousand pounds to keep the *United Irishman* and the voice of antiimperialism alive in Ireland.

# CHAPTER TWENTY

# Daughters of Erin

My back is to the wall;
Lo, here I stand.
O Lord whate'er befall
I love this land! . . .

This land to us Thou gave
In days of old;
They seek to make a grave
Or field of gold.

To us, O Lord, Thy hand
Put forth to save;
Give us, O Lord, this land
Or give a grave!

The poor farmers in Ireland saw their own plight dramatized by the farmers' fight in the veldt. At the Galway railroad
station countrywomen saying goodbye to husbands and sons
off to the front bade their men "not to be too hard on the
Boers." In January the separatists decided as a gesture of
defiance to support Major MacBride as a candidate in the
by-election caused by Davitt's resignation as M.P. from South
Mayo. On O'Leary's motion the Tranvaal Committee sup-

ported the Irish Brigade leader in absentia, but the United Irish League was split; William O'Brien, its leader, supported his agrarian candidate John O'Donnell, and although Griffith and the Fenians worked hard for the Major, he lost overwhelmingly to O'Donnell, 427 votes against 2,401. MacBride would not have been seated in Parliament if he had won—in British eyes he was a traitor to the Crown—but the UIL's failure to back the symbolic candidate earned MacBride's and Maud's enmity.

When she returned from America, Maud worked in Dublin to protect the raw recruits ignorant of their rights in an army that was shipping them off to be slaughtered. The Transvaal Committee printed her leaflets, explaining that it was illegal for any man to be sent to the front unless he had specifically volunteered for service against the Boers. She had help from Father P. F. Kavanagh, a Franciscan who worked with the committee, in presenting the religious justification for their position: "No human authority can justify those who take part in an unjust war. . . . All, who knowing a war to be unjust engage in it, are guilty of a grievous sin."

In one of her articles for the *Irish World*, Maud estimated that there were at least fifty thousand Irish troops with the British Army in the Transvaal: the Connaught Rangers, the Dublin Fusiliers, famous regiments that bore the brunt of the ill-planned campaign; "the Inniskillings going into action and coming out with five officers out of thirty; forty men out of five hundred." Winston Churchill, then a war correspondent, praised their coolness and bravery; the Queen was said to be upset by the Irish massacres. Were Maud's father still alive, would he be making antiwar speeches as an M.P. at Westminster? Or would Colonel Gonne have rejoined his regiment?

For the Irish were divided on the issue, and England's war against the South African Republics had the enthusiastic support of Protestant Unionists, so similar in temperament to the Afrikaners. Roger Casement of County Antrim, who was British consul in Cape Town, despised his countryman John MacBride for daring to recruit the Irish to fight for the Boers. Many Home Rulers found themselves emotionally tied to the Crown. Katherine Tynan Hinkson abandoned her independent Irish views and succumbed to the imperialist fever in London. While Lady Gregory wore an ivy leaf, Parnell's symbol, inside her cloak, her society friends were knitting socks for British soldiers and putting "little Union Jacks" on safety pins "for Tommy to fasten his bandages with."

"You must be much cheered by the war news to-day," Yeats wrote his sister Lily. "The spectacle of John Bull amassing 70 or 100 thousand men to fight 20 thousand and slapping his chest the while and calling on the heavens to witness his heroism has not been exhilarating. Ireland seems to be really excited and I am not at all sure that Maud Gonne may not be able to seriously check enlisting. She is working with extraordinary energy."

ENLISTING IN THE ENGLISH ARMY IS TREASON TO IRELAND
"Fellow-countrymen—The Irishmen in England's service who are sent to South Africa will have to fight against Irish Nationalists who have raised Ireland's flag in the Transvaal, and have formed an Irish Brigade to fight for the Boers against the oppressors of Ireland. . . . England's army is small. Englishmen are not good soldiers. England has to get others to do her fighting for her. In the past Irishmen have too often won England's battles for her and saved her from defeat and have thus rivetted the chains upon their Motherland. Let them do so no more. . . .

In its effort to spur recruitment the army had relaxed its regulation that the men sleep in their barracks, and at night parties of redcoats and their women made Sackville Street a rowdy promenade till the gas lamps grew pale in the dawn. Maud and her brigade of young women from the Transvaal Committee—Maire Killeen, Marcella Cosgrave, Mary and Margaret Quinn, Griffith's sisters, Rooney's sister and his fiancée—confronted the soldiers in the streets. Armed with their leaflets, they followed courting couples into the pubs, crying shame on girls consorting with the soldiers. Abusive language was exchanged, hair pulled, dresses torn. Griffith and Rooney often came to the rescue when fists began to fly.

Although she suspected that Griffith hated it, Maud wrote that "fighting soldiers became quite a popular evening entertainment with young men."

By the spring of 1900 the British, reorganized under Lord Roberts and Kitchener, were beginning to stem the Boer advance. General French's cavalry relieved Cecil Rhodes at Kimberley, defeated General Cronjé at Paardeberg, and went on to occupy Bloemfontein. Casualties were high— "not a knocker in London town without a bit of crepe on it" —and in Ireland enlistment came to a virtual standstill. The government decided that the old Queen should visit her subjects to the west again, to stir up some loyal enthusiasm. "Her visits to Ireland have indeed been unfortunate for English power," Yeats warned in an article he wrote for Griffith's newspaper, "for they have commonly foreshadowed a fierce and sudden shaking of English power in Ireland." In a letter of protest to the *Freeman's Journal* he pointed out that the Queen had chosen a "remarkable" date to embark on her good will tour, April 2, the hundredth anniversary of the Act of Union.

> I propose that a great meeting be summoned in the Rotunda on that date to protest against the Union and to dissociate Ireland from any welcome that the Unionist or the time-server may offer to the official head of the Empire in whose name liberty is being suppressed in South Africa, as it was suppressed in Ireland a hundred years ago. I propose that Mr. John O'Leary be the chairman and that all Irish members [of Parliament] be upon the platform.

At a meeting of the Irish Party April 2, Yeats tried "in vain to get Harrington to resign in favour of MacBride of the Irish Brigade." Maud's new hero was also Willie's, and his pro-Boer activity brought him closer to her again. His public protests were made at no small risk, as she knew; some of the wealthy patrons of his nationalist theater were bound to take offense. In the condescending tone Maud detested he wrote Lady Gregory: "In a battle, like Ireland's, which is one of poverty against wealth, one must prove one's sincerity, by making oneself unpopular to wealth. One must accept the baptism of the gutter."

He still feared guttersnipes and the riots that the Queen's visit would cause, but for the moment he could rest assured that Maud was out of harm's reach. She was in London, confined to bed with an intestinal illness and furious because, as Willie told Lady Gregory, she "will hardly be well in time to do anything with the crowds."

Dublin Castle went to great expense to put on a show of loyalty; special ships brought thousands of shipyard workers from Belfast to applaud the Queen; the workers in Guinness's great brewery had the day off and an extra shilling in their pay envelopes. To honor Victoria, a free treat was given in Phoenix Park to five thousand boys and girls commandeered from the Catholic and Protestant schools of the city. Street vendors hawked bunches of shamrocks as big as cabbage heads, tied up with Union Jack ribbons.

The government's appeal to popular sentiment did not alter Irish animosity, and on April 4 "a tiny lady, almost a dwarf, tossed and jolted to and fro by the movements of the carriage, dressed in mourning and wearing horn-rimmed glasses on a livid and empty face . . . the old queen of England entered the Irish capital in the midst of silent people." James Joyce witnessed Victoria's last Royal Procession in Dublin; apathetic, sullen, the hush was not one of awe. Yeats quoted Mirabeau: "The silence of the people is the lesson of kings." There were only a few outbreaks of violence along the route. A counterdemonstration by the Transvaal Committee was disrupted before it got under way. Both Connolly and Griffith were injured in the charge of mounted police.

From her sickbed in London, Maud made her presence felt in Dublin during Queen Victoria's visit:

> . . . Taking the Shamrock in her withered hand, she dares to ask Ireland for soldiers—for soldiers to fight for the exterminators of their race! And the reply of Ireland comes sadly but proudly, not through the lips of the miserable little politicians who are touched by the English canker, but through the lips of the Irish people: Queen, return

to your own land; you will find no more Irishmen ready to wear the red shame of your livery. In the past they have done so from ignorance, and because it is hard to die of hunger when one is young and strong and the sun shines, but they shall do so no longer. See! your recruiting agents return alone and unsuccessful from my green hills and plains, because once more hope has revived, and it will be in the ranks of your enemies that my children will find employment and honour.

Maud's article, "The Famine Queen," translated from *L'Irlande Libre*, appeared in Griffith's weekly on April 17. The Lord Lieutenant, Lord Cadogan, ordered the police to confiscate the entire issue of the *United Irishman*, and censorship boomeranged to give wide publicity to Maud's denunciation. Within the week she was in Dublin, where, as Yeats wrote Lady Gregory, "a number of her newspaper has been suppressed, to her great joy, as it will give a lift to the circulation, and where, not at all to her joy, the editor has been imprisoned for a month for horsewhipping the editor of the *Dublin Figaro*, who wrote something against her, but what she does not know. The *Figaro* is a kind of society paper and very loyal . . ."

On her arrival Maud saw the nature of the slander. Placards were hung all over Dublin advertising the *Figaro* scoop: Maud Gonne was in the pay of the British government. According to Ramsay Collis, a Castle hack, Colonel Gonne's army pension was being paid into the estate from which she drew her income. Infuriated, Griffith stormed into the *Figaro* office and assaulted the reporter. The "Dove" broke his stick, a South African "sjam-bok," and Collis was laid up for weeks. Griffith was arrested and imprisoned for a fortnight in Mountjoy Prison. Maud sued for libel. She appeared in court in a new hat bought for the occasion, and was represented by her old friend the silver-tongued J. F. Taylor. Collis's lawyer read "The Famine Queen" to the jury, hoping to turn them against Maud, but the people in the packed courtroom were as delighted as she to hear her attack on Victoria repeated aloud. Taylor won the case, and Collis was made to publish "a full and abject retraction and apology." After the trial his lawyer admitted to Maud that Dublin Castle had footed the bill for the *Figaro* defense and apologized to her. Amused, she thanked him for having furthered the antienlistment campaign.

It was Griffith who had paid the price, and Maud and her co-workers decided he should be rewarded. *Bean na hEireann*, "Women of Ireland," the first political periodical published by women in Dublin, told how they did it:

> Now there were some young girls in Dublin, chiefly members of the Irish classes of the Celtic Literary Society. They knew the man and felt sorry he had lost his stick. They resolved to replace it. They borrowed the key of the rooms at 32 Lower Abbey Street from a friendly Celtic member and held a meeting on Easter Sunday after 12 Mass. They subscribed the price of a nice strong blackthorn with a silver ring, bearing an Irish inscription . . . there were about fifteen girls present, and they discussed other things too . . . the best way for dressing hair . . . and the latest fashions, black and karkhi because it was the year of the Boer War. And then we spoke of Queen Victoria's visit to Ireland. One said it was a fine idea that, in the *United Irishman* of that week, of giving a treat to children who refused to go to the park and kow-tow to her majesty, and then the girls all looked at each other and said "Let us do it." They were (with one exception) all working girls.

Most of the women gathered at Abbey Street were younger than Maud. Some of them had just put up their hair and let down their skirts. They had proved their value to the Irish cause with their successful antienlistment drive, and, with Maud, they too "resented being excluded, as women, from National Organisations." Almost two decades had passed since O'Leary remarked, of the disbanded Ladies' Land League, "They may not have been right, but they were suppressed because they were honester and more sincere than the men." Twenty years, and a new generation of women had grown up to find themselves still disfranchised, still unrepresented by any member of their sex in government except for the Queen—"for after all," wrote Maud, "she is a woman." They had been influenced by the woman's suffrage movement and Emmeline Pankhurst's slogan, "Deeds not words." With Maud's leadership, that Easter Sunday of 1900 they decided to form their own organization, Inghinidhe na hEireann, Daughters of Erin.

Maud was elected president. Annie Egan (James Egan's wife), Jennie Wyse-Power, and Anna Johnston served as vice-presidents. The actress Maire T. Quinn (later Mrs. Dudley Digges), Maire O'Kennedy, and Dora Hackett were secretaries, Margaret Quinn and Sarah White treasurers. Other early members included Frances Griffith, Marcella Cosgrave, Sinead O'Flanagan (later Mrs. Eamon de Valera), Alice Milligan, and another actress, Maire nic Shiubhlaigh.

Unlike the members of the Irishwoman's Suffrage Association, most of whom came from the upper classes and were solely concerned with winning the vote (Hanna Sheehy and Louie Bennett were notable exceptions), Maud's Daughters of Erin placed women's rights in the context of nationalism. Their immediate objectives were

> to encourage the study of Gaelic, of Irish Literature, History, Music and Art, especially amongst the young . . . to support and popularize Irish Manufactures . . . to discourage the reading and circulation of low English literature . . . and to combat in every way English influence, which is doing so much injury to the artistic taste and refinement of the Irish people; to form a fund called the National Purposes Fund for the furtherance of the above objects. And its members, all of whom adopt a Gaelic name, are pledged to mutual help and support, and to work for the cause of Irish Independence.

The Daughters of Erin quickly took on other projects in addition to the antienlistment campaign. The first large one was their Patriotic Children's Treat, held to reward those who had refused to go to Victoria's celebration in April. On July 1, Maud and Maire Quinn, riding in an outside car, led a procession of some thirty thousand children through the streets of Dublin, from Beresford Place to Clonturk Park. They carried leafy branches. Douglas Hyde's "little green branch" of the Gaelic League, multiplied a thousandfold, formed a forest on the march. It took two hours for the procession to pass through the gates of the park. Marshaled by strapping hurley players from the Gaelic Athletic Association and young teachers from the Celtic Literary Society, the immense festival miraculously went off without a mishap or a single lost child. After the games and dances, and after all the casks of ginger beer and thousands of sandwiches had been consumed, Maud addressed the children. She told the boys they must never disgrace themselves by joining the English armed forces or police; she asked the girls to work to further the national ideal. "In a field beyond Drumcondra, and in the presence of a Priest of their Church, they swear to cherish towards England until the freedom of Ireland has been won, undying enmity," wrote Yeats, who could not help but wonder, "How many of these children will carry bomb or rifle when a little under or a little over thirty?"

Years later, strangers, middle-aged men and women, would stop Maud in the street and tell her, "I was one of the patriotic children at your party when Queen Victoria was over."

Women had shown the nationalists what efficient organization could accomplish. Maud and the Daughters of Erin had organized the largest peaceful demonstration ever held in the city. "Dublin has never witnessed anything so marvelous as the procession of 30,000 schoolchildren who refused to be bribed into parading before the Queen of England," Griffith wrote in the *United Irishman*. Hundred of letters poured into Inghinidhe's headquarters at 32 Abbey Street. A bricklayer wrote, "Her services to the land of the Shamrock have been unparalleled, and there is no name that will ever shine out with greater prominence in the history of our country than that of our beloved lady, Miss Maud Gonne."

The English *Daily Express* called for her arrest, and the

loyalists accused the Daughters of Erin of teaching little children a diabolical catechism: "What is the origin of evil? England." Maud needed the people's approval and accepted with pride the attacks from enemies that her success elicited. But it was difficult to countenance criticism from the very men who had sought women's help within the movement: "the most acrid invective was reserved for women in politics." Harpies, furies, hysterical females—rebel Irishwomen suffered the harsh treatment given to militant suffragists, and much of it came from their male colleagues. Even one of Griffith's comrades, the historian P. S. O'Hegarty, wrote, "They took to their hearts every catch-cry, every narrowness and every bitterness, and steadily eliminated from themselves every womanly feeling . . ." And liberal women who hid behind their husbands felt threatened by the new breed of Amazons. "Of late years the energies of the young women of Ireland have been absorbed in politics," wrote Katherine Tynan Hinkson, who had once followed Anna Parnell. "There is plenty of room for women in politics in Ireland as elsewhere . . . but a whole generation of political women would be a nightmare . . ."

"Mad Gonne" and "Maud Gonneing"—Maud's name was used to belittle women activists. Annie Horniman told Yeats to beware of "a beautiful woman screaming from a cart," the bugaboo of defenseless poets and children. Yet Oliver Gogarty, not a kindly wit, was surprised at Maud's gentle manner at a meeting of the Literary Theatre. "For one so tall and striking you would have expected a voice full and contralto: but no, hers was a small voice. And like the man in Douglas Hyde's song, she had a large heart—'I'd rather have if I got my choice, A large heart and a small voice.' A tall and tawny woman, the daughter of a colonel in the English Army," the ironic doctor wrote. "Greatly she inspired Yeats."

Many others were moved by that persuasive voice. It hit the right note at the right moment for the women of Ireland. It opened doors. Maud got Yeats to help her create pageants in celebration of the four seasons of Celtic lore: the winter of Brigid; the summer of Lug; Beltane, the spring; and Samhain,

All Soul's in November. She got AE, Padraic Colum, and other writers and artists to contribute their talents for the Daughters' performances. Ella Young, the mystic poet, a protégé of AE, taught Irish history and legend. The precocious young Gaelic Leaguer Padraic Pearse, also a gifted poet and a mystic, was the examiner for language studies. Affiliated clubs sprang up in Cork, Limerick, and Ballina after Maud's visits, and soon there were branches of Inghinidhe in Liverpool and in Brooklyn. Members came and went, paying dues when they could, leaving no permanent record; yet when Maud went to Paris to attend a ceremony for President Kruger, who was in Europe seeking aid for the South African Republics, she presented to him an address on behalf of the Daughters of Erin bearing ten thousand signatures.

Unable to vote, and also opposed to Irish representation in Parliament, the militant women nevertheless made their influence felt in local elections. Thomas Byrne, who had supplied horses and lorries for the Patriotic Treat, was returned for the North Dock Ward by a large majority. No wonder Arthur Griffith and Willie Rooney were more than willing to accept Maud's women's organization as a militant auxiliary wing. The shopgirls and students in long black serge skirts who parked their bicycles on York Street and climbed the wooden stairs to Inghinidhe's classrooms in the "Workers' Club" were to become participants in "the establishment of a permanent National Government, representative of the whole people of Ireland and elected by the suffrages of all her men and women."

Like Maud herself, the Daughters of Erin were imbued with a moral confidence approaching self-righteousness, with physical courage, enthusiasm, and a certain youthful bravado: "Respectable people who believe in no politics and the *Leader*, and lust after the flesh-pots of the Mansion House, say it is vulgar . . . Woman rushes in where man fears to tread, and makes him foolish and fall back on the apple theory to save himself. . . . I am weary living in a world ruled by men with mouse-hearts and monkey brains and I want a change."

Before she founded Inghinidhe na hEireann, Maud had lived her public life in a landscape peopled by men. During her motherless childhood, the early years when her devoted

Tommy was alive, in the garrison and the viceregal court, she had moved in a world where men were the dominant figures. The salons of her beloved Paris were run by women for men; the intrigues of the Boulangists, the politics of London and Dublin life were managed by men.

The women who worked in Inghinidhe and proceeded to take on its responsibilities provided Maud with something new, more tangible than the acclaim of admiring audiences and the evanescent attention which propagandists must constantly revive. The Daughters of Erin gave her an inner esteem based on the most supportive companionship she had ever experienced. With her new friends she went hiking in the Wicklow Mountains, waded in the fresh streams that raced through the glens. Sailing to Ireland's Eye with Ella Young and Helena Molony, she saw Innisfallen take shape from the spiraled mists that had shrouded her childhood view from Howth. "Amid the seagulls," she wrote, calling to mind the white birds in Yeats's poem, "we often lit the Beltaine fire of the old Gaelic festival, now represented by the fires of St. John's Eve. It served to boil our tea kettle and to destroy all vestiges of the picnic, for Ella was very careful that the land should not be disfigured. At the last she would kindle from it a tiny fire in which she burnt herbs she had gathered from different parts of Ireland, as she said, to unite all . . ."

The Daughters of Erin chose St. Brigid as their patron saint. In her Christian incarnation, the warrior goddess of pagan Ireland had led St. Patrick a merry dance through the Druids' territory. In the Dark Ages learning flourished in Ireland: Brigid was famous for her knowledge of the classics and the law, girls attended school with boys, and women headed the academies. Handed down from prehistoric Celtic peoples, the Brehon Laws remained in effect well into the Middle Ages, granting equal rights to women in marriage, inheritance to landed estates, and noble titles. Women were rulers and warriors, the equals of men as teachers, physicians, poets, lawyers and judges. Something of their spirit survived the subjugation of women by the church of St. Patrick. It lived on in those who fought side by side with their men in the rebellions and the Land Wars; it sang in the ballads of Lady Uillach in the first century and Liadan in the seventh, and in the works of Speranza, Fanny Parnell, Ethna Carberry, Alice Milligan, and Augusta Gregory. Ireland had as many heroines as heroes in its Castle. This was the lesson Maud set out to teach.

Girls and boys from the streets came to Inghinidhe's improvised classrooms scarcely knowing how to write their own names, but they were quick to add those of the great warrior queens, Maeve, Macha, Emer, to their imaginary battle games. Gaelic pseudonyms protected some of the Daughters of Erin who worked for Unionist employers and also served as a link with the tradition of powerful women. Marie Kennedy took the name of Queen Macha, Helena Molony chose Emer. Maud was Maeve. In Inghinidhe's classes children were not punished; rewards were expected to lead them to learning, according to the Montessori method which Maud had heard of on the Continent. The little singers and dancers, wearing green sashes clasped with golden badges, performed at local competitions. The prize winners were taken on excursions to historic shrines, to Tara, the magic hill of the High Kings, or to Wolfe Tone's grave. On their way "they talked in Irish to the great delight of the people along the roads . . . and loudly booed and hissed every English soldier they passed. They arrived back at Abbey Street . . . having had a very pleasant day."

When she had time Maud taught dramatics, the school's most popular class. Maire nic Shiubhlaigh, Sarah Allgood, Maire Quinn were among the apprentices who later became Ireland's stars in the Abbey Theatre. Members wrote their own plays and tableaux vivants; "Ireland Fettered and Ireland Free" was a favorite of the stage-struck adolescents. Ella Young saw Maud perform in *The Last Feast of the Fianna*, by Alice Milligan. "The raised curtain showed her, seated in an ancient carved chair, with an illuminated parchment book on her knee. She had a splendid robe of brocaded white poplin with wide sleeves, and two little pages in medieval dress of black velvet held tall wax candles on either side of her. . . . The quality of her beauty dulled the candle-flames."

# Broken
# Alliances

In July 1900 Maud led a delegation of men and women from the Dublin Transvaal Committee to France. England's imperialism in Africa had revived French sympathy for the Irish cause, and in an unprecedented gesture of harmony the Paris Municipal Council invited Maud's group of delegates— Arthur Griffith, Maire Quinn, and Mrs. Wyse-Power among them—to the Hôtel de Ville. On the eve of Bastille Day a banquet was held in their honor at the Restaurant Vantler on the Avenue Clichy. Maud sat to the right of Deputé Archdeacon, and her friend Augusta Holmes on his left, at the head of a long table of dignitaries. The deputy toasted the day when French and Irish, bound by their Celtic heritage, would see the end of England's tyrannical rule. Millevoye wrote an editorial for *La Patrie* welcoming the Irish delegates in the name "of the glorious memories of Castlebar . . . the names of Hoche, Humbert and the daring but unsuccessful heroes of a hundred years ago." Maud felt secure in their alliance.

Paris, which was still a home for Maud because of Lucien and Iseult, extended a gala welcome to her Irish friends. The boulevards in carnival dress were jammed with tourists visiting the Universal Exposition. Apotheosizing nationalism, the flags of every country in the world waved from the Trocadéro to the Grand Palais. Balloonists in tricolored gondolas floated around the Eiffel Tower; cascades of fiery carnations illuminated the night sky above the Arch of Triumph. The secretary of the Opéra invited the Transvaal Committee delegates to a performance of *The Valkyrie*, but they could not stay in Paris long enough to attend. Lucien and Madame de Ste. Croix shared Maud's box. Lucien had overcome his prejudice against Wagner to please Maud, who was amused to hear him criticize Bréval, the Brunhilde of the evening. He claimed that her voice was inferior to that of a young woman friend of his whose talent remained unrecognized because she would not give herself to certain Ministers. Avril de Ste. Croix remarked that the Opéra rarely took singers from café-chantants and, turning to Maud, whispered, "You are away from Paris too much, Maud chérie." Maud put the warning out of her mind as the flight of the Valkyries rose from the orchestra and swept her into another world. She had accomplished a great deal in the past few months; it was time to forget her troubles for a little while.

A few days later she was on her way to Switzerland to join Kathleen, who was vacationing at Vevey. She had not seen her sister for some time, and in the absence of Captain Pilcher, who was off with his regiment fighting the Boers, Maud could enjoy being with her and the little niece and nephews. Millevoye wrote her at Vevey asking her to meet him at Chamonix. Rested and in high spirits, Maud took the little steamer across Lake Léman.

All was serene in the Arcadian playground where, not so many years before, Byron and Shelley had traced the path of Rousseau's courageous heroine, Julie, through the groves of Meillerie. Even the reflection of the grim castle of Chillon floated gently on the surface of the lake. Lighthearted as a girl on a summer excursion, Maud went to meet her lover. As so often before, they would spend a few days together in the mountains.

The gentle slopes of Chamonix spread green at the foot of forbidding Alpine ranges. Like snow blown from the frozen summits, daisies drifted across the meadows. Thirteen years earlier Maud and Lucien had met for the first time and fallen in love in the shadow of the Puy de Dôme. Now on a blazing August afternoon they are walking below the great triangular mass of Mont Blanc, side by side, but too far apart to be taken for happy lovers. Maud does not look at the tall dark man beside her. She is twisting a folded newspaper in her hands as if she would like to destroy it.

That morning she had read an article in *La Patrie* which distressed her profoundly. Contradicting all they had worked for, it named Germany as the sole enemy of France. There was no mention of England. It was signed by Millevoye, but Maud knew it was not in his style. She had to deal with the portents and warnings she had ignored for so long. When she confronted Millevoye with the article as proof of her worst suspicions, he admitted that the author was none other than the young singer he had praised at the Opéra, a friend of Clemenceau and a woman "who loves Alsace-Lorraine as you love Ireland."

Maud now saw with utmost clarity that behind Lucien's long-standing criticism of her "absurd Irish revolution-aries," and behind the unprincipled editorial, lay the power of Clemenceau. So far *"l'homme sinistre"* had failed to break her influence on Millevoye. He had tried to destroy her through a corrupt doctor; he had tried to frighten her off with blackmail. Now he was using a woman to lure Millevoye into the pro-English party. Maud could forgive her lover for being unfaithful, but she would not tolerate his betrayal of their ideals.

Had it always been a fantasy, their alliance? Proud as he had been to flaunt his *belle Irlandaise* in public, eager to use her charm and talent for his own purposes, Lucien had begun to be embarrassed by her stubborn loyalty to Ireland. He could not estrange her from her revolutionary ideals, and her inde-pendent activities imperiled his career.

Seeing him so easily taken in by an ambitious woman, Maud realized that Lucien had never been sincerely involved with Irish freedom. His professed interest had been a ruse to hold her. His cause was counterrevolution in France, hers was revolution in Ireland. Now that his political advance-ment required a softening toward England, he could no longer deceive her. She must part with him. They would meet again but casually at public functions and speak of matters concerning Iseult. She would never mention their alliance again. Clemenceau had triumphed.

"I gazed at those cruel snow mountains which were turning my heart into stone in spite of the scent of the flowers and the hum of the wild bees around us, whispering of life," Maud wrote, remembering their parting at Chamonix. The first exaltation, the gradual disillusionment, the heartbreak, are all contained in her lines. Writing in her seventies, Maud still found inexplicable her passion for the tall adventurer, her faith in their political bond. One only dies of the first man, wrote Colette, the wise anatomist of the heart who was then still enslaved by her husband. "After that, married life—or a semblance of it—becomes a career . . ."

Iseult was the only surviving link to Maud's first love. Maud became increasingly protective and adoring, and valued every minute she could spend with Iseult. After the death of her old nanny at Howth, she brought Tommy's illegitimate daughter to Paris, and sixteen-year-old Eileen became a member of the household, a companion for little Iseult, a half-aunt with a striking resemblance to Maud. The girls were left in the charge of an elderly widow, Madame de Bourbonne, when Maud was away. In Ireland Maud could not acknowledge her true relationship to Iseult or Eileen, and they were known as her "kinswomen." Iseult was aware that Millevoye, who came for a visit now and then with gifts and a kiss, was her father. Later she considered him licentious, vaguely threatening. Maud herself, though she sometimes spoke of him with anger, pitied Lucien for being so weak and so ambitious.

In the fall Maud went to England, where unemployed Irish laborers were being herded into the army. In Lancashire she spoke against enlisting for the Boer War, and the campaign was so successful in the industrial districts that the government banned all pro-Boer meetings. Maud was pleased to think that hers were the first meetings banned in England for a generation. But they continued to be held despite riots by jingo mobs incited by the police. The labor leader Jim Larkin and a group of Liverpool dockers came to her rescue during one such mêlée; another time some Canadians on their way to fight for England in the Transvaal saved her from an angry crowd.

While she was in London she received a surprising and rather menacing message from Millevoye demanding her presence in Paris. Fearing some catastrophe, Maud agreed to see him. She waited for him in her Passy apartment with apprehension, which increased when he arrived with a captain from the French War Office who was introduced by his first name only, Robert. White with fury, Lucien accused the IRB of having betrayed a certain army officer who had been dispatched by French military intelligence to do espionage in London. Irish nationalists had some influence at the French War Office, which was still anti-English, and some months earlier, at Millevoye's request, Maud had supplied the agent, Colonel L., with introductions to her IRB comrades. In London Dr. Ryan had provided him with an English-speaking secretary, and soon afterward the Minister for Foreign Affairs, Théophile Delcassé, who was working for Anglo-French entente, had ordered Colonel L. arrested and brought back to France in disgrace. Obviously an informer had been at work. Lucien blamed the whole unfortunate affair on Maud. "See what your blind confidence in them has done," he said. "You have broken all your work in France; our Military Party will never trust the Irish again."

After the purloining of the Boers' two thousand pounds, Maud had to admit that Colonel L. might have been betrayed by an Irishman rather than the British Secret Service. Compared to her loss of trust in the IRB, Millevoye's scorn for her inept Irish colleagues, "a set of *farceurs,*" was trivial. Even if the informer was exposed, there was no way to repair the damage done to her reputation in France, or to Colonel L.'s career.

After a sleepless night Maud rose early and went to the Jardin des Plantes with Iseult and Eileen. At the zoo the three of them watched the lions and tigers pacing and fed the monkeys. They ate *gaufres* and went for a ride on the elephant. That night, with tearful farewells, Maud took the night train to London.

As always she turned to Yeats to help her get out of trouble, and as always he was ready to be of assistance. He discovered that F. H. O'Donnell, their old enemy the Mad Rogue, had recently come into funds and subscribed a hundred pounds to the Parliamentary Party, trying to buy his way back into its ranks. Armed with this highly compromis-

ing information, Maud had no difficulty making Dr. Ryan
confess that he had been stupid enough to entrust the Rogue
with information about her errand to Ambassador Leyds, and
had also been foolish enough to assign O'Donnell, who would
commit any treachery for a price, as secretary to Colonel L.
Under such lax leadership it was no wonder to Maud that the
Irish revolutionary movement failed again and again even in
the midst of "England's difficulty."

Yeats presented the facts of O'Donnell's larceny to the
Parliamentary Party, and John Dillon saw to it that the two
thousand pounds of Boer funds were returned to the Transvaal Committee. Some hotheaded members of the IRB
wanted O'Donnell shot for his treachery. Maud had met him
once in Arthur Griffith's newspaper office, an "old ruin of a
man" with foppish manners, wearing rusty clothes and a
monocle. She pitied and despised him. He had worked as an
agent for the French and Austrians as well as the British; his
execution would have no public significance for Ireland. This
man had slandered Davitt and Yeats and ruined others; he had
done irreparable damage to her reputation in France; he had
indeed sold "souls for gold"; yet when it came to the question
of taking his life in vengeance, Maud hesitated. "I had made
it a rule of life never to ask any man to do a thing I was not
ready to do myself or to take a risk I was not ready to share.
I was not ready to shoot this man." Relieved to see her compassionate—he had feared vindictiveness—Yeats joined her in
pleading for mercy. Thanks to their efforts, the Mad Rogue
lived on to write more slanderous articles, but his career as
a spy was ended.

Father Kavanagh, her colleague in the Transvaal Committee, had cautioned her: "My child, even if as a priest I was
not bound to disapprove of secret oath-bound societies because no one should surrender his free will, I would still
oppose them. I believe they are worse than useless for the
freeing of Ireland; the British Secret Service will always get
inside and use them."

Maud learned from experience that Father Kavanagh
was right. Secret societies were bound to fail. If she could, she
would have banished them altogether from this time on, as
the great flaw of revolutionary activity. She resigned from the

IRB and Willie followed suit. There was some doubt whether Maud, being a woman, had ever been a bona fide member. It was of no consequence. She had the satisfaction of telling Dr. Ryan and his followers the reason for her decision. For too long her life, both her political work and her personal relationships, had been circumscribed by secrecy, and secrets brought with them betrayal and pain. She would stop all clandestine activity. To be open, to be free—it was as if she glimpsed the sky at the end of a dark, tortuous passageway. From now on Maud Gonne would refuse to take orders from any organization, from any man.

# Major MacBride

By the end of summer 1900 the tide had turned in South Africa. The British, pouring better equipment into the Transvaal, and more troops (450,000 all told against the Boers' 75,000), drove toward victory under the unified command of Lord Roberts and Kitchener, the formidable conqueror of the Sudan. The Orange Free State and the South African Republic were annexed by England in September, but the Boer commandos refused to surrender, and President Kruger was still working to raise support for his homeland. His hotel in Paris was besieged by sympathizers who were outraged at Kitchener's scorched-earth tactics and his concentration camps. The English were waging a war of extermination. Livestock and grain were taken from the Boer farmers, their fields burned, the people of the veldt, mostly women and children, herded into compounds. Of the 117,000 behind barbed wire, at least 20,000 died of hunger and enteric fever.

In November the Irish Transvaal Committee sent another delegation to Paris to honor the stubborn "Oom Paul," and at a reception for him at the Hôtel de la Seine, Maud listened as a letter from General Botha thanking "Major M'Bride and the Irish Brigade for their valuable service" was read aloud.

Accompanied by Griffith, MacKenna, and members of

the Association Irlandaise, she was at the Gare de Lyon to welcome John MacBride on his return from the war. "He was a wiry, soldierly-looking man, with red hair and skin burnt brick-red by the South African sun. Griffith called him Rooinek, at which he laughed. It was the name by which the Afrikaaers called the English, because, while other races burn brown, they burn red . . . MacBride said the only nickname he ever objected to was one his school mates gave him—Foxy Jack. He was in great spirits and delighted to meet so many friends."

MacBride and Griffith dined with her that evening, two comrades reunited under her roof. Warmed by the fire in her grate and the ardor of their high spirits, they sat up all night talking. It was a soldier's dream of peace come true for MacBride—to rest at ease in the comfortable apartment in Passy, with his best friend and the celebrated woman rebel, perhaps, as Yeats had written, the most beautiful woman in the world.

John MacBride, the seasoned soldier of thirty-five, was a sentimental man; moved almost to tears, he told Maud how the flag sent to the Irish Brigade by Inghinidhe na hEireann had cheered their bivouac on the veldt. In the vast African night, by the light of the campfire, he had seen one or another of "our lads go up and kiss its folds." After their long retreat before the British, from Bloemfontein to the final evacuation of Pretoria in September, his brigade had been the last foreign commando to leave Johannesburg; eighty casualties suffered, fifteen prisoners taken including their chaplain, and MacBride himself wounded at the battle of the Tugela River. Why, then, after such brave sacrifice, had the Irish Brigade been disbanded? The Boers, led by General Botha and the elusive General de Wet, were engaged in guerrilla activity. Only men familiar with the veldt, who knew the farm people and their guttural language, could survive in daring raid, ambush and swift escape. Kitchener had 150,000 men and eight thousand forts to house his man-hunting troops. The small guerrilla bands were dependent on the support of civilians for smuggled arms and secret hideouts in burned-out barns and shelled villages. This kind of warfare was the only possible recourse against a superior force. MacBride and his men had had a taste of it, and the Major believed guerrilla warfare would serve Ireland well one day.

Maud was impressed by the expertise and resolution of the soldier who had risked his life on foreign soil in the battle against England. Smoking cigarette after cigarette, she listened to him with growing excitement. MacBride was eager to get back to work for the nationalist cause: the question was how.

In September Maud and Griffith had called together in Dublin representatives from the literary, athletic, and political societies dedicated to Irish independence, to form a national federation. At Maud's insistence, Cumann na nGaedheal was to be an open organization in which women would play an equal part with men for the "disciplining of the mind and the training of the forces of the nation." She and Griffith had worked out a moderate nationalist program within which strong revolutionary forces dominated by the IRB could function.

What role could MacBride have in it? If he returned to Ireland he was certain to be imprisoned, possibly even executed as a traitor. He must remain in exile, but in Paris he was hampered by his lack of French. Maud and Griffith suggested he go to America, to galvanize the Clan na Gael into pro-Boer activity and raise money for the *United Irishman* by lecturing, but MacBride was a man of action, not words. "You will have to write the lecture for me, then."

First of all, Griffith needed an article on MacBride's experiences, and as it was already dawn, the determined editor sat down at Maud's desk to take notes while she interviewed the war hero for the *United Irishman*. After breakfast she and MacBride set to work on his speeches for America. Only a few months earlier she had said goodbye to Lucien at Chamonix, her trust and her heart broken; now she was working with a man who seemed to her of an entirely different sort.

Late in November Maud and Griffith returned to Ireland for the first national convention of Cumann na nGaedheal. Willie Rooney presided. O'Leary, the necessary Fenian, now nearing the end of his life, was honored as president, Major MacBride as vice-president in absentia; and Maud, head of Inghinidhe and of the Cork Celtic Literary

Society, became an honorary secretary. The federation of Irish societies supported Irish industry, Irish control of public boards, and the development of an active foreign policy. To wear rough Irish cloth, smoke Gallaher's, sip Irish whisky provided virtue for revolutionaries. Self-denial, self-discipline, self-sacrifice—Griffith's characteristics put a stamp of middle-class morality on Cumann na nGaedheal. "It was a sober and sparsely-smoking movement." wrote P. S. O'Hegarty, "very much in earnest, and rather puritanical, which was one of its great strengths."

That winter in Dublin, Horace Plunkett gave a reception for Yeats and his wealthy patron, the playwright Edward Martyn, and their Irish Literary Theatre. The historian Standish O'Grady, his tipsy frame supported between two tables, addressed an inebriated audience of intellectuals: "We have now indeed a literary movement, it is not very important; it will be followed by a political movement, that will not be very important; then must come a military movement, that will be important indeed."

Major John MacBride, his spirit bolstered by Maud's encouragement and with her prepared speeches tucked away in his valise, undertook the lecture tour he had promised. Sailing from Le Havre on the *Bretagne*, he arrived in New York on December 9. In the grand suite at the Vanderbilt Hotel the Major received the press with the audacity expected of him: "Winston Churchill may say what he likes about the war in South Africa being over, but I tell you that the war is not over. The Boers will fight just as long as there is a man, woman or child alive . . . it will be found that President Kruger's prophecy has been fulfilled, and the British will have paid a price that will stagger humanity."

At a banquet given by "Irish Nationalists" at Sturtevant House on December 19, MacBride spoke with Maud's fiery rhetoric: "Irish blood has been shed freely on behalf of the South African Republic . . . The only regret being that those gallant lives were not offered up on behalf of their own native land. . . . Though at present the weapon has fallen from our hands, we hope to pick it up, in our own island home, and never let it drop till, by union and strength, we blot out the last vestige of the 'Empire of Hell.' "

John O'Leary had written Devoy that "my young friend, the Major . . . has done us and our country the greatest credit in the Boer War, everything that was done by the Irish Brigade . . . having been (as far as I can at all make out) mainly, if not entirely due to him. I knew him long before he went to South Africa, and then, as now, I found him a type of the best sort of young Irishman."

In spite of his warm reception, in spite of his brave speeches, MacBride was miserable. Accustomed to the simplicity of small-town life and the unpretentious camaraderie of miners and soldiers, the Major felt at a loss in the great city; the manners of his countrymen in the "New Island," the wealth they had so proudly acquired, the complexities of their politics, were as confusing as the traffic. Public speaking was more of an ordeal than withstanding a cavalry charge, and MacBride wrote Maud that he could not go on without her.

She sailed from Le Havre on *La Champagne*, and on February 10, overwhelmed with relief and joy, the Major met her at the pier in New York. She had been unable to resist his plea for help, but it was not generosity alone that had brought her to America again. She was counting on their joint appeal to draw huge audiences. The *Irish-American* announced their first appearance together on the platform. "Miss Gonne needs no eulogy . . . the Academy of Music on . . . February 17 will not be large enough to accommodate all who are anxious to hear Major MacBride."

Out of respect for the leader of the Irish Brigade, John Devoy put aside his distrust of upper-class women, women in general, and Maud in particular, and came to have tea with her at the Fifth Avenue Hotel. The elderly watchdog of the Clan was very nearsighted, and he tripped over a footstool, landing on his knees at Maud's feet. She and MacBride quickly got him settled in a comfortable armchair, but Devoy was "extremely temperamental and self-conscious and could not stand anything which upset his dignity," and it turned out to be "a most unsatisfactory interview."

From then on things began to go wrong. The turnout at the Academy of Music on the 17th was disappointing. Devoy and his cohorts were noticeably absent. The Irish-American press was critical:

> We hope that, with a little practice, the Major will
> be able to tell the story off-hand, for having to read
> it takes away very much from its interest. Miss
> Gonne was cheered on rising and a large harp of
> roses was presented to her. But her audience was
> evidently puzzled and disappointed when she
> switched off from the Boer War to make a bitter
> attack on the United Irish League that was most
> unfortunate. . . . Irish-Americans have been too anx-
> iously endeavoring to bring about a united Irish
> party to turn around now when unity is secured
> and listen to silly abuse of the United Irish League.
> If Miss Gonne cannot find some better mark for her
> abuse . . . she had better go back to Paris.

Maud Gonne and Major MacBride, for all their glamour,
could not effectively condemn a parliamentarian party to people who after years of subjugation were enjoying the benefits
of constitutional rights in their adopted land, and were no
longer much more anti-British than other Americans.

Once they left New York, however, their audiences were
larger and more sympathetic. In Kenosha, Bloomington, Chicago, St. Louis, crowds turned out to see them, and they were
entertained like royalty. There were friends she had made on
her previous tours, and everywhere MacBride ran into dis-
tant relatives and former neighbors from Mayo. "Willie
McLoughlin is city editor of the paper and he has been booming me ever since he heard I was coming to Chicago," he
wrote his mother. "They are joking me here about the number of my cousins in this city. The man in the ticket office on
Sat. evg. [said] about 500 told him they were cousins of
mine."

From Janesville, Wisconsin, he wrote like a seasoned
trouper: "We spoke in Detroit the night before last and in
Milwaukee last night and had splendid meetings notwith-
standing that the parliamentarians and the Catholic and Irish
press of the States are doing all they can to knock us down.
. . . I have been approached half a dozen times by different
people not to go for the parliamentarians but I let them have
it all the same."

During the hours they spent together on the west-bound train, MacBride, who had close connections with the rank and file, gave Maud an insight into the reasons for the IRB's failures in America. "The men in high places, distinguished lawyers and politicians, were not revolutionists and they had much control. It was inevitable that they should look on the organisation from an American point of view—the great voting power of the Irish."

After a month he was no longer so dependent on Maud, but still in awe. He wrote his mother from Marquette on March 20: "Miss Gonne astonishes me the way in which she can stand the knocking about. For a woman it is wonderful."

By the end of June, his speeches learned by heart and his delivery improved, the Major had arrived alone on the West Coast. On the hundred and thirty-seventh anniversary of the birth of Wolfe Tone, he spoke in San Francisco's Metropolitan Hall and made headlines in the *Chronicle:* "Veteran of the Transvaal War Arouses the Large Audience to Patriotic Enthusiasm by His Forceful Utterances."

Maud showed him the way and then found it necessary to leave him after their lecture in St. Louis. MacBride was in love with her and pressing her to become his wife. She told him there was no place in her life for marriage so long as the war continued, "and there was always an Irish war on." When Griffith wrote in May that his co-editor Willie Rooney was dying and begged her with uncharacteristic despair to return to Dublin, Maud grieved for Rooney and used his illness to escape MacBride's continual wooing. The crucial reason to cut short her lecture tour was the sense that she had failed this time. People would applaud MacBride's tales of daring and bravery and empty their pockets of sentimental change, but no more than that. For a brief moment the Boer War had revived her hope, the old dream of international cooperation against English rule. The moment had passed.

Maud remembered the poem that Alice Milligan and Anna Johnston had published in the *Shan Van Vocht,* verses translated from the Gaelic by Douglas Hyde:

Waiting for help from France, waiting for help
    from Spain;
       the people who waited long ago for that,
       they got shame only.
Waiting for help again, help from America,
       the lot who
       are now waiting for it, my disgust forever on
       them.
It is time for every fool to have knowledge that
       there is
       no watchcry worth any heed but one—Sinn Fein
       amhain—
       Ourselves Alone!

Maud sailed on the *Lorraine* from New York on May 13. When she reached her apartment in Paris she fell ill, exhausted by the months abroad. She did not get to Dublin for Willie Rooney's funeral. Maud had admired the young journalist and poet—"the greatest Irishman I have known or can ever expect to know," wrote Griffith. Not an English executioner but overwork for Ireland's freedom had cut Rooney down. To his fiancée, Maire Killeen of Inghinidhe, to all his friends and comrades—sons and daughters of working-class Dublin, the new breed of nationalists—he was as much an Irish martyr as the aristocratic Wolfe Tone, and many thought his death a fatal loss to the cause. Yeats wrote Lady Gregory, "Griffith has had to go to hospital for a week, so much did it affect him."

Yeats himself was gloomy. Much as he had raged against the Queen, when Victoria's death in January 1901 at long last bestowed the crown on her aging playboy son, it brought "new commonness upon the throne . . ." Life seemed petty, a reflection of dying light. His literary life was plagued with problems: George Moore was trying to dominate their collaboration on a play, Mathers was destroying the Golden Dawn. "I have been in rather low spirits about my Irish work," he told Lady Gregory. "I am in an ebb tide and must wait the flow."

He wrote Maud, hoping to revive her interest in their Celtic work, and she responded:

My dear Willie—Many thanks for your letter. I succeeded very well in America, but will tell you all about this when we meet. I got back very well but caught a bad cold and sore throat on arrival in France. I am well of that now and am engaged nursing my poor little sister who has been very ill indeed. . . . I shall stay about a week longer with Kathleen. My address will be Queens Hotel Norwood—then I am going to Ireland, 73 Lower Mount Street, but will only be there till first week July as I have to return to Paris for a meeting. I would like very much to see you and do a little occult work. I have not done much, but on the boat I did a little, writing down some of my visions which may possibly be of use in this life. I quite agree with your divisions of the ceremonies—I have a lot of writing to do for my sister—so can't add more now—What a great pleasure is the thought of seeing you shortly. I remain

> always your friend,
> Maud Gonne

# Cathleen
# ni Houlihan

Maud's reunion with Willie took place at the end of summer 1901 in the London house of her cousins, May and Chotie Gonne. The only happy companions of her childhood years in England had been leading "aimless lives," devoted mainly to decorating their house and to "Bridge," the popular Edwardian form of gambling. Now May was about to marry a young Englishman in the Indian Civil Service, and Maud had come from Paris for the wedding, hoping that the ancient curse on the Gonne women was no longer effective. Already her sister's marriage was blighted: Colonel T. D. Pilcher of the Fifth Fusiliers, now aide-de-camp to King Edward VII, was a negligent and unfaithful husband; and the compliant Kathleen, suffering in silence, devoted her life to their children. She and her sons and little daughter were also staying in May and Chotie's house in South Kensington.

Maud's arrivals, often unannounced, like sudden summer storms blowing freshets of rain through an open door, brought adventure and a frisson of danger into their lives. The cousins loved her, and in their decorous household all differences were forgiven; England and Ireland drank tea together and her niece and nephews crowded expectantly around Maud's chair. This time she brought them one of her prize-winning dachshunds. The children immediately made a pet of the puppy, but when they heard that Maud had brought an alligator all the way from America for Iseult, they were consumed with envy. Thora was promised that she could visit the alligator in the convent garden in Laval. The boys naturally would not be allowed.

When Yeats came to call after dinner, Maud was still in her dark traveling suit and veil. She bought her clothes in Paris and not all of them were of Irish tweed; she believed it did not help the cause to look dowdy. But she could not always find time to change for dinner, and she refused to be a slave to fashion or to maintain the bloom of youth.

Kathleen with her pale gold hair was in a white evening dress. On the sofa among the heaped silk cushions Maud and her sister, night and day, sat side by side. Willie's critical glance while he complimented Kathleen's gown and youthful appearance told Maud that he was, as usual, irritated by her tendency to neglect herself. Kathleen remarked that it was "hard work being beautiful." Maud assumed that her beauty could withstand the wear and tear of living. Willie wrote a poem about the evening's conversation; and years later, remembering their reunion, Maud quoted "Adam's Curse" in her memoirs:

> We sat together at one summer's end,
> That beautiful mild woman, your close friend,
> And you and I, and talked of poetry.
>
> I said, "A line will take us hours maybe;
> Yet if it does not seem a moment's thought,
> Our stitching and unstitching has been naught.
> Better go down upon your marrow-bones
> And scrub a kitchen pavement, or break stones
> Like an old pauper, in all kinds of weather;
> For to articulate sweet sounds together
> Is to work harder than all these and yet
> Be thought an idler by the noisy set

Of bankers, schoolmasters, and clergymen
The martyrs call the world."

                                 And thereupon
That beautiful mild woman for whose sake
There's many a one shall find out all heartache
On finding that her voice is sweet and low
Replied: "To be born woman is to know—
Although they do not talk of it at school—
That we must labour to be beautiful."
I said: "It's certain there is no fine thing
Since Adam's fall but needs much labouring.
There have been lovers who thought love
    should be
So much compounded of high courtesy
That they would sigh and quote with learned
    looks
Precedents out of beautiful old books;
Yet now it seems an idle trade enough."

We sat grown quiet at the name of love;
We saw the last embers of daylight die,
And in the trembling blue-green of the sky
A moon, worn thin as if it had been a shell
Washed by time's waters as they rose and fell
About the stars and broke in days and years.

I had a thought for no one's but your ears:
That you were beautiful, and that I strove
To love you in the old high way of love;
That it had all seemed happy, and yet we'd
    grown
As weary-hearted as that hollow moon.

Again Willie urged Maud to give up "the tragic struggle
and live a peaceful life." He asked her to marry him and again
she refused; there would be no happiness for him with her.
He countered that he was not happy without her. "Oh yes,
you are," she told him, "because you make beautiful poetry
out of what you call your unhappiness and you are happy in
that." Faced with proposals from the demanding poet and the

dependent Major, Maud clung to her freedom. Perhaps for all women the curse lay in the institution of marriage itself. "Marriage would be such a dull affair," she told Willie. "Poets should never marry. The world should thank me for not marrying you."

At thirty-six, his youthful intensity hidden behind an air of superiority, his vague nearsighted gaze through pince-nez exaggerating his aloof pose, Yeats had himself become a "Distinguished Person." Susan Pollexfen Yeats's death the year before, releasing her from her long, tragic illness, marked no great change for him, except that his father moved back to Dublin, where Willie's sisters pursued their handicrafts, and brother Jack, sponsored by Sarah Purser, was launched on his career as an artist. Yeats was his own man in London now, and 18 Woburn Buildings his permanent residence, the abode of a successful though still impoverished literary man.

Maud found his lodgings more comfortably furnished than before, thanks to Lady Gregory, who had given him the deep leather armchair and the prized Kelmscott Chaucer on its pedestal between two gilt candlesticks. Champagne and country delicacies from Coole enlivened the Monday nights when Yeats entertained, "talking, talking, but in an inequality of communication." Dorothy Richardson, the young writer who lived across the street but never dared enter the door of Number 18, saw from her window that his guests were "chiefly being talked to, by the tall, pervading figure, visible now here, now there, but always in speech."

Many of Willie's acquaintances were familiar. Arthur Symons and his wife; Florence Farr, Maud's old rival; Annie Horniman, who was trying to outshine Lady Gregory as the poet's patron—she had the money "but Lady Gregory had the brains." John Masefield and Robert Bridges had replaced the Rhymers in the poet's world, and luminaries from the theater had become of prime importance to him: Mrs. Patrick Campbell; Ellen Terry's son, Gordon Craig; and Shaw, who was leaving the Fabian soapbox for the larger platform of the stage. Maud congratulated Willie on the life he had made for himself without means and the respect his work had won for him among his peers. His friends saw in her the muse the poet had glorified. "Outrageously beautiful," Shaw told Joseph Hone, Yeats's biographer. "He remembered in particular coming on her and W.B. in Chancery Lane under the circle of light thrown on the pavement by a street lamp."

But where was Ireland, where was nationalism in Willie's new literary life? Now and then O'Leary, gaunt and stooped, a ghost of the past, climbed the curving stairs to see him, and from time to time Maud met young rebels from home and abroad at Woburn Buildings. Sarojini Naidu, the Hindu nationalist whom Willie called "the little Indian Princess," sat cross-legged at his feet and read her poems aloud. He chanted his own lines to the strumming of Arnold Dolmetsch's psaltery, and he still pursued his interest in the occult. But where were the poems for Ireland he had promised to write; where were the rituals for the Castle of the Heroes Maud had worked on with him not so long before?

She made Willie go with her to Westminster, where the Lia Fail, the Stone of Destiny, was anchored under the Coronation Chair. According to legend it had been stolen from the altar at Tara, where the High Kings had sworn their oath of office. Maud challenged Willie to use his power as a magus of the Golden Dawn to transport the massive stone out of England. Many had plotted to restore it to its rightful home, to no avail. Like their Castle of the Heroes, the capture of the Lia Fail remained a dream.

The Irish theater had become for Yeats what their Castle might have been, a stage on which to enact the drama of Ireland's destiny. In Dublin on October 21, 1901, the Irish Literary Theatre presented a double bill at the Gaiety. Sir Frank Benson's Shakespearean Company had been brought over from London to perform *Diarmuid and Grania,* the play that Yeats and George Moore had written in contentious collaboration. The second half of the bill was *Casadh an tSugain,* "The Twisting of the Rope." Douglas Hyde's dramatization in Gaelic of a short story by Yeats was directed by William G. Fay, an Irish vaudeville trouper who with his brother Frank had set up the Ormonde Dramatic Society.

"It was the first time that a play in Irish had ever been acted in a theatre, and the enthusiastic members of the Gaelic League stormed the cheaper seats," wrote Synge, who was in the audience with Maud and Yeats.

> . . . one could not help but smile at seeing all around the room the beautiful girls of the Gaelic League, who were chattering away in very bad Irish with palely enthusiastic young clerks. But during an intermission of *Diarmuid and Grania*, it happened that the people in the galleries began to sing. . . . They sang the old songs of the people. Until then I had never heard these songs sung in the ancient Irish tongue by so many voices. The auditorium shook. In these lingering notes, of incomparable sadness, there was something like the death-rattle of a nation. I saw one head bend down behind a program, and then another. People were weeping. Then the curtain rose and the play was resumed in the midst of lively emotion. One sensed that the spirit of a nation had hovered for an instant in the room.

It was a mystical moment for actors and audience. Yeats quoted Victor Hugo: "It is in the Theatre that the mob becomes a people," and resolved never again to engage an English company to perform for his theater in Dublin. Maud, in a dress chosen specially for the occasion, silver shot silk that changed color in the light, sat beside Willie, who wore his usual theater-going outfit: "a long black cloak drooping from his shoulders," as his erstwhile colleague George Moore described it, "a soft black sombrero on his head, voluminous black silk tie flowing from his collar, loose black trousers dragging untidily over his long, heavy feet . . ."

After the performance was over, Maud and Yeats, far more conspicuous than the actors, were mobbed when they got into their cab to go to a supper party. "The crowd from the gallery," he wrote, "wanted to take the horse out of the cab and drag us there, but Maud Gonne, weary of public

demonstrations, refused." The limelight belonged that night
to Yeats. Maud decided she must play a part in his theatrical
world or lose him for his country and herself. She agreed to
act in a play he would write for her on the condition that he
give her Daughters of Erin the right to produce it.

Yeats went to work and made a symbolic one-act play
out of a "dream almost as distinct as a vision of a cottage
where there was well-being and fire-light and talk of a marriage and into that cottage there came an old woman in a long
cloak. She was Ireland herself." *Cathleen ni Houlihan* was everything Maud had asked for. Set at the time of the French
landing at Killala during the '98 rebellion, the drama was both
patriotic and poetic. It would move unsophisticated audiences familiar with street ballads about the "Shan Van
Vocht," the poor old woman of Ireland who had lost her four
green fields. Dedicated to the memory of Willie Rooney, the
lines sang with the rhythms of Irish speech.

> *Old Woman:* It is a hard service they take that help
> me. Many that are red-cheeked now will be pale-
> cheeked; many that have been free to walk the hills
> and the bogs and the rushes will be sent to walk
> hard streets in far countries; many a good plan will
> be broken; many that have gathered money will not
> stay to spend it; many a child will be born and there
> will be no father at its christening to give it a name.
> They that had red cheeks will have pale cheeks for
> my sake; and for all that they will think they are
> well paid.

> (She goes out. Her voice is heard outside singing.)

> > They shall be remembered for ever;
> > They shall be alive for ever;
> > They shall be speaking for ever;
> > The people shall hear them for ever.

With Lady Gregory's help, Yeats had put the dialect of
the people, so long the butt of comedy on stage, into a poetic
form for the first time. *Cathleen ni Houlihan* would move the
hearts of the literati and the uneducated alike.

Maud was delighted with the role Yeats had given her, and the simple one-act form was suitable for her amateur actors. She had seen AE's *Deirdre* directed by the Fays at the Coffee Palace in Dublin, and she had no trouble persuading Willie that the brothers must also direct *Cathleen ni Houlihan;* he would agree to anything so long as he had her for the role: "Maud Gonne in my play would really draw a fine house—" he told Lady Gregory. A few weeks later Maud wrote from Paris:

My dear Willie—Many thanks for your letter. I am delighted to hear you have given *Cathleen ni Houlihan* to Fay. Did you write him that I would act the part of Cathleen? Have you another copy that you could let me have as I would like to learn the words here and then go over them with you in London. If you haven't got a copy I will write to Fay to get one made for me. They must begin rehearsing it without me—as they are very slow and take a great time rehearsing a play and I would not be in Dublin long enough to do all that with them. I have a lot of work here—a lecture on the 4th, one the 14th and one the 20 Feb. and another on the 4th March besides a lot of other work.

Easter I thought will be the best time for the play, but I will write Fay as soon as I hear from you. What have you arranged with him? The Society of St. Patrick is having such a handsome and such a comic row that I thought it best not to go to the assemble generale this year as I didn't want to take sides. McGregor wrote to me he wanted to see me, but I didn't answer his letter—I really can't afford to have charlatans about—people don't understand it. Martin [Martyn] is ridiculous—it is too provoking, giving up the literary theatre. I can't write more as friends have just come . . .

In haste,

Always your friend,
Maud Gonne

A little imperiousness went a long way, and Maud used her upper hand to good effect to keep her many activities going at the same time. In Dublin her drama students from Inghinidhe, Maire nic Shiubhlaigh, Maire Quinn, and others who would play an important role in the National Theatre, began to rehearse with William Fay.

In Paris Maud continued to lecture on behalf of the beleaguered Boers. MacBride, a veteran now of public meeting halls, had returned from America to share the podium with her. She coached him in French, and on February 14, at the Salle Wagram, the audience give him a standing ovation for his speech in praise of Colonel de Villebois-Mareuil, the French Brigade commander who had given his life for the Boers. Anti-British feelings still ran high in Paris, rabid enough to cause a furor over the official invitation of Swinburne to the Victor Hugo Centennial. Two thousand people gathered at the Salle des Agriculteurs voted to protest the attendance of England's poet laureate at the forthcoming ceremonies. Lucien Millevoye was among the deputies seated on the stage on February 20, when Maud rose with MacBride at her side to denounce the English for turning South Africa into "one vast concentration camp." Cries of *"Vive l'Irlande! Vive MacBride! Vive les Boers!"* rang in the great hall after she spoke, and she was more interested in the audience's reaction than in Lucien.

In March Maud was in Dublin rehearsing. Just two weeks until opening night, and the troupe was in confusion. Edward Martyn had indeed withdrawn his support; he considered *Cathleen* too poetical, "a silly little play." George Moore was fussing about the acting, "the silliest he ever saw," and criticizing the direction, which he thought parochial, although the Fays had been trained in the French style of Antoine and Coquelin. Maud was irritated when Moore tried to take over as director, ordering her not to "sit down by the fire and croon but to walk up and down in front of the stage, so as to dominate." Yeats, still in London at the end of the month, heard from his father: "Just a line to say I yesterday met Miss Gonne, who was very urgent for you to come over and look after the rehearsals."

There were too many would-be directors squabbling in St. Theresa's Total Abstinence Hall, and Maud escaped from the dust and controversy by going off by herself to the Wicklow Mountains to learn her part. Chanting the lines against a rushing stream, she made them her own. She needed the solace of the spring landscape because her friend Anna Johnston was dying of consumption a few months after marrying the young writer Seuman MacManus. The day after the play opened, the *United Irishman* carried Maud's elegy for "Ethna Carbury": "She is with the ever-living ones, and I think she is working and guiding in the great spiritual struggle for Ireland of which our material struggle here is but a reflection. . . ."

Yeats got to Dublin in time to take charge of the dress rehearsal, and Maud saw him in a new guise as the authoritative director. He too could be imperious. She put up with his orders gracefully and proceeded to play Cathleen ni Houlihan her own way. Breaking every rule, she arrived late on opening night. "Gleaming shirt-fronts mingled with the less resplendent garb of the Dublin worker in the tiny auditorium," wrote Maire nic Shiubhlaigh. "Before the footlights lit up the banner of Inghinidhe na hEireann—a golden sunburst on a blue ground hanging near the stage—the aisles were crowded with standing patrons." Then Maud in her dark, flowing costume strode through the hushed audience to the stage. Frank Fay, watching through his peephole, was annoyed by her unprofessional behavior, but she caused a sensation.

"Never again will there be such a splendid Kathleen as she," wrote William Fay, "a beautiful tall woman with her great masses of hair and her voice that would charm the birds off the bough." When Maire nic Shiubhlaigh played Cathleen ni Houlihan in later productions, she based her interpretation on Maud's: "Watching her, one could readily understand the reputation she enjoyed as the most beautiful woman in Ireland, the inspiration of the whole revolutionary movement. She was the most exquisitely-fashioned creature I have ever seen. Her beauty was *startling* . . ." wrote the young Daughter of Erin who became one of Dublin's great actresses. "In her, the youth of the country saw all that was magnificent in Ireland. She was the very personification of the figure she portrayed on the stage."

The *Irish Times* criticized Maud for simply acting herself on the stage, and the reviews were mixed, hot or cold according to the political stand of the newspaper in which they appeared. But Yeats was ecstatic about the acting; the economy of gesture and perfection of speech fulfilled his hopes. He told Lady Gregory that Maud had "played . . . magnificently, and with weird power."

On April 3, 4, and 5 the house, which held about three hundred, was sold out. "The effect of that play which nightly filled the little hall . . . was such that after the first week, powerful intervention was used to evict us . . ." Maud wrote. Without Edward Martyn's backing the Irish Theatre had been unable to rent St. Theresa's Hall for more than three nights, and lack of funds stopped the performances of *Cathleen ni Houlihan*. But it was never forgotten.

"Those who had the privilege of being present on that occasion will remember it as long as they live. I have never seen an audience so moved . . ." Seamus O'Sullivan remembered Arthur Griffith's reaction: "I can still see his face as he stood up at that fall of the final curtain . . ." Constance Gore-Booth Markievicz considered Yeats's only propaganda play a religious sacrament. For nationalists *Cathleen ni Houlihan* became a myth and a battle cry.

After the bloodshed of 1916 the playwright would ask himself about his responsibility: "Did that play of mine send out/Certain men the English shot?" But after the first performance, in 1902, Stephen Gwynn left St. Theresa's Hall asking "if such plays should be produced unless one was prepared for people to go out to shoot and be shot. Yeats was not alone responsible . . . above all Miss Gonne's impersonation had stirred the audience as I have never seen another audience stirred."

To the public Maud Gonne was now Cathleen ni Houlihan: "Did you see an old woman going down the path?"/"I did not; but I saw a young girl, and she had the walk of a queen." And to a large extent Maud herself identified with the role Yeats had created for her, and was disappointed that he could not or would not write another like it.

A few months after the performances at St. Theresa's Hall, the Fays' company joined with the Literary Theatre to form the Irish National Theatre. Yeats was president and Maud was on the board of directors with Lady Gregory, AE, and Douglas Hyde.

# The Great Storm

Maud wanted a place of her own in Dublin, a more permanent home than the rooms over Morrow's Bookstore that looked out on College Green. Of all her many lodgings in years of restless changes, they held the longest memories: tête-à-têtes and lovers' quarrels with Willie; comrades conspiring by her hearth; G men on watch at her doorway doused not accidentally by the faithful janitor boy's pail of water. Maud exchanged busy Nassau Street and the small hotel which Lady Gregory now frequented for suburban Rathgar, a small house at 25 Coulson Avenue with a yard for flowers, pets, and children.

The Russells lived next door, AE and his wife, Violet, an unconventional woman who smoked cigarettes and wrote on Theosophy, and their two-year-old son, Brian. Murals by AE depicting the invisible inhabitants of Ireland soon covered the walls of Maud's rooms with winged creatures in gauzy attire. John Quinn, the Irish-American lawyer and connoisseur, seeing them on his first visit to Dublin, thought the drawings exquisite. Convinced that art should serve spiritual rather than national or aesthetic purposes, George Russell, unlike Yeats, placed the creator above the work. More tolerant of aspiring artists than his old schoolmate and quasi-rival, he was generous to all who would listen to his flowing monologues and counted among his favorites the poet James Stephens, Padraic Colum, and James Joyce. There was still deep affection between AE and Yeats, for the shaggy mystic was as loyal to old friends as to the old clothes which looked to Stephens as if they had been put on with a shovel. AE welcomed Yeats's muse to his Sunday at-homes in Rathgar. A pastel sketch he drew of her, stern and strong-jawed, gave her classic profile an aureole of other-worldly light.

Mysticism drew Maud to AE, and their shared concern for Willie led her to confide that he was still determined to marry her despite her insistence that "he was not to expect anything." AE told her "she was ruining a man of genius" and must make him understand that his obsessive wooing was interfering with his art. Both deplored his neglect of poetry, whether because of his infatuation for Maud or for his National Theatre.

AE was less of a recluse now and more involved with his countrymen, riding around the countryside on his bicycle looking for likely creamery locations instead of faeryfolk. The Irish Agricultural Organization Society was growing, setting up cooperative credit banks to rescue debt-ridden farmers from the gombeen men, the money lenders and shopkeepers. Sir Horace, the patriotic Unionist, worked tenaciously for his organization, believing that Ireland's survival depended on improved agricultural economy, self-help and technology. By the early 1900s the IAOS had eight hundred branches and eighty thousand active members.

While Maud was in Roscommon during the last flare-up of the Land War, the government reinstituted strict coercion laws, alarming Unionists and nationalists alike. In the fall of 1902 John Shawe Taylor, Lady Gregory's nephew, called together a group of M.P.s, landlords, and tenant representatives to tackle the land problem. Their recommendations became the basis of a Land Purchase Act proposed by George Wyndham, Balfour's successor as Chief Secretary for Ireland.

With the promise of the land conference and the accomplishments of Plunkett's cooperatives in mind, Maud wrote on the issues which were closest to her: "I do not think it is Ireland's destiny to ever develop into a great manufacturing country like England with its great, black smoky cities where the lives of the workers are hell, but some industries and manufacturers are a necessity to the well-being of every nation, and in the present state of society they are a useful check on landlord greed." Although land reforms avoided the issue of independence, they fostered nationalism by making it possible for a large segment of the population to rise above a state of helpless destitution. Maud, who encouraged AE to continue his arduous materialistic work for the IAOS, wrote in the *United Irishman:* "Every effort which aims at increasing the productiveness of the earth and enabling more people to live on it seems to me the better way of checking emigration."

Maud contributed frequently to Griffith's paper, and her far-reaching activities were reported in its columns. The Boers were still fighting their doomed battle when she lectured in France on "British Concentration Camps." The *United Irishman* in its foreign notes described a dinner at her house in Passy to honor M. Baptiste Duffand for his painting, *Les Anglais en Irlande, 1798,* which had been purchased by the city of Paris. Major MacBride spoke a few words after Maud presented the Cross of the Order of St. Patrick to the artist. She denounced Catholic schools in England for serving as recruiting stations for the English army: "It is for Irish Nationalists to check this by forming National boys' brigades, where the boys should be taught to be soldiers of Ireland, swear allegiance to her and to her only." She hoped Inghinidhe would form branches in English towns to carry out this work. "There is an old prophecy which says that Ireland will be saved by the women, and if Irish women will only realise the importance of this work of National education for the children I think this prophecy may come true."

Although Maud's journalistic style shared the high seriousness of most nationalist propagandists, "their Intensities," as Joyce called them, her writing was often humorous and ironic. "Poor Edward VII! One cannot help feeling sorry for him, obliged to spend all his time in the society of his fellow countrymen in his own country which he always felt so insufferably dull." The aging playboy whose royal glance had spotted Maud at the viceregal ball was King of England but persona non grata abroad, and was condemned to stay on board his yacht with its cargo of lady admirers for fear of overt hostility should he step ashore at Biarritz or Monte Carlo. His subjects were still divided over the South African war, and with rising unemployment and labor strikes at home, the atmosphere in the British Isles was far from that of an Edwardian garden party. As for his projected royal visit to Ireland, "an angry murmur reached him from across the Sea of Moyle warning him that his presence is not desired . . ."

Inghinidhe circulated leaflets against the King's royal visitation. They continued their antienlistment campaign, despite the final defeat of the Boers, and their fund for organizing National Boys' Brigades to answer British recruitment was supported by contributions from women's auxiliaries in America.

Maud's house in Coulson Avenue soon became a rendezvous for nationalists, and Griffith spent many hours with her elaborating his "Hungarian policy," derived from Ferencz Deak, who had won the peaceful separation of Hungary and Austria by organizing a massive abstention of Hungarian representatives from the Imperial Parliament. Griffith did not as yet propose to go beyond the achievement of nationhood within the Empire, and his plan for the development of Irish industries under a protective tariff was by no means revolutionary. But it was a beginning for the formation of separate Irish institutions. Economic nationalism had a logical appeal for the independent shopkeepers, clerks, and small landholders attending the convention of Cumman na nGaedheal in October 1902. Griffith's following was still small, but a growing middle class in Ireland was ready for revolution by nonviolent means.

It was apparent to Yeats "that a new class, which had begun to rise to power under the shadow of Parnell, would change the nature of the Irish movement . . ." Unlike Griffith, he distrusted it. Maud could not tolerate Yeats when he separated himself from the common lot; as AE liked to point out, he and Yeats came from the middle class themselves. Maud argued with Willie about his values; and, disagreeing but still faithful to their friendship, they went their separate ways, Yeats to his theater, Maud on "the path of the patriot . . . the Thorny Path of Kathleen ni Houlihan."

In Paris that winter Maud saw John MacBride and went

with him to call on ex-President Steyn of the Orange Free State. Since his return from America the Major had been unable to find a way to use his energies for the cause, and he spent most of his time reminiscing with veterans of the South African war. Maud worried about his poverty but was uneasy when he went to work at two pounds a week as secretary to the pro-British correspondent of the New York *Sun*. She did what she could to help him financially and tried to improve his French and his savoir-faire. How shocked he was when, to save him the cost of a café, she insisted on having tea in his tiny attic room in the Rue Gay-Lussac! The woman he wanted as his wife should not be in his bedroom. Maud, however, adopted him as she might have a child or a pet, and, heedless of the consequences, lavished on him her customary warm affection.

People talked. Her new liaison caused scandalized speculation on both sides of the Channel. Nationalists in Paris and Dublin had frowned on her love affair with a Frenchman and looked the other way, but even the appearance of an affair with an Irish hero amounted to a dereliction of patriotic duty. James Joyce, who fled the stifling middle-class provincialism of his own country, associated Maud with the immoral image of the French capital: "Paris rawly waking, crude sunlight on her lemon streets. . . . M. Drumont, famous journalist, Drumont, know what he called Queen Victoria? Old hag with the yellow teeth. *Vieille ogresse* with the *dents jaunes*. Maud Gonne, beautiful woman, *La Patrie*, M. Millevoye . . . Licentious men. . . . Lascivious people."

Maud was interested in the starving young writer whom Willie considered a genius, but when he arrived at her door on his first visit to Paris she was unable to receive him.

My dear Mr. Joyce,

I was very sorry not to see you when you called last evening. The polite lie about my being in bed was diplomacy on the part of my concierge as at such an early hour I never retire to rest. The truth is that my little cousin who is staying with me took ill with diphtheria last Sunday, and I have been and still am nursing her and consequently am in

quarantine on account of the danger of infection.
. . . There would of course be no possible danger seeing me out of doors, and if I can be of any use to you, come up any day at about 2 o'clock and I will come out and see you in the Trocadéro Gardens.

This is a cold inhospitable welcome. I am very sorry, for Mr. Russell and Mr. Yeats have both spoken and written to me so much about you that I have been looking forward to making your acquaintance. However, as I hear you are thinking of staying in Paris for some time, it is only a pleasure deferred.

With kind regards,
Sincerely yours,
Maud Gonne

Stanislaus Joyce suggested that "some very unusual qualms regarding his shabby appearance" may have prevented his brother from following up Maud's invitation. But, although Joyce approved of Griffith's policies, he despised all super-patriots, and Synge, who was at the Hôtel Corneille while Joyce stayed there in February 1903, may have hardened his resolve not to meet the notorious rebel in the Trocadéro. His mother urged him to call again—"love making naturally kept her from looking after more serious business and you will make a big mistake by not keeping as yr Pappie says 'in touch with her.'" Joyce replied, "I have not gone to Miss Gonne nor do I have to go." Described by Lily Yeats as a shy apparition in white sneakers standing in the doorway, Joyce was not only diffident and arrogant; there was a strong puritanical streak in him, and yet he was broad-minded compared to the great majority of Dubliners.

Maud was all too aware of Dublin gossips. Under the circumstances she knew that her desire to settle in Ireland with Iseult and Eileen was an impossible dream. She had told MacBride she would never marry until Ireland's war was won, but now marriage seemed a possibility. They could do more for the Irish cause together than apart. Married, they would be safe from scandal. She was thirty-six, and MacBride, the same age, was attractive. His lack of worldliness made him seem, if not callow, a man she could manage. He looked to her for guidance and support; his dependence was seductive.

On February 14 the *United Irishman* announced a "forthcoming event which has occasioned great interest and pleasure amongst Irish Nationalists. Miss Gonne, who some time ago became a Catholic, will be formally received into the Catholic Church on Tuesday, at the Chapel des Dames de St. Thérèse, Laval, and her marriage will take place before the end of the month."

Canon Dissard received her into the Church at last in the chapel at Laval. The Carmelite nuns who had looked after Iseult and prayed for Maud's conversion were known as the Association of St. Theresa now that France had officially expelled their order. The Republic's long war with the Church had reached a climax after the Dreyfus case. As the government grew more sympathetic to England, Maud suspected a conspiracy between Edward VII, "Grand Master of English Freemasonry," and the French Masonic orders to persecute the Jesuits.

She had resigned from the Order of the Golden Dawn with its Masonic taint, but she still believed in reincarnation and in the spirit world she had explored with Yeats. Dissard, whose ancestors had roamed the Celtic highlands of the Auvergne, understood. Maud was not alone in combining pagan belief with the security of Catholic dogma. Joining the Church, she identified herself with the people of Ireland. MacBride was a Catholic. She was marrying a man of the people.

It was impossible to explain to Willie. She sent a telegram. He was about to give a lecture in Dublin when her message arrived. ". . . the ears being deafened, the sight of the eyes blind/With lightning, you went from me, and I could find/Nothing to make a song about . . ." He managed somehow to go on with his talk. The audience applauded his lecture, but afterward he could not recall a single word. He went out alone and wandered through the darkening city. Maud had sworn she would never marry; to Willie that meant she would never marry another. How could she have betrayed him? Why had she chosen John MacBride?

Everyone who knew them asked the same question.

*Maud at nineteen.* "My presentation dress, embroidered with iridescent beads, looked like a fountain . . ." Maud Gonne

*Lucien Millevoye.* "Every day at the springs and at the promenades I met M. Millevoye and we walked together . . ." Maud Gonne

*John O'Leary.* "Beautiful lofty things: O'Leary's noble head . . ." W. B. Yeats

*Portrait by Sarah Purser of Maud about 1888.* "There was a tale of her inviting all her friends to meet the chaperone who was arriving from Paris, and then walking in with a small gray monkey on her arm." Stephen Gwynn

*Willie at the age of twenty-one, from a drawing by his father, J. B. Yeats.*

*W. B. Yeats in his twenties.* "At that time he was all dreams and gentleness." Katherine Tynan

*The battering ram.* "It was the time of the evictions and I used to see people standing in front of their unroofed cottages from which the police held them back and weeping bitterly. I thought to myself, when I grow up I'm going to change all that." Maud Gonne

*W. B. Yeats shortly after meeting Maud in 1889.* "While still I may I write for you/The love I lived, the dream I knew." W. B. Yeats

*Maud at the time of her first visit to Willie at Bedford Park.* "A woman of so shining loveliness/That men threshed corn at midnight by a tress . . ." W. B. Yeats

*An Irish rebel.* "Maud Gonne at Howth station waiting a train/Pallas Athene in that straight back and arrogant head . . ." W. B. Yeats

Photograph by Desmond Barrington.

Courtesy of MacBride family. Reproduced by F. Czira.

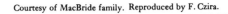

*Howth* Castle (ABOVE) and Howth Head. "I am haunted by numberless islands/and many a Danaan shore . . ." W. B. Yeats

Photograph by Desmond Barrington.

*La Belle Irlandaise. Maud at twenty-eight in Paris.*

*Maud at the time of the "spiritual marriage" with Willie.* "I thought of your beauty and this arrow/ Made out of a wild thought is in my marrow."
W. B. Yeats

*In the Paris apartment, Avenue d'Eylau, around 1902.* "At her handsome apartments in the Avenue d'Eylau are to be seen deputies, journalists and irreconcilables . . ." Arthur Lynch

RIGHT: *Maud sketched by J. B. Yeats, 1907, as Cathleen ni Houlihan.* "She was Ireland herself, that Cathleen ni Houlihan for whom so many songs have been sung and about whom so many stories have been told and so many have gone to their death."
W. B. Yeats

LEFT: *Maud in her thirties.* "But one man loved the pilgrim soul in you/And loved the sorrows of your changing face . . ."
W. B. Yeats

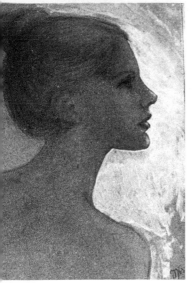

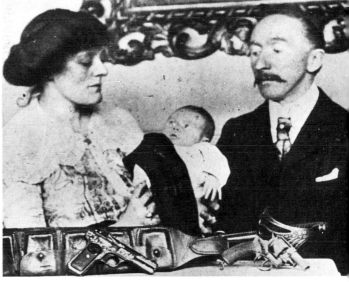

*Iseult Gonne:*
*drawing by Maud,*
*1906.* "Being young
you have not
known/The fool's
triumph, nor yet/
Love lost as soon
as won . . ."
W. B. Yeats

*Maud, Major John MacBride, and their infant son*
*Sean in his christening robes, about 1903.*

*Lady Gregory in bronze, by Jacob*
*Epstein, 1910.*

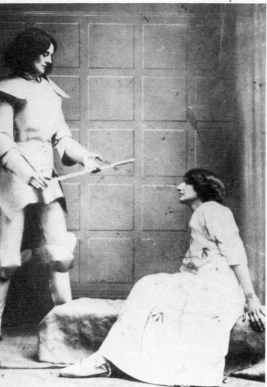

*Drawing of John Quinn by Augustus John, 1909.* "It looks harder than you do generally, but I have seen you look like that occasionally." Maud Gonne

*Constance Markievicz in linoleum armor as "Suffrage."*

*W. B. Yeats with Mrs. George Russell, Dublin, 1911.*

*British troops in Dublin during the Troubles.*

*Sackville Street during Easter Rising, 1916.* "There's nothing but our own red blood/Can make a right Rose Tree." W. B. Yeats

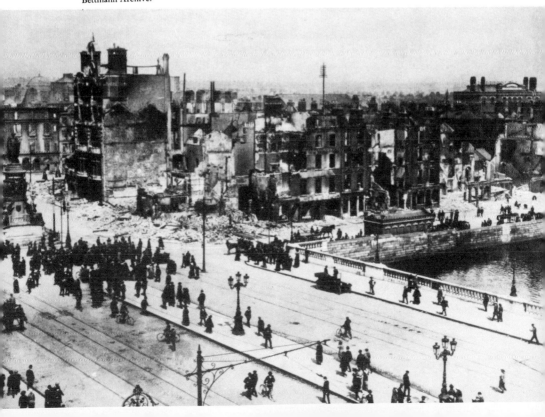

*Entrance to Kilmainham Jail, where John MacBride and the leaders of the 1916 Easter Rising were executed and where Maud was imprisoned in 1923 by the Free State Government.* "We had fed the heart on fantasies,/The heart's grown brutal from the fare . . ." W. B. Yeats

*W. B. Yeats and his wife, George, during visit to America in 1920s.*

*Roebuck House, Maud's home in
Clonskea, Dublin, for the last thirty
years of her life.*

*Passport photograph of Maud
taken around 1924.* "Remembering
what she had/What eagle look
still shows . . ." W. B. Yeats

*Drawing by Sean O'Sullivan, Maud Gonne MacBride.* "Her heroic and now cavernous beauty, made sombre by the customary black draperies she wore, was also illuminated by an increasing gentleness and humor. She had now what seemed a faint far-away amusement of life." Michael MacLiammoir

*In the garden at Roebuck House, 1937.* "Did I not tell you we have the most beautiful ruins in Europe ... there is the most beautiful ruin of them all." Mary Colum

*Maud speaking for prisoners in Mountjoy Prison, 1937.* "Or hurled the little streets upon the great,/Had they but courage equal to desire?" W. B. Yeats

*At the headquarters of the Women's Prisoners Defence League.* "Though she had young men's praise and old men's blame, Among the poor both old and young gave her praise." W. B. Yeats

*On her movable platform Maud holds up a copy of the Coercion Act.* "Owing to Article 2a . . . anyone arrested on suspicion of treason is submitted to the English prison laws of 1820."

*At street meeting of Prisoners Defence League, 1937.* "Why, what could she have done being what she is?/Was there another Troy for her to burn?" W. B. Yeats

*Willie at Riversdale, where Maud saw him for the last time in 1938.*

*MacBride family portrait in 1948, at time of Irish election. Maud seated with (LEFT TO RIGHT) granddaughter Anna MacBride White, Sean MacBride and his wife, Kid.*

*George Bernard Shaw.* "She was outrageously beautiful."

Photograph by Adolf Morath, 1948.

*In her eighties.* "That nobleness made simple as a fire,/With beauty like a tightened bow . . ." W. B. Yeats

*Sean MacBride in Geneva, 1968. Chairman of Amnesty International; Secretary General of the International Commission of Jurists; Chairman of Special Committee of International Conference on Human Rights; Nobel Peace Prize, 1974.*
"In my view it is the women of the world who can now create the climate of public opinion which can save the world from the nuclear catastrophe." Sean MacBride

Friends and relatives, seeing nothing but disaster ahead, did what they could to prevent it. Griffith, who had introduced them, was the first to warn Maud: "Queen, forgive me. John MacBride, after Willie Rooney, is the best friend I ever had; you are the only woman friend I have. I only think of both your happiness. For your own sakes and for the sake of Ireland to whom you both belong, don't get married. I know you both, you so unconventional—a law to yourself; John so full of conventions. You will not be happy for long."

"She will not make you happy," wrote MacBride's widowed mother, who approved of Maud's work but not her life. "You will neither be happy, she is not the wife for you." The patriarchal traditions of Catholic peasants were deeply ingrained in the Mayo family. John must be truly bewitched to propose to such a headstrong, independent woman. "She is accustomed to money and you have none; she is used to going her own way and listens to no one," MacBride's older brother, Joseph, cautioned him. "These are not good qualities for a wife. A man should not marry unless he can keep his wife . . ."

When Maud went to Laval to tell Iseult about the forthcoming wedding, the child wept. She had never liked MacBride; now she hated him with the fury of the dispossessed and clung to her mother as if to keep her safe in the convent. Maud wept too.

The day before her wedding Maud lay down to rest in her bedroom in the Avenue d'Eylau. The hearth was strewn with charred papers, the furniture draped, packing cases ready to move into the new apartment in Passy. She heard Tommy's voice: "Lambkin, don't do it. You must not get married." Years earlier she had heard his spirit tell her not to become Millevoye's mistress. She had disobeyed, and her romance had ended in disaster.

The wedding took place at noon on February 21, 1903, in the fashionable Church of St. Honoré d'Eylau. The best man, MacBride's friend Reginald Collins, "bore aloft the green flag of the Irish Brigade . . . the blue flag presented to Miss Gonne some years ago by Inghinidhe na hEireann was carried by the bridesmaid. . . . Both flags were reverently lowered during the Elevation." The bride wore a "simple costume of electric blue." Reverend Father Van Hecke, chaplain of the Irish Brigade, celebrated the marriage.

At their wedding breakfast in the Hotel Florence the newlyweds sat at a table decorated with shamrocks and violets. Father Van Hecke raised his glass to Major MacBride's bold exploits against the English: "We have slept side by side sometimes under the open sky, covered by the same rug, at times drenched to the skin, and I can bear witness that never did I hear a murmur or word of complaint for all he was enduring for the cause of freedom. It is with the greatest pleasure that I came from Belgium to unite him to that peerless woman of the Irish race . . ." The bride herself gave the final toast: "To the Complete Independence of Ireland."

Lady Gregory was among the first to send congratulations, and Maud thanked her promptly, knowing that her letter would be relayed to Willie:

> . . . I was married at the English consulate, as well as at my parish Church, so I think it is quite legal—
>
> We had heard there was a possibility of the English trying to arrest Major MacBride at the consulate, but I do not think it would have been really possible, as even if the consulate is English territory, which is doubtful, they couldn't have imprisoned him there for long and once outside he would have been free. No such attempt was made. The consul was rather rude and began asking irrelevant questions, but when Major MacBride refused to answer and told him it was no business of his, he went through the ceremony without further trouble.

On their wedding trip they went first to Spain, where in Barcelona MacBride met some members of the Clan come from America on a secret mission. They then traveled to Normandy and spent the rest of their honeymoon at a small country inn near Bayeaux. Maud was familiar with the seaside resort; Millevoye's family owned property there. Centuries before, the Norman invaders had launched their long-oared boats toward Ireland from that storied coast of abbeys and fortresses; centuries before, Iseult had watched the white gulls flying and wept for Tristan. Maud walked the esplanade where the salt wind blew from the Channel and dreamed of the future.

At the end of February a hurricane swept across the British Isles. Katherine Tynan saw oaks in London toppled like straws. In Dublin the great elms in Phoenix Park blew down, and trees littered the countryside like the limbs of prehistoric giants fallen in battle. "Something has happened in the elemental world," wrote Ella Young. "I think the Guards have changed. . . . Mrs. O'Grady reports from Achill that the faery-folk are no longer there. Journeying, later, to Achill myself I find this to be true. . . . It is strange what a difference it makes. The heather is still rose-coloured, the sphagnum moss marvelously green, the reeds are silver, but the magic has gone!"

When Lady Gregory went up to Galway she found her "place sadly changed . . . ten lime trees down between house and stables, and the big lime to the left (the greatest loss of all) and the big evergreen oak on the front lawn, and some parts of the wood laid flat. Many thousands of spruce and larch down."

Willie, who had gone to Coole to recover from the shock of Maud's marriage, wrote in the introduction for his book of poems published that summer, the last for many years: "I made some of these poems walking about among the Seven Woods, before the big wind of nineteen hundred and three blew down so many trees, and troubled the wild creatures, and changed the look of things . . ."

Nineteen three was long remembered as the year of the great wind, and Maud could well imagine that those forces, natural and supernatural, which controlled human destinies reflected her own stormy fate. The marriage she had entered into with such an independent spirit almost immediately became a prison. MacBride's expectations were not hers, and he was as stubborn and proud as she. After the first few months, she refused to share her bed with her husband. In March she went to Ireland and saw the Russells briefly on her way to Tralee. In April Yeats, who was in London, heard from AE:

On Tuesday last when I returned there was a wire from Mrs. McBride saying she would be home that evening. This was contradicted by another . . . I understand she will not be in Dublin until the 1st, or second of May . . . Would you like me to leave a note for her if I have to go away? My wife told me that Miss Young had a curious dream about Mrs. McB. seeing her all in gray with a darkness about her, and that she herself had a dream about ten days ago in which Mrs. McB. came to her weeping, and saying she did not know what to do or where to hide herself. My wife in the dream asked her was she not going to stay in her house in Coulson Avenue, but she said, 'No, he would find me there.' My wife had not the faintest idea who was referred to. . . . I think it strange as she has not the slightest knowledge of Mrs. McB's past relations with anyone, or any knowledge of Mr. McB.

In the spring Maud finally made her peace with Willie, explaining as best she could how the unhappy situation had come about. Yeats, who had endured so much pain for her sake, realized that she had risked her prized independence for respectability and idealism and had lost:

> Friend of these many years, you too had stood
> With equal courage in that whirling rout;
> For you, although you've not her wandering
>     heart,
> Have all that greatness, and not hers alone,
> For there is no high story about queens
> In any ancient book but tells of you;
> And when I've heard how they grew old and
>     died,
> Or fell into unhappiness, I've said,
> "She will grow old and die and she has wept!"

Lady Gregory was soon party to Maud's story. "It is very sad your friend should have taken such a step for what seems so slight a motive," she wrote Yeats. "It shows how hard it is for any of us to escape from our surroundings. What did it matter to her what Paris people thought or to me what Gort [Galway] people think, and yet there is an imperceptible influence closing round one all the time—a net to catch the feet."

Caught in a trap of her own devising, Maud tried to maintain the appearance of harmonious family life in elegant Passy, where secret gardens were guarded by spiked walls and balconies were screened with centennial wisteria vines. Eight-year-old Iseult came home from the convent to stay with her mother and Eileen, a beauty of seventeen. Still hoping her marriage could be an asset for Ireland, Maud continued her lectures and journalism. When the tension grew unbearable she would flee to her little house in Dublin, where MacBride, still under threat of arrest, could not follow.

The city was buzzing with rumors about Edward VII's plans to visit Ireland. Timed to coincide with the signing of the Wyndham Land Purchase Act and the lifting of the coercion laws, it would take place in July. In May Arthur Griffith heard that the Irish Party intended to present an address of loyalty to the King. He and Maud decided to expose the parliamentarians, hoping that public pressure would prohibit any official welcome. Maud sent out a dozen telegrams: "Without fail be at my cottage, Rathgar, three o'clock tomorrow afternoon. Meet Griffith, Martyn, Moore and others for most important conference. Maud Gonne."

The young writer Seumas MacManus received his telegram in Donegal and came down to meet at Maud's house with Griffith, Edward Martyn, AE, Alderman Tom Kelly, Father Anderson, Henry Dixon. She proposed that they crash a fund-raising meeting of the Irish Party and publicly raise the question of loyal demonstrations. George Moore, arriving late, "spick and span, exhibiting perfection in every tailored, barbered, manicured detail," excused himself from the venture; "after all, he was a literary man, not a politician." Griffith would remain behind the scenes, and Edward Martyn, the erratic nationalist playwright from Tulira Castle, agreed to confront John Redmond and Tim Harrington, now the Lord Mayor.

On May 18, Maud led "four hulking fellows" onto the

stage of the Rotunda, where Redmond was addressing an audience of several thousand. Harrington was in the chair, and behind him sat eighty M.P.s, "banked in rows, like so many geraniums in a hot-house," MacManus wrote. "Even apart from the cohort, the sight of Maud Gonne, stately, commanding, was to most of that reactionary gathering, the sight of a stormy petrel."

Martyn's hands trembled so that he was unable to hold the prepared statement, and taking over for him Maud asked Redmond in her most imperious tone if indeed he planned to advise his followers to welcome King Edward to Dublin. The party leader refused to answer. Over the uproar that broke out in the Rotunda, "the Lord Mayor . . . appealed to his 'pure record' as a Nationalist . . ." Angry loyalists rushed the platform, but Maud and Griffith had seen to it that members of Inghinidhe and Cumann na nGaedheal were in the audience, and now they came forward to protect their "delegation."

"Of the riot that then broke, I can hardly tell," MacManus wrote. "Maud Gonne [later said] that to her enraging I lifted her bodily, quite a feat, and carried her off the stage to safety . . . as we at length succeeded in getting out of the Rotunda, we met the ambulances tearing up to bear away the casualties which were many. . . . The press of the three kingdoms next morning blazoned forth the exciting account of the first Redmondite revolt!"

AE wrote Yeats that Maud had "rudely shocked last night in the most gorgeous row Dublin has had since Jubilee time. The Rotunda meeting was a free fight and two M.P.s are incapacitated." Her coup strengthened Cumann na nGaedheal and brought new affiliations with Bulmer Hobson's Dungannon Clubs in the North. New members flocked to Inghinidhe; Helena Molony was so impressed by Maud's intrepid performance at the "Battle of the Rotunda" that she became a devoted friend and political lieutenant.

On July 2, Griffith's National Council held a large public meeting at which Edward Martyn, having recovered his aplomb, put the resolution to protest against any presentation of loyalty by the Municipal Council. Amid tumultuous acclaim Maud rose to second the motion and point out that America was the real object of the royal visit. "Between the

English and the coveted alliance, stand the Irish in America
. . . the King of England comes to Ireland, hoping that by the
reception of addresses from the Dublin Corporation—bodies
supposed to represent popular feeling—the American-Irish
may be deceived into believing that the patent 'New Era' of
Sir Antony MacDonnell's [Wyndham's under secretary] is a
tangible thing."

A fortnight later the Dublin Corporation voted by a slim
margin of three against the loyal address to the King. Public
pressure was effective, as Maud had foreseen; for the first time
since the Norman invasion the capital had denied before the
world the right of the King of England to rule the country.

Yeats had spoken out on the occasion of the old Queen's
last visit; now he wrote a letter to the *Freeman's Journal* about
her son's. "Somebody has said . . . that the King has given us
the Land Bill. I have even read that he is going to give us
Home Rule." He recalled the false hope raised for Catholic
Emancipation at the time of George IV's visit in 1821: "Whenever Royalty has come to Ireland rumours of this kind have
been spread and spread with an object. The Land Bill has not
been given to us by English Royalty but won by the long
labors of our own people."

On July 21 the royal entry, "guarded by 20,000 armed
men . . . whilst the guns of his Majesty's fleet commanded the
capital of Ireland," was either a triumph or a fiasco, depend-
ing on whether one stood in College Green among cheering
well-dressed throngs or "along the line of quays, where from
the people along the sidewalks not a cheer arose and scarce a
hat was lifted."

Pope Leo XIII died while Dubliners gathered to "honour the head of the English Protestant Church." Maud objected to the gaily illuminated city as a sacrilege and for the
first time took a public stand on the religious issue. Leo XIII,
the "liberal Pope," had not always been liberal with his Irish
flocks, but at this moment his death provided an irresistible
opportunity for dramatic propaganda. The Daughters of Erin
distributed copies of the Coronation Oath, which linked the
English King with the Church of England.

The next morning, instead of the obligatory Union Jack

a black flag hung in front of 25 Coulson Avenue. Unionist neighbors complained, and five Dublin policemen were sent out to Rathgar to tear it down. The next day Maud hung half of a black petticoat out of her window at the end of a broomstick borrowed from the Russells, and, in a game of seize the flag, each time the police managed to pull it down, another appeared from Maud's seemingly endless supply of petticoats. Mrs. Fitz, her charwoman, and the actress Maire Quinn, "a fine strong lump of an agricultural girl," stood guard as Dublin detectives rounded up a gang of street urchins to besiege the house. Griffith sent athletes from Cumann na nGaedheal and women from Inghinidhe to protect Maud. When a policeman climbed up on a neighboring rooftop and tried to lower a noose around the flag, Maire Quinn felled him with a lemonade bottle. Maud warned her guardians to avoid more violence, and eventually the crowd outside grew bored and drifted away. After cordoning off the area, the police gave up the game. Maud's black flag for the Pope stayed aloft for the duration of the King's stay in Ireland.

While Maud enjoyed her street theater, Yeats was in difficulties with his literary theater. He needed wealthy sponsors; his players needed their own hall. Miss Annie Horniman, with her Hudson's Bay stocks, her chains of pearls and opals glimmering like fantasies of the Golden Dawn, took Edward Martyn's place as patron. But she was no nationalist. Along with her inheritance from the Manchester industrialist she brought into his theater a strong mind and a dislike for poor people in general and the Irish poor in particular. "Willie got the money from those not interested in Ireland's freedom," wrote Maud, "and this led up to our first quarrel."

That old bone of contention, art versus propaganda, hardly a lovers' quarrel, flared into a public debacle in the fall when Yeats, overriding strong opposition by members of his company, insisted on producing John Millington Synge's first play, *In the Shadow of the Glen*. Maud sided with those who thought it utterly unsuitable and resigned from the board.

Synge had come home from Europe to discover his métier for drama in the lives of country people, the Aran Islanders, the poor tillers of the soil in his native Wicklow. His use of poetic dialect was innovative, the stark realism and the subject matter of his simple play shocking. A young farm wife, Nora Burke, trapped in a loveless marriage to a much older husband, escapes her harsh and monotonous life in the poverty-stricken glen by running away with a wayfaring man. "Nothing more or less than a farcical libel on the character of the average decently raised Irish peasant woman"— Synge's work was condemned by the *Irish Daily Independent* even before it opened. Yeats urged tolerance so that "the half-dozen minds who are likely to be the dramatic imagination of Ireland for this generation may put their own thoughts and their own characters into their work." But the traditionalists saw Synge only as a young man with a raffish beard who had returned from bohemian life in Paris to ridicule his Irish countrymen.

On October 8 Maud was in Molesworth Hall when *In the Shadow of the Glen* opened to a full house of three hundred people. Chief Secretary Wyndham's seat of honor offended the nationalists, which added to the feverish atmosphere, and Yeats dashed about the theater anxiously keeping an eye on everyone. Maire nic Shiubhlaigh played Nora; W. G. Fay was the tramp. Faint applause was interrupted by angry boos and hisses, and Fay saw the audience "convulsed with what Oscar Wilde calls 'the rage of Caliban at seeing his own face in the glass.' "

In the middle of the performance Maud rose from her seat and walked out of the hall, followed by two of the company's best actors, Maire Quinn of Inghinidhe and her fiancé, Dudley Digges. The damning reviews next morning were less crushing than the blow Maud gave Yeats in public that night.

Synge's *Shadow of the Glen* was attacked from right and left. "A licentious play, an evil compound of Ibsen and Boucicault, a Boccaccio story": Arthur Griffith's epithets were chosen to inflame the collectors of insults to Ireland. In self-defense Yeats cited *The Red-Haired Man's Wife*, the ancient Irish song of a woman with a will of her own, but Griffith countered that that did not "alter the fact. . . . that Irishwomen are the most virtuous women in the world." He would not go so far as to impugn Yeats's sincerity but asked why his theater should call itself Irish or National if it had no propaganda save that of good art.

Maud was more discriminating and less moralistic than Griffith. She had encountered the reality of life on the land and was too honest to concur that "no one could be found in Ireland like the characters in this play." It was the tyranny of an alien culture that she objected to:

> It is for the many, for the people that Irish writers must write, and if the Irish people do not understand or care for an Irish play, I should feel very doubtful of its right to rank as national literature, though all the critics in England were loud in its praise and though I myself might see beauty in it. Few of us who have been educated abroad or in schools where English thought is predominant can escape entirely from that influence. . . . The best and truest writings of our greatest living poet, W. B. Yeats, are understood and appreciated by the people; the poems and essays they do not understand are those touched by foreign influence, from which Mr. Yeats has not altogether escaped, having lived long out of Ireland.

As Griffith predicted, the Irish National Theatre was dissolved as a result of the row. Yeats walked an uneasy path, holding on to Miss Horniman and her stocks, which were yet to be converted into funds to buy him the old Mechanics' Hall on Abbey Street, and trying to appease Griffith for the sake of the theater's future. For love's sake he forgave Maud. A few weeks later, escaping the dissension, he was on his way to give a lecture tour in America.

Maud had walked out of his theater and gone back to her unhappy life in Paris. Nine months after her wedding, her difficulties were no longer secret. From John Quinn's apartment on West 87th Street in New York City, Yeats wrote Lady Gregory, "I have just heard a very painful rumour—Major MacBride is said to be drinking. It is the last touch of tragedy if it is true. Mrs. MacBride said in one of her last letters that he has been ill all summer."

# The Red-Haired Man's Wife

I have taken that vow!
And you were my friend
But yesterday—Now
All that's at an end;
And you are my husband, and claim me, and
    I must depend!

Yesterday I was free!
Now you, as I stand,
Walk over to me
And take hold of my hand;
You look at my lips: your eyes are too bold,
    your smile is too bland! . . .

I am separate still!
I am I and not you!
And my mind and my will,
As in secret they grew,
Still are secret; unreached, and untouched,
    and not subject to you.

"Maud Gonne's house in Passy sits green-shuttered and demure beyond a stone-flag courtyard and a clipped lawn. A stout oaken door, flanked by a high wall, shuts all view of it from the street." Visitors, relatives, friends from Ireland, couriers from the Daughters of Erin, found Maud surrounded by "beautiful things: carved wood, Russian embroidery, Oriental rugs—all thrown together carelessly." Ella Young described it: "There are mirrors everywhere reaching from floor to ceiling. Maud Gonne likes the effect of light and space they can give. There are many dogs, large and small: Great Danes, Toy Pomeranians, haughty court-bred Pekinese, and one Persian cat. There is a parrot that curses in Spanish, and a comrade that yells in a language of its own. There are many servants. Everyone speaks French. The center of delight in the household is Maud Gonne's son . . . a golden-haired boy."

Since Iseult's birth nine years earlier, Maud's thoughts had turned to the needs of children everywhere, and she delighted in them for their own sake—"the cascades of Italian children," she told Willie after a trip to Italy, "the large families so much like those in Ireland." Her optimism expressed itself in a desire to nurture the future generation. Inghinidhe's educational program must expand, and from Paris Maud wrote Lady Gregory requesting an autographed copy of her *Cuchulain* for a fund-raising lottery to extend free classes in the Dublin slums and "to give bread and butter to some of the very poor children before the classes."

As a child she had mothered her baby sister, and as a young woman had taken on responsibility for her father's illegitimate daughter and for her own. Homeless tenants, prisoners, indigent protégés, even her animals and caged birds had been the beneficiaries of humanitarian and maternal impulses. For twelve years she had grieved for Georges. Now at last she had another son.

The love Maud felt for him became a center, a reason for life as demanding as the Irish cause itself. No lover had been able to contain her restless spirit; no friend could divert her for long from the exhausting and often dangerous career of an activist. The threats of England's secret agents, the slanders of her enemies could not stop her. But in subtle ways Maud's life was changed by her little boy.

In an early photograph, Maud, her luxuriant hair in a chignon, looks down like a Roman matron on the child in her arms. His christening dress is draped with the flag of Inghinidhe. The Major, in a dark suit, stands beside his wife and child behind a table where, in metallic splendor, his gun belt and holster and two pistols are on display with the sword of honor presented to him on behalf of the nationalists by John O'Leary. Maud painted her baby on a round canvas as a della Robbia cherub. Iseult called her little half-brother "Bichon," after the French for a curly-haired puppy. Maud spelled his name in Irish, Seagan.

When Maud took her son to Ireland to be baptized, MacBride's mother overcame her distrust and came from Westport for the ceremony. MacBride was unable to be present, and the parents' choice of O'Leary as godfather almost prevented the ceremony from taking place at all. The priest at the Church of the Three Patrons in Rathgar refused to accept him. Maud finally found a sympathetic young priest willing to accept the old agnostic, who had not been to mass for fifty years. O'Leary's name was not entered on Seagan's baptismal certificate, but it did appear in the police report, and the christening at the Church of the Three Patrons became part of Dublin Castle's dossier on the MacBride family.

If Maud had had her choice they would have lived in Ireland, but MacBride was in exile. She was torn. Reluctant though she was, in June she left five-month-old Seagan with his nanny and was in London for the annual Wolfe Tone celebration, sharing the platform again with decrepit John O'Leary. Henry Nevinson, champion of the independent women Emma Goldman, the Pankhursts, and Annie Besant, was in the audience and reported that Maud Gonne, whom he had not seen for ten years, was as beautiful as and more commanding than before. Yeats, in London for the première of his first tragic drama, *Where There Is Nothing,* and absorbed in theatrical business, could not attend the ceremonies. "It was really very fine. I hear," he wrote John Quinn, "quite self-restrained for her, at least, as eloquent as ever." Yeats had been presented to Queen Alexandra at Lady Cromartie's garden party while children danced with long white muslin scarves à la Isadora. He still smarted from Maud's public defection at the performance of Synge's play, and there was mischief in his letter to Quinn about his brush with English royalty: "I have been waiting to see if the rumour reaches the *United Irishman* and in what form . . . I am looking forward to seeing the effect of it on Mrs. M[a]cBride. (I shall tell her as soon as I can . . . )"

Lovers but not lovers, friends but not on friendly terms, Maud and Willie continued to spar with each other. Aware that her upper-class background had always been one of her attractions for him, Maud was amused at the thought of the absent-minded poet in his old blue jacket at a soirée for the Queen. But the news that he had raised the price of admission to his theater was another matter. Miss Horniman was renovating Mechanics' Hall and paying for sets by Gordon Craig. Sarah Purser's stained-glass works was making windows to enrich the dark lobby, and Lady Gregory's "barmbracks," huge cartwheels of fruitcake, would nourish the underpaid actors. Maud's prime concern was the kind of audience the Abbey Players would attract, and tickets at the new rate, six shillings a seat, would keep many Dubliners away from the theater that should be theirs.

"I have had a letter from Paris that rather irritates me," Yeats complained to Lady Gregory. "It speaks of my once having thought that our literature should be national but having given up that conviction. I replied on the first day of my cold and was somewhat vehement, and am now sorry that I was. One doesn't mind the misunderstandings of the indifferent world but one is hurt by the misunderstandings of friends."

While Yeats's dream playhouse was under construction in Abbey Street, the players continued to use the more modest quarters acquired some time before by the Fays and Inghinidhe in Lower Camden Street. On the makeshift stage behind a butter-and-egg shop, Sara Allgood rehearsed Synge's new play, *Riders to the Sea*, and James Joyce with his drinking companion Oliver St. John Gogarty ("Buck Mulligan" of the pink waistcoat and flashing wit) paid an unexpected visit. One of the actresses, Vera Esposito, stumbled over the intoxicated Joyce, who had passed out in a passageway filled with egg crates. "O, the night in the Camden Hall when the daughters of Erin had to lift their skirts to step over you."

A few days before, Joyce had met an auburn-haired

young woman from Galway who worked at Finn's Hotel and fallen in love. Nora Barnacle, "with her country strength, stood for Ireland for him much as Maud Gonne, the single-minded aristocrat, stood for Yeats." That summer Joyce was about to leave Ireland for good, taking Nora to share his life in Europe. The single-minded aristocrat found the Dublin of 1904, which Joyce memorialized in *Ulysses*, more congenial than Paris. The city of gray buildings flanking the Liffey, of bridges and steeples and green parks, was still small enough to nourish strong personalities, and in its mingling of politics and daily life to produce a unique and exciting ferment. George Moore lived behind a green door in Ely Place with his spurious paramours and authentic French paintings, the silver Manet, the mauve Monet. J. B. Yeats, in a studio at 7 St. Stephen's Green, was painting a portrait of Lady Gregory's niece, sister of the art collector Hugh Lane, and waiting hopefully for a commission from the Chief Secretary to paint Mrs. Wyndham. Lily and Lolly Yeats were printing their brothers' poems and drawings on their hand press at the Dun Emer Guild out in Dundrum. Sarah Purser's wit made up for the meager refreshments she served at her Tuesday salons. Young Dr. Gogarty held forth at the Bailey. The classicist Stephen MacKenna, back from Paris, spoke only in Greek or Irish to his guests. AE's satellites gathered in Rathgar on Sundays, and he published an anthology of their works, *New Songs*. The Celtic revival had reached a peak, and behind the flood of talk and publication a new drive for Irish separatism was in the making. Everyone was reading Arthur Griffith's pamphlet, *The Resurrection of Hungary*. This was the time and Dublin was the place Maud wanted to be. With servants in Paris to look after her household and her husband, a *bonne* for little Seagan, she saw no reason not to come and go as she chose.

Maud took Iseult to Ireland in October 1904. Ella Young saw Maud Gonne's daughter and George Russell's son playing with snails on the wall between their gardens, and overheard Iseult tell incredulous little Brian that in France they ate the slimy creatures as a great delicacy.

John Quinn had come from America to collect paintings, books, and gossip. At the Standish O'Gradys' he and Yeats were told that "M.G. had come down there and had been perfectly charming and had insisted on addressing Mr. O. as Edward or King Edward or as Edward 7th—all laughed very pleasantly and said that a man should take anything from a handsome woman."

Maud and the dry, irascible lawyer finally met at AE's, where Synge, Gogarty, Colum, Maire nic Shiubhlaigh, and other members of the artistic coterie had gathered to welcome their benefactor from New York. Most elegant among them were Count and Countess Markievicz, who had recently moved with their three-year-old daughter, Maeve, and a large staff into a Victorian mansion in Rathgar. "The Gore-Booth girl who married the Polish count with the unspellable name" was AE's new neighbor. A willowy beauty like Maud, though on a smaller scale, determined and independent, though not yet converted to the Irish cause, Constance Markievicz at thirty-six was on the brink of becoming a full-fledged rebel.

Maud made one of her late entrances, arriving just before midnight to face the curiosity of old friends and acquaintances, many of whom she had not seen since she became Mrs. John MacBride. High-spirited as ever, and more devious, she parried their questions about her husband: "did not know exactly when M. had gone to U.S.," the visitor from New York noted. "Did not know whether he was writing for any American paper, but heard he was doing some such thing." Quinn thought she looked "very charming," and Maud thought the opinionated bachelor as humorless as he was handsome. Her own self-confidence and deliberate gaiety dispelled speculations about her domestic troubles in Paris. In Dublin she was still Maud Gonne.

John MacBride was humiliated by a wife who was more active in the movement than himself. "Mrs. MacBride got back from Ireland a few weeks ago," he wrote John Devoy from Paris, "and she gives a very encouraging account of the state of affairs there. She finds fault with our friends for not being as active as they might be; but women are never satisfied." MacBride traveled once to Westport to see his ailing mother, and during his short stay managed to elude the authorities, who were not eager to resurrect memories of the Boer War. He went to New York for a briefing at Clan headquarters, but in Paris he remained a hero without a function. "I started my account of the Irish Brigade a short time back," he told the leader of the Clan, who was now publishing the *Gaelic American*, "but with one thing and another I never got very far."

Maud's frequent absences heightened the resentment he already felt, adding insult to negligence and rejection. What had seemed to him so romantic in her past life—the many admirers, the love of a poet—now became sinister. Joseph MacBride visited Paris and was alarmed to see that his predictions had come true. His promising younger brother, his comrade in the IRB, was seeking solace in drink with lost soldiers of fortune in the cafés, returning late at night with his rowdy companions to shatter the peace of his home. Ashamed of her husband's betrayal of the IRB code, Maud blamed his drinking on British agents taking malevolent advantage of MacBride's weakness.

Work was the drug for Maud. From her desk in Passy she sent articles to the *United Irishman* and continued to direct the activities of the Daughters of Erin. To banish worries that lay too heavily on her spirit she set herself to write a play for Inghinidhe. *Dawn, A Play in One Act and Three Tableaux* was published in the fall of 1904 in the *United Irishman*. One-act plays modeled on *Cathleen ni Houlihan* were popular in Dublin, and Maud's was easy and inexpensive to produce: Bride, a self-sacrificing mother, spurs the men in her family to rebel against the Stranger, who has stolen their land and freedom, put their homes to the torch, and murdered their children. Maud's piece of propaganda was saved from banality by a sensitive rendition of Irish speech. Ella Young wrote two poems for the play, and Maud chanted them "to music that came to her in a dream—music out of the faery world": "They have bright swords with them that clash the battle welcome,/A welcome to the red sun, that rises with our luck."

*Dawn* was Maud's response to all she found objectionable in Synge. It expressed her compassion for her countrywomen, her faith in their potential leadership, her hope for Ireland. For herself she had no hope. Her luck had run out. The Great Shield of Lug, the magic of the gods which she had boasted of to Willie, no longer protected her. MacBride's behavior affected her whole household. It upset the baby, and Iseult and Eileen were terrified.

When drunk he attacked Maud. Wife beating, all too common in Ireland, was intolerable, utterly degrading; but the ultimate disaster occurred late one winter night when MacBride came home and, totally out of control, assaulted Eileen.

Forced to put the welfare of her ward and her own children above all other considerations, Maud was a tigress defending her brood. To salvage her half-sister's future, she insisted that Eileen marry MacBride's brother Joseph. The desperate situation—the ruin of a national hero, the despoiling of an innocent girl—required a desperate solution. Even the cloistered secrecy of a convent could not be trusted to hide the dishonor of the family. Instead of taking the veil, Tommy's eighteen-year-old daughter was married in Paris in December 1904 to the forty-three-year-old man from Mayo. Maud took some comfort in the fact that Joseph was loyal and good-natured; she was convinced that he would be devoted to his beautiful young bride, who had looked on him as a kindly uncle whenever he visited Passy. Eileen, like legions of women, the Noras of Ireland, had no choice. Her problem was resolved in a compromise, ruthless yet conventional, but for Maud no compromise was possible. Life with MacBride was unbearable for Maud and for her children. In the full knowledge that a suit for separation would seriously damage their work for Ireland, she sought legal means to terminate her marriage.

She went to London to see Yeats for comfort and help. Lady Gregory suggested they consult the nationalist lawyer Barry O'Brien. As friend and biographer of Parnell, O'Brien was well qualified. He drew up a separation agreement which Maud was willing to sign. When, much to everyone's disappointment, her husband refused, she was left with no alternative but to start a public action for separation. In February she and John MacBride appeared together before a magistrate in Paris. The machinery of the law took over, and the tragedy of their lives became the property of the court and the press.

Yeats went back to Paris with Maud to give her his

support. He saw her stunned, wounded, isolating herself at home, making a feeble attempt to distract herself by painting. "Dear friend," he wrote to Lady Gregory, "I turn to you in every trouble. I cannot bear the burden of this terrible case alone—I know nothing about lawyers and so on. When you know the story you will feel that if she were the uttermost stranger, or one's bitterest enemy, one would have, even to the putting aside of all else, to help her."

Cousin May came to stay with Maud in Passy and suggested that their influential lawyer friend Quinn might have some suggestions. Yeats relayed the message, for it seemed to him as to all her friends that she was headed for some catastrophic dénouement. In a letter blotched with ink stains, written in the minute uneven hand that revealed his stress, he asked for help, describing Maud's trouble as the most painful event of his own life. MacBride's unconscionable act could only be the result of drink, Yeats told the lawyer, and impressed on him that the trial would have to be held *in camera*, to protect the reputation of the innocent and for the sake of the Irish nationalist movement itself. Yeats mentioned with wry humor that MacBride in a jealous fit had threatened to shoot him some while back. The mad charges, he assured Quinn, were as empty as the maddened husband's revolver, and the part he himself had played in the melodramatic tragedy was minor. His concern for Maud sprang from an affection in no way passionate, he wrote; he felt as he would for an unfortunate sister.

In her determination to keep Seagan from his father's influence, Maud convinced herself that a cause as great as the nationalists' could not suffer from one member's lapse, and was prepared to expose MacBride's ill-doing if it should prove necessary in obtaining custody of her son. Memories of the Parnell divorce haunted her nationalist friends, who feared vengeful scandal, but so far, Yeats told Quinn, it was not Maud who had instigated publicity, but MacBride and his partisans, who were circulating stories about her unconventional life.

The obliging American hired private detectives to investigate MacBride's conduct on his visit to New York the previous year. "None of the Clan men here would want to appear in the matter, but I do not think they will oppose my getting the testimony," Quinn wrote Yeats. "In fact, I have assurances from [Judge Daniel] Cohalan who is the chief that they will not oppose it although he himself does not want, because of his past relations with MacBride, to appear personally in the matter." Quinn was on good terms with Tammany Hall, knew its tactics, but had no real standing with the Clan na Gael nor awareness that the lips of men in a secret society were sealed to suppress any discreditable word about a brother. Quinn told Yeats that his efforts for Maud were made "out of regard and friendship," and suggested that "some day I might pick out of her sketch-book a picture to frame for my apartment, and that if she would let me do this we would call accounts even." Quinn was finally unable to obtain any affidavits in America for Maud's Paris lawyers and could only report the discouraging truth: backed by the IRB, MacBride would fight and make countercharges.

"You must keep out of this," Maud told Willie; she had "brought this trouble on myself and must fight it alone." But in the end she had to accept every assistance. Her French confessor, the faithful Canon, circulated a letter among the clergy in Ireland justifying her action. Yeats rallied his friends to support her.

Lady Gregory went to London to confer with lawyers and Fenians, and even Miss Horniman, refusing to be left out, undertook a mission for Maud. For the poet's sake the Manchester heiress journeyed to Westport to investigate the MacBride family and its environs, hoping to bolster Maud's petition for custody with evidence of lower-class impropriety. The thin spinster in her stiff, high-necked traveling costume raised no suspicions as she snooped about the shops on the steep streets that led down to the quay, or sat over tea in the lounge of the Railway Hotel.

> Whilst waiting for my meal I heard three men, without mentioning names, speaking of the coming trial.... One said that he had been "in love with her for twenty-four hours and had then got over it—" ... When they spoke of the husband they spoke so that I could not hear at all. At the end the oldest

man said something about thinking that a woman is "better minding the shop than in public life."

Like Quinn's sleuths in America, she was faced by the silence of partisans. The MacBride family's general store betrayed no evidence of being a "low public house," and when she called on the only two solicitors in the small county seat, they had nothing of ill repute to contribute. Annie Horniman, private detective, hoped to circumvent the curiosity of the postmistress by sending her reports to Lady Gregory. "I don't think your name and address would be as interesting to anybody as that of Mr. Yeats." "Says he drinks not," she telegraphed Lady Gregory in German from Westport; *"Der auder auch sagt dass er sauft nicht."* In a following letter she added, "Both solicitors openly own to having been in love with Mrs. McBride. Mr. Garvey asked me whether she took herself seriously, as no one else does. I said that she did." Finally Miss Horniman saw MacBride, who had come home to get advice from his comrades. "He does not look a nice sort of person or rather not a pleasant character, but that without drinking would not be considered important."

"John MacBride has come again from Paris . . ." P. T. Daly, a member of the Supreme Council, wrote to John Devoy. "How have Miss Quinn and Digges got on?" he inquired about the young actors who had gone to New York after resigning from the National Theatre with Maud. "And is she backing her goddess very much?"

Maud Gonne needed no press service now, and all her publicity was bad. From far-off Trieste, James Joyce wrote his brother: "I have read in the *Figaro* of the divorce of the Irish Joan of Arc from her husband. Pius the Tenth, I suppose, will alter Catholic regulations to suit the case: an Italian comment says Irish genius is not domestic." Griffith, whom he still admired, was to be pitied; Joyce remarked to Stanislaus, "Poor little U.I.; indignant little chap." Griffith's *United Irishman* avoided any mention of the disgrace that had overwhelmed the editor's two dearest friends. In late February the *Irish Independent*, a conservative nationalist paper owned by the wealthy industrialist William Martin Murphy, took full advantage of the cause célèbre for its middle-class Catholic

readers: "MRS. MAUD GONNE MACBRIDE—THE DIVORCE CASE—IN-
FLUENCE OF FRIENDS UNAVAILING—CUSTODY OF THE BOY IN DIS-
PUTE." Under a Paris dateline it quoted the *London Daily News:*

> The husband is charged with cruelty, infidelity and
> drunkenness. He is at present living apart from his
> wife, but she alleges that on several occasions when
> she was away from home he brought home tipsy
> Irishmen who slept in her bed.
>     The main bone of contention is the child of the
> marriage. The Major denies his wife's charges, and
> brings a counter-action, but is willing that his wife
> should have the custody of the child, on condition
> that the boy spends at least nine months of every
> year in Ireland, "in a national and Catholic atmo-
> sphere." At the end of six years he asks that a coun-
> cil be held to decide the boy's future.
>     Mrs. M'Bride insists upon the charge of the
> child, and alleges the dissolute and vicious habits
> unfitting the father to control the boy. He retorts in
> kind.

MacBride, trying to protect his reputation, started a libel
suit against the *Independent.* While it was pending, newspapers in Great Britain were prohibited from reporting the
case, but the Irish, French, and American press kept on the
trail.

Irish-American and Catholic newspapers in New York
were discreet, John Quinn wrote Maud. "I must say that the
Nationalists have behaved very well as a rule and have all
apparently desired only to keep the matter out of the papers.
. . . The last rumor I heard (and it was only a rumor—nothing
in print) was that you were going back on, or had already
gone back on, all of your Nationalist principles and were
allying yourself with the English part from which you had
come, or words to that effect. This remark undoubtedly emanated from McBride or some of McBride's friends and I denied it."

There was nothing to do but ride out the storm. Maud
had lost control of her life, and it took all her resolve, all her

pride to withstand the storm that her suit for separation had loosed. She wrote Willie:

> All this time I have not written ... but I was waiting to have news of my divorce to tell and even now I have none. In vain my lawyer tries to get Mac-Bride's lawyer to fix the date for the final hearing. ... MacBride evidently wants to delay in hopes of winning his libel action against the *Independent* in the meantime, which if by any chance, he does succeed in winning, would prevent the publication of the trial and verdict in the English and Irish papers. My lawyer says there is no hope that case will be heard now till the *middle of May* as when the lawyers don't agree the judge cannot fix a date out of turn. This waiting is most wearisome . . .

There was too much time for reflection, for self-examination and regret. Cut off from her Dublin life, Maud read of struggles in which she could no longer take part. The same issue of the *Independent* that ran the story of her divorce case told of rejoicing in Roscommon, where once she had seen the smoldering thatch roofs and the scorched limbs of little children. In February 1905 old John Fitzgibbon, her guide three years before, stood on the hill of Fairymount to announce to joyful tenants that Lord de Freyne had capitulated. The last great estate was up for sale to the Congested Districts Board, and from all the surrounding hilltops bonfires lit the night in celebration. The Woman of the Sidhe was present only in spirit.

The lawyers, M. Cruppin representing Maud and M. Labori for MacBride, continued to delay the case through the spring of 1905 while they fought over custody terms. Mac-Bride was now willing to settle out of court if Maud would withhold the most damaging evidence and allow the question of the child to be arbitrated later. Maud maintained that as a mother she had no right to surrender her claim. Finally, in August 1905, the court granted a separation decree. The *New York World* reported:

Major John MacBride and his wife, who was Maud Gonne, the "Irish Joan of Arc," were separated by the Civil Tribunal of the Seine today on Mrs. MacBride's petition for a divorce. The Court decreed only a judicial separation at this time, and left the question of absolute divorce for a future hearing.

Their son, Sagan (John), a year and a half old, was given into his mother's custody, but Major MacBride is privileged to visit the boy at certain times.

The case came before the court on July 26, Maitre Cruppe [sic] appearing for the wife and Maitre Labort [sic] (who defended Capt. Dreyfus) for the husband. The two lawyers eloquently presented reasons why the pair should or should not be divorced.

Maitre Cruppe pictured MacBride's return from South Africa, where, commanding the Irish Brigade, he fought bravely with the Boers, meeting Maud Gonne and firing her affection and imagination by his heroism and patriotism. Together they went to America on a lecture tour, and seeming to be congenial, they were married in Paris Feb. 21, 1903.

"Soon Mrs. MacBride was disillusioned," her lawyer declared. "She discovered her husband to be a roisterer and a rake. For their child's sake she bore with him until she could do so no longer."

"Major MacBride admires feminine beauty, as do all brave men, but he is no rake," retorted Maitre Labort. "His wife is insanely jealous, but without just cause. Nor is he a drunkard. He is what we call here in Paris a 'rude buveur'—he can drink heavily without getting tipsy. He was known in the army as a strong drinker. But his brain is always clear, nay, brilliant. He has collaborated with his wife in her literary work; indeed he wrote some of the most striking passages in her lectures and books."

"Major MacBride has no literary ability whatever," returned Maitre Cruppe. "He can write only the roughest sketch of an article."

Maitre Labort declared that "the Irish Joan of Arc, the apostle of Irish liberty, was born of English parents in England."

"She has no Irish blood at all," he exclaimed.

Mrs. MacBride's advocate ridiculed this statement.

"She is a thorough Irish woman," he cried. "Born in Ireland, she has consecrated her life and work to Ireland's cause."

"But she brings here not one proof that she was born in Ireland," said Maitre Labort. "Let her produce her birth certificate. It will show she was born in England. Nor was she a Roman Catholic until she became one for love of MacBride, that she might marry him."

After the hearings on her divorce petition in November and December, and all the unpleasantness of accusations and counteraccusations—for MacBride had instituted a countersuit charging defamation of character—Maud was again refused a divorce, but the separation was reaffirmed. Her charges of "intemperance" testified to by witnesses were considered sufficient cause by the Tribunal in view of the couple's *"éducation"* and *"rang social."* All concerned were greatly relieved that no other justification was necessary. MacBride's claim of grave injury from defamatory statements by his wife was dismissed as the court found Maud's charges made without malice, and he was made accountable for the court costs. A divorce was not granted, because in marrying an Irishman Maud had taken on his status, and under Irish law she could be granted only *"a mens à et toro"*—analogous to *"la séparation de corps"* of the French civil code. As she explained to Quinn, an Irish judicial separation was all the judge could grant because of international law. MacBride was given permission to see his son once a week for two hours at a time, and after Seagan reached the age of six his father would be allowed to take him for the month of August.

Maud was dismayed at the visitation rights, but MacBride made no attempt to interfere with Maud or see his son. Impoverished, crushed by defeat and the breakup of his family life, he remained in Ireland trying to earn a living and reestablish himself in the Irish movement. The storm that Maud's marriage to MacBride unleashed had created havoc. Like the big wind that toppled the trees in 1903 and changed the look of things, it changed their lives irremediably, and for the time being removed each of them from the mainstream of events.

That fall Griffith proposed to the Cumann na nGaedheal his fifteen articles for a new, united revolutionary organization, Sinn Fein, "We Ourselves." Maire Butler, a Daughter of Erin and one of Maud's protégées, had suggested the Gaelic slogan signifying self-reliance for the new program. The use of the name honored Willie Rooney, who had proposed it before he died.

On November 25 in the Rotunda, Griffith faced a sparse audience alone. Edward Martyn took the chair in O'Leary's usual place. The time of the old Fenian was running out at last. "He was a figure from a world which had disappeared," Joyce wrote in an article called "Ultimo Feniano." "He would often be seen walking along the river, dressed in light colored clothes, with a shock of very white hair hanging down to his shoulders, almost bent in two from old age and suffering. He would stop in front of the gloomy shops of the old book dealers, and having made some purchase, would return along the river. Aside from this, he had little reason to be happy. His plots had gone up in smoke, his friends had died, and in his own native land, very few knew who he was and what he had done."

In his old age O'Leary, who had never shown sympathy for "those dreadful people called teetotallers," became a heavy drinker—the proscription against alcohol was a latter-day rigor of the Brotherhood—and one of his favorite companions was John MacBride, whom he had always trusted. Maud's flamboyant politics were never O'Leary's style, and in the MacBrides' marital dispute he had sided with his IRB comrade. The two men were photographed together in Belgium—O'Leary in his frock coat, more than ever the bearded Old Testament prophet; MacBride with his jaunty mustache, arms crossed against his tweed jacket. The camera caught them en route to the unveiling of a monument in honor of the Irish Brigade, sitting in their railway carriage at the depot of Fontenoy, in an elegiac mood.

It was the Major, the "traitor," who could now travel freely. The Liberals were back in power, and, with the lifting of the coercion laws on the eve of the general election, he felt safe enough in Ireland. Maud was trapped in Paris. Her marriage to MacBride had been legalized at the British Embassy; should she return to Ireland with Seagan, the father could claim his son, for English laws on divorce did not extend to Ireland. As she waited through the months of legal wrangling for the civil dissolution of her marriage, Maud's irrepressible spirit failed at the thought that to keep custody of her boy she might be condemned to live in exile with him.

In her house in Passy she reconciled herself to practicing the gentler arts which she had learned from her aunts and Mademoiselle. Music, painting, embroidery; she took pleasure in creating a special dish for a guest or sketching a portrait of a friend. But endless domestic life could not satisfy her.

> My dear Willie, I have just read the *White Cockade*
> ... Lady Gregory knows the soul of our people and
> expresses it as no one else does. Through the surface
> of triviality, of selfish avarice, of folly which often
> jars on one, she never ceases to see and to express
> in her writing that deep passion which only heroic
> action or thought is able to arouse in them. . . . It
> is a play that will live and I know I shall often have
> the opportunity of seeing it which consoles me a
> little for missing its first production. It is a play that
> will be popular—don't look contemptuous—such
> plays are needed for your work and for the public.
>
> I sent off my little drawing of Iseult for you.
> Tell me if you like it. She had her hair twisted up
> for her bath which makes her look too old but other-
> wise it is like her.

Requests for funds, weekly directives to the assistant head of Inghinidhe, "Emer" Molony, reports to Griffith—the letters Maud sent from 13 Rue de Passy were written on stationery engraved in blue with her crest, the Red Hand of Ulster with the motto "In Fighting and Hoping." Slowly she recovered her old optimism, and when she finally received the official separation decree in August 1906, she prepared to re-enter the scene of action.

In the eyes of the law and the Church Maud was still married, and in Ireland her separation was an outrage. Some Dublin gossips had accused Maud of manipulating the marriage to better her standing; the fact that MacBride too had much to gain by it had not been seen as a reason for criticism. Now that Maud had dissolved their union, she was doubly culpable. When "Mrs. Gonne MacBride" returned to Dublin her reception was hostile. On October 20, 1906, a young woman was in the pit waiting for the curtain to rise on the opening night of Lady Gregory's play *The Gaol Gate* when Willie Yeats entered, accompanied by a marvelously tall woman dressed in black, and as the sound of hissing spread among the audience and she heard the shout, "Up John MacBride!" she realized she was sitting near the woman who had been presented to her since childhood as a living legend, Maud Gonne, Cathleen ni Houlihan, the poet's Aoife in *On Baile's Strand* and his Dectora in *The Shadowy Waters*. "Her height would have drawn attention anywhere, but it was her beauty that produced the most startling effect. It was startling in its greatness, its dignity, its strangeness. Supreme beauty is so rare that its first effect is a kind of shock."

Smiling and unperturbed, Maud faced her attackers. "A counter-hissing set up, the first hissers being drowned." The crowd who had come to the theater to jeer at Maud were stopped by her strength, and the curtain went up.

Yeats watched in admiration. Her lack of bitterness, her act of faith was an awesome achievement, "a purity of natural force" he could not emulate but only praise. Later he spoke for his phoenix at the time of her disgrace:

> "The drunkards, pilferers of public funds,
> All the dishonest crowd I had driven away,
> When my luck changed and they dared meet
>     my face,
> Crawled from obscurity, and set upon me
> Those I had served and some that I had fed;
> Yet never have I, now nor at any time,
> Complained of the people."

# CHAPTER TWENTY-SIX

# Reconciliations

A little girl in a grieving household heard her father say, "You must never be afraid of anything . . ." and in the years that followed her mother's death Maud taught herself to be fearless, staring wide-eyed in the dark at her nightmare visitors, exploring alone the haunted passages of childhood. Later she faced violence with desperate men and women and took foolhardy risks, flouting the voices of authority and of her own common sense. Many times she pretended a calm she did not feel, but the "strange aloof power" which rises from the total absence of fear was hers. "It is the young who ARE afraid, and yet take risks, who are brave."

Maud was photographed for an article about her which appeared in the French magazine *Femina*. How calm she looks, seated in her salon, a dog on the rug at her feet. Behind her the clutter of pictures in carved frames, table tops covered with *objets*, bouquets of lilies and carnations might have been painted by Vuillard, the richness and mystery of a complex life. Dressed in flowing dark lace, Maud stares at the camera, but her gaze is intent on something far beyond the secluded room. "My dear Mr. Quinn . . . for the sake of a peaceful life I find it better to live with my son in France." From her desk in Passy she sent her letters on the blue-crested stationery out to the world she had abandoned, and revealed a wistful impatience between the lines about her thoughts on Ireland and the pleasures of motherhood. "My dear Emer," "My dear Ella," "My dear Willie."

Her dear Willie above all, for his devotion meant more than ever. During the past year they had become lovers, and their desire for each other, so long repressed into dream and fantasy, was at last consummated. Although he knew she was not free to marry again, he crossed the Channel to be with her frequently. He was forgiving and still in love. In the summer of 1908, Yeats was staying nearby at the Hôtel de Passy, and they were at one as they had never been before.

But the sense of complete possession which Yeats longed for and which Maud evaded remained unfulfilled. Physical intimacy fell short of the dream. In June Yeats was writing in his journal: "June—At Paris with P I A L [Maud's Golden Dawn initials] on Saturday evening (20th) she said something that blotted away the recent past and brought all back to the spiritual marriage of 1898. . . . On Sunday night we talked very plainly. She believes that this bond is to be recreated and to be the means of spiritual illumination between us. It is to be the bond of the spirit only and she lives from now on, she said . . . for that and for her children."

Although by now Willie too had had other sexual experiences, the "spiritual marriage" of their younger years still had meaning for him, and they both could still imagine themselves as lovers in mythical landscapes of grottoes and airy castles where spirituality disguised eroticism. In Paris the perpetual twilight of the decadent period spilled into the twentieth century, "swollen with masks and voodoo, black Masses, blissful decapitated women whose heads float among narcissi and blue toads." In the Musée Gustave Moreau, Maud and Willie could still immerse themselves in an atmosphere "of beautiful and impossible things, of things that are lovely and never happen, of things that are not and should be."

She gave Willie a notebook bound in white calf with brown leather thongs, and the unlined pages were soon filled with cryptic references, drafts of poems, joint records of their attempts to reach each other by meditation and thought transference past "barriers that are not broken when lip touches lip . . ." On June 26 she wrote Willie, who had left Paris for London:

> Friend of mine—It was sad you had to leave Paris so soon—there is so much I wanted to talk to you about and which we had not time for. Next time you come you must arrange to have a little more time to spare. I was so tired last night when I got home I could not do much but several times I felt your thoughts with me quite distinctly. . . . I think a most wonderful thing has happened—the most wonderful thing I have met with in life. If we are only strong enough to hold the door open I think we shall obtain knowledge and life we have never dreamed of. The meanings of things are becoming very clear to me. I shall work it all . . .

Above the fragment of Maud's letter in the white calf journal, Yeats wrote: "Think meditation shows the repetition of initiation in the coffin of Father Rosy Cross. Must work out relation between this and mystic marriage." Meditating according to methods learned in the Order of the Golden Dawn on symbols of the sun and moon, two overlapping circles, he evoked a vision of being with Maud. On July 25 she wrote again, and when he concentrated on the red and green globes of Mars and Venus, their zodiacal signs, he saw cascades of roses and apple blossoms, and experienced "a great union with P I A L." The following morning he recorded it in the white notebook and noted that he felt unusually well and "for the first time in weeks physical desire was arrested."

On the same day Maud, at her desk in Passy, wrote Willie that during the night when her house was quiet, children and servants asleep, she had sent her astral body to his rooms in Woburn Buildings.

> I must know at once if it affected you and how . . . I don't want to do anything which will take you away from your work—or make working more arduous—that play is going to be a wonderful thing and must come first—nothing must interfere . . .

(it was not working hours and I thought I might even be able to share with you some of my vitality). . . .

I had seen the day before when waking from sleep a curious somewhat Egyptian form floating over me (like in the picture of Blake the soul leaving the body). It was dressed in moth-like garments and had curious wings edged with gold in which it could fold itself up—I had thought it was a body in which I could go out into the astral—At a quarter to eleven last night I put on this body and thought strongly of you and desired to go to you. We met somewhere in space. I don't know where—I was conscious of starlight and of hearing the sea below us.

You had taken the form I think of a great serpent, but I am not sure. I only saw your face distinctly and as I looked into your eyes (as I did the day in Paris you asked me what I was thinking of) and your lips touched mine we melted into one another till we formed only *one being, a being greater than ourselves* who felt all and knew all with double intensity—the clock striking eleven broke the spell and as we separated it felt as if life was being drawn away from me through my chest with almost physical pain. I went again twice. Each time it was the same—each time I was brought back by some slight noise in the house. Then I went upstairs to bed and I dreamed of you, confused dreams of ordinary life.

We were in Italy together . . . We were quite happy and we talked of this wonderful spiritual union I have described—you said it would tend to increase physical desire—this troubles me a little— for there was nothing physical in that union. Material union is but a pale shadow compared with it.

Years before she adopted the Catholic faith, Maud had dreamed that in a past life she and Willie had been brother and sister. Now he was dear friend and spiritual lover, Iseult's

"Uncle Willie," and, mingling the Christian dogma with belief in reincarnation, Maud maintained the illusion that they were too close to be married. In the white notebook she could read the first draft of his "King and No King" as his answer:

> . . . Whereas we that had thought
> To have lit upon as clean and sweet a tale
> Have been defeated by that pledge you gave
> In momentary anger long ago;
> And I that have not your faith, how shall I know
> That in the blinding light beyond the grave
> We'll find so good a thing as that we have lost?
> The hourly kindness, the day's common speech
> The habitual content of each with each
> When neither soul nor body has been crossed.

Yeats was no longer willing to take shadow for substance. A young woman, a medical masseuse in London, had become infatuated with him, and he fancied her devotion and her athletic figure. On the very day Maud told him they must relinquish physical love, he wrote Mabel Dickinson:

> My Dear Friend— I have spent my days at the Louvre for most part. I have seen a good deal of Maud Gonne. She thinks she will not make another attempt to get rid of her husband (as she can in three years) unless he makes more trouble. She is content and I think happy. We have talked over old things sadly perhaps, but always as old things that have drifted away. I shall return to London on Monday morning. . . . I am hoping to hear from you in the morning. It is so long since I have heard . . . For the moment I am tired of modern mystery and romance and can only take pleasure in clear light, strong bodies—having all the measure of manhood— . . . Ten years ago when I was last in Paris, I loved all that was mysterious and gothic and hated all that was classic and severe. I doubt if I should have liked you then . . . I wanted a twilight of religious mystery . . .

Maud, at forty-one, was no longer the impetuous girl in love who flung herself into Millevoye's arms. Her experiences with her lover and her husband had made her attitude toward sexual pleasure more ambivalent. She told Willie that shortly before she married MacBride she had a vision of an inverted sword, and thought it must have been a symbol of the suffering to come. Willie argued that it must be a sign for her to leave her violent external life, and in their white notebook wrote that he alone knew "enough of her nature and of the past errors of her nature . . . her marriage and its unhappiness" to help her. That year each of them consulted astrologers; each had Maud's horoscope cast, she going to the famous Ely Star in Paris. J. R. Wallace, in Manchester, told Yeats that in the "1866 case . . . there never was, or will be, happy marriage . . ." In October 1908, when the white notebook was in Maud's keeping in Paris, she described in her fine slanting handwriting her waking vision of themselves as Maeve and Aileel:

I was reading this book and other records of old visions last night when suddenly Aileel who was in Liverpool at the time came to me and we became one being with an ecstasy which I cannot describe. The intensity of the spiritual union prevents it lasting long or one would die. I looked at my watch— it was past one. Keeping the books beside me I put out the light and either in sleep or vision I saw Aileel [D E D I] looking very beautiful and happy and triumphant. I dreamed a great deal I think but I can remember little. I was awakened by a great gust of wind blowing through the room. I thought there was some great presence, but could see nothing; half-sleeping, half-waking these thoughts came to me. I saw Aileel's love for me lighting the years like a lamp of extraordinary holiness, and voices said, "You did not understand so we took it from you and kept it safe in the heart of the hills for it belongs to Ireland. When you were purified by suffering so you could understand we gave it back to you. See you guard it for from it great beauty may be born." We stood with hands clasped above it in that white radiance and again the white shining bird flew up from it and a voice said, "It is the image of Forgael's harp which nothing can destroy."

Reunited but not united—the old inhibition was the sword between them. Yeats wrote in another journal on January 21, 1909:

> We are divided by her religious ideas, a Catholicism which has grown on her—she will not divorce her husband and marry because of her church. Since she said this, she has not been further from me but is always very near. She too seems to love more than of old. In addition to this the old dread of physical love has awakened in her.
>
> This dread has probably spoiled all her life, checking natural and instinctive selection, and leaving fantastic duties free to take its place. It is what philosophy is to me, a daily rooter out of instinct and guiding joy—and all the while she grows nobler under the touch of sorrow and denial. What end will it all have? I fear for her and for myself. She has all myself. I was never more deeply in love, but my desires must go elsewhere if I would escape their poison. I am in continual terror of some entanglement parting us, and all the while I know that she made me and I her. She is my innocence and I her wisdom. Of old she was a phoenix and I feared her, but now she is my child more than my sweetheart. . . . Always since I was a boy I have questioned dreams for her sake—and she herself always a dream . . . the phoenix . . . when she is reborn in all her power to torture and delight, to waste and to ennoble. She would be cruel if she were not a child who can always say, "You will not suffer because I will pray."

Maud knew that Willie had suffered since her marriage to MacBride. He had gone from deep despair to a peak of happiness which dissolved again in torment. Success with his theater had been followed by ignominious failure. In 1905, when Yeats reorganized the Abbey into a limited society that would pay actors out of Miss Horniman's endowment fund, nearly all the original members had resigned, protesting that the company could not serve Ireland as a private enterprise. Maire nic Shiubhlaigh, Padraic Colum, and AE were among those who left in 1906 to start a rival company: the Theatre of Ireland, Edward Martyn, president. By 1907 the Fay brothers had been ousted, Miss Horniman had withdrawn her patronage, and Yeats, Lady Gregory, and Synge controlled the Abbey. But the riots at the opening of Synge's *Playboy of the Western World* almost broke up the group. In desperation Yeats called in the Dublin police to try to keep order, running the risk of alienating his public completely. He was determined to preserve his artistic ideals against the Dubliners' fury at what they saw as an insult to the Irish character. Griffith was again in the forefront of the protests against Synge, and Yeats angrily compared him to the eunuch in *Don Juan*, castrated by hatred.

Although Maud did not like Synge's presentation of a parricide and a liar as the hero in the *Playboy*, she herself thought Griffith's attacks on the theater overvindictive. "He is too suspicious of people's motives," she wrote Quinn. "That is the greatest misfortune, I think, of belonging to a conquered country . . . one grows suspicious and narrow . . . because life is hard and treason and meanness well-paid." It was Yeats's misguided use of Castle protection against the crowds that infuriated her, and she was not alone in her concern over his blind involvement with his theatrical ambitions. AE, Quinn, and Helena Molony were similarly distressed about the poet lost to poetry.

In her most rhapsodic letters Maud would interject practical advice, messages of loving concern, proprietary as well as understanding. In June 1908 she wrote to Willie:

> I am thinking it would not be right for you to give
> up your London life completely yet—there are
> some elements in it which you still need. The

theatre is the millstone from which you must try to get free, at least partially free. I understand how you feel about the responsibility toward the players who depend on you—it is kind recognition of responsibility which I always admire in you and which is such a rare quality in our country, *but* for the sake of Ireland, you *must* keep your writing before all else. A great poet or a great writer can give nobler and more precious gifts to his country than the greatest philanthropist ever can give. Your own writing, above all, *your poetry* must be your first consideration. Anything that takes you from it, or makes it less intense, is wrong and must be shaken off. You remember how for the sake of Ireland, I hated you in politics even in the politics I believed in because I always felt it took you away from your writing and cheated Ireland of a greater gift than we could give her, and this theatre is just as bad or worse. For it brings you among jealousies and petty quarrels and little animosities which you as a great writer should be above and apart from. It is because you vaguely feel this that you are exasperated and often very unjust to our people. It is this exasperation that has made you take up old class prejudice which is unworthy of you and makes you say cruel things which sound ungracious—though you are never ungracious really. . . . Forgive me Willie for writing all this which may make you angry. I ought to have *said* it—but I was so taken up by other thoughts when you were here that I had not time—everything else seemed too important to waste the short time we had together in discussing and indeed even now I know these outer things are of little importance, but even in little things I don't want there to be the least jar between us. I know on many things we think differently but only when you spoke of these things I felt a slight surprise, a disappointment, as though it was not you yourself who was speaking.

She continued her efforts to woo Willie away from the Abbey and enlisted the support of Quinn, who thought Yeats's poetic dramas were quite impossible and was also tired of being asked for funds for the Abbey. "Willie Yeats was in Paris for a short time last month—" Maud wrote the reluctant angel. "I think he is weary of the theatre and feels as we do that it is keeping him from his own work . . ."And again, in January 1909, she told Quinn: "Willie Yeats spent Xmas in Paris; he has just returned to Ireland and that terrible theatre."

Although Yeats continued to visit Maud, he was still involved with Mabel Dickinson and quite determined to pursue his life in the theater. The spiritual marriage could not withstand the flawed realities. When Sarah Purser came to visit Maud, Yeats saw her in Passy, "characteristic as ever, as like herself as a John drawing. Maud Gonne had a cage full of canaries and the birds were all singing. Sarah Purser began lunch by saying 'What a noise! I'd like to have my lunch in the kitchen!' " He was annoyed as always by many of Maud's opinionated friends. They exacerbated "everything that had ever divided P I A L and myself," he wrote in his journal, "by continually giving occasion to discussion, which brought out the old trouble. P I A L, when under the influence of external things, [judges people and things] by an exclusively inexcusably political measure[s], which I cannot accept as complete."

> My dear is angry that of late
> I cry all base blood down
> As though she had not taught me hate
> By kisses to a clown.

Maud was trying to establish a life of her own in Paris, studying Gaelic again and painting. She illustrated Ella Young's book of Irish fairy stories, *The Coming of Lugh*, with black-and-white renderings of Celtic iconography, serpents coiled, peacocks and embracing swans. Her old well-disciplined habits returned as she worked on her assignments. She frequently got up at five and worked till midnight to meet her deadlines. She began to entertain again, a few journalists,

artists, young Indian nationalists who had sought refuge in
Paris under the wing of her friend Madame Cama. Her cook
Josephine prepared excellent meals, and the table talk rivaled
the best of Dublin. Yeats heard one of Maud's guests tell a
"strange heroic story" about Oscar Wilde's death. "He died
in great agony, thrusting his hand into his mouth to stop his
cries. He was in great poverty, often without money for food,
and declared that it was his wallpaper that was killing him.
'One of us had to go,' he said." Wilde had died eight years
earlier in poverty in Bagneux, but now Joseph Epstein was
making a monument for his final resting place among the
great at the cemetery of Père Lachaise, in Paris. The son of
Speranza had written his own epitaph:

> And alien tears will fill for him
> Pity's long-broken urn
> For his mourners will be outcast men,
> And outcasts always mourn.

In December Maud took Yeats and Ella Young to
Rodin's studio in the cloistered building that had been a nun-
nery in the days of Richelieu. The bronzed, bearded sculptor
was working on his statue of Saint Theresa, and under his
chisel the marble reflected the light of the snow outside the
long windows. On the paneled walls they saw his sketches;
too erotic, thought Maud, who preferred the Leonardos and
Botticellis in the Louvre. Willie, accompanying her and Iseult
to the museum, would pause in wonder at the resemblance
between his two lively companions and the attenuated dancing figures of the quattrocento. Iseult enchanted him with her
grace and oddly archaic smile. He held forth on poetry, art,
magic; and because he spoke to her as if she were grown up,
turning on her the same rapt attention he gave her mother,
Iseult adored her "Uncle Willie." She wooed him by telling
him that "she disliked plays in modern dress and preferred
the *Iliad* to any other book," and when she was not yet fifteen,
proposed that he should marry her. Yeats declined politely:
there was too much of Mars's warlike influence in her horoscope. Maud's daughter had her mother's insouciance and
self-possession. "Dear Mister Quinn . . . 'Bichon' is delighted

with his fairy book," she wrote in a letter after Christmas 1908, when the Seine, swollen by unusual snows, poured over its banks and flooded the streets. Maud, who was working with the relief committees, told Quinn, "Paris, beautiful Paris is a wrecked city," but Iseult was thrilled: "The Seine's inundation is most interesting, but I regret that we are much too high up for it having a chance to come in our house; the idea of having a little black boat to walk about in the room is most exciting."

The lawyer remembered to send gifts to Maud and her children on every anniversary: New York State apples, American books, and now and then a contribution. He also sent his mistress to Paris, and Dorothy Coates, who was drawn to Maud, caught some of her enthusiasm for Symbolist paintings, Wagner's operas, and Willie. Yeats boasted about his attraction for the attractive Miss Coates, and Miss Coates boasted too. Quinn, who was possessive of his artists and his women, assumed that Willie had attempted a seduction and was furious with the poet he had sponsored. Maud did her best to restore their valuable friendship; she wrote to Quinn from Aix-les-Bains: "The light went out in the railway carriage the other night which destroyed for me the power of Boehme as a heavy sleeping draught." Willie had wanted her to read one of his favorite philosophers, but Maud was preoccupied with mundane concerns. "I thought a lot and the more I thought the more certain I became that you ought to see Willie and hear his explanation. There has certainly been misunderstanding . . . I know he is incapable of deliberately making mischief."

A month later she wrote again: "You say I being a woman could easily forgive if he had done something like that to me. I do not know—for though Willie Yeats and I have been friends for *23 years* and though we have differed often on things and even said hard things to each other I have always found him a very loyal friend whom I could trust and capable of great unselfishness. I know it is very difficult for Willie not to talk freely of everything that interests him, but if he realizes the importance of a thing he can keep quiet."

It took years for Quinn to forgive Yeats the imagined wrong, but he remained cordial with Maud. She sent him a picture she painted of Brigid, scholar, woman warrior, Ireland's first Christian saint. Maud's starry portrait of the patron saint of Inghinidhe went with the Augustus Johns, Pissarros, and Matisses into Quinn's collection.

Painting, sightseeing, charitable works, personal intrigues began to pall. Iseult was almost grown up, Seagan getting ready for lessons. When the return of bronchial illness sent Maud to Switzerland, she complained in a letter to Quinn from the Hotel du Midi in Bernex that even a walk with the children exhausted her. "Being old and rheumatic I have done little else than sit in the sun and watch them play and my letters are written in my thoughts . . ."

Maud met Sir Roger Casement on one of his stops in Paris between South America and England, and painted a portrait of him which revealed the intensity of a Spanish fanatic in the swarthy Ulsterman. The civil servant who had been knighted for his investigations of the Belgian Congo horrified Maud with tales of the brutalities committed by the Portuguese against the rubber workers in the plantations of Putumayo. The atrocities he had witnessed in the outposts of imperialism had opened his eyes to the desperate conditions of the peasants in his native land, and Sir Roger had become a fervent nationalist. During the Boer War he had been enraged with John MacBride and his Irish Brigade; now, although he was still serving the Crown, Casement praised the Brigade and urged MacBride to write its story. "It was a fine fight and should be told." Maud had tremendous admiration for the rebel civil servant, but Yeats, who had met him in the studio of William Rothenstein while two Putumayo Indians sat dressed in a few bright feathers for their portraits, felt that Casement typified "something new and terrible" for Ireland, "the mood of the mystic victim."

Each time Maud visited Dublin she thought Paris more dull. Only the children brought her back to the house in Passy. Only the fear of losing custody of Seagan kept them in exile. She had gone back to court three years after the separation decree to have his father's visitation rights reduced, and MacBride lost the right to have his son in Ireland for the month of August. At the same time she appealed for a complete divorce, which was refused with a clause allowing her to reopen the case another three years later. She wrote Quinn: "As long as Major MacBride does not attempt to interfere with me or my child I don't think I will take the trouble to go to law again." But she could not make a home for herself with Seagan and Iseult in Ireland, and for the time being she was forced to depend on others to keep her in touch with events.

Helena Molony was now secretary of Inghinidhe na hEireann. Every week "Emer" sent a report to her president, and she frequently visited Paris to consult with Maud. *L'Irlande Libre* had been discontinued, and Maud conceived the idea that Inghinidhe should have its own publication. The first issue of *Bean na hEireann,* "Women of Ireland," a penny monthly of a dozen pages, appeared in February 1909. Its heading, a drawing of a peasant woman against a round tower and a rising sun, was contributed by a new Daughter of Erin, Constance Markievicz, who had followed Maud's footsteps from Castle society to militant nationalism. Influenced by her sister Eva, who had left Lissadell to organize working women in Manchester with the suffragist and pacifist Esther Roper, Constance began to see her country in a new light, and, the year before, she had finally broken with her conservative Anglo-Irish heritage.

At the invitation of Helena Molony she arrived at a meeting of Inghinidhe one rainy night in March 1908, astounding the assembled women in her silk gown and furs, for she had come straight from a Castle ball. Ten days later she made her first appearance as a Sinn Feiner on a public platform. Although Griffith did not accept the Countess as readily as he had Maud, Constance rose in the ranks and soon overstepped the little editor's pacific policies by becoming a strong disciple of another hero of Maud's, James Connolly. By 1909 Constance had put into practice Maud's proposal that young people be trained to fight for Ireland. She named her youth organization the Fianna after the legendary warriors and, still a tomboy at forty, taught them how to shoot. The Countess left her charming dilettante husband and gave away her ball gowns. Dressed in breeches or heavy tweeds, she drove her motor car around the countryside, setting up camps for her rebel boy scouts. The youngsters who had attended

Maud's classes in the Workers' Hall in York Street and had
seen her as Cathleen ni Houlihan had grown up to found their
own schools, their own militant organizations. In a little
tobacconist's shop on Parnell Street, Maud's last prisoner out
of Portland jail, Tom Clarke, returned from America, had set
up an unofficial headquarters for the IRB where he inspired
men and women like Constance and Padraic Pearse and Patrick McCartan, a medical student who had joined the movement after hearing Maud speak at the Academy of Music in
Philadelphia.

These new developments gave Maud hope. She took a
house near Vierville, in Normandy, where she spent sum-
mers with her children. The rest of the year, except for holidays, she left them in Paris and took up the nationalist cause
again in Dublin. It was not easy to face the resentment about
her "divorce" from a hero. It was hard to leave Sean and
Iseult. Later, in a letter to Constance Markievicz's husband,
Maud defended her militant friend for having left her own
little daughter to be brought up by Lady Gore-Booth.

> Constance loved children and it was a *great* sacrifice
> when she sent Maeve to be brought up by her
> mother because life's evolution had made things too
> strenuous for the child at home. I have heard people
> criticize Con for this and speak of her being a ne-
> glectful mother. Nothing could be falser than that,
> but she was so unselfish she sacrificed everything
> for Ireland, and in this case did what she thought
> best for the child. Only people who knew her very
> closely and intimately knew how deeply she felt, for
> with all her open exuberant manner and frank way
> of speaking she was very reserved about her per-
> sonal feelings and kept things deep hidden in her
> heart.

Maud spoke for herself as a mother too, and it was her
concern for children that now claimed her energies. She
wrote John Quinn from Paris on October 29, 1910, that she was
leaving for Ireland the next day, "not to rest this time. I was
terribly troubled this summer at the way the children in

Ireland have to work in the schools when many of them are always starving. I believe it is that which is filling our lunatic asylums."

Dublin had the highest infant mortality rate in Great Britain, 142 per thousand compared to 103 in London. Women worked ten hours a day for less than five shillings a week; there was no food for the children's breakfast, and the schools provided no lunch or time for a meal at home had any been waiting for them. Maud wrote articles for *Bean na hEireann* condemning the appalling conditions, and in the *Irish Review*, edited by Thomas MacDonagh and Joseph Plunkett, Sir Horace's nephew, she quoted medical authorities on the physical effects of malnutrition. Dr. Oliver Gogarty had examined thousands of Dublin children in the city dispensaries. "The greater part of their suffering and ailments could be traced to the continued strain of long hungry school hours on their childish systems." And she wrote Quinn asking for help: "It is horrible to think that Ireland is the only country where education is compulsory where nothing is done to provide food for the bodies as well as the minds of the children . . . It is one of the most vital natural questions—If we are to get free and keep free, we must keep up the strength of the race and compulsory education and compulsory starvation is sapping it—" In three months' time Maud's first school canteen was set up in one of the poorest parts of the city. The staff of her soup kitchen included Constance Markievicz, Helena Molony, Hanna Sheehy-Skeffington, and the three Gifford sisters—Muriel, Grace, and Sydney. Assisted by members of Hanna's Women's Franchise League, they served hot lunches every day for a year to two hundred and fifty pupils at St. Auden's. Their program expanded when Helen Laird, Madeleine ffrench-Mullen, and Mrs. Tom Clarke joined it. Maud was accepted once more. No longer hounded by the disapproval of her old comrades, she could rejoice that the British Secret Service was on her track again:

> Arrived at Kingston from Holyhead on evening of 31st October last and proceeded to the Nassau Hotel, Nassau Street, where she remained until 19th inst. when she left for London.

During her stay she was seen to attend meetings of the Sinn Fein League, at which Arthur Griffith, T. S. Cuffe, and other suspects were present. She is said to have interested herself on behalf of "Major" John McBride who is a candidate for position of Water-bailiff in Dublin Corporation, but this does not appear to have brought about a reconciliation between them; on the contrary "Major" McBride is alleged to have resented her interference in the matter.

The "interference" which helped secure the position for MacBride was purely practical. Unforgiving, still Maud pitied him and wanted the father of her son to be honored in Ireland. MacBride was active again in the IRB with Tom Clarke and Hobson, and with a decent job he might regain the stature he once held. She also realized that a generous gesture toward the man whom many thought she had wronged could help restore her own popularity. But when their paths happened to cross, they did not recognize each other, not even by a look. The actor Harry Hutchinson recalled seeing Maud on the street while he was talking with MacBride in the doorway of the Bailey. MacBride continued the conversation without a pause; and, head held high, Maud strode past.

She enjoyed visiting Pearse's experimental secondary school in the park of Cullinswood, an old manor out in Rathmines. The students at St. Enda's were instructed in Irish as well as English, encouraged in self-discipline in the Montessori method Maud had used in Inghinidhe's classes. "The factor of nationality is of prime importance," wrote Pearse, and the staff was imbued with the poetic idealism of the Irish Renaissance. Young Thomas MacDonagh, already the author of two books of poetry, was Pearse's right-hand man. Maud saw him dressed in his saffron kilt walking with his students on St. Enda's lawns.

She bought an allegorical picture of a hooded figure of Cathleen ni Houlihan which had been painted at Sarah Purser's stained-glass works and gave it to St. Enda's. A large painting of the youthful Cuchulain bearing the spear and sword of a full-grown warrior hung in the front hall. Around the frame was an inscription in Gaelic: "Though I live but a year and a day, I will live so that my name goes sounding down the ages." Here indeed was a Castle of Heroes; Maud longed for the day when Seagan could come to Ireland and be educated at Pearse's school.

# CHAPTER TWENTY-SEVEN

# A Separate Peace

Yet she, singing on her round
Half-lion, half child is at peace.

Les Mouettes, Maud's summer place in Normandy, was on the coast between Honfleur and Bayeux. Named for the gulls that circled ceaselessly over the salt meadows, the big, rambling house was a heaven for her children on school vacations: Seagan home from Saint Louis de Gonzague in Paris, Iseult from the convent in nearby Caen. Maud's red-haired cousin, now Mrs. Clay, shared Les Mouettes with them, and there was always room for another guest along with the Gonne menageric of rabbits and chickens, birds, dogs, and the black Persian cat, Minnaloushe.

Maud planted a garden at Colleville, vegetables in neat rows like Mademoiselle's in Provence long ago; and she set out flowers as Tommy had taught her to do in the potting shed when she was a child in County Kildare. Here, close to the earth and the water, her own children could wander through orchards and fields of poppies and run free on the long, dark gray sand bars. The house had its necessary mystery, a haunted painting in an upstairs bedroom, and the fertile provinces of the Normans and Bretons held storybook landscapes of castles and Gothic churches built on the ruins of ancient Celtic civilizations.

Mont St. Michel was "the most magical place in France," Maud wrote John Quinn, urging him to visit Les Mouettes. "Long ago there was a Druid temple to the sun there. Then St. Michael who was a sun force too ordered a temple to be built there for him. It is called La Merveille. . . . The English tried time after time to take the abbey fortress and left thousands of dead under its walls but never succeeded. It is invincible in its perfection of beauty . . ."

Quinn consistently refused all Maud's invitations. Having adopted more of the Irish than he could handle, he had become wary. J. B. Yeats had visited Quinn in New York in 1908, but unlike his son, J. B. stayed on and on. Lily Yeats, who had accompanied him, returned to her press in Dundrum after five months, but the old artist remained as Quinn's protégé, lodging at Petitpas in Chelsea, enjoying the bohemian frequenters of the little French café, John Sloan, Alan Seeger, and Van Wyck Brooks.

Willie's father had an eye for good-looking women, and his portraits of them were always "full of respect and understanding." He sketched Maud as Cathleen ni Houlihan reaching for the stars but never painted her; perhaps J. B. was not interested in classic beauty; no doubt he found Maud too independent. In his seventies he was just discovering the new woman in New York.

> The American girl is in revolution. She means to be quite good-humored about it, even gay, and certainly will not permit any blundering such as the men have made in their bloodthirsty revolutions. . . . Just consider it—the woman interested in herself, surely it is a new thought. She is now leading herself, according to the dictates of her own heart, and not according to the will and opinion and caprices of the man . . .
>
> Meantime there is one good result already apparent: the women here in America are continually drawing toward one another in close alliance and friendship.

The "father of all the Yeatssssss's," as Ezra Pound called him, was the least of the Irish problem cases for Quinn, who was weary of doling out funds and acting as a lecture bureau. He would rather think of Maud as an Irish myth than a real woman; the attractive wealthy bachelor was especially wary of unattached beauties. William Morris's daughter May, whom Shaw had loved, was pursuing Quinn, and he was determined to avoid an emotional entanglement with Yeats's inamorata. Even in his letters to Maud he followed the advice of the Irish playwright Dion Boucicault: "Never fornicate through an ink bottle."

Like other beneficiaries of Quinn's largesse, Maud saw him as myth and symbol of American power, but this time she did not succumb to hero worship. She appreciated his support of Irish artists and was still trying to heal his breach with Yeats. She wrote from Les Mouettes in the fall of 1909, "I think this thing with you must have distressed Willie a great deal . . . for though he wrote to me about the triumph with the Viceroy over Shaw's play, his letter seemed to me rather sad and not as triumphant as I expected, for from all the papers he has scored a real triumph over Dublin Castle."

*The Shewing-Up of Blanco Posnet* had been banned as immoral and irreligious in London. Through some anomaly of the law, English censorship did not extend to theater in Ireland, but the Lord Lieutenant had the power to revoke the Abbey's license. Yeats and Lady Gregory decided to take the risk, and the Abbey produced Shaw's theological satire. True to form, Griffith called *Blanco Posnet* a "London monstrosity," but most nationalists applauded the defiance of Dublin Castle. The Abbey had enough public support to weather Miss Horniman's angry withdrawal when a matinee was given on the day Edward VII died. *Sinn Fein*, Griffith's newly renamed newspaper, praised the Abbey's affront to royalty. Ironically, the director himself was in no way responsible for the performance on May 7, 1910. Far from the tribulations of the theater, he was with Maud at Les Mouettes, flying kites with Seagan on the tide flats and writing poems again, as if to prove that his recently published *Collected Works* was by no means his epitaph.

"Such a delicate high head,
All that sternness amid charm,
All that sweetness amid strength?"
Ah, but peace that comes at length,
Came when Time had touched her form.

Enveloped in Maud's considerate hospitality, he had the pleasant illusion that he was a member of the family, and the sense of harmony recalled his muse. Maud helped him work out an essay on Synge and Ireland, her different point of view as valuable as her sympathy. "Yesterday afternoon, there being much wind and rain," he wrote in his journal, "we all stayed indoors—Mrs. Clay, Iseult, Maud Gonne; and Maud Gonne and I got into the old arguments about *Sinn Fein* and its attack on Synge. . . . I notice that this old quarrel is the one difference about which she feels strongly. I for this very reason let myself get drawn into it again and again, thinking to convince her . . . it was fundamental. . . . My whole movement, my integrity as a man of letters, were alike involved. Thinking of her, as I do, as in a sense Ireland, a summing up in one mind of what is best in the romantic political Ireland of my youth and of the youth of others for some years yet, I must see to it that I close the Synge essay with a statement of national literature as I would re-create it."

Inevitably the sun came out again after the summer squalls, and Maud had many marvels to show Willie in William Morris's "happy poplar land," above all Mont St. Michel. The abbey in the sea was another incarnation of their Castle of the Heroes: "all that majestic fantasy, seeming more of Egypt than of Christendom . . . the places of assembly, those cloisters on the rock's summit, the church, the great halls where monks or knights or men-at-arms sat at meals, beautiful from ornament or proportion."

Maud would kneel and pray in every church they visited; and Willie, seeing her light a candle in "the ancient chapel of Saint Michel . . . where Montaigne's old woman offered a candle to the Dragon and a candle to the Saint," asked her what she prayed for. She was preoccupied with the recently established National University of Ireland. At last Irish youth could get a college education in an institution that was not hostile to Catholics, and she prayed for its success. Willie heard her priest exclaim: "What faith you Irish have!"

Iseult and Seagan often went along on the excursions. Listening to the poet's monologues and recitations, the children received a heady introduction to the beauty of the English language. Maud had marveled at her little son's uncanny knowledge of ancient battles fought beside streams that were now dry ditches, his awareness of places she had visited on the coast of Normandy long before his birth. Now the seven-year-old was losing his gift of extrasensory perception, or hiding it behind the shy pride of a growing boy.

At fifteen Iseult thought of Willie as more friend than uncle, and Maud did nothing to discourage a naive flirtation. Her middle-aged lover rediscovered the Maud Gonne he had met twenty years ago in her daughter, whose placid brow and laughing lips "smoothed away the violent heartache of youth." At Les Mouettes Maud created a sanctuary for herself and the people she loved. When the summer holiday was over they scattered, and she went back to Dublin and her work for school children.

In Paris for Christmas with Iseult and Seagan, she sent season's greetings to Quinn from the house in Passy, along with a report on her project. She planned to return in February to organize another canteen, "and above all to shake up our M.P.s to get a law passed enabling the school children to be fed in all the schools in Ireland."

She was in Ireland during the general election in November 1911, "the Great Home Rule Election," as John Redmond called it, for after years of futility the Irish Party again held the balance of power in Parliament. The Orange Lodges in Ulster, seeing the bulwark against Home Rule weakening, sent out an urgent call for members; there were rumors of arms being bought and cadres trained. But Dublin seemed "wonderfully peaceful," Maud wrote Quinn, and when she returned to Paris and read news stories of an imminent civil war in Ireland, she could only believe that the English were deliberately creating a scare to hinder the passage of a Home Rule bill.

"From talk I had with Unionists . . ." she wrote, "I

gather that they are afraid of a home rule bill which would make the Irish government tax collectors for England and end in bankruptcy and ruin in Ireland, but that if there was a real good measure of home rule and proper financial arrangements and an Irish parliament with *real* power to govern and develop the country, they would be anxious to take part in the government." Sir Anthony MacDonnell, once Under Secretary for Ireland, admitted the long scandal of overtaxation of the Irish by English administrations. Among the liberal nationalists who advocated full fiscal autonomy for Ireland was the Anglo-Irish Erskine Childers, a clerk in the House of Commons, amateur sailor, and author of *The Riddle of the Sands* and *The Framework of Home Rule*. The movement for Home Rule was becoming a mass movement. Sinn Fein's policy of abstention from Westminster became impolitic, and Griffith bided his time. John Redmond began to claim the hope of the people, as Parnell had before him. Maud told Quinn, "It is no use weakening him in any way just now. If only he were a strong man what a wonderful chance he has now! But I feel the Liberals will cheat him and play with him as they have done in the past." Members of the IRB, radical Republicans like Rory O'Connor, and the Socialist James Connolly were convinced that Redmond was too weak and conciliatory. In secret, uncompromising separatists prepared to defend themselves against the Northern Unionists.

From her semibanishment in France Maud watched and waited and held her Irish-French soirées and musicales. Her articles appeared in the new republican paper *Irish Freedom*, founded by Bulmer Hobson, Sean MacDermott, and Patrick McCartan. *Bean na hEireann* published her pieces on education and nourishment. She wrote Quinn that much of her time had been spent at her painting. "My master Granié and Hughes the sculptor who I think you know say I am improving in spite of my inconsequent interest in things outside art."

Early in the summer of 1911 Maud took Seagan to Italy. Rome depressed her with its weight of Renaissance and baroque architecture, and she longed for time enough to replenish her spirit in the hill towns—Siena, Perugia, Assisi. She wrote Quinn that art could reach no greater height than in the work of Giotto, Lorenzetti, and Cimabue—"there is much in their drawing that reminded me of the Chinese painting." She added that she trusted her Italian trip had not been a total waste of time. She had met some sisters of a religious order "who took a great fancy to my little Seagan and I profited of this to try and enlist their sympathies in the cause of the Irish children and get their Brothers to say a word to the Irish Bishops on the matter. If this is done it will mean an end to the secret opposition which we are meeting from some of the clergy in Ireland who seem to think it dangerous and subversive to feed starving children."

Maud flattered Quinn as an art connoisseur and a great politician who must give his valuable time and energy to prevent an alliance between King George V and President Taft. Foreign relations were of increased importance to England, and America's alliance was as weighty a prize as Russia's had ever been. Asquith's Liberal government was faced with a threat of civil war over Home Rule, shaken by labor strikes and militant agitation for women's suffrage. George V's empire was menaced by the Kaiser's imperial ambitions in Morocco. The Edwardian garden party had faded away, if indeed it had ever been more than an illusion.

Still president of Inghinidhe, though often in absentia, Maud was pleased to report that King George received no loyal address when he made his first official visit to Dublin in the summer of 1911. The Daughters of Erin were out in force, demonstrating for Home Rule, and two of Maud's friends were picked up by the police. "I think the inner meaning of the arrest is amusing . . ." wrote Maud, referring to the rumor circulating in the press that the King had been married before he married Princess Mary of Teck.

> None of us care about attacking the King of England because of his private character, if he were a saint we should object just as strongly to his receiving loyal addresses from Ireland—it is no concern of ours that he is a bigamist. The English authorities know that Madame de Markiewicz knows the real story of George's first marriage, and when Helena Molony got up to speak and began by quot-

ing the words of Mr. Carpenter, a Socialist who is still in prison for objecting to loyal addresses, "George of England may be the greatest ruffian in Europe but all that matters to us is that he is the scoundrel of the British Empire," the police, who must have had orders to prevent at all costs any word of the bigamy story coming out, heard the word ruffian and fearing it was coming, rushed in and arrested Helena Molony and Countess Markiewicz who was presiding at the meeting.

Yeats was in Paris early that summer with his new acolyte, twenty-six-year-old Ezra Pound, the poet-critic from Idaho, and the American pianist Walter Rummel. He had only a few weeks to spend at Les Mouettes before he left for America to arrange a tour for the Abbey. In Normandy the childless bachelor was entranced once more by Maud and her family. He was full of his latest enthusiasm, Rabindranath Tagore. When Iseult heard Yeats read some of the works written in English, she was inspired to learn Bengali so that she could help translate his serene, idealistic prose poems. Evenings by the fire, the troubles in Great Britain and Europe forgotten, Maud listened to Willie's stories of the fabulous and would-be fabulous characters who inhabited his literary London: Henry James, Wyndham Lewis, the engaging neopagan Rupert Brooke, the sociable painter William Rothenstein, and Augustus John.

Maud reported none of Willie's gossip to Quinn for fear of arousing his lingering anger against Yeats. She told him instead about the poet's old rival, George Moore, who left Dublin for good in 1911. The publication of *Ave*, his first volume of Irish memoirs, hastened his departure from the whispering gallery. "It is certainly clever and amusing reading," Maud wrote, "but it is yellow journalism turned into a novel and all pleasant social intercourse would come to an end if many people were like George Moore. He called to see me in Paris several years ago and after drinking his tea, he began in quite a businesslike way—'Now I want you to tell me all about it, just why did you get married? I can understand the separation but I want to know all about that too.' " Maud asked if he wanted to know for his book, and talked about the weather, "as dull and sleepy as possible," she added, "for I felt the only way to escape Moore books was not to interest him in the least."

Once again she was staying in the Nassau Street Hotel. Having given up the little house in Coulson Avenue, Maud moved her carved oak furniture into Ella Young's house in Temple Hill. The first time she stayed at Ella's, she arrived late at night in a jaunting car and was immediately aware that the place was haunted. The next morning she described how the ghost had shown her a secret passage under one wing of the tall derelict building, but she was not at Temple Hill long enough to explore the hidden storeroom behind the wine cellar which her friends later found an ideal cache for smuggled arms.

Walking across Stephen's Green in the prosperous center of Dublin, on her way to see Hanna at Women's Franchise League headquarters, Maud saw a little girl picking pieces of bread out of the Black Pond. "That's not stealing," the child told her. When there was nothing to eat at home after school, she brought her brothers to the Green to get bread from the ducks.

Hanna drafted a bill to extend the School Meal Act to Ireland, and Maud presented it to Stephen Gwynn, M.P., but no action was taken. Maud and her assistants from Inghinidhe continued on their own. They started another school canteen in John's Lane, and after a month the teachers noticed more life and noise in the playground. Pearse called the Irish school system The Murder Machine. Maud saw minds murdered in starving little bodies while public money supported the victims in workhouses and asylums. "Revolutions have been made for less valid causes," she wrote in December for the *Irish Review*, "and I do not think we can entirely shift the responsibility for our supine indifference."

It was her own son and daughter, Maud explained to Quinn, who called her back to Paris again and again. "I have been in Dublin for the last three weeks and am beginning to want to get back to Paris and the children, but I can't stir till the second school is in good working order—and in the meantime it is very pleasant seeing all my old friends. I love Dublin. People are all so keen on things here."

That summer the British Parliament Act, which curbed the veto power of the House of Lords, seemed to assure passage of the Home Rule Bill. If voted for by the House in three successive sessions, it would by-pass the Unionist House of Lords to receive the Royal Assent. Early in 1912 Redmond shared the podium at a monster rally in Dublin with the firebrand Pearse, who spoke in Gaelic: "Let us unite and win a good Act from the British; I think it can be done. But if we are tricked this time, there is a party in Ireland, and I am one of them, that will advise the Gael to have no counsel or dealings with the Gall [foreigner] for ever again, but to answer them henceforward with the strong hand and the sword's edge. Let the Gall understand that if we are cheated once more there will be red war in Ireland."

Within two weeks Asquith introduced his Home Rule Bill. The Unionists saw it as an act of war and flocked to the orange colors of their new leader, a Conservative M.P. from Dublin, Sir Edward Carson, once Solicitor General, an imposing lawyer remembered for his relentless cross-examination of Oscar Wilde. The northern counties, with a million and a half people both Protestant and Catholic, became identified as Unionist under Carson's leadership. "Home Rule is Rome Rule" was revived in the industrialized North, where any unity of Catholic and non-Catholic workers posed an additional menace to propertied Unionists on both sides of the Irish Sea. The Ulster Unionist Council prepared to take over the province should Home Rule be enacted, but few could believe that the government would allow Carson's disruption to succeed.

Maud remained hopeful, and her only fear was that the Liberals had become so unpopular in England that they might not stay in power long enough to pass the Home Rule Bill. She found it more and more difficult to get any accurate news in Paris, where she was confined that winter. Seagan was stricken with appendicitis in January. Nursing and worry brought on Maud's lung trouble again, and in April, still weak from months of illness, she was writing Quinn from her new apartment in Passy at 17 Rue de l'Annonciation.

She praised him for having defended *The Playboy of the Western World* in America, where it had had unexpected opposition from the Clan and the Irish-American press. Lady Gregory and the players had been attacked with more virulence in New York and Philadelphia than in Dublin. "I can't understand why Devoy was so foolish . . ." she wrote, and the Clan "only showed their weakness and their want of sense. Lady Gregory was very plucky and deserved to win and I am glad you helped her."

Quinn came to Paris to buy paintings—Cézanne, Gauguin, Van Gogh—and Maud took him to her favorite little museum near the Luxembourg Gardens to show him the wonders of Moreau, but she still could not entice him to Normandy. In any case his visit would have been quite impossible; Willie was at Les Mouettes again during the rainy summer of 1912. James Cousins and his wife, young friends of James Joyce from Belfast, were looking for miracles among the Celtic ruins near Bayeux when Maud sent them a penciled note: "As we are all evidently destined to be drowned, you might as well be drowned with friends instead of alone in a strange village hotel. So come over here." She met her Irish friends at the railway station in St. Laurent. "When we alighted," the Cousinses wrote, "I saw Yeats standing like an elongated rook in rain . . . near a donkey cart in which Madame Gonne was apparently trying to pack things. She greeted us warmly. A young lad, thin, pale and dreamy, was introduced as Shawn." They arrived at Les Mouettes with a pet bantam cock in the cart and were welcomed by Iseult, "accompanied by a dog and two cats. There were cooings in the background mixed with chirpings in different keys and a sharp parrot-like exclamation." Cousins, who soon became acquainted with the sources of the sounds, was also introduced to "a dormouse asleep in his sanctum, and a family of white rats. When Gretta entered, one of the doves, with a little gurgle that sounded like happiness, alighted on the rim of her hat . . ."

At the dinner table the bantam roosted on Maud's shoulder, and Yeats displayed his customary absentminded habit of gathering all the dishes in front of his place as he talked. When Maud dropped a laughing hint that there were other hungry guests, the absentminded poet distributed the plates indiscriminately and without apology.

Maud took her friends to Bayeux, where through her friendship with priests and custodians she had access to the treasures of the cathedral. They traveled through the moist countryside in a *voiture*, a large farm cart with a hooped canvas covering. Yeats "stowed away as conveniently as his inordinate length would permit, on the back seat at the end of the canvas tunnel," and the rest of the human cargo included Maud herself, equal in length but more flexible; Iseult; and two young Celtic scholars from the Sorbonne.

At Les Mouettes, Yeats would sit for hours alone by the kitchen stove, chanting in a strange monotone the lines of the poem he was working on, and when Maud came in from her household chores or from Mass, she would ask him how he was getting on. That summer he wrote his first poem for Iseult:

> Dance there upon the shore;
> What need have you to care
> For wind or water's roar? . . .
> Being young you have not known
> The fool's triumph, nor yet
> Love lost as soon as won,
> Nor the best labourer dead
> And all the sheaves to bind.
> What need have you to dread
> The monstrous crying of the wind?

He also wrote his last Rosicrucian poem, "The Mountain Tomb." Yet his interest in spiritualism had not died, and in the evenings Maud, whose faith in the spirit world never faltered, would gather the household around the open fire, and talk would center on astrology and the power of mediums to foretell the future.

In London long before, Maud and Willie had seen kingdoms rising and falling in the flames. Now violence was spreading across Europe like wildfire, and Ireland was on the brink of civil war. The Home Rule Bill had passed two readings in the House of Commons. An amendment proposed in order to pacify the Unionists by excluding four northern counties placated no one and enraged the nationalists with the shadow of Partition. It was defeated in committee. On September 28, 1912, Unionists in Belfast defied Parliament with a huge, well-organized demonstration. Under the largest Union Jack ever to fly in the United Kingdom, Carson led a great procession to Belfast Cathedral. On that one day alone, to the rattling of drums and fanfares of trumpets, more than two hundred thousand signed the Ulster Covenant, "to defeat the present conspiracy to set up a Home Rule Parliament and in the event of such a Parliament being forced upon us, we further solemnly pledge ourselves to refuse to recognize its authority."

By the beginning of 1913 the Ulster Volunteers numbered sixty thousand men and women. Wealthy Unionists in England sent arms and money; the British League for Ulster counted over two hundred M.P.s and Lords among its members. Not even the veto of the first Home Rule Bill by the House of Lords in January could stem the armed insurrection in the North. And the government, as if to prove that there was one law for Ulster and another for the South, took no steps against Carson under the Crime Acts. Militant separatists saw the day for action drawing near; the IRB laid the groundwork for an armed force of nationalist volunteers, but the public initiative had to come from a less revolutionary source. Redmond was under pressure to call Carson's bluff.

In Ireland the young were getting ready to fight in battle for their beliefs, and their poets celebrated a coming rendezvous with death: ". . . the joy that laughs and sings/Where a foe must be withstood," wrote Thomas MacDonagh; and his young student, Joseph Plunkett, filled his verses with a burning mysticism: "Praise God if this my blood fulfills the doom/When you, dark rose, shall redden into bloom."

In the summer of 1913 in Normandy, the Channel breaking on the shingle close to Maud's house seemed a narrow moat. Off to the east were the deep fortifications between France and Germany. Iseult had discovered the poems of the Catholic Charles Péguy and read them aloud in French to Maud and Willie: "Happy are those who have died in a just war,/Happy the ripe stalks and the harvest grain."

That fall labor disputes held Dublin in a bitter impasse and led to an acceleration of martial preparation. The Irish Transport and General Workers Union was on strike against the United Tramway Company. The police charged workers' mass meetings; on August 31 three people were killed and scores injured, and James Larkin was arrested and jailed. Sympathy strikes followed, and in retaliation four hundred employers organized by William Murphy, head of the Tramway Company, and his lawyer, the anti-Parnellite Tim Healy, instituted a massive lockout. More than twenty thousand men and women were out of work and 150,000 people, nearly a third of Dublin's population, were affected. As Maud pointed out in a letter to Quinn, "the trade of the City is going over to England." Dublin was starving.

Maud agreed with Sinn Fein policy, protesting against oppression and injustice as Griffith did, and like him she resented the intrusion of international labor leaders in what she saw as a national problem, not a class war. Larkin was a *"painful* necessity, but a *necessity* . . . it was necessary to wake people up in Ireland to the condition of the working people . . . the sleepy indifference of comfortable people to the sufferings of the poor is very bad in Ireland but most of it comes from the fact that we do not govern ourselves." She wrote an article for Larkin's *Irish Worker* and titled it "The Real Criminals."

James Connolly, having started the Irish Labour Party the previous year, was Ulster organizer for the ITGWU, and now he came to headquarters in Dublin's Liberty Hall to take charge while Larkin was imprisoned. Constance Markievicz, running a soup kitchen in Liberty Hall for the needy and evicted workers, was helped by Helena Molony, Helen Laird, and other Daughters of Erin who had gained useful experience in the school meal program. Maud continued to campaign for a bill to provide free meals. "It has become such a necessity," she wrote Quinn, "that everyone is with me now over it, every school is giving dinners and many breakfasts to keep the children alive." She hoped to find further means to help the starving families of the locked-out workers, but was called back to Paris at the end of October because Seagan was ill again.

Diseases of childhood—measles this time—always brought back Maud's terror of loss, and she was compelled to nurse Seagan day and night herself. Her health failed with anxiety and overwork. Recuperating from pneumonia at a sanitarium near Lourdes, in the village of Dax, "a place no one would come to except they were nuns . . ." she wrote to Yeats, feeling cut off from the world and bored. "I walked with two rheumatic nuns . . . but they have left and I fear I am scandalizing the hotel now for yesterday I walked in the park with a rheumatic actress who wears silver rings on her ankles and has a strange deep voice. I like the nuns best—for I don't think there is very much under the actress's paint or it may be I have not found it—" She longed to be back at work in Ireland, where the lockout dragged on and rumors of deals between Redmond and Asquith spread after Carson was invited to meet the Kaiser at luncheon in Hamburg.

Maud wrote despairingly to Quinn from Paris, "The Ulster affair would be only funny if one were sure the Liberal government would not get excited and lose their heads. They are doing so, I fear. Talk of concessions, which will mean lots of trouble later on, is in the air. . . . The Royal Irish Constabulary would be well able to deal with Carson and his crowd, including all the Protestant clergymen who are masquerading as warriors, but I hear the English Gov't. is seriously anxious over the indiscipline of the English army . . . many of those belonging to conservative families are threatening sending in their commissions so as to be able to go over and fight for Ulster. A nice sort of army, isn't it?"

There was talk of secession by Ulster, threat of an alliance with Germany. Lord Roberts, who had led British troops against the Boers, was organizing a hundred thousand Ulster Volunteers. But a Protestant in Dublin who had also fought the Boers answered the northern challenge; Captain Jack White urged the beleaguered working men and women to form a Citizen Army. Connolly helped in the organization, to which Constance Markievicz added her Fianna boys, and soon the Irish Citizen Army was drilling at Croydon Park with Captain White. AE designed their blue and green banner of the plough and the stars, although he was too much a pacifist to join up. By December 1913 there was another paramilitary group. The Gaelic scholar Eoin MacNeill had organized the Irish Volunteers; MacNeill, Roger Casement, and Padraic Pearse were on its ruling committee.

In the spring fifty-eight British officers stationed in the Curragh threatened to resign rather than face the possibility of being ordered to "coerce" Ulster, and the government in a shocking capitulation pledged not to use troops against a revolt in the North. The conspiracy in high echelons, organized by General Henry Wilson and backed by the landed classes of Britain, sent repercussions around the world. "March 21, 1914," wrote Lenin, "will be an epoch-making turning-point, the day when the noble landlords of Britain smashed the British Constitution and British Law . . ." In Ireland the Curragh Mutiny propelled nationalists of all persuasions to join the Volunteers. The extremist wing feared the influx of recruits would give John Redmond control.

By May 1914 the Irish Volunteers numbered seventy thousand, according to police reports, but they lacked the essential guns and ammunition. The Clan set up a Volunteer Fund Committee to provide funds from America, and England issued an order forbidding the importation of arms. Already Ulster Unionists had fifty to eighty thousand rifles and revolvers.

John MacBride wrote to his old comrade in America, John Devoy, "The Volunteer movement will be a tremendous force in national life over here, if properly handled. The country people are at last commencing to kick against the Home Rule bluffers."

The Daughters of Erin were becoming warriors. *Bean na hEireann* carried the message: "Arms, discipline and tactics should be the one thought, the one work, the one play of Irishmen and women." When a women's auxiliary of the Irish Volunteers was created in 1914, Inghinidhe voted to amalgamate. Cumann na mBann, the League of the Women, was an ally, not a subordinate group, preparing to take charge of medical work, food, and equipment. Maud was an honorary president.

At the end of the year Maud had written Quinn from Paris trying to reassure him about the situation. He had entertained Padraic Pearse in his apartment overlooking the peaceful Christmas-card scene of Central Park in the snow. The headmaster and Volunteer was in America raising funds for his young Cuchulains, but the New York lawyer was against Irish patriots in either Dublin or Belfast arming themselves and had no faith in Irish politicians. "This Home Rule bill is a step in the right direction and can be improved on," Maud insisted. "In the future I think we shall see the British Empire, as it exists today, disappear . . ."

By the spring of 1914 the situation was ominous. A consignment of 35,000 rifles and 2,500,000 rounds of ammunition originating in Germany arrived at northern ports for the Unionists. The government seemed impotent, but there was strong pressure on Redmond to accept a compromise Home Rule bill. The Irish party leader was indeed trying to control the Volunteers. In March, Maud still believed Home Rule would pass into law before the general election, but feared that Redmond was no match for Asquith and the foxy Lloyd George. At Douglas Hyde's in Dublin she had seen and coveted a drawing of Quinn by Augustus John, which brought her close to hero worship. "It looks harder than you do generally, but I have seen you look like that occasionally," she wrote, asking for a copy of the portrait. "It has all that strength and determination, which makes me feel wild that you do not belong to Ireland *entirely*, for you would have led the people and made history as Parnell did."

Quinn and Yeats were friends again after their five-year estrangement, and the poet was in America on another lecture tour. Fed up with Dublin's problems, Yeats retreated to his literary life, leaving the Abbey in Lady Gregory's charge. Class warfare, secret factions arming against each other! "Romantic Ireland's dead and gone." His elegiac refrain signaled his further withdrawal from public life. At Stone Cottage, Sussex, with Ezra Pound as his secretary, he entertained lovely intellectual young women: Olivia Shakespear's daughter, Dorothy (whom Pound married in March); and her cousin, Georgiana Hyde-Lees, a dark, handsome girl with a musical flair and an interest in astrology. Once more Willie was consulting mediums and spiritualists, stimulated by the widespread interest in psychic phenomena that, like cubist painting and futurist poetry, expressed the undercurrents of frenzy among people waiting for war.

In May he asked Maud to go with him and the Hon.

Everard Feilding, head of the Society for Psychical Research, to witness a miracle reported from a small church town near Poitiers. Spring was made poignant by presagements of doom as they climbed the blossoming slopes above Mirebeau to Abbé Vacher's farmhouse. Maud, Yeats, and Feilding saw drops of blood form on his oleograph of the Sacred Heart. On their second day at Mirebeau the Abbé was not present, and there was no fresh blood. The evidence was weird, inconclusive, but the simple faith of the old priest moved Maud deeply, and she spent much time on her knees praying in his chapel. "Dear, good, charming creature," said Feilding of her to Willie.

Maud kept a record of their pilgrimage in a brown leather journal, another of her presents to Willie from Florence. "After Mass Abbé Vacher said pointing to W. Yeats: 'Tell him, our Lord says he must write for him . . .' " Asked if the message came from the Sacred Heart, the priest told Maud, " 'Our Lord will help him. He never fails anyone, but if he does not use his great gifts for God, our Lord will take from him his intelligence and leave him at the mercy of his heart.' He then went up to W. Yeats and trying to make him understand in French he touched his head then his hand then his heart. . . . Turning to me he said, 'I have a message for you too, you will come back here . . . you will have to leave Paris —Paris will be destroyed— . . .' then pointing to me he said 'Elle est le Coeur—' and to Mr. Yeats, 'Il est l'intelligence.' "

Mr. Feilding had introduced Yeats to the Abbé as a great writer, and Maud, "not wishing the credit should go to England, said 'a great Irish writer' . . . The voice from the tabernacle had said 'Germany will come here first, then England, then the other Northern countries.' "

Yeats wrote it all to Lady Gregory when he went back to London. Maud hoped to return to Mirebeau that summer, but family cares interfered, and she never saw Abbé Vacher again. On what was to have been a brief visit to the Villa Castiglioni in Florence with Cousin May, Seagan got chicken pox. Iseult, now nineteen, was difficult, moody. She had her mother's strong will and delicate health. The doctors diagnosed a weak heart and ordered her "to give up smoking, to eat meat and to keep her window open, all of which," Maud wrote Willie from Paris, "she refuses to do." Iseult was studying Eastern literature with Diva Brat Mukerjea, a young

Brahmin who had fallen in love with her. Helena Molony had been sick and was recuperating at the apartment in Passy. Maud decided to take all her charges as soon as possible to a resort she had discovered in the Pyrenees. Iseult would be unable to find her favorite cigarettes in the remote village, Helena could help chaperone the young couple, and she herself would gain vigor for the work ahead.

Taking advantage of Yeats's paternal feeling, she urged him to have Tagore use Iseult's translation of *The Gardener*. Willie recommended Iseult's literal text and tried to obtain a professorship for Mukerjea in the colonial school system in India. Nothing Maud asked of him was ignored, from an acting part at the Abbey for Helena Molony to legal aid for Maud's newest political prisoners, Savakar Hyardal and the Indian scholar and nationalist B. Tilak, recently released after seven years in jail. She sent Quinn a letter from her friend Madame Cama, editor of *Baud Mataram*, a revolutionary Indian paper, announcing that Hyardal was out on bail and in safety.

The Home Rule Bill, which passed its final reading in the House in May, carried with it an amendment that allowed for the partition of Ireland. William O'Brien called it the most cruel fraud upon popular credulity by which Irish leaders had ever disgraced themselves. Whatever the Lords did, it would receive the Royal Assent. They could not veto, but in July they amended the amendment to exclude the nine counties of Ulster. Sir Edward Carson was silent; John Redmond refused to accept the bill as amended: events in Europe moved inexorably toward conflict with Germany (the Archduke Ferdinand had been assassinated at Sarajevo). Asquith advised the King to call a conference. Redmond was weakening.

In a letter to Quinn on May 12, 1914, Maud was forced to admit: "Events in Ireland are quickly bearing out what you foreshadowed in your letter. Redmond's consenting even to a nominal compromise was a mistake for which we shall, I fear, have to pay heavily in the future."

Erskine Childers proposed a plan for the Irish Volunteers to obtain arms, and it was carried out by a committee which included his American wife; Sir Roger Casement, now a confirmed separatist; his friend the Irish historian Alice Stopford Green; and Mary Spring-Rice. Purchased in Hamburg, nine hundred rifles and twenty-nine thousand rounds of ammunition were landed at Howth from Childers' yacht, the *Asgaard*, and unloaded by hundreds of Volunteers who swiftly transported the cargo to hiding places by lorry and cart and on foot. In Dublin, crowds hearing the news of the landing gathered at Bachelors Walk to cheer, and were fired upon by a troop of passing Scottish Borderers. Three civilians were killed and thirty-two wounded in the first bloodletting of the new resistance movement. Four days later Maud was writing from the Pyrenees:

My dear Willie,

When I read of the splendid coup of the volunteers and of its tragic sequel I nearly rushed over to Dublin to be present at the funeral of the victims but the difficulty of leaving Iseult and Bichon alone in France with the chance of war being declared which would probably make my return to them impossible stopped me. How I love and reverence the Dublin crowd, they are always fearless and heroic when ever a national or religious idea is before them . . . The war scare and the sacrifice of those poor Dublin men, women and children should make it possible for Redmond to obtain a great deal for Ireland. I am waiting for the paper with breathless anxiety. I can hardly sleep for thinking of it all — How are you, where are you and why don't you write to me? In spite of the condition appearing so promising for Ireland I had a haunting sort of vision yesterday of death and famine which put me in very low spirits, but today I try to explain it to myself by thinking I was desperately moved and excited by the thought of what had happened in Dublin and by my powerlessness to help or be with the people and this may have drawn to mind thoughts and memories of scenes of famine and misery I have witnessed long ago. I think it would be that. Write to me soon.

Always your friend, Maud Gonne

A few days after England declared war, Yeats wrote from London to Lady Gregory at Coole:

> I have just left Stephen Gwynn, we lunched together and I send you his gloomy prophecy as much in his own words as I can. "Churchill and Grey have won Asquith over to a postponement of the Home Rule question. . . . The position will become very difficult but if there is a cataclysm of some kind and a Conservative Government elected it will become desperate. The Conservatives are pledged against Home Rule. Should that happen, Ireland will have been betrayed by the Liberals; and the Irish party" (and this, he adds, "is Redmond's position") "will cease to exist. It will leave all political power to the Volunteers and let them make what terms they can. The Ulster Volunteers will then be formed into Yeomanry by the Unionists, and as they are better drilled and armed, they will be more than a match for the National Volunteers."

Redmond had stood up in the House of Commons on August 3 to pledge that his Volunteers, now 180,000 trained men, would guard Ireland's shores in cooperation with Carson's Covenanters. Twelve thousand disowned Redmond, and under the nominal leadership of Eoin MacNeill became known as the Irish Volunteers or the Sinn Feiners, as opposed to Redmond's National Volunteers, who were joining the British Army. There were now four armies in Ireland: the Redmondite National Volunteers; the Irish Volunteers; the Irish Citizen Army, led by James Connolly; and the Ulster Covenanters. And Home Rule remained frozen on the statute books. "This hateful issue," as Winston Churchill called it, "was drowned in the cannonade of Armageddon."

Equinoctial storms swept down on Maud's mountain retreat. Farmhouses around the small town of Arrens were devoured by avalanche and flood. The country people told her that no such onslaughts of nature had been seen since the Franco-Prussian War. Weird noises rang on the hillsides; spectral drums, a muted hammering, wild bells, disturbed the night. "I cannot work, I cannot read, I cannot sleep," Maud wrote Willie on August 26.

> I am torn in two, my love of France on one side, my love for Ireland on the other. . . . An inconceivable madness which has taken hold of Europe—It is unlike any other war that has ever been. It has no great idea behind it. Even the leaders hardly know why they have entered into it, and certainly the people do not. (I except England from this, she, as usual, is following her commercial selfishness getting others to fight . . .). It is race suicide for all the countries engaged in it who have conscription, only the weaklings will be left to carry on the race, and their whole intellectual and industrial life is already at a stand still. The victor will be nearly as enfeebled as the vanquished.

The mails were slow and Maud begged Willie for news. "Are the channel steamers running?—Write to me often . . . send me an Irish paper." Helena Molony was eager to get back to be with her sweetheart, Sean Connolly, and to work with the Countess Markievicz, who had donned the uniform of the Citizen Army. Travel was almost impossible in France. Maud did not dare leave Iseult and Seagan. Cut off from her friends in Dublin, she felt a strange despairing hope: "Who is to end it? In France, in Germany, in Austria only the old men, children and women are left . . ." As always she thought of the women as the guardians of the race. "Soon they will be in a terrible majority unless famine destroys them too. I always felt the wave of the women's power was rising. The men are destroying themselves and we are looking on—will it be in our power to end this war before European civilization is swept away—"

# The Terrible Sacrifice

Take care! The dead are strong persuaders. One must pay attention to the dead . . . I tell you the primary fact of politics today is the inevitable revolution which is preparing . . .

They think that they have foreseen everything, provided against everything; but the fools, the fools, the fools!—they have left us our Fenian dead, and while Ireland holds these graves, Ireland unfree shall never be at peace.

As the German army rolled westward, the wounded and dying flowed into overcrowded hospitals. All over France public buildings were being commandeered for medical care. Maud went down to Argelès-Gazost in the Pyrenees to work as a Red Cross nurse. "In such a terrible upheaval it is too awful to stand by and watch suffering." Iseult and Helena were working as nurses' aides and eleven-year-old Seagan was a page. Their hospital work was onerous and distressed Iseult, but, as Maud wrote Willie, it brought the indolent, fanciful girl into "contact with real life."

Yeats, insulated in a London that believed Germany would be defeated in a few months, seemed to Maud "to have escaped the obsession with this war." To her it meant "destruction for Germany and France if it goes on, only England, where there is no conscription, will profit by it—"

While strange white zeppelins loomed above London and searchlights crisscrossed sinister skies, Yeats was writing his autobiography, *Reveries Over Youth and Childhood.* "I wonder," he wrote Lady Gregory, "if history will ever know at what man's door to lay the crime of this inexplicable war? I suppose, like most wars, it is a big man's war, a sacrifice of the best for the worst. I feel, strangely enough, for the young Germans who are being killed. The spectacled, dreamy faces, or so I pictured them, remind me more of men I have known than the strong-bodied young English footballers . . ."

Maud felt for them all; French and German, English and Irish, the young were being mutilated and killed. Toby, Kathleen's eldest son, was carrying dispatches in Belgium for the British forces. In Ireland, encouraged by their leaders to believe they would be fighting for the freedom of small nations, men responded enthusiastically to England's call to arms. Home Rule was promised, soldiers' pay was steady, and recruiting surpassed expectations, although Kitchener's High Command treated Catholics as second-class citizens and discriminated against them in promotions. A euphoric war spirit seized Ireland. The Abbey Theatre even considered "putting down red carpets and playing the National Anthem" when the Viceroy attended.

"England's Difficulty—Ireland's Opportunity"—fifteen years earlier, Maud and the Transvaal Committee had conducted their antirecruiting drive under the slogan of Irish insurrectionists. Now it seemed to have been forgotten except by the small band of Volunteers led by Eoin MacNeill but in fact controlled by the IRB. Shortly after England declared war, the IRB's Supreme Council held a secret meeting and decided upon an insurrection before the war was over. Devoy's Clan na Gael supported the decision, and directives went back and forth across the Atlantic between New York and Berlin, where Sir Roger Casement was negotiating for more arms. Emulating MacBride in the Boer War, he tried to organize an Irish Brigade in Germany, but the Irish prisoners of war he approached showed little interest in fighting England. In September 1914 the IRB formed an undercover military command: Tom Clarke, Sean MacDermott, and Joseph Plunkett, later joined by Padraic Pearse and Thomas Mac-Donagh. The Irish Volunteers would be the spearhead of the insurrection with the support of the much smaller Citizen Army. Connolly favored a rising now, hoping that the Irish would inspire socialist risings in Europe and stop the war. He wrote in the *Irish Worker*, "I know of no foreign enemy in this country except the British Government. Should a German army land in Ireland tomorrow, we should be perfectly justified in joining it . . ."

Surrounded by so much pointless suffering, Maud could see one thing clearly, and wrote Willie in November from Argelès:

> Ireland should keep every man she has at home. She has nothing to gain from this war except perhaps extra tillage and employment for her people. I am nursing the wounded from 8 in the morning to 8 at night and trying in material work to drown the sorrow and disappointment of it all—and in my heart is growing up a wild hatred of the war machine which is grinding the life of these great nations and reducing their populations to helpless slavery—and among all the wounded I have nursed I have only seen one man who spoke with real enthusiasm of returning to the front . . . but all pray for the end of the war and hope it will be before they are recovered, and in the hearts of some there is a terrible secret bitterness. Among the women it is the same—

Maud recalled her early involvement with secret diplomacy and the international alliances that had paved the way for the devastation of France and Germany. Princess Radziwill, who had assisted her almost thirty years before, had recently published her memoirs under the pseudonym Count Paul Vassili, borrowed from the indomitable Juliette Adam. Maud remembered with what high hopes she had carried a draft of a Franco-Russian treaty for the Boulangists to St.

Petersburg, and how well she had been received as an Irish nationalist in the northern capital, now Petrograd. The secretary of the Pan-Slavist movement had urged on her the importance of reviving the Irish language when the Gaelic League was still only a dream of Douglas Hyde's. *My Recollections* brought the whole adventure back to her, and Maud reminded Willie that the English had resented the Franco-Russian rapprochement: ". . . open and secret intrigues against it were extraordinary. J. F. Taylor and I came across some of these in the Ivory trial, through their fear of exposure Taylor was able to get Ivory acquitted—" Now the treaty with the Czar was working to England's advantage, "and to France and Germany's undoing, for however this war may end," wrote Maud, "France and Germany will be of little account in Europe after it is over—at least for some generations—"

After three months of nursing at Argelès, Maud returned to Paris in January 1915. There too she found work in the wards, "patching up poor mangled, wounded creatures in order that they may be sent back again to the slaughter." She was "terribly depressed," she wrote John Quinn after a Christmas which seemed a mockery. "I feel I would be better employed in feeding my children in Ireland, but I can't make up my mind to leave Seagan alone in France during the war, when German submarine activities may possibly render return difficult, and MacBride and the English law make it impossible for me to have him in Ireland until he is old enough to defy both."

Helena Molony had managed to get back to her work for Cumann na mBann, and Sean Connolly was training in the Citizen Army. Constance Markievicz was a commissioned officer, holding open house in Rathmines for conspiratorial Republicans, including her young Fianna chief, Liam Mellows, and James Connolly. Helena took on the additional job of secretary to the Women Workers' Union. Over Trades-Union Congress headquarters at Liberty Hall, Connolly hung a long banner proclaiming: "We serve neither King nor Kaiser, but Ireland."

Paris seemed more dreary to Maud without Helena's vivacious company. When Kathleen came to stay with her,

Maud was concerned about her sister's shattered nerves. She had quietly divorced Captain Pilcher in 1912 and he had since remarried. Her young daughter was at school in London, her sons fighting for the British at the front; always frail, Kathleen was worn out with anxiety. Their beloved Toby was killed in action at Neuve Chapelle in March, and Kathleen collapsed. Maud took care of her until she was strong enough to rejoin the countless bereaved mothers who were nursing other women's sons.

In the spring Maud had a new visitor in Passy, Gwen John, the sister of Augustus. Quinn, who much admired the young English artist's work, had long hoped she would meet his faithful correspondent, and Gwen John wrote him that she found Maud "beautiful and charming" but was "frightened and chilled" to hear about her experiences in the wards. Maud liked Gwen's independence and sincerity, but after their tea together the shy young woman disappeared again into the privacy of her studio at Meudon.

Paris was a city of the maimed and mourning. Maud's old friends, MacGregor Mathers and his wife, had moved out to St. Cloud. The magician was failing, poverty-stricken. "He believed he was bewitched . . . and he looked haunted." Maud had seen him going into a Catholic church "seeking refuge." Most of Maud's Irish colleagues were leaving for home. The Association Irlandaise no longer existed. The poet James Stephens and his wife lived for a few more months in the France they loved, but finally went home to Dublin. Maud's sense of isolation grew. Her friends were for the most part engaged in secret operations, and wartime censorship was rigorous. Under the Defence of the Realm Act, passed in late 1914, England banned all publications considered seditious. Griffith's *Sinn Fein* and Connolly's *Irish Worker* were suppressed, and the little underground sheets that took their place never reached Maud across the Channel.

In July she went to Paris-Plage with Kathleen and Iseult, to work in Military Hospital No. 25, which held 1,100 beds. Transferred to No. 72, a new infirmary for 400, which was short of nurses, Maud wrote John Quinn thanking him for his "generous cheque"; he was now sending her ten or twenty pounds every few months for French war relief. His gifts of

New York State apples, which had seemed superfluous in peacetime, were priceless now, and the American books he sent were treasured in a country where the pleasures of civilized life, the luxuries and soon the necessities, were rapidly disappearing. "Yes, I am very low-spirited about this war and think more than ever that *peace* is the only thing worth striving for—but how to work for it is what I do not know." Could America show the way? she asked Quinn. Carson had been appointed Attorney General by Asquith, who ignored John Redmond's protests against the inclusion of the rebel Unionist in the new cabinet. "The English-made Ulster revolt is quite triumphant in the Coalition Govern't, and Home Rule is again far away. Once again Ireland has been deceived and cheated."

There was no holiday at Les Mouettes that summer, and Yeats could not get over from London to see Maud. When the *Lusitania* was sunk by German submarines near Cork Harbor, Hugh Lane was among the victims. Yeats went to Coole to comfort Lady Gregory and support her in the controversy over her nephew's collection of great French paintings. He had bequeathed it to Dublin, and the city fathers refused to accept his conditions for housing it.

Overwhelmed with her hospital duties, Maud, nearing fifty, began to feel her age. "It is a strange and absorbing life," she wrote Quinn, ". . . the long hours and the routine tire one physically so much, one has little time for thought. Iseult says it is an *'abrutisement* life and leaves no room for the intellect,' but she makes a very good nurse all the same and the soldiers love her."

For the first time Maud did not fret at Willie's withdrawal—perhaps art was the only worthwhile effort in a world gone mad. She wrote Quinn of her sorrow that "All the young art and intellect of France is being killed in the trenches." Yeats would go to his club and read the news about the war, "the most expensive outbreak of insolence and stupidity the world has ever seen, and I give it as little of my thoughts as I can." He ended up reading Keats, and when Henry James invited him to contribute to an anthology of war poetry Edith Wharton was editing, he wrote from Coole Park to refuse:

He's had enough of meddling who can please
A young girl in the indolence of her youth,
Or an old man upon a winter's night.

But the young poets in Ireland who had committed their lives to a rebellion were singing a different tune:

I have turned my face
To this road before me
To the deed that I see
And the death I shall die.

Slaughter at the front and Asquith's coalition with the Unionists swelled the ranks of the Irish Volunteers with disillusioned patriots. Sinn Fein became more popular. O'Donovan Rossa, the old Dynamitard Maud had met in America, died, and the Clan shipped his body home for a great funeral in August. Multitudes followed his hearse to Glasnevin, where Pearse, in the gray-green uniform of the Volunteers, spoke on behalf of "the new generation re-baptized in the Fenian faith."

Irish Volunteers in slouch hats, the women of Cumann na mBann, and the Citizen Army marched openly in small battalions in Dublin that fall. The Royal Irish Constabulary and the British garrisons ignored them. England was too close to losing the war on the Continent to risk a crisis over a handful of uniformed men and women parading about with more flags than rifles. Few people in Ireland and America took them seriously, and only the inner circle of the IRB had reason to. Maud in Paris was no more ignorant of the coming revolution than most Dubliners going about their business in a city that prospered with war trade and soldiers' pay.

In Europe the nightmare continued through the winter of 1915–16. Maud wrote Quinn on February 4: "The attempted advance in Champagne at the beginning of the winter packed the Paris hospitals. They are beginning to empty now, in provision, I am told, for Spring fighting." Seagan had been sick, Maud ill for weeks with influenza. Kathleen, whose second son had been badly wounded, had great difficulty getting permission to travel with her daughter to a sanitarium in

Switzerland. "I don't suppose United States citizens are treated in the same way!" wrote Maud. She doubted if she herself would ever be allowed a passport to leave France, and told her lawyer friend:

> I believe I shall come after this war to America with Iseult and the boy and get naturalized, for Europe won't be a place to live in for generations. If the allies win, only England and Russia will be strong and the vilest jingoism and imperialism a la Rudyard Kipling will prevail. France is wonderful in her courage and her calm. She just sets her teeth and refuses to look at the ruins, but her loss of population cannot be made up and England is taking all her markets. As for Ireland, God help her after the war!

A month later Pearse delivered a farewell speech to his students at St. Enda's: "As it took the blood of the Son of God to redeem the world, so it would take the blood of Irishmen to redeem Ireland." At University College, Thomas Mac-Donagh startled his English class by laying his revolver on the desk before him as he said to himself: "Ireland can only win freedom by force."

The IRB's Provisional Committee set the date for the insurrection. Connolly pledged his Citizen Army. MacNeill, chief of staff of the Volunteers, was informed at the last moment and complied only because of a false rumor that the police were planning mass arrests to disable the whole organization. Old Tom Clarke, young Sean MacDermott, and Joseph Plunkett drew plans of key points circling Dublin to be held by the rebels. Cumann na mBann sent couriers by tram and bicycle to battalion leaders outside the city. Maud's former colleagues in Inghinidhe were involved: Helena Molony; Maire nic Shiubhlaigh; Dr. Kathleen Lynn; Mrs. ffrench-Mullen; Helen Laird; Nora Connolly; Grace Gifford, Joseph Plunkett's fiancée; Muriel Gifford, now Mrs. Thomas Mac-Donagh and the mother of his two children. Roger Casement was in a submarine escorting the German ship, the *Aud*, and its cargo of 20,000 rifles, ten machine guns and 4,000,000 rounds of ammunition, due to land at Tralee.

At Easter Maud took Seagan and Iseult to Les Mouettes. She was in Normandy when the insurrection began on April 24, Easter Monday. The military council carried out its plans despite serious setbacks. The *Aud*, intercepted by the British Navy, had been scuttled, and Casement was arrested on the coast near Tralee. Hearing the news, Eoin MacNeill counter-manded the call to the Volunteers, and only 1,100 men re-sponded out of a possible 16,000. With the 200 members of Connolly's Citizen Army, they marched in small contingents along the streets of a city deserted on a holiday morning; the usual crowds, including the English officers on patrol, were forty miles away at the annual Fairyhouse races. Meeting no resistance, the rebels swiftly occupied their assigned posts. John MacBride, although not in the military council, had been alerted by Sean MacDermott; MacBride was on his way home from a wedding when he saw Thomas MacDonagh entering Jacob's Biscuit Factory and joined them. Maire nic Shiubhlaigh was in the building when MacBride rallied the little band by his brave action. A marked man, the traitor leader of the Irish Brigade, he knew he faced certain execu-tion if caught, and he was unarmed.

At noon curious passers-by paused on Sackville Street. The Republican tricolor—green, white, and orange—flew against the blue sky over the General Post Office, and Padraic Pearse stood on the stone portico reading aloud the Proclama-tion of the Irish Republic: "Irishmen and Irishwomen: In the name of God and of the dead generations from which she receives her old tradition of nationhood, Ireland, through us, summons her children to her flag and strikes for her free-dom." Pearse's face was cold and pale. As he finished reading, "a few thin, perfunctory cheers" rose from the listeners on the wide avenue. A man in the watching crowd saw the fulfill-ment of years of dreams. Stephen MacKenna, Maud's friend from Paris, Synge's lighthearted companion, had been a war correspondent during the 1905 Revolution in Russia. Now, seeing the tricolor fly above his native city, armed men half-hidden by sandbags at the windows of the General Post Office, he turned to Austin Clarke, nationalist and poet, and said: "At last!"

Sean Connolly led the attempt to seize Dublin Castle. The first shots of Easter Monday were fired at the guards, killing one of them. Helena Molony saw her fiancé, dashing across the roof of City Hall for reinforcements, shot dead by a sniper from the Castle.

That afternoon 2,500 British troops were ordered into Dublin. The Republicans held their posts: Commandant MacDonagh in Jacob's Biscuit Factory with Major MacBride; Eamon de Valera in Boland's Bakery; Eamon Ceannt in the South Dublin Union; Edward Daly in the judicial buildings, the Four Courts. The Citizen Army, under Michael Mallin and Constance Markievicz in her slouch hat, was entrenched in Stephen's Green.

There were only a few skirmishes in the country at large, but Dublin was at war. In Galway, Lady Gregory heard wild stories: "terrible slaughter," the Castle captured, the Germans landing. By mid-week the British had 5,000 soldiers in the city and began shelling from the gunboat *Helga* on the Liffey and field guns at Trinity College. George Russell, returning from County Clare on April 25—the last fourteen miles on foot, for all transportation was paralyzed—saw "smoke and fire rising from ruined buildings in the city centre and gunfire resounding in the streets as British troops closed in on the strongpoints held by the hopelessly outnumbered soldiers of a stillborn Irish Republic."

For almost a week the first guerrilla fighters of urban warfare, outnumbered twenty to one by British troops, held Dublin. The English soldiers, trained for the trenches, were stymied by barricades, confused by an enemy in uniforms now more gray than green, and in the dust of rubble difficult to distinguish from civilians. Tragic killings, some by mistake, many vengeful, took place Easter week: Francis Sheehy-Skeffington, the pacifist husband of Maud's friend and colleague, was picked up by the British while trying to stop looting in the streets, and shot to death in the barracks with two other noncombatants. Incendiary shells set fire to tenements along the Liffey; Sackville Street, one of Europe's great thoroughfares with its majestic buildings of the eighteenth-century Ascendancy, was in flames. James Stephens watched the "red glare that crept to the sky, and stole over it and remained there glaring . . ." The General Post Office was burning. The death toll rose.

On April 29, knowing they faced imprisonment and death but wanting no more lives lost, Connolly and Pearse decided to surrender. The order went out to the entrenched battalions. Constance Markievicz gave up her revolver but refused to be taken away in a British Army car. "I will march at the head of my men," she said. Major MacBride helped the Cumann na mBann girls leave Jacob's Factory; he gave Maire nic Shiubhlaigh a message for his friends: "Tell them, too, that we had a good week of it." Michael Collins, a young IRB militant from Cork, was utterly realistic. And when released from prison he reorganized the Volunteers—the beginning of the Irish Republican Army. General Sir John Maxwell was placed in command of Dublin, the mopping up, the retribution that followed the wartime revolt.

"I can write, think of nothing but the tragic events in Ireland," Maud wrote John Quinn from Normandy on April 30. On the Western Front the battle of Verdun went on. Mourning for the dead in Dublin, Maud raged at the news, so sparse, so horrifying, that leaked through the censors. "The papers say my old friend James Connolly is killed, Pearse wounded and a prisoner with John MacBride. They were the men I esteem and like the best in Irish politics. Countess Markievicz also is arrested and she is my great friend. I feel so wretched and powerless. I doubt if I shall be able to get a passport to go to Ireland. I shall try to get one to London and from there try to get over."

Martial law was enforced throughout Ireland; 3,430 men and 79 women were brought into custody and imprisoned. Many who had no connection with the rebellion were slowly released; Griffith was in jail till Christmas. Courts-martial were held; 170 men and one woman were tried and sentenced; seventeen of the leaders were condemned to die. Constance Markievicz's death sentence was not carried out because she was a woman, and De Valera, an American citizen, was also spared. Each dawn of early May, signers of the Republican Proclamation were shot by British firing squads: Joseph Plunkett, who had married Grace Gifford in his prison cell; Connolly, so badly wounded he had to be strapped to a chair to face the death volley; MacBride, refusing the customary blindfold, for he had faced British fire before.

"Tragic dignity has returned to Ireland," Maud wrote to Yeats in London, reminding him of the nightmare vision that had come to her on the outbreak of the Great War: "Ruined houses about O'Connell Street and the wounded and dying . . ." Yeats grieved for her, not knowing, he wrote Lady Gregory, if she yet knew that her husband had been executed. He was sending Maud newspapers and hoping she would not try to leave France until the trials were over. The Easter Rising had moved him more deeply than he had thought he could be moved by any "public event," and he was "trying to write a poem on the men executed—'terrible beauty has been born again.' "

All was changed in Ireland. The insurrection had taken place without the support of the people, but England's harsh retaliation, the executions, and the ruin of the capital shocked the country. Public opinion began to swing toward the "Sinn Feiners." The martyrs of the failed, unpopular rebellion were, as martyrs must be, victorious in defeat.

On May 11, Maud wrote Quinn from Paris: "My dear friend, I have seen the English papers now and know the ghastly extent of the tragedy—" The French people around her were horrified, but the press was silent because of France's alliance with England. Americans must speak out for Ireland and condemn England's "latest crime against civilization and humanity," she told Quinn. "Most of my best friends have been executed in cold blood. You know many of them I think. MacDonagh, a great friend of Willie's . . . Pearse and Skeffington, Heuston and Plunkett. You must have met them all at Russell's—I spent so many pleasant evenings there with them all. Constance Markievicz was like a sister to me."

When her death sentence was commuted to life imprisonment the Countess wept, despising life while her comrades, including her beloved hero James Connolly, met death in the prison yard.

Helena Molony was in Kilmainham, the man she loved dead. Mrs. Pearse had lost two sons. Maud's friends were bereaved: Grace Plunkett, Muriel MacDonagh, Kathleen Clarke, Helen Ceannt, Hanna Sheehy-Skeffington—the widows of Erin.

"My husband is among those executed . . ." Maud wrote. "He has died for Ireland and his son will bear an honoured name. I remember nothing else."

But rumor was there as always to remind her of the past: "It is characteristic of the English to insult a fallen adversary —so the *Daily Mail,* Paris edition, announcing his execution, had an article full of lies which I had to contradict in the French papers. I could not bring myself to write in an English paper." She collected evidence disproving the story that Mac-Bride had joined MacDonagh as a lark on his way home from a wedding. For Seagan's sake she showed that the contemptuous Tim Healy was lying when he reported that MacBride's behavior was cowardly and opportunistic at his court-martial. She received a flat denial from Father Augustine, the Franciscan who had attended MacBride in his cell at Kilmainham. It was untrue that MacBride had refused to see him, Maud wrote. "He made a fine heroic end which had atoned for all — It was a death he had always desired—"

MacBride's death was the tragic irony. There was nothing to stop her from returning to Ireland with their young son, nothing but England's Defence of the Realm Act. As she had feared, the English refused to issue her a passport for re-entry. Perhaps, she thought, if she was employed as Irish correspondent for an American newspaper, the government would feel obliged to let her return. She asked Quinn to help her find work as a journalist, in a letter written from Passy in August, in which she also praised his efforts to save Sir Roger Casement from being executed. Conan Doyle, Nevinson, Shaw, Hearst in America, sympathetic South Americans and Africans who appreciated his work for the victims of colonization, Alice Stopford Green and her committee for Ireland—all their pleas for a reprieve were rejected by the Cabinet. On August 3, Casement, found guilty of treason, was hanged. "I only knew him slightly," wrote Maud, "and his death was a less terrible blow to me than the deaths of Pearse, MacDonagh, and Connolly who were dear old friends, but he was a brave and clever man and loved Ireland and his death is a national loss."

Her thoughts were with the dead and the meaning of their sacrifice. In her impatience to get back to Ireland to help rebuild, Maud decided to send Iseult, who as a French citizen was allowed to travel, to get Yeats's help in obtaining a passport. She also wanted him to find a lawyer for Helena Molony, who was still in prison. In the middle of the summer Iseult made the dangerous crossing. Excited by the adventure, she embroidered Maud's requests with romantic notions of her own. Her mother was very upset, she told Yeats, sleeping badly and very lonely.

Out of Maud's shadow, Iseult appeared to Yeats in a new light. Her emotional innocence and intellectual sophistication charmed him and impressed his friends. Lady Cunard wanted to know who she was: "Never in my life have I seen such a complexion." When Iseult went with Yeats to Stone Cottage, Ezra Pound thought her worthy of a troubadour's romance. His wife and Georgie Hyde-Lees found her enchanting, distinguished. "She is beautifully dressed though very plainly," Yeats wrote Lady Gregory. "I said, 'Why are you so pale?' And she said, 'Too much responsibility.' She makes me sad, for I think that if my life had been normal I might have had a daughter of her age. That means, I suppose, that I am beginning to get old." He had passed fifty.

He came back to Normandy with Iseult in August as Maud had wished, but her relief at their return, her daughter safe at home and her aging lover with her again at Les Mouettes, did not compensate for her disappointment that they had been unable to get her a passport.

# CHAPTER TWENTY-NINE

# Transformations

Was it needless death after all?
For England may keep faith
For all that is done and said.
We know their dream; enough
To know they dreamed and are dead:
And what if excess of love
Bewildered them till they died?
I write it out in a verse—
MacDonagh and MacBride
And Connolly and Pearse
Now and in time to be,
Wherever green is worn,
Are changed, changed utterly:
A terrible beauty is born.

Maud wore mourning for Ireland's loss, she told Willie, not for her own. MacBride's death was part of a larger sacrifice. That she was free to marry again meant nothing to her. It meant a great deal to Yeats, who had come to Les Mouettes to comfort her and to ask her again to be his wife.

This other man I had dreamed
A drunken, vainglorious lout.

He had done most bitter wrong
To some who are near my heart,
Yet I number him in the song;
He, too, has resigned his part
In the casual comedy;
He, too, has been changed in his turn,
Transformed utterly;
A terrible beauty is born. . . .

For the sake of the Abbey Theatre, dependent now on rich Unionists, and also admittedly seeking "a refuge from some weakness in myself," Yeats had promised Lady Gregory before he left for France not to marry Maud unless she "renounced all politics, including amnesty for political prisoners."

The poet, who worried about whether his own words had sent men out to be shot, and Maud, who gloried in being Cathleen ni Houlihan, walked together on the beach in Normandy. Her black veil fluttered over the collar of her heavy black wool coat. In her long dark garments she looked taller than ever, and somber. They traced and retraced their footsteps on the wet gray sand while Willie recited his poem to her:

Too long a sacrifice
Can make a stone of the heart.

He implored her "to forget the stone and its inner fire for the flashing, changing joy of life . . ." Maud found his mood hard to understand. For her, life and politics were one. "Easter 1916," with its terrifying refrain, showed her "the struggle of his mind."

Willie received a letter from Lady Gregory, a gentle echo of Maud's concern about his views. "I had been a little puzzled by your apparent indifference to Ireland after your excitement about the Rising. I believe there is a great deal you can do, all is unrest and is discontent, there is nowhere for the imagination to rest; but there must be some spiritual building possible just as after Parnell's fall, but perhaps more intense . . ."

How Maud envied his freedom to go back! Consumed with her desire to end her exile and bring Seagan up in Ireland, she was oblivious to the pain her rejection caused Willie and wondered vaguely why week after week he lingered at Les Mouettes. He wrote Sturge Moore, who designed covers for his books: "I am living in a house with three and thirty singing birds which for the most part have the doors of their cages open so that they alight on the table during meals and peck the fruit from the dishes."

Yeats was continuing his autobiography, working on the decade before the turn of the century, when Maud was at the peak of her acclaim and they were both in Ireland. She helped him recall the eventful years after Parnell's death when they had worked together in the nationalist movement and the Irish Literary Society. It was all still so vivid in her mind— the Jubilee riots when they marched side by side in the Dublin crowd, the committee meetings, the huge demonstrations of the '98 Centenary. He was sounding her memory.

"Willie Yeats is staying with us here," Maud wrote Quinn from Les Mouettes, "and my friend Madame de Ste. Croix. Willie and Iseult are both very interested in reading Péguy and Claudel, and Iseult is translating Péguy into English." Maud's daughter was twenty-one, the same age Yeats had been when he first heard of Mallarmé and Verlaine. While black Minnaloushe slept under the table, dreaming of free-flying wings, Iseult introduced him to French Catholic poetry. She read aloud from Francis Jammes a dialogue between a poet and a bird that made them all cry, "and a whole volume of Péguy's 'Mystère de la Charité de Jeanne d'Arc.' " Willie reconciled himself to Maud's insistence on returning to Ireland by imagining how the three of them might work together to "civilize Dublin Catholics" through the poetic influence of the French Catholic mystics. Dreaming of another Castle of the Heroes, he decided to give up Woburn Buildings and settle down in the country of his birth. But he could not tear himself away from Maud and her family, and in mid-August Ezra Pound was writing Quinn that Yeats was still in France, "feeding young rabbits with a spoon."

Yeats wrote to Lady Gregory, "I believe I was meant to

be the father of an unruly family. I did not think that I liked little boys but I liked Shawn. I am really managing Iseult very well. The other night she made a prolonged appeal for an extra cigarette. . . . I have stayed on much longer than I intended, but I think you will forgive me under the circumstances—as father, but as father only, I have been a great success."

> O you will take whatever's offered
> And dream that all the world's a friend.
> Suffer as your mother suffered,
> Be as broken in the end.
> But I am old and you are young,
> And I speak a barbarous tongue.

Maud paid no attention to Willie's infatuation for her daughter. She was sure the romance between age and youth would end as soon as they could leave for Ireland.

The days grew shorter, autumn gales blew from the sea, and still she had no news about her passport. She worried about her friends and comrades still in prison, fifteen hundred men and women held without trial. Griffith was in Reading Gaol while Sinn Fein, the movement he had started, became endowed in the public mind with the Republican spirit of the Easter martyrs. Delay and frustration drove her fury at England to the pitch of a personal vendetta. Even the fall of her beloved France would not be too great a price to pay for the defeat of the Empire. Yet in September she saw nothing to do but return with her family to Paris. Yeats accompanied them and left them at last with a promise to do everything possible to influence the War Office, Maud's last hope for release.

She moved into a much smaller apartment on an upper floor of 17 Rue de L'Annonciation. From now on she would live chiefly in Ireland, she wrote Quinn in a sanguine mood on October 8, and a pied à terre would be sufficient. "It is nearer heaven and has a roof terrace from which the sunset on the chimney tops of Paris looks wonderful." She enclosed a copy of "Easter 1916" in her letter to America. Yeats had asked her to forward it in the hope that French censors would be more lenient than the English. "I don't think he need fear either in the very least," wrote Maud, "as the poem is not worthy of Willie's genius, and still less of the subject. England and Ireland are too far apart for a writer to be able to keep one eye on one and the other on the other without a squint."

Winter set in, and still she had no word from London. Paris was dark and cold, and her cramped quarters made the delay more exasperating. In November her passport finally arrived. She had it signed and countersigned, bought tickets to Ireland for Iseult, Seagan, and herself; wrote Quinn to address his next letter to her in care of George Russell in Dublin.

The day before they were to leave, she received a message from the British Control Bureau—an order had been cabled by the War Office: Madame MacBride was permitted to live in England, but she would not be allowed to return to Ireland. Stunned, she argued to no avail; she would have gone to London to protest but Major Lampton at the Bureau in Paris warned her that once she was in England she might not be allowed to return to France. "Such is the liberty of the world we live in!" she wrote Quinn.

She wrote letters protesting the ruling, "this monstrous and stupid piece of tyranny . . ." Lloyd George, who would soon become Prime Minister, did not respond, and the Irish M.P.s were not cooperative. Tim Healy told her that John Redmond was the only person who could help if he would, and Redmond wrote that he would not. John Dillon said he would do his best. Stephen Gwynn, fighting at the front, wrote that he would try to help if she would support the Irish Party. Yeats, who had done his utmost, forwarded the most enraging information: the government would allow her to return to Ireland if she would take no part in politics.

Maud prepared to wait out the winter. "It is not gay!" she wrote Quinn. In the streets, the blind and the crippled shivered and begged; housewives huddled in queues for sugar and meat, until meat and sugar ran out. The sight of starving children, of women in rags heaving coal, reminded Maud of famine-stricken Donegal.

Just before Christmas she and her children came down

with *"la grippe"* in the cold apartment. In March, weak from a winter of illness, she wrote Quinn that however bad things were in Paris, they were worse in Ireland. Inflation and rationing to feed England's armies were bound to cause another famine, and as after every insurrection the prisons were full. Joseph MacBride, Eileen's gentle husband, had been held in solitary confinement in Wakefield after the Rising and then sent to Reading. According to reports smuggled out of prison, where no visitors were allowed, Joseph had been broken by his brother's execution and was very ill. Maud was told he had no coat and lay shivering in his cell, listening to the screams of fellow prisoners being kicked and lashed in the prison yard.

She could do nothing to help Joseph MacBride or the hundreds of men and women herded into British internment camps. She could only report what she knew to Quinn, in a country without censorship. He had praised an article of hers on the Easter Rising which was published in the *New York Sun* on July 16, 1916, and now as the Allies suffered defeat after defeat the Irish situation was crucial. The truth must be known, because England's repression was a prime stumbling block in Anglo-American relations. America's entry into the war was at stake. General Maxwell, who had had a pit dug at Arbour Hill Barracks to receive the bodies of 150 men he intended to execute along with the leaders, was removed from command. One of Lloyd George's first gestures on becoming Prime Minister in December 1916 was to grant a Christmas amnesty to some six hundred political prisoners. Among those who came back to a Dublin still under martial law was Michael Collins, who had been organizing his fellow prisoners in Frongoch, Wales. Arthur Griffith resumed publishing his newspaper, now called *Nationality*. But all Maud's requests to return were ignored.

The English were using against the Irish the cat-and-mouse tactics they had used against the suffragists. In the spring of 1917 Sinn Fein, beginning to show its political strength, was repressed in a new wave of coercive acts. Released prisoners were rearrested, and at the same time Lloyd George made another move to win Irish and American approval. A Home Rule Bill giving Ulster the choice of exclusion was proposed. Redmond turned it down. "If he had walked out of the House of Commons years ago it would have been better . . ." Maud wrote Quinn. In April 1917, when America declared war on Germany, her feelings were ambivalent. The slaughter would be prolonged and England would be the victor, but France would be saved, and, like many of the Irish, she read President Wilson's statements about democracy and the rights of small nations to mean that Ireland would have a powerful guardian at the peace table.

At Easter Maud went alone to plant her war garden at Les Mouettes. As she dug the rows for beans and potatoes in the dark wet earth, she grieved for the thousands dead and the thousands still to die, the soldiers in the trenches, the civilians murdered and bereaved, the children lost and starving, all for no cause. Alone on the beach at Colleville, she mourned the Easter martyrs who had given their lives for freedom.

When she returned to Paris, the mail brought a copy of *Vanity Fair* from Quinn, with his review of *A Portrait of the Artist as a Young Man.* Quinn's praise of Joyce seemed to her unmerited. "While he has portrayed himself with curious frankness and probably photographic accuracy, he has failed I think in drawing vividly any of the other characters . . ." Although she knew many of them, she could not recognize them in "the nonentities presented by Joyce," and missed the heroic type of young Irishman like Pearse or MacDonagh.

The days of Joyce's youth, when men and women wept and argued about Parnell's fall, were far removed from the turbulent summer of 1917 in Dublin. Threats of partition and conscription caused many protests, and there were large demonstrations for the release of all political prisoners, De Valera with his fellow republicans still at Lewes in England and Constance Markievicz still alone among English criminals in the women's prison, Aylesbury. Cumann na mBann had elected her president in absentia, and De Valera had been nominated Sinn Fein candidate for the East Clare by-election. In June their life sentences were rescinded. On the seventeenth, cheering multitudes welcomed Constance back to Dublin, as a great procession carrying the republican tricolor and thousands of red flags escorted her from Kingston to Liberty Hall. Helena Molony, released from prison earlier, went with Constance to electioneer for Sinn Fein. Maud's friends were active again in Dublin and in America, where Hanna Sheehy-Skeffington had gone to lecture.

In July Maud was writing Quinn from Les Mouettes: "So here we are, Iseult, Seagan and I, again spending our holidays by the sea shore in Normandy." In the third summer of the war, food supplies were so scarce they were living entirely off the garden she had planted at Easter, beans and potatoes, "and the torpedoed fish and washed up treasures the sea brings us—coal, wood, etc." Lying sleepless at night, Maud heard the big naval guns pounding in the Channel and felt the house shake. "I don't know what anyone is fighting for," she wrote Quinn.

> Why go on wasting all those lives and piling up evil, when conversation and Peace Congress could settle everything. The famine and the Socialist movement that will follow peace inevitably will make all re-turn of war impossible for several generations. I think that is what all the governments are really afraid to face, but face it they will have to before long as even the soldiers are all sick of the butcher-ing and even America will not be able to galvanize them for a long continuance of this Hell before they turn. But you I believe, still see beauty in war; I did once, but hospitals and broken hearts and devasta-tion and destruction of all art and beauty have changed me and I bow to any peace advocate—

Yeats came back to Normandy in August. Maud decided that when he left they would all go back with him to London, where she would fight in person for permission to live in Ireland. Yeats had also come to a decision. He would overlook the difference in their ages, forget the melancholia he saw in her horoscope, and ask Iseult to marry him. Surprisingly, Lady Gregory was backing his suit; she thought Iseult would keep him close to Ireland. Maud raised no objection, but her daughter's response was vague. "Iseult and I are on our old intimate terms," Yeats wrote Lady Gregory, "but I don't think she will accept. She 'has not the impulse.'"

Iseult kept him uncertain, and in September, when they all returned to Paris, nothing was resolved. Maud was annoyed with Willie for suggesting that London would be a better place than Dublin for Iseult to live, but she was too preoccupied to be either jealous or amused at her old lover's proposal to Iseult. Excited about crossing the Channel, apprehensive over the problems of legal permission, impatient to get Seagan in school in Ireland for the fall term, she was busy closing up her Passy apartment. Yeats wrote Lady Gregory that Maud was "in a joyous and self forgetting condition of political hate the like of which I have not yet encountered."

Before they left Paris, Willie delivered his ultimatum: if Iseult would not accept him, he would marry Georgie Hyde-Lees. Iseult turned him down. At Le Havre, she wept. She was ashamed, as Willie wrote Lady Gregory, " 'at being so selfish' 'in not wanting me to marry and so break her friendship with me.' " He promised her his friendship; he had always felt like a father to her and always would. Iseult cried all the way across the Channel.

At Southampton they met all the difficulties Maud had anticipated. She and Iseult were served with a notice under the Defence of the Realm Act forbidding them to proceed to Ireland, and they were told they would not be allowed to go back to Paris. The train was held up while they were searched as possible spies by shamefaced policemen. Maud was furious. Seagan was delighted with all the excitement. England, which he was seeing for the first time in thirteen years, had turned out to be just what he expected, filled with fog and great engines and secret service men. Willie, exhausted, was full of foreboding for himself and his little band of returned exiles.

"Yeats is back from Paris," Ezra Pound wrote John Quinn from London, "bringing Maud Gonne, 10 canary birds, 1 parrot, 1 monkey, 1 cat, two members of M.G.'s family and the hope that she will lead a tranquil life."

Now that she was able to fight for her rights in person, Maud could be more patient. She told Willie, who had expected her to "do something wild," that she would take a flat in Chelsea for six months and study design at a London art school." He found a job for Iseult as assistant librarian at the School of Oriental Languages. Ezra Pound would tutor Seagan. When all this was arranged, Yeats burst into tears of relief.

On October 17 Yeats married Georgie Hyde-Lees. There was much curiosity about Maud's reaction. Arthur Symons sent Quinn an extravagant report: "Wish you had heard Maud laugh at Yeats's marriage—a good woman of 25—rich of course—who has to look after him; she might either become his slave or run away from him after a certain length of time!" Lily Yeats wrote that both Lady Gregory and Maud seemed pleased. "And why shouldn't they be? They have both, so to speak, had their 'whack'—the latter a very considerable 'whack' of her own choosing, but she will live forever in Willie's verse . . ."

Maud would always have his devotion, and his marriage put an end to his troublesome wooing of her and of Iseult. Her daughter was still hers. To everyone's surprise, Willie's most of all, Iseult and Georgie became great friends. Close in years, they had similar interests—astrology, Sanskrit, and clothes. Iseult spent Christmas with the newlyweds at Stone Cottage. Yeats continued to feel responsible for Maud's illegitimate daughter, half-waif, half-woman. Although he was "extremely happy" in his marriage to George, as he called his wife, he felt at first that he might have "betrayed three people."

Later that winter, when Yeats took George to oversee the restoration of the old Norman tower he had bought near Coole, Maud and her children moved from Chelsea, into his lodgings at Woburn Buildings. Minnaloushe could sleep on his velvet sofa, the dogs guard the landing, and the birds fly about Willie's twilit study, while Iseult worked at the School of Oriental Studies and Seagan studied with Pound. Maud did some painting and was pleased to see her daughter enjoy the company of London artists and intellectuals. For them she became an object of adoration, as Florence Farr had been. The prodigal actress who had charmed so many a generation earlier had died in April in Ceylon, where she had gone in 1913, knowing she was incurably ill, to be principal of a girls' college. Symons found Iseult "strangely exotic," took her out every week to some bohemian gathering, and dedicated his collection of essays, *Colour Studies in Paris*, to "the adorable Iseult Gonne." Pound was infatuated, and there were rumors of a liaison between Iseult and the scintillating red-bearded egotist.

Maud found a few distractions in wartime London— some old friends and relatives, the theaters and galleries that carried on through air raids and blackouts. She went with Symons and Iseult to see Augustus John's exhibit and, not caring for his portraits of society ladies, as she wrote Quinn, preferred "some most beautiful little pictures of John's wife, Dorelia, in the cornfields or in the mountains . . . Now John has gone to the front in khaki uniform to paint soldiers." She had attended a small dinner party on the eve of his departure. "Five people and five hours! Much reading aloud of Baudelaire and Verlaine." Symons described Maud, "majestic, speaking rarely, seeing always visions; still with some of her strange beauty; saying, 'I am old . . . old. My heart is for Ireland and my love for France.' "

She wrote Quinn about her feeling for the two countries, "France for what she *has* been, Ireland for what she *will* be." Her benefactor in America had been campaigning for Home Rule among powerful politicians and diplomats in Washington; Theodore Roosevelt and William Howard Taft offered statements in favor of it, and Quinn led a deputation of prominent Irish-Americans to urge the case on Arthur Balfour, now Foreign Secretary, who was visiting the capital. Lloyd George, continuing the long rule of repression and appeasement, had set up a convention to solve the Irish problem, while hundreds of nationalists were arrested, released, and jailed again. Maud complained that Quinn did not realize the full infamy of the English: "A good part of my early youth was spent fighting Balfour's regime," she wrote, thinking of "the thousands and thousands of Irish tenants evicted under his administration. . . . All that can be said for the regime is that Maxwell's was worse and Mahon's is as bad." Maud could not convince Quinn, who was working so hard for peaceable solutions, that Home Rule would no longer satisfy the swiftly growing and changing movement for Irish nationhood. By October 1917 membership in Sinn Fein had reached a quarter of a million in twelve hundred branches throughout the country. Eamon de Valera, with Arthur Griffith's approval, was elected president and at the same time became president of the Volunteers. As M.P. from East Clare, he demanded sovereign independence. Outside Mountjoy, where Thomas Ashe, chief of the IRB's Supreme Council since the Rising, was on hunger strike, De Valera had quoted one of President Woodrow Wilson's Fourteen Points: "That no people shall be forced to live under a sovereignty under which it does not desire to live." The mass movement De Valera led was now giving at least lip service to secession.

Maud was not resigned to being banned from participation. In her black dress and veil she haunted the War Office asking for her right to be in Ireland. She attended meetings of the Women's Social and Political Union, the radical splinter group of militant suffragists, and at the Women's Freedom League she met Mrs. Charlotte Despard. In barefoot sandals and black dress, with a lace mantilla pinned to her graying topknot, the eccentric patrician sister of Lord French, Field Marshal General at the battle of Ypres, looked as unusual as she was. For many years she had worked for suffrage and women's rights. Her socialism was a source of great embarrassment to her brother, and she was considered a dangerous influence by the upper class she had deserted. Vera Ryder, the great-granddaughter of Sir Francis Cook—Maud's Great-uncle Frank of Doughty House—was dragged away swiftly by her nurse when Mrs. Despard happened to pass by in her voluminous black skirts. "Really most attractive, for a witch," thought the overprotected little girl. "But nannie thought otherwise . . ."

Lord French's sister was small, handsome, and inclined to be pugnacious. A distant forebear of her husband's, a Colonel Despard, had been a Republican, hanged for his part in a conspiracy to blow up George III in 1802, when Robert Emmet was planning his ill-fated rising in Ireland. Charlotte Despard could not claim that violent inheritance, but she was a confirmed Irish separatist. Her zeal for human rights matched Maud's, and her energy too, although she was ten years older. They could rejoice together on December 7, 1917, when the Representation of the People Bill, which enfranchised six million women, passed the House of Commons. The irrepressible, outspoken socialist helped restore Maud's spirits, and she was ready to "do something wild." "My dear Mr. Quinn," she wrote, "I am still held up in London, and longing to be among all my friends in God's own country, Ireland."

By February 1918 she was. The *Irish Nation* reported her presence at a Sinn Fein meeting expressing sympathy to the Bolsheviks in the Lord Mayor's Hall on Dawson Street: "Two new forces made their appearance on the platform at the Mansion House on Monday night week. Mrs. Maud Gonne MacBride may not be responsible for the Bolshevik incursion, and the Bolshevik ideal may not be responsible for Mrs. Mac-Bride's return to Ireland, but the advent of either or both is —to say the least—significant."

Maud had made her getaway from London in disguise. With rags stuffed under her black skirt, a shawl over her head, and carrying two shabby valises tied up with string, she escaped notice by the police as she climbed the gangplank with the other passengers boarding at Holyhead. A young British soldier inadvertently helped her by calling out from the rail above, "Here comes Mother," and making space for her baggage on deck. The plainclothesmen paid no attention. She was just another poor old Irishwoman hunched over her rosary, but her heart never stopped pounding. "The harder part was yet to come, for the authorities in Dublin would be watching the ports . . ." But "indeed, I might not have worried so much, because I was so well disguised that my friends were unable to recognize me."

Maud was welcomed quietly behind closed doors, where she was reunited with her old friends and comrades. She was recognized then, although at fifty-one she looked older than her years. Her tall figure was gaunt; her face, translucent to the bone, radiated an enduring strength. Her long black widow's weeds added mystery. But she was still Maud Gonne.

> There is gray in your hair.
> Young men no longer suddenly catch their breath
> When you are passing;

But maybe some old gaffer mutters a blessing
Because it was your prayer
Recovered him upon the bed of death.

For the first time she began to call herself Mrs. MacBride instead of Maud Gonne, and she was criticized for using the name of her husband now that he was among the honored dead. She ignored the accusations of hypocrisy as she ignored suspicions that Iseult was not her adopted niece. It was important for Seagan that she have his father's name in Ireland. The boy had come over from London to be with her in a city transformed from the bustling peacetime Dublin she had known—fire-gutted buildings, rubbled streets patrolled by British soldiers and cruising police cars.

She rented a house at 73 St. Stephen's Green and began to pick up the pieces of a life she had left thirteen years before —her work for school meals, amnesty for prisoners, relief for their dependents and the families of men on the run. She did what she could to help the children of the dead. Once more she was active in Sinn Fein. Griffith had stepped down for the time being, and Maud was no longer participating in top-level decisions, but she was campaigning for the major party in Ireland. The Parliamentary Party was dead and John Redmond a disillusioned, broken-hearted man, sick and dying.

When Maud shared the podium at the Mansion House with Socialists who praised the new constitution of the Bolsheviks, she spoke not as one of them but as a nationalist, sympathizing with their humanistic goals, what James Joyce referred to obliquely as "the generous idea." Although her friend Charlotte Despard's theories were contagious, Maud was more interested in the success of a people's revolution. Approval of the Bolshevik state was not Sinn Fein's official policy, but many who were far from being revolutionaries— liberals, trade unionists, Fabians—supported the overthrow of the Czar's despotic regime. AE, the dreamer who could also be practical, believed bolshevism would usher in an international era of agricultural cooperatives. Only a few, Sean O'Casey among them, saw a class struggle in Ireland. James Connolly, the sincere Marxist, had recognized this and put the nationalist cause first. Lenin had defended Connolly but regretted his timing: "The misfortune of the Irish is that they have risen prematurely, when the European revolt of the proletariat has *not yet* matured." Now the bravest man Maud had ever known was dead; Connolly, who had the vision to unite the forces of class and national revolution, was lost, and Ireland's fight for freedom continued to be led by many leaders not often united, except against England.

The meeting halls and small committee rooms Maud frequented were under police surveillance, but for the moment the British authorities kept hands off. They had far graver problems. In the spring of 1918 Ludendorff's massive offensive pushed the Allies back to within forty miles of Paris and cost the British forces such losses that despite warnings from America—and in the face of open rebellion—the Conscription Act for Ireland was passed in April. Lloyd George had promised to give the Irish Home Rule first, and Home Rule was still a dead statute. The Irish closed ranks, resolved to resist; even the Catholic hierarchy opposed conscription. Ireland had given enough men for England's war.

Lady Gregory's only son had been killed in action, his plane shot down, in January. That spring Maud went to Coole to offer her condolences. While she was in Galway she visited Yeats and George at Ballylee, their "Castle" by a stream in the rolling meadows. Soon afterwards, Yeats, anticipating fatherhood, wrote a friend in London that he felt he could not "encourage men to risks I am not prepared to share or approve. If the Government go on with conscription there may be soon dangerous outbreaks . . . the old historical passion is at its greatest intensity."

In its drive to repress disaffection and enforce conscription, the government appointed Lord French the new Lord Lieutenant and Governor General of Ireland. On flimsy evidence Dublin Castle constructed a "German plot" which gave them a pretext for wholesale arrests that could be justified to America. While Yeats was writing of dangerous outbreaks, Maud was arrested, picked up as she was leaving AE's house one evening with Joseph King, M.P. She was one of seventy-three men and women rounded up on the night of May 17 by order of Lord French and deported to England. Nearly all the leaders of Sinn Fein and the Volunteers were imprisoned "for an indefinite time" without charge or trial.

Maud was held in Holloway, where many English-women had spent long terms for the right to vote. Constance Markievicz and Tom Clarke's widow, Kathleen, were her cellmates. A whole landing was cleared and heavily guarded for the "three wild Irishwomen." Although they were only internees, they were treated as ordinary prisoners, locked up for twelve hours every night in total darkness, only one hour's exercise at noon in the yard. At last Maud experienced the confinement and the humiliation of prison life, the suffering she had felt for others through long years of work for prisoners. The worst anguish was her isolation. Her last sight of Seagan had been of him running after the Black Maria that carried her away, and she was racked with anxiety about her headstrong young son. She was not allowed to draw a check to send him any money, and she had no news of him. She and her two cellmates chose not to receive any visitors, because, as Constance explained in a letter to her sister Eva, "They want us to promise not to talk about politics. Today life *is* politics. Finance, economics, education, even the ever-popular (in England) subject of divorce is mixed up with politics today." On principle Maud agreed with Constance, and the three women spent their time discussing politics with one another. They had no books—not even St. Augustine's *Confessions,* which Maud had requested—no news to ease their concern about what was happening to families and friends.

Constance, a hardened convict with a prison term behind her, knew enough to pay for meals from outside, which was a privilege of internees, but Maud and Kathleen, insisting that the government had the duty to feed them, sickened on the prison diet. Maud's nights were an agony of sleeplessness, and her cough kept her cellmates awake. Kathleen Clarke had not been well since the shock of her husband's execution. Eventually all three were transferred to the hospital wing and allowed some books, paper and pen, gifts of food and cigarettes. Maud was permitted to have her pet canary, but nothing eased her claustrophobia, and unlike Constance, who painted forty watercolors and scrubbed floors with equanimity, she could not concentrate on any work or pastime. When mail was at last allowed, Maud learned of Lucien Millevoye's death in Paris. His son, Henri, had been killed at the front in 1914. Lucien had been dismissed from her life for eighteen years, but the news of his death brought memories of betrayals and lost hopes.

"All she'd do was talk to her canary . . ." said Kathleen Clarke. "She was like a caged wild animal herself, like a tigress prowling endlessly up and down. We were given the chance to apply to the Sankey Commission for release, and in her misery, she said she would—said she'd point out she hadn't been in Ireland during the war. Con said: 'If you do that, you need never come back to Ireland,' and she tore the application up."

Maud had been in prison three months when Hanna Sheehy-Skeffington was arrested upon her return from America, where she had interviewed President Wilson for the *Irish World* and lectured for Irish freedom and women's rights. Hanna was put in their cell at Holloway—four "wild" women cooped up together—and Maud saw how prison could be a school for rebels. The plucky suffragist immediately went on hunger strike and won a release after a few weeks. Maud did not feel physically strong enough to follow Hanna's example. Her heavy cough and her loss of weight alarmed her cellmates, and Republican women's organizations began to agitate on her behalf.

In October Maud was informed that Kathleen had died in the sanitarium at Davos. She fell into a deep depression. Iseult was in despair about her mother's health. Yeats feared the worst and wrote "On a Political Prisoner," telling his wife in his anxiety that he was writing a poem "on Con to avoid writing one on Maud. They are all in prison . . ."

> She that but little patience knew,
> From childhood on, had now so much
> A grey gull lost its fear and flew
> Down to her cell and there alit,
> And there endured her finger's touch
> And from her fingers ate its bit.
>
> Did she in touching that lone wing
> Recall the years before her mind

Became a bitter, an abstract thing,
Her thought some popular enmity:
Blind and leader of the blind
Drinking the foul ditch where they lie?

Yeats asked Lady Cunard and others to apply pressure in England. In late October Maud was finally permitted to have a medical examination by a Harley Street specialist, who reported "a recrudescence of her former pulmonary tuberculosis" and recommended "active medical and open air treatment in a suitable climate without delay." Pound sent the doctor's report to Quinn, who cabled Colonel Sir Campbell Stuart, assistant to the influential newspaper tycoon Lord Northcliffe, that Maud Gonne's "death or serious illness while detained in English prison . . . would produce worst possible effect this country." A similar message went to T. P. O'Connor, M.P. On November 7 Quinn received a cable from O'Connor that Maud had been released. He wrote Iseult at once that he hoped Maud would go "to a high and dry mountain climate like the Pyrenees or Switzerland" and that "as an old friend" he would be glad to help with expenses. "The climate of Ireland is bad, not to be thought of for her at the time being."

After five and a half months Maud was released from Holloway and sent to a London nursing home. She refused to stay there, and five days later was at Woburn Buildings, "worn to a 'skeleton' and ill," but overjoyed to be reunited with Iseult and with Seagan, who was back in London.

While Maud was in prison Seagan had been in school at Mount St. Benedict in Gorey, County Wexford, and spent holidays in Galway with Willie and George. Yeats had grown very fond of the "gentle solitary boy." Pound, on the other hand, saw in Maud's son the worst of Irish "monomania." He wrote Quinn that the months in Ireland had ruined the mind of the fourteen-year-old, and left him, as might be expected at his age, doomed to political futility. "He is a walking give-away of the real state of feeling there. . . . talking of arrest as necessary to his career." Like mother, like son—Maud laughed at Quinn's orders that she not go back to Ireland and its "unsuitable" climate. She had been initiated into prison life and had no desire to endure it again, but she was as determined as ever to get back to her poor unhealthy country.

Maud was still in London when the Armistice was signed. The sound of jubilation rang bitterly in her ears. Men had died by the thousands, and there was no real peace in the world—only more death, more hunger, more prisoners. She was pleased to see youngsters stripping the King's poster from Nelson's column in Trafalgar Square and argued with Pound that the crowds cheering in front of Buckingham Palace were flunkies. In Dublin the Armistice called forth the same screaming sirens, pealing church bells, wild crowds. The streets were lined with the red, blue, and white of Union Jacks. Women whose husbands had served in the British forces led demonstrations against Sinn Fein headquarters. Forty-nine thousand Irish citizens and thousands more Irishmen from America and Australia had died in the war. After the peace celebrations, Maud wondered what hope the Peace Conference would hold for Ireland. A year ago she had asked Quinn, "When Wilson in his pronouncement for small nationalities mentioned Poland, why did he not mention Ireland too by name?"

Lloyd George, seeking reelection in December for his coalition government, refused to put the Home Rule Act into effect without Partition; he could "support no settlement which would involve forcible coercion of Ulster." Sinn Fein, the party of secession, was proving its strength in one by-election after another. Arthur Griffith, while still a prisoner in the summer of 1917, had defeated his Parliamentary Party opponent in East Cavan by over a thousand votes. Now women over thirty had the ballot, and their votes combined with labor's to assure victory for Sinn Fein, although more than a hundred of its leaders were in prison. The country was under military rule—87,500 troops were stationed in Ireland as the election campaign began.

At the end of November, Maud learned that passport requirements for Ireland had been lifted and immediately made plans to return, although her detention under the Defence of the Realm Act was unchanged, and according to Pound she was "somewhat scared at the risk she was about to take . . ." This time Iseult and Seagan accompanied her, and she had no difficulty passing herself off as an emaciated Red Cross nurse.

"Maud, as you probably know," Pound wrote to Quinn on December 2, "did a bunk to Ireland nine days ago." He had heard from Iseult that she herself "fixed it up with the Lord Mayor . . . Maud is to be left in peace."

Her troubles began in front of her house on Stephen's Green. While she was in Holloway she had rented it to Yeats so that he and George would have a place to stay in the city, which was overcrowded with British military personnel. Early on the cold November morning of her arrival, she knocked at the door of Number 73, assuming her prerogative as old friend and landlord. George was asleep, convalescing from pneumonia, and Willie was taking no chances with the safety of a young wife seven months pregnant. Maud's presence could bring on police raids that would endanger George's health and his unborn child. Furious at Maud for disobeying everybody, he refused to let her in. Hurt and indignant, she left. Angry accusations followed: he was an unpatriotic coward—she had a "pure and disinterested love of mischief." Their friends took sides. Iseult told Pound they were "equally to blame and both in need of keepers."

The row could not remain private and was soon taken up as a political cause. Cumann na mBann charged Yeats with conspiring with the Chief Secretary, Mr. Shortt, to keep Maud shut up in the London nursing home so that he could stay on in her house. Mr. Shortt showed no interest in the case, and Maud went out to the Wicklow Mountains, the most peaceful place she could think of, to try to forget the whole ugly episode. She spent a fortnight with Ella Young near Glenmalure, where a small colony of artists had settled—the poets Austin Clarke and Joseph and Nancy Campbell.

By Christmas Yeats had found other quarters. Maud moved into her own house. The row was forgotten, yet there was more than a subtle shift in their relations. At one time he would have defended her political activity: he had quoted the son of Speranza to Lady Gregory: "Someone said, 'A woman after twenty years of public life is a ruin.' Oscar Wilde said, 'And a woman after twenty years of domestic life is a public building.' " Now he rebuked Maud and all militant women. "It's certain that fine women eat/A crazy salad with their meat," he wrote when his daughter, Ann, was born in February 1919.

> May she be granted beauty and yet not
> Beauty to make a stranger's eye distraught . . .
>
> An intellectual hatred is the worst,
> So let her think opinions are accursed.
> Have I not seen the loveliest woman born
> Out of the mouth of Plenty's horn,
> Because of her opinionated mind
> Barter that horn and every good
> By quiet natures understood
> For an old bellows full of angry wind?

After thirty years, Maud and Willie knew a great deal about each other, took much for granted, and understood each other less. In her singularly graceful manner Maud kept Yeats as her friend, but their passionate friendship was ended.

# CHAPTER THIRTY

# The Terrible Necessity

It is possible to believe that they too, while recognizing the inevitability of violence, nevertheless admitted to themselves that it is unjustifiable. Necessary and inexcusable . . . Mediocre minds, confronted with this terrible problem, can take refuge by ignoring one of the terms of the dilemma. They are content, in the name of formal principles, to find all direct violence inexcusable and then to sanction that diffuse form of violence which takes place on the scale of world history. Or they will console themselves in the name of history, with the thought that violence is necessary, and will add murder to murder, to the point of making of history nothing but a continuous violation of everything in man which protests against injustice.

In Ireland at last; Madame Gonne MacBride, the polite form of address, honoring years of work, was hers, and she was living with her children and her pets in her own house on Stephen's Green in the heart of Dublin. Seagan was attending the National University. Iseult was often at home from her studies in London. To the embarrassment of her brother, Lord French, head of government in Ireland, Charlotte was staying with Maud. Josephine, the cook from Paris, ran the kitchen with her rough *patois* and flair for *haute cuisine;* 73 Stephen's Green became a Republican meeting place, and once again Maud had a salon—conversation Irish, family life European, and the gracious hospitality especially hers.

Maud's guests, new friends and old, were greeted at the painted Georgian doorway by the housemaid, Kathleen Kearney. Her son, Brendan Behan, often heard his mother tell how the great poet Yeats himself would pause to chat with her when he came for tea, always a little early, to see Madame MacBride and eat the cakes before the other guests arrived.

"It was at one of Madame's At Homes that I was first introduced to Yeats," wrote Cecil Salkeld.

> There then was certainly no constraint between them. She received Yeats with the gay good-humor characteristic of her. I fancy the place she occupied in his verse had placed them both beyond possibility of any prolonged quarrel. Behind his aloofness I was soon to discover one of the most touching traits in his character: his instant recollection of, and unfailing courtesy to, anyone who was a friend or protégé, or even a dependent of Madame Gonne MacBride . . . I have often heard distinguished men and women regret Dr. Yeats's "short-sightedness," or "forgetfulness," when they found themselves unrecognized in the street. Yet an ailing old servant or a penniless art-student (as I was at the time), were never passed by without a greeting or a kind inquiry—if they were friends of Madame Gonne MacBride.

Pity for all she had gone through tempered Willie's disapproval, and now it was he who tried to mend a rift with Quinn. He wrote the lawyer, who was still furious at Maud's refusal to go to a sanitarium: "Pound must have been mistaken about her laughter—I imagine all she meant was that it was incredible to her that Ireland should be bad for the health. She looks ghastly. I heard a young English officer speak of her the other day as a tragic sight."

She still had the walk of a queen. What a sense of *déjà vu* she evoked when she entered the Abbey Theatre the evening of March 19 to see a production of *Cathleen ni Houlihan*. Her part was being played by Lady Gregory, substituting at the last minute for Maire nic Shiubhlaigh. Maud sat in the audience with Iseult, Mrs. James Stephens, and Alice Stopford Green. Listening to lines she had made her own, she heard the audience applaud: "They are gathering to meet me now."

The Abbey had had its financial difficulties during the war, but it had kept its popular repertory, and *Cathleen ni Houlihan* always drew crowds. After the performance Yeats said coldly to Lady Gregory, for it was always hard for him to see anyone but Maud as Cathleen: "Very nice, but if I had rehearsed you it would have been much better." It sounded like old times, yet Willie's lock, falling over his forehead like a boy's, was silvered, Augusta Gregory needed no wig to look like an old woman, and the coils of hair Maud wore at either side of her face were gray.

Dressed in black, tall, fragile, always in motion, she still drew attention. People in the street would stop to stare as they had when she was young. On her way to Sinn Fein headquarters she would cross Stephen's Green, where three years ago, entrenched behind the barricaded gates with her Fianna troops, Constance Markievicz had shot down a British soldier. Under the peaceful trees hungry urchins stole bread from the ducks on the Black Pond as always. Along the river the sky showed through gaps in buildings left unrepaired since the shelling in 1916. "We are reeling back into the middle ages without growing more picturesque," wrote Yeats.

Maud saw it in a different light. The ragged, bony children would be clothed and fed, the ruined walls rebuilt. Despite martial law, censorship, imprisonment, the Sinn Fein Party had won the parliamentary elections in December 1918. Of the seventy-three Republican candidates, only twenty-six had been at liberty to campaign. Constance Markievicz was still in Holloway when she was put up for Dublin's St. Patrick's Division. Mrs. Despard, the suffrage candidate in North Battersea, was defeated, as were the seventeen other women candidates in England, and Madame Markievicz was the first woman ever elected to Westminster. Even if she had been free, she would have refused, along with the other victorious Republicans, to take her seat. The people, by a majority of 70 percent, had given Sinn Fein's program for a separate government a sweeping mandate.

Maud went to work for Sinn Fein's Press Bureau, headed by Robert Brennan and later by Erskine Childers and Desmond Fitzgerald. " 'The people have voted for Sinn Fein,' said Father Michael O'Flanagan. 'What we have to do now is to explain to them what Sinn Fein is.' "

For Maud there was no ambiguity about the meaning of the victory. The path of Cathleen ni Houlihan had led inevitably to the moment on January 21, 1919, when she sat in the Mansion House among the jammed spectators in the Round Room, while the throngs overflowed into Dawson Street; the first Meeting of Dail Eireann, the Assembly of Ireland.

"No day that ever dawned in Ireland had been waited for, worked for, suffered for like that January Tuesday . . . Never was the past so near, or the present so brave, or the future so full of hope . . . there was no going back," wrote Maire Comerford, who sat in the audience with the Wexford contingent of Cumann na mBann. Cathal Brugha, standing in for De Valera, read the Declaration of Independence in Irish and English. When the roll was called, *"Faoi Glas ag Gallamh"*—"Imprisoned by the foreign enemy"—was given in response to thirty-six names, including Griffith's and De Valera's. Only thirty-seven elected representatives were present. They voted for an all-Ireland republic in which "all right to private property must be subordinated to the public right and welfare." It affirmed the right and duty of women to serve the Commonwealth. The unresolved problem of the northern counties would be presented to the Peace Conference at Versailles. Griffith, De Valera, and Count Plunkett were elected delegates to the conference from the newborn, unrecognized Republic.

Their envoy to Paris, Sean T. O'Kelly, knocked at many doors to secure admission for the Irish delegates, sent letters to the European newspapers, wrote Clemenceau that Ireland's case must be heard. He could not breach the wall of silence. The Peace Conference would deal with the minorities of defeated powers only.

That Clemenceau did not respond was no surprise to Maud. Her old enemy was now in thrall to England. The question of Ireland's fate at the peace table rested with President Wilson, who still spoke of making the world safe for democracy, and in America the Irish Republic's "Ambassador," Patrick McCartan, was making headway. The Clan supported an Irish Race Convention organized by Joseph McGarrity; five thousand delegates from Irish-American groups met in Philadelphia in February. The House of Representatives passed a resolution, 261 to 41, urging the Peace Conference to consider favorably Ireland's claim to self-determination. The Irish lobby put strong pressure on President Wilson in Washington and in Paris. The French *poilus* did not forget the Irishmen who had fought and died on every battlefield of the Great War. Socialists and Syndicalists supported the provisional republic. The Second International, meeting at Amsterdam, recommended unanimously that the Peace Conference "make good this rightful claim of the Irish people." But popular feeling, that best hope of propagandists which had counted in the world Maud worked in before the war, was no longer so potent. International power politics dominated the peace. President Wilson, fighting for his League of Nations, would not risk alienating England. Lloyd George maintained that the Irish problem was an internal affair of the British government. And so it remained.

Dail Eireann held sessions throughout the summer of 1919: Constance Markievicz and Robert C. Barton, Erskine Childers's cousin, from the Anglo-Irish landed gentry; Count Plunkett from the Catholic aristocracy; and Joseph MacBride, Maud's brother-in-law from West Mayo, white-haired after his prison ordeal, representing the old Fenian tradition. The Irish Labour Party had thrown its support to Sinn Fein and had no representation; most of its strength was in Unionist Ulster. Constance Markievicz, Connolly's former aide, was appointed Minister of Labour; but otherwise, in spite of the tremendous contribution made by Cumann na mBann, women were absent from the Irish Parliament.

The Dail filled and emptied as deputies were released

from jail only to be arrested again, as the English tried to maintain their system of law and order while the Republicans administered Irish law and order themselves. Their alternate judicial system consisted of a Supreme Court, district courts, and parish courts, the latter presided over by men and women elected by local Sinn Fein clubs. The Republic adopted the ancient Brehon legal code. "When a woman was being tried, it was customary to have a woman among the judges on the Bench." Maud and Kathleen Clarke, her cellmate from Holloway, served as magistrates in Dublin, and in June 1920 Maud was elected a judge. Hearings were broken up by British authorities, documents seized in the effort to destroy the new system of justice which was undermining English law. But the Irish courts avoided circumvention by keeping on the move and meeting secretly, and the people flocked to them to resolve their disputes.

Griffith's theories of passive resistance were being put to the test. Nationalists in African and Asian colonies—Gandhi, Nehru and Tikal of the Indian Congress Party—saw how civil disobedience could weaken imperial rule. But the period of nonviolence was brief. In the first six months of 1919 the English made many arrests. Cumann na mBann, the Volunteers, the Gaelic League were banned; Republican newspapers suppressed. In September Lloyd George declared the Dail illegal. Deputies went underground and met in secret. The Volunteers, now the Irish Republican Army under General Richard Mulcahy, although ill prepared, were more than ready to fight.

Already impatient guerrillas had fired the first shots, killing two police in Tipperary. Dan Breen, Tom Barry, Ernie O'Malley, Liam Lynch led their flying columns against the Royal Irish Constabulary and British troops. Like their predecessors, the wild hillside men, the IRA leaders, most of them not much older than Maud's son, felt no moral hesitation at using physical force; the British army of occupation was a continual form of aggression. The women of Cumann na mBann risked their lives as couriers and saboteurs. In November there was a failed attempt to kill Lord French. The English forces struck back, shooting up villages, raiding homes and attacking civilians. Tomas MacCurtain, Lord

Mayor of Cork, was shot. "Active Defensive Strategy" became Sinn Fein policy; Griffith was no longer leading a passive resistance movement.

In urban hideouts bands of Republican gunmen were directed by Michael Collins, Minister of Information, determined to put out "the eyes of the British," the Intelligence Service indispensable to imperial control. The British forces in Ireland began to crack. R.I.C. recruiting dropped; several units defected to the side of their countrymen. The Dominions watched. In India a battalion of Connaught Rangers mutinied in protest against oppression in Ireland.

Lloyd George offered another "Partition" bill—two separate Parliaments with restricted powers, one for the South, the other for the North. De Valera escaped from prison and toured America as President of Dail Eireann, winning widespread support in the land of his birth.

Erskine Childers, working with Maud at the Press Bureau, answered Lloyd George's threat of reprisals for any attempt at "secession" with words familiar to Maud since she first sat at O'Leary's feet: "The Irish answer to this declaration of war—this heroic defiance of the weak by the strong—is something like the following: We do not attempt secession. Nations cannot secede from a rule they have never accepted."

Maud's son, Seagan MacBride, found his "Romantic Ireland" with the Republican students at Dublin University. In the underground network he met the men and women on the run: young Ernie O'Malley, who had known and worshiped Major MacBride of the Irish Brigade, and Constance Markievicz, like his own mother a legendary woman. On September 26, 1920, Seagan was driving Madame Markievicz and Maurice Bourgeois, the French writer, into Dublin when the police stopped the car in Rathmines because the tail lamp was out. They recognized Constance Markievicz and arrested all of them. Seagan had his first taste of prison at Bridewell, and Bourgeois, who was reviled and bullied by the military in his filthy cell, became a stout champion of Irish republicanism. He and Seagan were released in a few days, but Constance was sent to Mountjoy and held without charges until December, when she was tried by court-martial for conspiracy for having organized the Fianna, her "open" scout troops, ten years before. Constance was sentenced to two years' hard labor. Maud and her other friends were not allowed to speak to her at her trial.

At AE's home, Iseult had met a tall young Republican from Ulster, a poet eight years younger than herself, with a shock of golden hair cut in a fringe, eyes like a faun's; at eighteen more naïve than she had ever been. Francis Stuart had read his Yeats and was predisposed to fall in love with the young woman whose very name rang with romance. He was soon a steady visitor at Maud's house on Stephen's Green. Iseult, who heard Yeats praise the green youth's poems while considering their author a "dunce," insisted on marrying Francis: if not for love, at least to escape from the difficulties of a life dominated by overwhelming personalities. Maud saw that Iseult needed no family curse to doom her marriage to the insecure adolescent, but Francis became a Catholic and Iseult married him early in 1920.

At Stephen's Green the young husband observed Maud and her circle with the "swift, unflinching, terrible judgment of the young." He heard his wife and his mother-in-law call his idol "poor Willie." He was critical of Maud for being possessive of Iseult, and for her overriding hatred of the English. He felt threatened by positive political women like Helena Molony and Hanna Sheehy-Skeffington. Apolitical, introspective, he rebelled against all authority and was a Republican partisan more out of a fondness for adventure than for the issue at stake. "So medieval and so skeptical," Yeats wrote of Stuart and the generation of writers growing up in Ireland in the aftermath of the Great War. Maud and Iseult called him "Grim."

In March Sir Nevil Macready was appointed Commander-in-Chief of the British forces in Ireland under Sir Henry Wilson, a Unionist and chief of the Imperial General Staff, who believed in "stamping out rebellion with a strong hand." Unemployable ex-soldiers in England, the raggle-taggle survivors of the war, were recruited to serve as military police and began to arrive in Ireland in late March. Their dark trousers and khaki tunics, resembling the motley coloring of a pack of hounds from Limerick, the Scarteen Hunt, earned them the name Black and Tans. They were augmented by the Auxiliaries, a force of ex-officers whose semiofficial position gave them the prerogatives but none of the discipline of their rank. Lloyd George maintained that the government could not be held responsible for the spontaneous actions of the Black and Tans, the massacres, the looting, the assault on civilian life and property by unruly mercenaries.

Maud suggested to Griffith, President of the Dail in De Valera's absence, that the women of Ireland organize to aid the victims. The American Committee for Relief in Ireland contributed some five million dollars, and the Irish White Cross was established by the fall of 1920. Maud served on the executive, her particular projects being the feeding of school children and providing employment where industries had been destroyed. At last her school-meal program was generally accepted, and it was found necessary to feed children of impoverished families during school holidays to prevent them from starving. She had set up cottage industries before in the rural wastelands. Now she found jobs for garment workers in Dublin in shops with union rates and directed the distribution of piecework to be sewn by women in outlying districts.

Maud had written John Quinn, "God help Ireland after the war," but in her most terrifying nightmares she could not have foreseen such devastation. In Galway Lady Gregory kept her journal as each day brought another horror story: "In Cromwell's time there wasn't half as much done because they hadn't the way of doing it"—airplanes to swing low and machine-gun the streets, lorries to drag the half-living bodies of young IRA men through the street, rifle butts to beat the innocent. "And there is a woman, an O'Donnell, over there in Peterswell, and she having but the one son, and they pulled him out of the bed and brought him abroad in the street and shot him, and they brought her out that she'd see him shot ... Out in Shanaglish they burned a picture of the Redeemer —'Is this another Sinn Feiner?' says one of them."

Yeats, who managed to keep his family out of danger by taking them to live in Oxford, was deeply disturbed by Lady Gregory's reports. He feared for Coole and for his tower at Ballylee. Maud saw him briefly when he came to Dublin in

September to have his tonsils removed by Dr. Oliver St. John Gogarty. She invited him to visit her in the "water-filled silences" of the Wicklow Mountains. Maud was taking a respite with Seagan and their young friend Cecil Salkeld in a lonely cottage, "the last in the glen," where Synge had set his play about Nora Burke, the play Maud had walked out on years before. Yeats, grown attentive to proper clothes, had visited Lady Ottoline Morrell that summer and strolled with the Bloomsbury set in his gray suit and pearl-gray hat beside his hostess in her lilac silk and red-heeled slippers. He arrived at Maud's cottage in a jaunting car in his "country get-up," having "pulled his ordinary socks up outside his immaculate tweed trousers." Salkeld rose early the next morning to find the poet already up; "coming down to breakfast, Madame Gonne MacBride smiled at me and said: 'Willie is booming and buzzing like a bumble bee . . . that means he is writing something. . . .' " The poem turned out to be a hermetic paean to poetry, Ireland, and Maud: "I have loved you better than my soul for all my words . . ."

She wore widow's weeds all the time now, headdress and flowing veil in the French style. Since the war her income had decreased considerably; there was no extra money for luxuries, nor did she have time for Paris couturiers. The long black or midnight-blue crepe dresses she designed for herself were as elegant as Yeats's fawn vests and well-cut jackets and far more dramatic. Three decades earlier, at the time of Parnell's death, she had been the talk of Dublin for her theatrical display of grief. Now she was accused of capitalizing on her widowhood, but Maud continued to wear mourning for Ireland.

On October 31, 1920, Terence MacSwiney, the Republican deputy who had succeeded the murdered Tomas MacCurtain as Lord Mayor of Cork, died in Brixton Prison, London, after seventy-four days of hunger strike. The next day Kevin Barry, a student at the National University and member of the IRA, was hanged for his part in an ambush of British soldiers. Maud saw Cullinswood, where Pearse had started his experimental school, reduced to ruins by drunken English soldiers, the paintings slashed, stained glass shattered. Here Maud had hoped to have Seagan educated by the schoolteachers of the Rising. Thomas MacDonagh's two young children, Donagh and Bairbre, aged eight and six, their mother dead of a heart attack, were wards of the Republic. Maud looked after their welfare and would have liked to adopt all the orphans of the Rising and the Troubles. The White Cross had established a special Children's Fund of £150,000, but love and security and laughter were not easily provided. Maud held open house for the destitute and wounded.

On November 21, fourteen British intelligence officers were assassinated in one day by Michael Collins's squads. That same Sunday afternoon the police fired into a crowd of thousands at a football game in Croke Park, in Dublin, killing twelve, wounding sixty; hundreds were injured in the ensuing stampede. Tommy Whelan, a mere boy, was arrested for complicity in the assassinations, and although he had evidence to prove his innocence, he was sentenced to death. Mrs. Whelan came down from Galway to stay at Stephen's Green, and Maud was with the anguished woman outside Mountjoy when her son was hanged.

Maud's heart ached with pride and fear for her own son. At sixteen Seagan was already a leader of an IRA squad. He had helped Ernie O'Malley escape arrest on Bloody Sunday by hiding him in Lennox Robinson's flat. While "steel plated Lancias and armoured cars with swinging turrets rolled through the streets, the director of the Abbey Theatre played Beethoven on his pianola while O'Malley showed Seagan how to work a 'Parabellum,' " an automatic rifle.

The British were rounding up men and boys suffering from bullet wounds: they invaded the hospitals that refused to turn them over. One of Seagan's squad lay helpless, his leg amputated, in Mercers Hospital. The young lieutenant lived up to his father's reputation for bravery by leading his men on a daring raid to hold up the medical staff, carry their comrade to a car, and drive him to a private house to be nursed back to health.

Maud worked on her own and with members of Cumann na mBann trying to save the lives of the hunted and imprisoned. Sometimes she acted on flashes of insight; Maire Comerford called them "brain waves." After the roundups following Bloody Sunday, Maud greeted the journalist Dorothy Macardle, who had just spent a day of scouting on her bicycle, with instructions to go to London immediately with a message for Lady Asquith. A young man Maud knew was about to be hanged. Dorothy did not have time to change her clothes or pack. "Off she went, and arrived at Asquith's residence with papers and a letter from Maud. Margot Asquith, having heard her mission, came down the great stairway and greeted Dorothy warmly. Maud's messenger returned from London with great tales of how the British government operated. 'All the members hated each other and worked against each other.' " The rebel prisoner won a reprieve.

"Here we are having a very strenuous and trying time, but the heroism and courage of everyone makes one proud . . ." Maud wrote Quinn in February. "The English may batter us to pieces but they will never succeed in breaking our spirit." The American lawyer had crossed Ireland off his list for being pro-German, but De Valera had softened Quinn's heart toward Irish causes again, and Maud hoped he would be receptive to her appeal. She wanted him to find an American publisher for her articles. It was important that Americans realize what was really taking place in Ireland. Maud and Charlotte Despard had toured the devastated areas of the South. "With her I was able to visit places I should never have been able to get to alone in the martial areas," Maud wrote Quinn. "It was amusing to see the puzzled expressions on the faces of the officers and of the Black and Tans, who continually held up our car, when Mrs. Despard said she was the Viceroy's sister." Quinn sent her piece, "Devastation," to a literary agent with a letter stating that the truth about conditions in Ireland was not generally available in the American press. Even though he stressed Maud's cosmopolitan background and her friendship with Lord French's sister, the article did not sell.

Iseult, expecting her first child in March, was staying with Maud. "Luckily her nerves are good," Maud wrote,

> for Dublin is a terrible place just now. Hardly a night passes that one is not woke up by the sound of firing. Often there are people killed, but often it is only the crown forces firing to keep up their

courage. One night last week there was such a terrible fusillade just outside our house that we all got up thinking something terrible was happening. That morning, when curfew regulations permitted us to go out, we only found the bodies of a cat and dog riddled with bullets. Seagan is working at his law course in the National University. There again it is hard for boys to work, with raids and arrests among the students going on continually. The English are particularly down on the students. Lots of them are in jail. One quiet boy of 17, a divinity student, Lawler, was beaten to death by the Black and Tans.

Iseult's daughter, born at Eastertime, lived only three months. When the baby died of spinal meningitis, Maud relived the anguish she had felt at the death of her first child and felt it the more keenly for Iseult's sake. Her old sleeplessness returned, and the nights were made more hideous by searchlights and guns.

By midsummer the Republicans were running out of resources, but the English government had lost both international standing and political support at home. De Valera had returned from America, and although the fearful warfare continued through the spring of 1921, peace overtures were being made. Lord French, his career blighted by the rumor of scandalous orgies in the Castle, was removed in April. He was replaced by Lord Fitzalan, a confirmed Unionist but the first Catholic to rule at the Castle since the Flight of the Earls. General Macready had convinced Lloyd George that unless a peaceful solution could be reached, it would not be safe to keep the troops in Ireland another winter without calling in large reserves. Moreover, to save his coalition Lloyd George wanted to hold off definitive peace negotiations until after the general elections in May; by then the Better Government Act would be in effect. Protected by military police sent over to reinforce the Ulster Volunteers, the Unionists won in the six northern counties, and when King George crossed the Irish Sea to address the new Parliament at Stormont, with Sir James Craig as Prime Minister, Winston Churchill declared from the Colonial Office that "the position of Ulster became unassailable." In the twenty-six southern counties Sinn Fein won unopposed, and the Second Dail, similar in makeup to that of 1919 but with five women deputies, had no intention of swearing allegiance to the Crown. According to Winston Churchill, Lloyd George had two alternatives: "War with utmost violence or peace with the utmost patience." In mid-July the truce was signed.

It was time for a respite. "During a terrible fit of insomnia, after the storm of the Black and Tan War," Maud wrote, "I went to Bavaria for a holiday to hear music." Seagan and the Stuarts were along, and they enjoyed the visit—Wagner, art, and café life. Maud had never felt any antipathy for Germans, and after the hazardous underground life of Dublin it was pleasant to see that "people, many of them, looked happy even after defeat, and it was marvelous traveling in a country where all officials on seeing Ireland on our passports said 'Casement,' and made everything easy for us, hardly examining our baggage, while making blustering English travelers turn out everything." She did hear some complaints about foreigners enjoying Bavarian food and music for nothing; quite justified, she wrote, "as only the rate of exchange had enabled me to take that holiday, for after our war, I had very little money left. I felt rather ashamed and tried to make a little restitution by giving as much as I could to the Collections held for the Wounded and the Orphans between the acts at the Opera house."

In Munich she ran into Walter Rummel, the musician she had known in Paris days. In Francis Stuart's mind Isadora Duncan's aging lover represented the decadence of Iseult's early years on the Continent, her illegitimacy, her relationship with Ezra Pound. He wished he were on the Italian side of the Alps, where Mussolini's socialists were marching, instead of tagging after his wife and mother-in-law on museum tours and shopping expeditions.

Seagan had to leave after a week or so to return to his IRA duties. Maud and the Stuarts stayed on, but after a month Maud grew impatient with her daughter's marital difficulties and, anxious about the peace talks in London, left Iseult and Francis in Europe and returned home.

After preliminary discussions between De Valera and Lloyd George, the Dail sent envoys to negotiate the peace. De Valera did not go; as President he wished to remain uncompromised. Griffith, Collins, Barton, and Erskine Childers were in the group. Seagan MacBride went as Collins's aide-de-camp.

The Irish delegates were determined to win a treaty that would lead to the creation of a united Republic in "external association" with the British Commonwealth. The goal of "external association" had been worked out in great detail as Draft Treaty A by De Valera and Erskine Childers. After eight weeks of negotiations under Lloyd George's threat of "immediate and terrible war," Griffith agreed to a treaty at 2:30 A.M. on December 6, 1921. A great advance over nationalist aspirations for Home Rule a decade before, it was nevertheless a setback for the Republic. The treaty did not guarantee a free, united Ireland but provided for dominion status; it granted naval and air bases to England and recognized Partition by creating a commission to settle the boundary should the Ulster Parliament vote to remain outside the Free State. The most controversial of all the Articles of Agreement which Griffith brought back for ratification by the Dail was the stipulation that, as officials of a Commonwealth country, officers and representatives of the Free State must take an oath of allegiance to the Crown.

Griffith and Collins, the pragmatists, announced that they had won the freedom to achieve freedom, but privately Collins asked himself: "Will anyone be satisfied at the bargain? . . . early this morning I signed my death warrant." Maud saw confusion over the treaty spread a "wizard's mist over the country, obscuring both the stone and the glory and joy of changing life."

The Dail was split in two. Constance Markievicz and the women deputies were among the passionate speakers against the treaty. Maud, who thought it betrayed all they had fought for, nevertheless believed its rejection would create two warring camps. On her side was Patrick McCartan, who said, "We are presented with a *fait accompli* and asked to endorse it, but I will not vote for chaos." The IRB and the IRA officially endorsed the treaty, although internally both were divided. Cathal Brugha, legendary survivor of the Easter Rising, acting president of the Dail and Minister of Defense, was vehement against the treaty and predicted that ratification would "split Ireland from top to bottom."

In England, where his second child, Michael, had been born on August 22, Yeats feared it would be impossible to raise his children in the "blood and misery" of Ireland; "they would inherit bitterness." In December 1921 he wrote Olivia Shakespear that he expected ratification but saw no "escape from bitterness, and the extreme party may carry the country. When men are very bitter, death and ruin draw them on as a rabbit is supposed to be drawn on by the dancing of the fox."

On January 7, 1922, the Dail voted on the treaty: sixty-four for approval, fifty-seven against. Griffith became President. Michael Collins, William Cosgrave, Gavan Duffy, Kevin O'Higgins, and General Richard Mulcahy were his ministers. De Valera and Constance Markievicz resigned. The anti-treaty deputies left the Dail and formed a new political group, Cumann na Poblachta, the Republican Party. At its convention on February 5, Cumann na mBann rejected a motion to support the treaty, 419 to 63. Constance Markievicz was elected president. Pro-treaty members were asked to resign. Maud remained neutral.

British troops were leaving, the lorries rolling away as people cheered with relief. Four hundred political prisoners sentenced before the truce returned to a country reduced to economic ruin, ripe for civil war in the aftermath of an unfinished revolution. The thought of Republican fighting Republican was anathema to Maud. She "bowed to any peace advocate," as she had once told John Quinn, and now became one herself. She went to Paris for Griffith to work for unity at the Irish Race Convention in January 1922. A year before, a great gathering of delegates from all over the world had been planned to demonstrate Sinn Fein solidarity. Now separate transportation had to be arranged for the warring delegates by Robert Brennan, the director who was himself anti-treaty.

In Paris Maud and Constance agreed that for all the fine talk—Yeats lecturing on the Abbey, his brother Jack on painting, Douglas Hyde on the Gaelic League—no cultural or racial harmony could mend the factionalism. "The Congress was a hotbed of intrigue," wrote Brennan, and in the gilded salon of the Grand Hotel, Maud recognized the red-draped dais and throne she had seen almost forty years earlier at the fancy-dress soirées of the Association du St. Patrice. The old Duke of Tetuan had come from Madrid to preside at the congress.

> He knew nothing of Ireland except its horses and had bought some good ones for the Spanish Government. It hardly seemed to me or to Constance Markievicz sufficient reason for erecting a throne in his honour . . . I had laughed gaily at the gilded throne in de Cremont's drawing-room; I could not laugh at that throne in the Grand Hotel, and the sneers and mockery of the reporters of the French newspapers *("Voilà les Républicains Irlandais!")* worried me. De Valera seemed quite content . . . At that very time, our Republic was being bartered in Hans Place in London.

Michael Collins was meeting with Winston Churchill, the Colonial Secretary; and Sir James Craig, Ulster's Prime Minister, trying to settle the boundary question. Already there were border skirmishes between the IRA and the Ulster Volunteers, and in the northern counties Protestant and Catholic clashed again.

When Maud returned from Paris she was amazed to find that the White Cross had been severely curtailed. "A terrible pogrom was raging in Belfast; every train from the North brought wild-eyed refugees." Maud saw "women half demented and children sick with terror" huddled in forlorn groups in the bare rooms of Fowler Hall, which had been commandeered as a temporary refuge by the IRA. As president of the Dublin Relief Committee, Maud went to see Griffith in the Provisional Government office in Merrion Street to ask him to allot some of the beds from the barracks evacuated by English regiments. "Arthur looked pale and harassed; his first words were: 'The IRA have no right to bring down refugees from the North; it is not our policy and we are the government.' "

Maud found herself pleading for mercy for the pitiful refugees who reminded her of the homeless she had seen camped in the Gare St. Lazare in 1914. Griffith, adamant, replied that the IRA had only made trouble by seizing Fowler Hall, which belonged to the Orange Order. "Can't you understand that *until we can show we have established order here we can't expect the plebiscite in the North Lloyd George has promised . . .* " Michael Collins at Dublin Castle gave her the same response and urged her to send the refugees back North, but eventually Maud won a hostel for the Belfast refugees. The Provisional Government was walking a tightrope between the Unionists in England and the North and the anti-treaty Republicans, and Maud was contemptuous of the leaders' faith in Lloyd George. The IRA split—the Free State Army under General Mulcahy against the Republicans, the "Irregulars," under Liam Lynch.

Maud's son was with the Republicans in April, when their Council occupied a number of strong points in Dublin, and he and his friend Ernie O'Malley were in the squadron under Liam Mellows and Rory O'Connor that took over the seat of juridical control of Ireland, the great domed building on the Liffey called the Four Courts. Just before elections were held in June, Collins and Griffith made a pact with De Valera which seemed to assure that the opposing wings of the IRA would not fight each other. The pro-treaty forces won the election. Maud went to Paris for Griffith's Publicity Ministry, run by Desmond Fitzgerald after Childers resigned to publish *Poblacht na hEireann* for De Valera's party. Her mission was to write about the renewed attacks on Catholics in the North and to expose English support of the Orange persecutors.

While she was in Paris the Unionist Sir Henry Wilson was assassinated in London. The murderers were hanged without revealing who had assigned them. Assuming that the Irregular IRA executive lodged in the Four Courts was responsible, England ordered General Macready to attack; then, realizing that such action could reunite the Irish, the British canceled the order and pressured the Provisional Government to send its own troops against the Four Courts.

On June 29 Maud read the Paris news reports. The Four Courts had been shelled by the Free State Government. She rushed to the Irish Office so early that Colonel Maurice Moore received her in his dressing gown. George Moore's brother showed Maud a telegram from Griffith instructing him to inform the press that the Irish government had acted on its own, not on orders from England. Maud left for Dublin immediately.

When she reached Dublin the thick walls of the Four Courts were being shelled by English guns lent to the Free State Army. The building was filled with ammunition, and every exit was surrounded. There were four hundred IRA men inside, Seagan among them, and women from Cumann na mBann were nursing the wounded.

Maud went to the Lord Mayor of Dublin. Laurance O'Neill, "that man of peace," was in despair. At any moment the besieged building would explode. Maud got together an emergency committee of women to go with him into the Four Courts and ask for a truce. Before they left the Mansion House, news came that the building was in flames. Rory O'Connor's brigade threw their arms into the fires and marched out under a flag of truce. Seagan and his comrades were taken to Mountjoy with their commanding officers. Ernie O'Malley was among six who escaped.

O'Neill agreed to be chairman of the Women's Peace Committee, which included Mrs. Despard, Hanna Sheehy-Skeffington, Nora Connolly, and Louie Bennett, the trade unionist. They drew up a peace proposal to present to both sides: immediate cessation of all hostilities so that the conflict could be settled at the July 2 meeting of the Dail; during the truce all combatants should return home; there should be no arrests. Oscar Traynor, for the anti-treaty IRA, accepted the conditions but refused to ask the Irregulars to give up their arms.

Maud headed the delegation to Provisional Government headquarters, where the peace proposal was rejected by Griffith, Collins, and Cosgrave. She insisted on seeing Griffith in person. Her son, the son of his friend John MacBride, was one of his prisoners—how could he refuse? Griffith came to the door of his office; he would not let her in. She stood in the corridor, the women in dark clothes behind her, and asked for a truce. She begged Griffith to be lenient with the prisoners. Many were scarcely more than children; they had fought the English in the war for independence; the abuses of imperial oppression must never be used by the Irish Free State against Irish men and women. Griffith's rejection was curt and final —he had said it before. "We are now a Government and we have to keep order."

Labor leaders, clergymen, representatives of the great majority who wanted peace in which to rebuild their lives, all tried to bring about a truce. Although the Catholic hierarchy supported the pro-treaty forces, the Archbishop of Dublin conferred with the opposing forces. The anti-treaty command, in their headquarters in the Hamman Hotel, refused to give orders to surrender arms. The Provisional Government would settle for nothing less, and General Mulcahy's troops closed in on Republican outposts in Dublin. On July 5 the Hamman Hotel was in flames and the last defenders were forced out. Amid a volley of shots Cathal Brugha fell dead. In one week of fighting, sixty men and women were killed in Dublin and over three hundred wounded. The east side of O'Connell Street was reduced to a smoking ruin, as the west side of the broad thoroughfare had been in 1916. Ten thousand rifles had been provided to Michael Collins by the British government. Cork, Limerick, Waterford—civil war spread through the South. The Provisional Government, at peace with England and Ulster, sent troops around Ireland by sea to attack Irregular strongholds.

Maud saw Arthur Griffith become England's pawn, trapped in a tragic situation. They had faced each other in the government offices across an incomprehensible gulf; she never again saw the man she had once so admired for his integrity. On August 12, a month after the shelling of the Four Courts, Griffith was dead of a cerebral hemorrhage. Not quite fifty, overworked, disappointed, he died broken-hearted. Ten days later his most brilliant minister, Michael Collins, was shot down in ambush. Three young men, William Cosgrave, General Richard Mulcahy, and Kevin O'Higgins, took over the government. Cosgrave was elected President; his government instituted martial law with special emergency powers to its armed forces. A Civil Guard, the Gardai, replaced the Royal Irish Constabulary, an armed police to augment the Free State troops; and the Criminal Investigation Department, the new G men, took the place of the British Secret Service. The Republican court system was abandoned, and military tribunals were empowered to inflict death sentences on any man or woman connected with the anti-Treaty IRA. In October, De Valera, refusing to recognize the Cosgrave government's right to rule, set up a rival government, but he had no effective control over his anti-Treaty IRA supporters.

In November Erskine Childers was executed by the Free State government. The unrepentant Republican propagandist whom Griffith had referred to contemptuously as "that Englishman" for his opposition to the treaty, and whom Churchill called a "renegade" Englishman, wrote a last letter to his American wife from his death cell. "I die full of love for Ireland. . . . I die loving England and passionately praying that she may change completely and finally toward Ireland."

Casualties in the Civil War approximated three hundred a month for both sides. Maud turned her house in Stephen's Green into an emergency hospital. She put on the Red Cross cap she had worn when she worked in the wards of the huge infirmary at Paris-Plage in 1915 and, with Iseult and Helena Molony, nursed the wounded. The young women from Cumann na mBann came to help, and Francis Stuart carried slop pails afloat with blood-stained swabs.

That winter Francis went to Belgium to get desperately needed arms for the Republican IRA. Shortly after his return, he was picked up by Free State troops and interned. Seagan was still in Mountjoy prison with a hundred captives from the Four Courts. Catalina Bulfin, who had been arrested with him, was interned in Kilmainham, where more than three hundred women prisoners were held. The twenty-one-year-old daughter of a well-known Irish journalist went on hunger strike with women whose names were already famous in the Republican roll of honor—Mary MacSwiney, Grace Plunkett, Nora Connolly.

The prisoners were Maud's chief concern. According to official estimates, eleven to twelve thousand military prisoners were held by the Free State during the year of the Civil War. Unofficial figures, which included civilians, were much higher. Their confinement in cold, overcrowded, unsanitary cells and barbed-wire-enclosed camps equaled the barbarity Maud had witnessed years earlier in English jails. She went to Mountjoy with a group of wives and mothers, their arms full of linen and food which they were not allowed to take into the filthy cells.

Maud realized that to be effective they must organize. She called a meeting at the Mansion House, at which Mrs. Despard was elected president of the Women's Prisoners' Defence League. The only qualification for membership was a familial relationship to some prisoner and payment of one half-penny a week. "Our offices were in the open street outside the jail gates . . ." Maud wrote. "We pooled all information . . . and little went on in the jails we did not hear of. Often we were able to assist anxious families find out the whereabouts of missing ones who had been arrested."

The women demonstrated, visited jails, sought legal aid, sent bulletins to the press. Years of experience working for amnesty for political prisoners in English jails helped Maud now; she knew the techniques of protest and propaganda. On November 10, 1922, she headed a deputation to the Dublin County Council. The flustered officials complained that they were turning the Council meetings into "bear gardens," but Maud calmly announced that "Mary MacSwiney in Mountjoy was on hunger strike since Saturday morning and might end as Terry did."

A few days later in O'Connell Street she held a meeting for the sister of the dead Lord Mayor of Cork. With Charlotte Despard at her side, Maud was addressing the crowd from a heap of rubble in front of the ruined Royal Hibernian Bible Society when an armored car pulled up and a government patrol "proceeded to search a large number of men." Remembering the helpless tenants surrounded by police in Mayo, Maud tried to get her audience to disperse calmly, but the soldiers opened fire. Fourteen people were wounded and hundreds hurt in the crush.

"The Mothers," as the women of the Prisoners' Defence League were called, were "shot at and hosed on," wrote

Maud, but their numbers grew, and "nothing stopped our work." She led a demonstration outside General Mulcahy's residence in Portobello to protest the executions. Free State guards were massed along the railings; "some shots had been fired over our heads; a woman's hat had been pierced by a bullet. I heard an order given and the front line of soldiers knelt down with rifles ready—some of the young soldiers were white and trembling. I got up on the parapet of the railing and smiled contempt at the officer. He had curious rather beautiful pale grey eyes and a thin brown face. We gazed at each other a full minute. The order to fire was not given."

De Valera was in hiding; the intrepid Constance Markievicz was picked up again while canvassing with petitions for the WPDL. Maud escaped arrest. Considered a pity-crazed crank, an avenging fury, a relic from another time, by the Provisional Government, she benefited from her time-honored connections with the party in power and the fact that Lord French's sister, Yeats, AE, Gogarty, and Lady Gregory were her friends. However, Cosgrave's government kept her under strict surveillance, and her house on Stephen's Green was searched while she was absent. She had moved out to a house which she and Mrs. Despard bought in Clonskeagh, a green suburb about ten miles from the center of Dublin, where she was closer to the Dublin hills and her pets could run free. On November 13 the *Freeman's Journal* carried the headline: "BONFIRE OF PAPERS, Sequel to Search of Madame MacBride's House." Maud had lent the top floor of Number 73 to Dorothy Macardle, whose own home had been raided. Dorothy had been arrested, and in her absence the "Staters" burst open the painted Georgian door and ransacked the house. Reporters arrived to find papers strewn about: ". . . in the upper rooms, presses and cupboards were pulled open and the contents left lying about. The military were on the scene for some time, and before leaving they piled up a heap of papers on the center of the road and set them ablaze."

Treasure salvaged from a lifetime on the move, irreplaceable notebooks, clippings, precious bibelots and pictures that decorated her desks and tables were stolen. Messages from comrades, the first scrawls of her children, the faded envelopes addressed to her by men and women she would never see again—all had gone up in flames. Reduced to a fine ash and blown away into the sere brown leaves of Stephen's Green, her letters from Willie and drafts of poems he had sent her disappeared forever.

In her youth Maud had wanted to travel light, unburdened by the past. For safety's sake she had found it necessary to dispose of documents that might incriminate her or others, bait for political blackmail. When her exile in Paris ended in 1917, a box of correspondence from Ireland—Willie's letters among the communiqués from Helena Molony and her Irish colleagues—was left behind with her concierge in wartime France.

Yeats believed that records must be kept; their stories were part of Ireland's history and must be preserved "to set the past in order" for future generations. To this end he helped Lady Gregory with her journals, and until his father died in New York in 1922, Willie had urged the painter who could never complete his self-portrait in oils to write his memoirs. At Les Mouettes he had asked Maud to write a political appendix for his own autobiography, and she, objecting to his plan to deposit his papers in an English library, had refused. Now an Irish government had destroyed her own records. Yeats's poems were preserved in his books, but the thoughts and dreams he had written in his letters, the unformed creations of daily life, would never be reread, and her documents of political life were gone forever. "About the letters," she wrote Joseph Hone when he was collecting material for a biography of Yeats, "alas I have not been able to find any." Some had vanished in Paris, and the rest, "letters from Willie and from Pearse and Connolly were all burned when the Staters shot up my house in St. Stephen's Green in 1922 and made a huge bonfire of all my papers."

# The Fanatic Heart

She wasted no tears over the loss of her papers. The burning of records, the destruction of archives were overshadowed by the suffering and death of the Civil War.

On December 8, 1922, Sean MacBride heard the shots in Mountjoy prison yard at dawn when Rory O'Connor, Richard Barrett, Joseph McKelvey, and Liam Mellows, his officers from the Four Courts, were executed. The order was given by Kevin O'Higgins, Minister for Home Affairs. Less than a year had gone by since Rory O'Connor had stood as best man at O'Higgins's wedding.

In accordance with the treaty, the Irish Free State had been officially recognized by England in early December, and immediately the Stormont Parliament exercised its right to "option out." King George approved the appointment of Parnell's old foe, Timothy Healy, as Governor General of a Free State sworn to the Crown. Among the senators were people Maud had known over many years: Andrew Jameson of the distillery family who had lived next door when she was a child, Dr. Sigerson, Colonel Maurice Moore, Dr. Gogarty, and Jennie Wyse-Power, a charter member of Inghinidhe na hEireann. Appointed to the powerless upper house of the Irish Parliament to represent Unionists and other minority groups, men and women of good will, distinguished in public life and the arts—they were all, thought Maud, manipulated by England.

Her old neighbor George Russell was editing the pro-government *Irish Statesman* but kept his theosophical distance by refusing an appointment to the Senate. Yeats accepted, and Maud could not forgive him. He turned away from her and the Irish people, she wrote, "when he became a Senator of the Free State which voted Flogging Acts against young republican soldiers still seeking to free Ireland from the contamination of the British Empire." In an angry letter she let him know that she would renounce his society forever unless he denounced the government. Jack Yeats, the free-spirited painter, sided with De Valera's Republicans, and he too refused to see Willie.

Years before, Yeats had refused a knighthood, not wanting, as he told his sister, to have his nationalist colleagues say, "only for a ribbon he left us." Now he accepted homage from Irish politicians whom Maud considered traitors. Pleased with the honor, Yeats noted that the stipend would "compensate me somewhat for the chance of being shot," or for a few bullet holes in the windows of his house in Merrion Square. The Free State provided an armed guard to protect the Senator's household, and Yeats divulged a secret weakness for detective stories, one he held in common with Maud, when he gave his favorite thrillers to the guards, "to train them in the highest tradition of their profession."

In 1923 Yeats won the Nobel Prize for Literature; £7,500 was a great fortune in a career that had rarely brought in more than £200 a year, and it would help support his new life style, the velvet jackets and top hats, the country retreat, the Georgian residence in town in the Berkeley Square of Dublin. Fancying himself an Irish D'Annunzio, poet-statesman, Yeats felt that the recognition included the resurgent nation he had helped to form. His laurels, which irritated many English writers, pleased the Irish Free State. Maud, who had always wanted Yeats honored for Ireland, did not congratulate him now.

Willie the dreamer had become a public personage and, dreamer still, hoped to make a positive contribution to his country. "Certainly peace seems coming," he wrote. "Only isolated shots now at night; but one is sure of nothing." Fighting against impossible odds, Republican troops continued trying to sabotage the Free State's power to rule. They attacked barracks, destroyed government property, and set private dwellings aflame in "a chain of bonfires through the nights. . . ." The houses of thirty-seven senators were demolished; nothing was left of Dr. Gogarty's Renvyle in Connemara but the charred central beam and ten tall chimneys. Sir Horace Plunkett's great house was razed. "People whose families had lived in the country for three or four hundred years realised suddenly that they were still strangers . . ." Sir Horace's sister-in-law, Lady Fingall, who had danced at the viceregal court when Maud made her debut, saw the barriers dividing the liberal order from the rebel republic, "immovable as those hills brooding over an age-long wrong," and wrote, "It was those who had tried to atone for that wrong and to break down that barrier who did most of the paying."

Maud saw the heavy price: Maire Comerford wounded by a prison guard's random shooting; Mary MacSwiney on hunger strike; Constance Markievicz in solitary confinement. She saw the anguished families of boys tortured by government agents; nine Republican soldiers captured in Tralee, tied to land mines and blown up; five dynamited on a bridge at Killarney. Fifty-five prisoners were executed by the Free State that winter. Maud was overwhelmed by the horror, while Yeats, her old comrade and lover, no longer stood aside from violence but had become associated with it.

Yeats's Castle in Galway was threatened by Republicans when they dynamited a nearby bridge, and the stream, dammed by debris, flooded the cellar. Lady Gregory's Coole Park was spared, although Roxboro, her ancestral estate, was raided. Not all the vandals were members of the IRA; some were jobless, land-hungry farmers trying to take advantage of chaos. "Everything good and bad in Irish character has boiled up," wrote AE's secretary, Susan Mitchell. "We are under no illusions now; our vanity is punctured; we have seen our ugly faces in the glass . . . the undoing of 700 years of idiotic government . . . could not fail to be terrifying."

In January 1923 the government cracked down on Maud's Prisoners' Defence League. She herself was arrested and held without charges in Kilmainham. Charlotte Despard and her friends kept loyal watch round the clock at the prison gate with its two locked dragons carved in stone overhead. Iseult was beside herself with anxiety. Francis and Sean were still interned, and now her mother was in prison again, her health endangered. Although she knew Maud would object, she appealed to Yeats for help. When he intervened on Maud's behalf, explaining that she had always been in delicate health, Cosgrave told him that "women, doctors and clergy ought to keep out of politics, as their business is with the sick." Yeats wrote Olivia Shakespear, "I am afraid my help in the matter of blankets, instead of her release (where I could do nothing), will not make her less resentful. She had to choose (perhaps all women must) between broomstick and distaff and she has chosen the broomstick—I mean the witches' hats."

Four years earlier, in Holloway, Maud had been too ill and afraid to go on hunger strike with Hanna Sheehy-Skeffington. Since then she had seen the dreadful results of starvation and forced feeding. But in Kilmainham, inspired by Mary MacSwiney's courage, she refused all nourishment. To her surprise it was easy, and she experienced a strange release in the euphoria of purposeful self-denial. The prison doctor told her she "was the most cheerful hunger striker he ever met, always laughing. Why wouldn't I laugh," Maud asked, "when I won either way?" After twenty days she was freed, on the side of life, but so weak she had to be carried out on a stretcher.

In March the Vatican sent Monsignor Luzzio to Dublin on a peace mission. Maud went with a deputation from the Peace Committee of Sinn Fein to call on him. The Free State Government, confident of victory, had no use for a peace negotiator from Rome. On May 24, ceding defeat, Frank Aiken, Republican chief of staff since the death of Liam Lynch, gave the order to cease fire and dump arms. Overt hostilities ceased, but very few IRA men were willing to give up their guns, and the war dwindled into sporadic clashes. The government, fearing new outbreaks, did not open the prisons, which still held almost twelve thousand Republicans. Their detention, now that a state of emergency no longer existed, was legalized by a new Public Safety Act.

A mandate from the people was still needed to implement the treaty, and a general election was called for August 1923. Constance Markievicz went to Scotland to campaign. The "Red Countess" was now safer from arrest in England than in Ireland. When De Valera came out of hiding to electioneer for his old seat in County Clare, Free State troops broke up a meeting of ten thousand people. In an article in *Sinn Fein*, Maud denounced Cosgrave and his "constitutionalists" for "attempting to shoot down President De Valera at the opening of his first election speech at Ennis (attempted murder prevented by the brave women who flung themselves over his body, some actually receiving the lead intended for him) . . ." De Valera was arrested and placed in solitary confinement in Arbour Hill Barracks.

With so many Republican candidates silenced, the Women's Prisoners' Defence League became the most vital voice of the opposition. In the press, in leaflets, on street corners, Maud and her intrepid women spoke out against Cumann na nGaedheal. No witches' broomsticks, but stubborn discipline and clever planning enabled them to avoid arrest. The "Mothers" held each meeting at a different coffee shop or private house, and kept the authorities guessing what hoardings would be plastered and replastered with their handbills. Maud would appear on a different street corner each day. Perched on a cart, addressing a handful or a mob, she became, like the ruins of O'Connell Street, part of the Dublin scene, familiar as the seasons. Mrs. Despard, also dressed in black and looking half Maud's height, was usually at her side. Terence de Vere White never forgot his first sight of Maud and her elderly companion letting themselves out of a cab when the driver failed to open the door for them. The young Dublin writer was even more shocked when one of his schoolmates spat on the pavement at Madame MacBride's heels as she passed by them on College Green.

Maud ignored the harassments as she ignored the mud underfoot and the weather in the streets. Maire Comerford saw her "always surrounded by enemies," yet her very way of walking made her seem impervious. Tall though she was, in the low-heeled shoes she wore now, Maud "always looked rooted to the ground."

She kept her gaiety, her sense of mischief. When the

local bishop called at Roebuck House, he was informed at the door that he could not come in unless he would speak in French or Irish, as Madame Gonne MacBride and Mrs. Despard refused "to sully their lips" with the English language.

On August 17 *Sinn Fein* reported "an attempt to set fire to the house of Mrs. Despard on Tuesday night . . . followed by the planting of a bomb in one of the outhouses during Wednesday night. It was found on Thursday morning by a gardener. Madame Gonne MacBride brought it to Rathdrum Police Station and handed it in, saying, 'I return your property. You will be able to send it on to the particular force that placed it in Mrs. Despard's outhouse.' Mrs. Despard, sister of Lord French, is speaking at election meetings in the south."

The Republicans did better than expected at the polls on August 27, winning forty-four seats, a gain of eight, but on the basis of Sinn Fein's objection to the Oath, the deputies refused to take their places in the Dail. With sixty-three members Cumann na nGaedheal remained in power, the prisons full and fear in the countryside. Lady Gregory railed against the "insincere" Oath, and Yeats made a vain attempt to influence President Cosgrave to negotiate with England for the abolishment of the main stumbling block to political amity.

"The Free State fears nothing so much as peace," wrote Maud, who saw no political solution so long as Cosgrave was the president; "turmoil and disturbance in Ireland being British policy. Seated in an English aeroplane, hurling insults at the enemies of the British Empire in prison, Mr. Cosgrave is the fitting worthy symbol of the Free State."

The onset of another winter made the long confinement in unheated cells and camps ever more intolerable. After sixteen months Sean MacBride escaped from an ambulance transporting him and other prisoners from Mountjoy to Kilmainham. Before he went underground, Maud was reunited briefly with her *"Bichon,"* no longer a curly-headed student but an IRA leader schooled by guerrilla warfare and prison life.

In October four hundred prisoners in Mountjoy went on hunger strike. Day after day Maud carried the banner, "Freedom or the Grave," demonstrating for their release. Constance Markievicz, having returned home only to be arrested again, joined the strike. By the end of November two hunger strikers had died; others, weakened and hopeless, had defected. A few weeks later the Republicans called a halt to the long fast, and the Free State, fearing epidemics of influenza in the overcrowded jails, granted amnesty to three thousand of the prisoners, including all the women, at Christmas time.

For the first time in many years there was reason to celebrate. Maud lit candles in the tall windows for her first Christmas at Roebuck House. Friends arriving at the twin glass doors were greeted by assorted dogs and puppies and led into the high-ceilinged, sparsely furnished parlor where they found warmth and nourishment by the fireside. Sean and his young woman friend Kid Bulfin were still in hiding, working at IRA headquarters, but Francis Stuart came home to Iseult at Roebuck after his fifteen-month internment.

The Released Prisoners' Committee of the WPDL met every train carrying the freed Republicans home at railroad stations haunted by waiting wives and mothers. By the first of the year Roebuck House had mattresses in every room; there was a constant coming and going; cars, motorbikes, and bicycles parked in the circular drive. Maud was running a hospital for ex-prisoners—men like Batty Noone from Sligo, one leg blown off, the other riddled with bullets. After months of negligent treatment in the Curragh Isolation Ward, he was nursed back to life. "A little happiness and ease . . . an artificial leg . . . life would still be possible," wrote Maud, "and his great child-like faith in the Republic which had kept him alive through everything cheered and encouraged us all."

Early in 1924 the Stuarts moved from Roebuck to a thatched stone cottage at Glencreagh, where Francis worked on a novel and Iseult, pregnant again, planted a herb garden in the peaty Wicklow soil, raised wild rabbits, and wrote articles for journals of Eastern studies. Occasionally Yeats would drive out over the dusty lanes to visit. "Uncle Willie" once more, he kept an affectionate watch over Iseult, his "tame hare." Maud avoided his visits, and there was no way he could keep in touch with her except through Iseult.

The "sixty-year-old smiling public man" could not forget the past, and Maud's image haunted his work. On an official inspection of a Montessori school, he was reminded of her concern for school children and, looking at the "paddlers" lined up before him, wondered "if she stood so at that age," and thought of her present image: "Hollow of cheek as though it drank the wind"—and of the broken dreams that had caused their quarrel.

The WPDL was involved in rehabilitation. Maud set up a dispensary and what she called a "vestiare" at the old offices of Sinn Fein on Harcourt Street, where exhausted men in tattered uniforms and sick, haggard women received first aid, food and clothing. There was no way for them to earn a living. Kevin O'Higgins estimated that crushing the resistance had cost the Free State Government about seventeen million pounds. The people paid in inflation and unemployment, and it was the twice-defeated Republicans who were charged most heavily. Hanna Sheehy-Skeffington lost her job as a German teacher in a technical school for having opposed the Treaty, and no jobs were available for the ex-prisoners or their families.

The outbuildings at Roebuck House were turned into shops for piecework. As a properly brought up young lady Maud had learned to embroider and to make floral decorations from sea shells and twigs. Now she taught her skills to Republican women and the wives and daughters of ex-prisoners. Their needlework and opalescent flowers were sold in fancy Dublin shops. They made preserves from crab apples and quinces that grew in the orchard, and "Roebuck Brand Jam" marketed by local greengrocers added to the WPDL relief fund.

Maud had only her energy and talent for organization to contribute; the Gonne estate could scarcely cover the upkeep of Roebuck. There were no relief funds from America. Maud's benefactor in New York had removed himself from politics into a personal fury at Germans and Jews. A sick man, Quinn was absorbed in the final disposition of his art collection, and his gifts to his Irish friends had ceased. He died on

July 28, 1924. The golden flood from the coffers of the Clan na Gael had diminished during the Civil War. The impoverished Sinn Feiners had only one newspaper in which Maud could publicize the prisoners' plight, but she saw to it that almost every issue carried an article about the WPDL, or one of her letters or columns.

In the tense aftermath of the Civil War, Dublin life resumed at a swifter pace. At the Abbey, now a truly National Theater dependent on a government subsidy, there were new plays on the boards. Lady Gregory, still active in her seventies, brought her "barmbracks" down from Coole to feed the new actors in the green room. Sean O'Casey, workingman turned playwright, listened in the wings while Sara Allgood and Barry Fitzgerald played in *Juno and the "Paycock."*

Big Jim Larkin, returned from America, was back with the ITGWU at Liberty Hall. Inspired by the Third International Congress in Moscow, he was trying to galvanize the sluggish Irish labor movement with romantic dreams of revolution: "Perhaps the Red machines would fly soon in Northern skies, and then they would order England in decided tones to clear out of Ireland."

The government instituted a revival of the Tailteann Games, an ancient Celtic festival, and Yeats persuaded the Royal Irish Academy to participate by giving awards to Irish writers. Stephen MacKenna, steadfast since the days of Maud's Association Irlandaise, refused a gold medal on political grounds. At the Tailteann ceremonies in August, Yeats depicted the end of a democratic era. He acknowledged the advent of national socialism with Mussolini's phrase, "We will trample on the decomposing body of the goddess of liberty," and paraphrased Lenin in the same speech by demanding authority and discipline to give society "a life sufficiently heroic to live without the *opium dream.*"

Maud's closest friends in the WPDL were socialists; Helena Molony, trade unionist; Hanna Sheehy-Skeffington, feminist; Constance Markievicz, James Connolly's disciple; Charlotte Despard, Marxist. They were all Catholics: Maud, Constance, and Charlotte were converts. Their Church equated their Republican ideals with bolshevism. The red scare of the twenties was in full swing in Ireland, but Maud was surprised that George Russell should attack communism in the *Irish Statesman* while supporting the Free State in the name of humanism. She wrote an angry rebuttal for *Eire* in which she accused him of opportunistic deception: "Humanism applied to the Free State! Kevin O'Higgins, the strong man of the Free State, quoted as a type of the 'Humanist'!— No, AE, your mantle of beautiful words is not shining enough or magic enough to cover this knight of capitalism . . ." Had he forgotten the great strike in 1913, when intolerable conditions in the Dublin slums made him denounce "a society which permitted such horrors to exist? The Free State is the perpetuation of that order." In the name of the Republic and humanism, Maud argued for a new order. "In Ireland an obscure prejudice, born of slave teaching, surrounds the words Socialism and Communism, which even the clear thought and noble life and death of James Connolly failed to entirely dispel. Humanism in this case would be a true title, for Communism is the apotheosis of Christ's teaching of the brotherhood of man and the upraising of humanity. As a triumphant world wave, it will eventually reach Ireland and will find no contradiction in the Republican ideal . . ."

But she knew there was division in the ranks of the Republicans, and from her son she learned of the rifts in the IRA which reflected the split in Sinn Fein. Sean MacBride, displaying a precocious gift for arbitration, took a middle stance between the extreme left and the moderates. To Maud the alleviation of suffering was primary, and she believed De Valera offered the only peaceful hope for a change for the better.

She went into the west of Ireland again, canvassing for candidates in the 1925 by-elections in County Mayo among the people who had voted for the Major and Joseph MacBride. Many families had no food at all; the dole was "four shillings a week for a widow with 7 children!" Relief work was available only to men who joined Cumann na nGaedheal by subscribing a shilling or the equivalent in eggs. With no credit at bankrupt shops and two bad harvests, famine was spreading from one devastated community to another. The fish-curing station at Belderrig that Maud had helped establish years before was shut down, and along the coast English steam trawlers, by permission of the Free State, were fishing inside the three-mile limit. Their huge nets "dragged the bottom out of the sea," and the fishermen's little boats lay idle.

When Maud returned on the train from Mayo she heard women keening; "the emigrant 'Caoine' . . . it is hard to forget, it tears one's heart out." In an article, "Famine in the West, 1897–1925," she described the "crying of the mothers as the train bears off their dear ones to foreign slavery . . . The 'Caoine' echoes right along the line to be taken up again at the next station." In 1924 there had been under twenty thousand emigrants; a year later there were over thirty thousand.

Unemployment, increasing poverty helped the Republicans in the by-elections. In December the Boundary Commission collapsed. Negotiating for adjustments in liability payments due England since the truce, the Cosgrave government accepted Partition and relinquished the predominantly Catholic and nationalist counties Tyrone and Fermanagh to the North. Maud's Prisoners' Defence League had an overburdened branch in Ulster, where large numbers of dissidents were being jailed. In Dublin the "Mothers" protested the continued mistreatment of prisoners of the Free State.

De Valera, taking advantage of widespread disillusionment with Cosgrave's Cumann na nGaedheal policies, had formed his own party, Fianna Fail, Warriors of Destiny, to enter the political arena with some formula that would enable its members to be seated despite the oath of allegiance. The die-hard Republicans, the irreconcilable women in Cumann na mBann saw this as a defection. The IRA, trying to remain united, supported no party and became an invisible army. The Cosgrave government became increasingly oppressive against Fianna Fail and the IRA; the Treasonable Offences Act of 1926 replaced the Public Safety Act, restoring power of detention and suspension of habeas corpus. The Church issued pastoral letters denouncing Fianna Fail and the Republicans. Parishioners who objected risked excommunication as well as arrest, and prisoners who demonstrated their disapproval of political sermons by walking out of prison chapels were put in solitary confinement. Many Catholics, like Dorothy Macardle, left the Church, but Maud adhered to her faith while condemning the inhumane policies of the hierarchy.

She wrote to the press and to the Catholic College at Maynooth protesting the "intrusion of party politics into the holy
service of the Mass."

As the Catholic middle class gained power, Senator
Yeats felt increasingly uncomfortable in an administration
that bowed to clerical dictates. In Leinster House on June 11,
1925, he spoke with impassioned conviction against legislation
that would make divorce impossible. His impolitic plea for
the preservation of the Protestant tradition, his defense of the
aristocratic, intellectual Anglo-Irish, hampered his battle
against all censorship of the arts, whether by government,
Church, or dogmatic patriot.

In 1926 Yeats had to protect the Abbey players from
physical assault when they produced O'Casey's *The Plough and
the Stars*. On February 10, the third night after the opening,
the performance was disrupted by outraged Republicans organized by Hanna Sheehy-Skeffington and Frank Ryan.
Speeches quickly deteriorated into insults; rotten fruit and
stink bombs were hurled at the actors, and some of the protes-
tors rushed the stage. Yeats called the police, then came out
in front of the lowered curtain. "I thought you had got tired
of this which commenced about fifteen years ago. You have
disgraced yourselves again." White with fury, he tossed back
his long hair and harangued the rioters. "Is this to be an
ever-recurring celebration of Irish genius? Synge first and
then O'Casey?"

Since the night Maud walked out on the *Shadow of the
Glen*, suspicion and prejudice had become worse in Dublin.
After two violent decades a new generation of partisans was
driven to fury by another Nora. O'Casey's Nora Clitheroe,
railing at the power of "Cathleen ni Houlihan" to lead her
men to slaughter, mocked their ideal of Irish womanhood.
Black-gowned, silent, Maud remained seated in the turbulent
audience, and it was Hanna, widow of the pacifist Francis
Skeffington, who stood up and spoke for everyone who felt
that *The Plough and the Stars* belittled the Easter Rising.

Griffith's heirs were offended by "the moral aspect of the
play," the naturalistic portrayal of Dublin tenement life with
its prostitutes, saloons, and squalor. But Hanna took up
Maud's old argument with Yeats. "On National grounds

only," she objected to an Irish theater "that helped to make Easter Week, and that now in its subsidized sleek old age jeers at its former enthusiasm . . . The only censorship that is justified is the free censorship of popular opinion."

Maud confronted O'Casey in a public debate Hanna arranged at the Universities' Republican Club. O'Casey maintained that he "was not trying and would never try, to write about heroes," but only of the life and the people he knew, and he distrusted all Republicans who wanted to make Ireland "the terrible place of a land fit only for heroes to live in." He defended his right to express his views on the stage; politicians had platforms of their own. Ill with silicosis and tortured like Joyce with eye trouble, O'Casey looked at Maud sitting beside Hanna and "felt a surge of hatred for Cathleen ni Houlihan sweeping over him." No longer the bright-faced girl with hair flying over her shoulders, the heroine of the Transvaal Committee driving with James Connolly in the runaway brake down Dame Street, "she sat silent, stony; waiting her turn to say more bitter words against the one who refused to make her dying dream his own . . . her deep-set eyes now sad, agleam with disappointment; never quite at ease with the crowd, whose cheers she loved; the colonel's daughter still."

Within the year O'Casey's antiwar play, *The Silver Tassie*, was refused by the Abbey. Yeats used his own aesthetic censorship against it, saying that O'Casey had sacrificed his character to the message. The rejected playwright said goodbye to Irish restrictions and, fleeing the establishment, exiled himself to England. The daughter of the English colonel went on fighting the establishment in Ireland from every platform she could find.

When he first came to live in Dublin, in 1927, Francis MacManus, teacher and novelist, was twenty-two. As a boy at Griffith's funeral he had seen the capital a burned-out shell; now new life was rising from the rubble. Near the Parnell Monument he heard a burst of cheering. His view down a side street was blocked by several hundred people, but above the "clatter and rumble of the trams and the grind of wheels on the wooden setts" he could hear Maud's voice as she addressed the crowd: "It was a voice no man forgets . . . What she said

I never remembered as words but only the effect of it: an effect of fluent, stern, and even slightly theatrical speech; and more than that, an effect of intense feminine vitality and of great hope."

Maud was sixty; 1927 hardly a year of hope. A tyrannical government held the country in a semblance of peace. In the June election Fianna Fail won a few more seats, forty-four to Cumann na nGaedheal's forty-seven, but was still barred by the Oath. On July 10, Kevin O'Higgins was murdered on his way to Mass. The assassins were never caught, and it was never known whether they were enemies from his own police force, avenging members of the old IRB, or IRA Republicans. O'Higgins, who was found dying on the roadside by Eoin MacNeill, had prophesied his brutal slaying: "Nobody can expect to live who has done what I have."

Yeats, who thought of O'Higgins as the "Irish Mussolini," mourned the loss of "the one strong intellect in Irish public life," and when the Free State retaliated, the Senator wrote Olivia Shakespear, "Next week I must go to Dublin to help vote the more stringent police laws the government think necessary. I hear with anxiety that they will increase the number of crimes punishable by death, and with satisfaction that they will take certain crimes out of the hands of jurors."

Maud considered the new laws a fitting memorial for Cosgrave's strong man, and she saw no other reason to mourn the death of Kevin O'Higgins. He had held her son in prison, executed the commanders of the Four Courts, and ordered the killing of seventy-seven men under the 1922 Free State Emergency Act. In August the government passed two more bills severely restricting constitutional liberties; every candidate, when nominated, would have to swear to take the Oath if elected. De Valera took the only step possible for political survival. He brought Fianna Fail into the government by signing the Oath as a mere formality, the Bible pushed aside along with his principles. The Republican deputies followed suit and were seated in Leinster House, all save Constance Markievicz.

The rebel Countess had died five days after the murder of Kevin O'Higgins. She was spared the humiliation of swearing allegiance to the Crown; even a meaningless gesture would have been agonizing for her. At the end of June she had entered Sir Patrick Dun's Hospital for an appendectomy, choosing to be treated in the public ward. Constance had drilled her Fianna boys on the rough hillsides, sniped at British soldiers from Dublin rooftops; she had scrubbed prison latrines and never spared herself any duty, however menial, to serve the poor. During the coal shortage of the previous winter she had driven into the country to collect turf for the heatless Dublin tenements and carried the heavy sacks up the steep flights of stairs to people who had no fuel. But she was fifty-eight and her physical strength was gone. She did not recover from complications following the operation and died in the hospital on July 15. While official Dublin wore mourning, and flags hung at half staff for the Minister of Home Affairs, the other Dublin mourned Constance's death.

"Poor Mme. Markievicz also gone," wrote Lady Gregory in her journal. She had seen the "hoyden" of Dublin society, "a jealous meddler" in the arts, transformed by her involvement in the labor movement. "There was something gallant about her. We were each working for what we believed would help Ireland . . ." Yeats and the Irish theater had enlarged Lady Gregory's life, but she had never forsaken her family or class. The poet had seen her steady courage during the Troubles.

Augusta Gregory seated at her great ormolu table,
Her eightieth year approaching:
"Yesterday he threatened my life.
I told him that nightly from six to seven I sat at
   this table,
the blinds drawn up"; . . .

At Constance's funeral Maud headed the WPDL in the somber procession of Republican organizations and labor unions swollen by crowds of the Dublin poor. The streets were lined by Free State troops alerted against a potentially revolutionary mob, and guards at Glasnevin prevented a volley from being fired over Constance's grave. De Valera gave the oration: "Madame, the friend of the toiler, the lover of the poor. Ease and station she put aside . . . Sacrifice, misunderstanding and scorn lay on the road she adopted, but she trod unflinchingly."

Maud remembered the merry young Countess with the unspellable name, but the Constance she mourned was the emaciated prisoner in the North Dublin Detention Camp, refusing food but accepting the warm clothes Maud took to her cell during the 1923 hunger strike. Maud had admired her independence for twenty years. Constance had taught herself to carry out her assignments with the selflessness of a martyr, and Maud, who had less of the self-sacrificial impulse, revered her. She had never heard her friend complain, yet she knew how much had been renounced along with the "ease and station" of the Gore-Booths and Lissadell:

> Great windows open to the south,
> Two girls in silk kimonos, both
> Beautiful . . .

Constance and Eva had remained close in spirit and purpose, and Eva's death the year before had been heartbreaking. Constance had sacrificed the comfort of a family, the nourishment and support of personal love, when she became a nationalist. Constance's brother, her husband, her stepson, and her daughter Maeve, who had been brought up by Lady Gore-Booth, gathered at her grave, but she had been apart from them for many years.

Thomas MacDonagh's daughter Bairbre, one of the youngest members of Cumann na mBann, only thirteen when Madame Markievicz died, could never quite remember her looks but sensed something hard in her manner. Mary Colum, seeing Constance for the last time at AE's, pitied her: "The outline of her face was the same, but the expression was different; the familiar eyes that blinked at me from behind glasses were bereft of their old fire and eagerness; she gave me a limp hand and barely spoke to me . . . she was obviously a dying woman, sunk in dejection, a dejection resulting either from her imprisonment or from the loss of her hopes." Constance died a disappointed woman, her ideals unfulfilled, Ireland partitioned, the Republic a lost cause.

The Countess had carried out her assignment; Maud played her role and was more fortunate. She was often disillusioned but never cynical. She had not undergone sudden conversion in middle age. The colonel's daughter, uprooted, orphaned, never bound by the past, rebelled against convention as a girl, and like an artist created her own pattern, taking from the world around her what she needed to make it coherent. The strong will cultivated since childhood enabled her to maintain her consistent faith in herself and her purpose.

Maud was a rebel seeking redress for wrong rather than the establishment of a new system. She was not a revolutionary, although Yeats, taking delight in outrageous juxtaposition, likened her to Ezra Pound, " 'the revolutionary simpleton' . . . He has most of Maud Gonne's opinions (political and economic) about the world in general . . . The chief difference is that he hates Palgrave's *Golden Treasury* as she does the Free State Government, and thinks even worse of its editor than she does of President Cosgrave. He has even her passion for cats . . . [who] belong to the oppressed races."

Maud's love for living was her good fortune, and her feeling for people was always for the individual, each unique and precious life. She called the young women who worked on her committees "Daughter." "You felt loved," said Bairbre MacDonagh, "when that long arm of hers was placed around your shoulder."

# La Grande
# Patriote

Years before in France, Maud's children had missed her when she went off on her mysterious errands. In those uncertain days Sean and Iseult, lonely and sometimes resentful, called her "La Grande Patriote." Their childhood name for their mother had become a family joke; now that they had children of their own and Maud was a grandmother, they still spoke of her to each other as "the G.P."

Sean and Catalina Bulfin had been married in secret very early on the morning of January 26, 1926, at the University Church of Dublin. After their first child, Anna, was born, they came to live at Roebuck House. Kid's proud spirit prevented Maud from overwhelming her, and her devotion to Sean and the Republican cause endeared her to Maud. Sean was away a great deal on missions for the IRA, while his wife and his mother ran the busy household, a nursery and a Republican office.

Iseult and Francis had two children, and in 1928 the cottage in Glencreagh became too small. Maud gave them the purchase price for some property near Glendalough, with its sway-backed churches and shining lakes. Proceeds from the sale of Les Mouettes, which Maud had invested, she now turned over to Iseult, because the house in Normandy had been her daughter's gift from Millevoye. The money would pay to renovate the old walled ruins. Originally a blockhouse built by the English in the eighteenth century, when the rebels of '98 roamed the Wicklow glens, the Stuarts' new home had survived evil days. The Military Road from Dublin to Laragh cut through bogland where present-day fugitives, wanted men of the IRA, could hide in an ancient network of gorse-covered gullies. Ian and Kay Stuart grew up with the scents and sounds of heather in the wind that Maud had loved as a child, and their granite fortress, embellished by a late Victorian landlord with crenellated turrets and climbing roses, resembled Sleeping Beauty's castle. Alas, in reality Iseult and Francis did not "live happily ever after," and Iseult and her children were often with Maud at Roebuck.

Josephine, the tyrant of the kitchen, might complain that all Maud's "geese were swans," but for Maud no child's demand was too great, no disorder too trying. The affectionate patience she lavished on her animals and birds was always there for her grandchildren: Ian, the sensitive towhead; Kay with Maud's radiant complexion; long-legged Anna, whom she called Gray Eyes; and Sean's son Tiernan, the youngest and her favorite. Reincarnation, Maud's comfort in the past, had become as simple as a small hand holding hers, as she walked the brick path that led from the back porch of Roebuck House to the kitchen garden.

Eileen and Joseph MacBride still lived in Westport, and their five children were growing up in Mallow Cottage, once the home of the Land Leaguer and M.P. William O'Brien. People in Major MacBride's home town were proud of their hero, and still would not accept his widow. The prejudice Miss Horniman had felt in 1905 was still strong. Although Madame Gonne MacBride disapproved of drinking and scolded girls for being "flappers," she smoked, was too dramatic, was far too outspoken for a woman. In the early days of her marriage Maud had visited her in-laws, and Joseph MacBride, not knowing what a bad sailor she was, had taken her yachting in Clew Bay as a special treat. Now Sean, who loved to sail, could take Eileen and his half-cousins out for a day in the boat he kept on the Shannon. But Maud stayed away from Westport to avoid embarrassing her half-sister. She kept in touch with Eileen by mail, sent her money when she had it to spare and new Irish books and the latest whodunits.

The postmistress in Westport was more intrigued by the mysterious mail with Russian and Estonian stamps addressed to Mrs. Joseph MacBride. Just before the Russian Revolution of 1917, the Baroness Budberg had sent Margaret Wilson to one of the family's estates in Estonia, and she had stayed on there as caretaker when the Baroness's children no longer needed her as a governess. Eileen never saw her mother after 1892, when Maud had found her a job with a noble family in St. Petersburg, but once when she was living in Paris, Moura Budberg's father had called on her with messages, and over the years letters with foreign stamps continued to arrive in Westport. Some of the MacBrides thought Eileen even more beautiful than Maud; her touch of glamour, vague rumors of far-off places and unhappy times, were all that linked her to her notorious sister-in-law.

Except for Cousin May and Kathleen's daughter, Thora, London had no attractions for Maud. There were more theaters in Dublin now; magic lantern shows had been replaced by newsreels and talkies. The opera at Bayreuth, the Comédie Française were pleasures foregone. When she could afford it, she went back to Dax seeking relief for the rheumatism that plagued her increasingly. From the spa at the foot of the Pyrenees she could make a brief pilgrimage to Lourdes, where in the summer before the Great War she and Helena Molony had been inspired by a Eucharistic Congress—the pageantry, and the humble hordes gathered at the shrine. She could revisit the little town of Arrens, hanging peaceful as a church bell on the mountain wall, and the infirmary at Argelès, where she had seen soldiers dying, now once more a resort hotel filled with tourists.

She had put down roots at last. In Ireland with her work and her family, she had what she had always wanted; not permanence, which would be boring, but her own life in her own place. Roebuck House had become her center. The world moved and changed ever more swiftly around it, and she herself, as on some whirling planet she had discovered, moved too.

Disappointed by the mediocre standards of the Free

State, all that he despised of middle-class morality, Yeats still tried to ignore the sacrifice of the Civil War, the dead Republicans, the seventy-seven executed men. "These dead cannot share the glory of those earlier dead," he wrote, "their names are not spoken aloud to-day except at those dwindling meetings assembled in O'Connell Street or at some prison gate by almost the sole surviving friend of my early manhood, protesting in sybilline old age, as once in youth and beauty, against what seems to her a tyranny."

Yeats realized he was jeopardizing his seat in the Senate when he fought the Censorship of Publications Bill, paraphrasing Wilde: "There is no such thing as a moral or immoral book. Books are well written or badly written."Although he was not reinvited to the Senate, he did not sever his ties with the government, hoping it might yet provide the elite authoritarian rule he favored. Maud continued to ignore him; and, confused by a political situation in which he was an honored outcast, Yeats was vulnerable to her reproach. Her integrity had never ceased to astound him, and he paid it homage in the preface to his revised edition of *A Vision*, the metaphysical summation of the psychic studies begun long before in the Golden Dawn. Again he compared Maud and Pound, seeing her this time "as unlike him as possible . . . grown gaunt in the injustice of what seems her blind nobility of pity: 'I will fight until I die,' she wrote to me once, 'against the cruelty of small ambitions.' "

She rode the Goatstown bus back and forth between Roebuck and the WPDL office on Lower Abbey Street. She led meetings on street corners, petitioned government officials, besieged newspaper offices with her delegations of "Mothers." Almost every issue of *An Phoblacht*, the Republican paper, carried her articles on political prisoners held in solitary confinement, tortured and humiliated by their countrymen. It had been nearly forty years since her first visit to Portland Jail, and it was as if she had never recovered from her initial shock of pity and anger. In April 1929 she went back to England on behalf of four Irish prisoners of war who had been held in Dartmoor and Maidstone since 1922. She toured London, Glasgow, Liverpool, Manchester, and at Lancashire, with the Indian Nationalist Saklatvala, she addressed a meeting demanding the release of both Indian and Irish hostages.

Her campaign was taken up by Roger Baldwin, chairman of the American branch of the International Committee for Republican Prisoners, who petitioned the Free State Embassy in Washington. Token reprieves were won, prisoners on the verge of insanity or death were freed, but Maud's unending propaganda accomplished less for the prisoners than for the political parties opposing Cosgrave and Cumann na nGaedheal.

With Sean, Maud had joined the short-lived Comhairle na Poblachta formed after the IRA convention in January 1929 to unify the non-Fianna Fail Republicans. The Free State police looked on the Council of Republicans as a plot to overthrow the State by "force of arms." But its membership was too broad to present any coherent political program, much less a revolutionary threat, and it soon dissolved into its disparate elements.

During the Great Depression of the thirties the problems of workers and farmers were taken up as they had not been since the days of James Connolly. There were many left-wing leaders now, like George Gilmore, Frank Ryan, and radical new land reformers such as Peadar O'Donnell, who had sparked the rural movement against payment of land annuities due England under the Free State agreement of 1926. In Ireland as in other countries, political and parapolitical groups committed to social change proliferated. Mrs. Despard sponsored a Workers' College in a building she owned on Eccles Street and founded the Friends of Soviet Russia. Hanna Sheehy-Skeffington and Nora Connolly, now married to William O'Brien, a labor leader, were active in the Women's International League for Peace and Freedom and the International Anti-Imperialist League. The Depression swelled the ranks of the National Unemployed Movement, the Irish Workers' and Farmers' Party, and the Irish Communist Party. The Commissioner of Police, General Eoin O'-Duffy, knew how to deal with the home-grown variety of IRA subversive, but the "imported" type spelled danger, and the Irish Criminal Investigation Department was busy investigating and intimidating. "The number of these revolutionary organizations, all of which have something in common, is bewildering . . . It is also of interest to note that much the same people appear to be behind several organizations, Mrs. Maud MacBride being as ubiquitous as it is possible to be."

The annual commemoration at Wolfe Tone's grave in July drew a crowd of fifteen thousand Republicans who faced down a cowed array of police at Bodenstown. While De Valera waited on the sidelines, IRA and Fianna Fail members heard O'Donnell prophesy the dawn of radical republicanism. The unresolved antipathies of the Civil War released a new wave of shootings. Police infiltrators found dead in alleyways were tagged: "Spies and informers beware.—I.R.A." Wardens known for cruelty were manacled to prison bars; jurors were intimidated. In the summer of 1931, Sean MacBride and seven other IRA leaders were arrested in Kerry and tried for treason. The judge ruled that police could not arrest on grounds of suspicion or depend on documents alone for proof. The courts and the guardians of justice were subject to public pressure and the forceful persuasion of the IRA. Frustrated, the police stepped up their persecutions.

At seven-thirty on the morning of July 17, thirty C.I.D. men with a warrant under the Treason Act battered their way into Roebuck House. "Armed with revolvers, electric torches, long iron rods with wooden handles and in some cases with ordinary walking sticks, the raiders ransacked every room in the house." Maud was away, but Mrs. Despard saw the drawing room walls gutted in a vain hunt for a weapons "dump." Letters and documents tossed out on the lawn blew away across the fields.

Alarms of civil war at home and abroad brought on a full-scale witch hunt. The clergy saw in the establishment of the Spanish Republic a dire prediction of the "red menace" vanquishing a Catholic state. From Maynooth, Irish bishops issued a joint pastoral linking the IRA and its political organizations with bolshevism. On October 17 a new Public Safety Bill, which Police Commissioner Eoin O'Duffy had urged, became Article 2A of the Constitution.

Excessive repression served only to make the Cosgrave regime more unpopular, and the economic crisis, with a hundred thousand unemployed, insured victory for Fianna Fail, with IRA support, in the general election of February 1932. No landslide vote, no radical change; De Valera took over the government from his old enemies like a driver seizing reins midjourney, and the Irish breathed a sigh of relief at a peaceful change of party rule. Fianna Fail was led by the wiliest constitutionalist since Parnell. Maud and her friends saw a revival of Griffith's early Sinn Fein policies in President de Valera's program to abolish the payment of land annuities to England and encourage an independent economy.

The Public Safety Act was suspended, and amnesty granted to the men and women sentenced by the infamous Military Tribunal. *An Phoblacht* resumed publication, and Maud wrote for it in high expectation: ". . . the work of the WPDL will be concluded and the 'Mothers' can take a rest— the opening of the jail gates will have accomplished what machine guns and proclamations failed to do—perhaps O'Connell Street will feel just a little lonely for us on Sunday mornings."

The next day hundreds of released prisoners assembled in College Green were cheered by a rally of thirty thousand, the largest gathering "in living memory." Maud, on the speakers' platform in veil and dark fur-trimmed coat, spoke for the first time in her life through a microphone. Sean MacBride read greetings from the Clan na Gael in America, then described the IRA's goals and the aspirations of the 1916 Volunteers, "the hope that all the national forces in the country would unite in marching forward towards achieving a free Irish Republic for the whole of Ireland."

De Valera moved too slowly to satisfy Republicans, who longed for more direct action against British imperialism. Cumann na mBann instituted boycotts of British goods. No longer outlawed, the IRA began to drill again; membership grew, but there was confusion about its function, and some units attacked members of Cumann na nGaedheal. Right-wing paramilitary organizations sprang to the defense of the former government party, foremost among them the Army Comrades Association, headed by Dr. T. F. O'Higgins, brother of the assassinated Minister of Justice.

Three months after Maud's appearance in College Green at the jubilant welcome for the released prisoners, she was back at her vigils. "The C.I.D. are reverting to their old methods of persecution," she wrote. "Next Sunday the Women's Prisoners' Defence League will resume the weekly Prisoners' meetings in Cathal Brugha Street and continue them while the necessity remains."

But attendance at her street-corner meetings was dwindling. The security measures skillfully imposed by De Valera were accepted as necessary for the new prosperity he promised Ireland. In 1933, Eoin O'Duffy, dismissed by De Valera as Commissioner of the Gardai, assumed leadership of the Army Comrades Association, and the sound of the goose step was heard in Ireland. O'Duffy's followers adopted blue shirts as their uniform and proclaimed themselves the new National Guard._They were backed by members of the clergy and the business community, to whom De Valera, who still allowed the IRA to bear arms, posed a vague "communistic" threat. Blue Shirts and IRA, both self-proclaimed defenders of their country, sparred with one another in the streets. When Blue Shirts set fire to Mrs. Despard's Workers' College in Eccles Street, IRA men ran to put out the blaze. Such confrontations gave De Valera a reason to reinstitute the notorious Article 2A with its Military Tribunal. In a memorial article about Constance Markievicz, Hanna Sheehy-Skeffington pointed out that De Valera's attitudes toward republicanism and toward women had never been those of James Connolly. To Connolly "woman was an equal, a comrade; to the other, a sheltered being, withdrawn to the domestic hearth, shrinking from public life."

Three decades earlier, Maud and her contemporaries had witnessed a renaissance for Irishwomen: Inghinidhe na hEireann and Cumann na mBann had given them a political foothold in national affairs. Now the strutting men in the streets, the crowds that listened to the promises of economic well-being for the common man, looked with suspicion at women who overstepped the bonds of domesticity. Many people thought the WPDL was obsolete and comic. According to the actor Michael MacLiammoir, what he termed "Dirty Dublin" had its epithet for the leaders: "Maud Gonne Mad and Mrs. Desparate." Whether or not they approved her current street appearances, old-timers in the nationalist movement still respected Maud. Her friends decided the time had come to honor her years of service to Ireland. She remonstrated at the fuss, but was finally persuaded to accept a watch and a gold key brooch symbolizing her efforts to open prison gates.

Women fighting for their rights admired her, and to the young intellectuals, artists and students, the legendary Maud Gonne was irresistible. Joseph Campbell, the poet of the Wicklow Mountains, was infatuated, and so was Dr. Patrick McCartan, who had succumbed to her spell thirty years before in America. Michael MacLiammoir endeared himself to her by forsaking his early success on the London stage to work in Dublin's Gate Theatre. "I had expected a tall rose; I was confronted by a black orchid," he said, remembering his first sight of Maud at the time of her return from exile in France. Now, twenty-five years later, she seemed no older to him except for the fine tracery of lines on her face. Her entrances were still theatrical—her tall, thin figure poised for a moment in the doorway, her presence felt, then a graceful gesture. Maud published a newssheet, *Prison Bars*, in the thirties, signing her column "A Woman of No Importance." Roger MacHugh, who helped her edit it, came to a party at Roebuck with a pretty young actress—the center of attention until Maud entered the room and all the young men deserted her to sit at Maud's feet. One of her young admirers, the actor Liam Redmond, who married Bairbre MacDonagh, described her chain smoking, handling her cigarette the way women in an earlier age flirted with a fan.

She had such tales of the past: at a banquet in the days of the Land League she had been seated between John Redmond and John Dillon, and each would speak only to her; but later, when she became a Sinn Feiner, neither of them spoke to her but only to each other. She liked to tell how she and Frank Harris had plotted to help Oscar Wilde escape from prison by sending him files baked into loaves of bread. She wished she could find that letter from Wilde: "Your suggestion is most romantic and kind, but I really feel too depressed in body and mind to undertake such strenuous exercise as your adventure seems to me to suggest." It was Willie Yeats who had inspired her with the idea when he asked her to sign a petition stating that Wilde had been wrongly accused. "Willie," she had said, "Mr. Wilde is not innocent but I will sign it because it will be a blow against England." The plan was to row Wilde down the river to the Channel, and Yeats had said, " 'Yes, in a boat with painted oars,' and I said, 'Willie, Willie, we must be practical.' " Was Maud forever telling him to be practical? The young, who wished above all to hear about her romance with Yeats, learned less from her than from his poems.

For more than ten years Maud had refused to see Willie. Even after he left the Senate, his support and semiofficial association with the Free State enraged her. His defense of *The Plough and the Stars*, his choice of an English artist to design the new Irish coinage, had made her feel that Yeats was lost to Ireland. But now, in 1933, he showed signs of becoming a rebel again. The old dream of Ireland governed by an elite was still foremost in his mind; if it was not to be political, and De Valera fell short of his standards, then it must be intellectual. Shortly before Lady Gregory's death in 1932, Yeats and AE had discussed with her the need for an Irish Academy of Letters. Such a body could resurrect the excitement of the Irish Renaissance. Yeats thought an Academy could safeguard Ireland from the deadening effects of censorship by Church and Government. By the end of the year he had made a successful lecture tour in America and with the help of McCartan had raised enough money to get the project under way. The first members included Shaw, Gogarty, AE, Peadar O'Donnell, James Stephens, Austin Clarke, Sean O'Faolain, Liam O'Flaherty, and Francis Stuart. To Yeats's delight, the conservative press and the Church attacked them; he still enjoyed a scrap with the mob. "If I were a young man," he wrote Olivia Shakespear, "I would welcome four years of conflict, for it creates unity among the educated classes, and force De Valera's Ministers, in all probability, to repudiate the ignorance that has in part put them into power." His reasons for disliking the establishment were not Maud's, but she was reassured to see him fighting for his own beliefs with a devil-may-care spirit.

Yeats, deeply grieved by Lady Gregory's death, felt the loss of the tradition, the center which had held him for so long. Coole Park itself, the symbol of aristocratic Ireland. He had already given up Thoor Ballylee as unsuitably damp. In 1933 he settled with George and their two children in a small house with a large garden, Riversdale, in Rathfarnham, just outside Dublin, beyond the abandoned campus of Pearse's school. "The garden is full of roses and there are lilies in the lily pond and the croquet goes on from day to day and I can still beat my family. All is well . . . I am revising a one-volume edition of my poems . . . and have made peace with ____ ____ who has suddenly and inexplicably turned amicable."

Young Michael Yeats would bicycle to Roebuck from Rathfarnham with messages for Maud and, wobbling precariously in the drive, would be met by the bounding force of one of Dagda's successors. Rescued by Maud from the blandishments of her black-and-white Great Dane, Michael would return to Riversdale with her reply.

Any guest, child or potentate, tramp or curious tourist, who breached the first fierce assault found welcome and asylum at Roebuck House. The dog's bark was friendly. The same did not hold true for Charlotte Despard. She could not tolerate Yeats. He could not tolerate her. She left Roebuck House in 1933 for Ballycastle, outside Belfast, to take up a strenuous campaign for civil rights in Northern Ireland. The ninety-year-old freedom fighter told Brendan Behan, then a young IRA recruit, that "the next move in Irish revolutionary politics would be made by the Northern worker." Her departure made a rapprochement between Maud and Willie easier.

It took no more than a return of his old bravado to interest Maud again, and in one of his periodic attacks of politics he was in a lively rage. The man she met now at tea or an occasional lunch in town was unwell, aging and yet somehow undefeated. Under the suave appearance, the fine clothes, was the naïve boy she had known. He made the mistake of inviting her for tea at the Kildare Street Club, and she made the mistake of going. Women were not allowed in the inner sanctum, so they sat in the gloomy hall under a portrait of a beribboned viceroy, and Yeats made an uncomfortable situation worse by introducing her to some Anglo-Irish peer. They parted in a huff, but they continued to meet and, inevitably, to argue.

Yeats thought O'Duffy's Blue Shirts could give Ireland what he had so often prescribed: "The despotic rule of the educated classes . . ." To Maud, O'Duffy was the tool of her old enemies in the Free State. She could not conceive of trusting a man who had headed the police for twelve years. The Blue Shirts planned a great march on Dublin in August, and Yeats was exhilarated at rumors of an impending coup. However, De Valera reinstituted the Military Tribunals and alerted the police, and the armed IRA was ready for action. O'Duffy canceled the march. Having written marching songs for the Blue Shirts, Yeats decided that O'Duffy was a weakling and turned the songs into unusable parodies. George, who hated the Blue Shirts, was immensely relieved. Later O'Duffy aligned himself with Cosgrave's party and the conservative farmers to form a new coalition of the right called Fine Gael, and Yeats saw him for the ordinary politician he was. It seemed to Maud that her old friend was still playing at politics like a butterfly.

As Yeats approached seventy he and George spent much time abroad, seeking warmth and peace in southern Europe. More and more he believed in a link between sexual and creative powers, and he made up his mind to undergo the newly discovered Steinach rejuvenation operation at a London clinic. Dr. Gogarty, informed only after the event, was appalled, but whether the monkey glands restored sexual potency or not, the psychological effect was beneficial. Yeats was at work on poems that gave him great satisfaction, his creative energy at a peak.

In December 1935 Maud went to Belfast, where Charlotte Despard was caring for victims of new pogroms. "Few people realize just what life is like under Orange terror in the North," wrote Maud. "One time I counted 5 children on crutches in the garden recovering from bullet wounds." To help her indomitable old friend, Maud crossed the invisible boundary surrounding an Ulster she refused to recognize. Yet she gave it practical recognition by not bothering to purchase a return ticket. She was to lecture in the linen manufacturing town of Lurgan, where George Russell had been born sixty-eight years earlier. He had died that summer of cancer, just a year and a half after the death of his wife Violet; gone off to his Karma or to the Gaelic heaven world, Tir na nOg, where he would bend the ears of the gods with his tales. Now his birthplace was wracked with sectarian strife and still under British rule.

After she had given two lectures, Maud was arrested in the middle of the night at the home of friends in Lurgan. Just as she had anticipated, she was shipped back to Dublin at government expense.

In the old days, before the Treaty created a monstrous reality out of the six northern counties, she had spent happy, peaceful days in the North with Anna Johnston and Alice Milligan of the *Shan Van Vocht*, evenings at meetings of Bulmer Hobson's Dungannon Clubs. The North had given the nationalist movement great leaders; new leaders were rising in the ferment over Partition. The IRA was supported by the Church in Ulster, where the Catholic Irish once more faced starvation or emigration.

De Valera dragged his heels on Partition. His immediate concern was to strengthen his government, and most people in the South were interested only in bettering their own lot. Yeats expressed a not uncommon attitude when he told Maud "he found the inhabitants of the lost province of Ulster so disagreeable that he hoped they would never reunite with the rest of Ireland." As popular feeling against Partition diminished, the IRA became a peripheral force. *An Phoblacht* ceased publication in 1935 from lack of support. Uncoordinated acts of violence led to arrests, and De Valera used the Military Tribunal against his old comrades in the IRA as he had earlier against the Blue Shirts. The IRA was outlawed in June 1936; its chief of staff, Maurice Twomey, was sentenced by the Tribunal to three years' hard labor. The extremist wing, about four hundred in all, followed Frank Ryan to fight fascism abroad in Spain, forming the James Connolly Battalion of the International Brigade. O'Duffy had taken about seven hundred Blue Shirts to Spain to fight for Franco, but their record was inglorious, and they returned home to fight with words for recognition of Franco's regime.

In 1936, shortly before her seventieth birthday, Maud ran for public office. Sean MacBride, steering his way among the more extreme Republicans, those who argued for physical force, formed another radical political party, Cumann Po-blachta na hEireann. Maud ran in the general election from Area 5, and like the other candidates put up by the Republicans, she made a very poor showing. She did what she could for Sean's sake, but with this second defeat, it was clear that no united front was possible for the IRA. There was no common base from which to oppose De Valera. The "devil" had shown his true color: not red, not even Republican pink, but bright green, a shade that pleased the small farmer and middleman, the patriotic man in the street. In 1937 De Valera's new constitution, written in Gaelic, cemented the ties between Church and State and weakened the ties to England. Maud's old teacher from the Gaelic League, Douglas Hyde, was honored by being made the first president of Eire. De Valera was Prime Minister, and in one of the great stratagems of his career he made an economic settlement under which Neville Chamberlain, Prime Minister of England, gave the Free State control of all the military bases England had taken under the Treaty.

After the failure of Cumann Poblachta na hEireann, MacBride broke with the militants, men like Tom Barry who were all for physical force in the North, firebrands like Sean Russell who were planning a campaign of terror in England. In 1937 Maud's son retired as a commanding officer—at thirty-three he had spent almost half his life in the IRA—and took up the practice of law. When he was called to the bar he began defending cases in which but a year earlier he might have been the defendant. With the further decline of Maud's income in the thirties, Sean's earnings as a barrister when he was fortunate enough to be paid were essential for the support of the family and the maintenance of Roebuck House.

Maud had always managed to keep servants, but after Josephine died it became more difficult. Kid, who had taken over most of the housekeeping chores from Maud, had her hands full, and to make matters worse, Anna, now going on twelve, was constantly ill with bronchial trouble. Many times Maud had wished she could earn money from her journalism. Writing had always been easy for her—to tell a good yarn, to describe, embellish, evoke. In 1936 she started to work on her reminiscences. She might conceivably enjoy the task she set herself as a way of making money, and she might be able to answer once and for all some of the questions people were always asking: Why had she become an Irish rebel? Was it true the Prince of Wales had danced with her? What had it been like to work for the Boulangists, to travel to St. Petersburg in the eighties? And what of O'Leary, Parnell, Connolly, Clarke, Griffith, Davitt, John MacBride? And what about Willie Yeats?

She wrote in bed every morning in her sunny room with her plants and caged birds. As time went on she came down later and later for lunch, and sometimes she would not appear till teatime. The job was more difficult than she had imagined. So many of her papers had been lost or destroyed; some memories were clouded with pain, some had faded. She and Willie were in truth the last survivors. They had outlived most of their contemporaries, and there were very few to whom she could turn for help when memory failed her. Her friend Dorothy Macardle, who had just completed her monumental account of the first fourteen years of the Irish Republic, was always there to encourage, edit, and advise. But as in everything she had ever undertaken, Maud wrote in her own inimitable fashion. She was not subjective, she was not literary, she was not careful about dates and sequence; she simply told the adventure that life had been for her. She enclosed her memoirs in a vision she had once experienced on her way home from a famine relief mission to Mayo:

> Tired but glowing I looked out of the window of the train at the dark bog land where now only the tiny lakes gleamed in the fading light. Then I saw a tall, beautiful woman with dark hair blown on the wind and I knew it was Cathleen ni Houlihan. She was crossing the bog towards the hills, springing from stone to stone over the treacherous surface, and the little white stones shone, marking a path behind her, then faded into the darkness. I heard a voice say: "You are one of the little stones on which the feet of the Queen have rested on her way to Freedom." The sadness of night took hold of me and I

cried; it seemed so lonely just to be one of those little stones left behind on the path.

Being old now and not triumphant I know the blessedness of having been "one of those little stones" on the path to Freedom.

Dorothy Macardle sent Maud's manuscript to her publisher in London, Victor Gollancz Ltd. By the spring of 1938, after the Irish novelist L.A.G. Strong had written a favorable report, Maud had a contract. Gollancz, the founder of the Left Book Club, was enchanted with his fiery author and heroine. Cautious about possible libel suits, he asked Maud to drop certain names from the text. Maud told Bairbre MacDonagh over coffee at Bewley's shop in Dublin that her publishers did not want her to tell the full story of her "scandalous" past, but her own discretion was an equal deterrent. Nevertheless, it seemed a pity one couldn't print the truth about people, she wrote her publisher. She doubted that in the current state of opinion any of the old evictors would want to draw attention to their acts of the past by the extra publicity of libel action. But she bowed to the demands of lawyers, disguising a few characters and taking Dr. Mark Ryan's name out of the chapter called "Betrayal." To get Dr. Ryan's permission would be difficult, she wrote Gollancz, because the incident in question had ended their friendship. She thought his objection would be, not to having contemplated sinking an English battleship, but to having trusted Frank Hugh O'Donnell with matters he should not. O'Donnell was long since dead. She had also written to Yeats for permission to use his poems and did not anticipate a refusal.

Yeats was, as she expected, generous. "Yes of course you can say what you like about me." But he corrected her appraisal of his views: "I have never felt the Irish struggle 'hopeless.' Let it be 'exhausting struggle' or 'tragic struggle' or some such phrase. I wanted the struggle to go on but in a different way. You can of course quote those poems of mine, but if you do not want my curse do not misprint them. People constantly misprint quotations."

Her title was chosen only after much discussion. Gollancz warned Maud that any mention of Ireland would put off the English reader. After her suggestion of "One of Those Little Stones" or "Laughing and Fighting," and his of "The Battles I Fought" were discarded, the book was finally published at the end of the year as *A Servant of the Queen*, a puzzling title with its associations with Victoria; but Maud meant Cathleen or Queen Maeve. Even her signature was problematical. In August she had written Gollancz that she agreed with him about the shorter use of Maud Gonne. She had always used it during her married life, but Ireland was conservative about such matters, and she thought it might be grounds for attack if she did not sign her name in full. She told him she would consult her family, and since the book was to be serialized in the *Irish Press*, she decided to be Maud Gonne MacBride.

All the annoyances of being a published author were hers. She wrote Gollancz that she had seen that her book had been advertised under its first title: *One of Those Little Stones*. It seemed to her a pity, as he had made her change the title. She also regretted his decision not to use any of the battering ram eviction photos, for those scenes of horror were what had turned her into such a bitter enemy of the British Empire. The book had no index for the cast of illustrious characters; two chapters were out of sequence; and the absence of dates gave the predictably hostile English critics reason to question her accuracy. Irish reviewers acclaimed the story of Maud Gonne's conversion to the nationalist cause. In England her "mystical" politics seemed dangerously similar to the emotional racism of the Nazis, or as Geoffrey Grigson put it in *John O'London's Weekly*, "that kind of mess from which 'revolution backwards' may spring."

Maud's severest critic never read *A Servant of the Queen*. In 1938 Yeats's health was failing and he husbanded his energies. After an illness that summer, he wrote to Maud: "When I got better I thought of asking you to dine with me, then I put it off till *On the Boiler* is out . . . The first number will be published in about a month. Perhaps you will hate me for it. For the first time I am saying what I believe about Irish and European politics. I wonder how many friends I will have left. Some of it may amuse you."

In his new series of essays, Yeats discussed themes that

had engaged him for years but which he now reexamined in the light of Europe's upheaval, refining his philosophy of civilization and decay: "Plato's Republic with machines instead of slaves" might dawn under national socialism; C. H. Douglas's Social Credit might benefit the common man ruled by some form of dictatorship. "The drilled and docile masses may submit, but a prolonged civil war seems more likely, with the victory of the skilful, riding their machines as did the feudal knights their armoured horses." In a bitter mood, mocking yet strangely gay, Yeats felt exhilarated by the prospect of war; he had come to believe that without a sense of terror there could be no rediscovery of the elite, without warfare no renewal of the race. Pound had introduced Yeats and his friends some years past to Major Douglas's economic theories, and racial prejudices like Pound's were voiced from Rome to Berlin, from Heidelberg to Oxford. But it was Yeats's aesthetic philosophy—art for art's sake—which underlay his dismissal of democratic principles in education and eugenics. Although he recognized the great changes in the world with all the prescience of his poetic sensibility—"Ireland is getting a proletariat," he wrote a friend in England, "which in Dublin is pushing aside the old peasant basis of the nation"—his romantic attachment to the land and his belief in rule by an elite remained unchanged. He was still at heart a nationalist, a Fenian of O'Leary's school. His last essay, "Ireland After the Revolution," had a note that rang in Maud's heart: "Indeed I beg our governments to exclude all alien appeal to mass instinct. The Irish mind has still, in country rapscallion or in Bernard Shaw, an ancient, cold, explosive, detonating impartiality. The English mind, excited by its newspaper proprietors and its schoolmasters, has turned into a bed-hot harlot."

His indignation at England had flared up during a renewal of controversy over the suspected forgery of Roger Casement's incriminating diaries. Despite deep friendships with English men and women and his admitted debt to "Shakespeare, Blake and Morris," Yeats had never put aside the passion against English tyranny which had made him join the IRB as a young man. "The Wild Old Wicked Man," as he now saw himself, took up once more the rebellious exaltation he had experienced with Maud when they marched together through Dublin in the Jubilee riots.

Maud never lost that fury. All her feelings about international politics sprang from her undying hatred of British imperialism. She regarded fascism and communism with an impartial curiosity. The prejudices against Jews, moneylenders, and Freemasons which she had picked up from Lucien Millevoye and the anti-Dreyfusards came to the fore when she wrote about the two "warring social systems." Attacking England's "alliance with the Jewish money powers and her proficiency in their unholy science of Usury . . ." she wrote, "this control of finance has been England's great weapon in fomenting war."

As a Republican she suggested that the Irish look at fascism and communism for "the good points where the two contrary systems agree." Planned economy; control of finance; state care for children, prospective mothers and workers; science serving the nation: such programs would be beneficial. Like Yeats she feared for her country's future. "The Proclamation of the Republic embodied a social policy based on equal rights and opportunities for all citizens, men and women. It left no place for land-grabbers and usurers. When this generation abandoned the Republic it seems to have abandoned all constructive thought. Youth encouraged to drown thought on the playing fields and middle age to goggle after pensions dangled by two political parties . . . Surely no way to build a nation."

Late that summer Maud went to call on Yeats at Riversdale. She walked over the bridge across the stream and up the path through George's well-kept wilderness of shrubbery. The old gray house was set behind an orchard heavy with apples; the croquet lawn was off to one side, and beyond were the blue hills. The heart-shaped knocker on the door was inscribed simply "Yeats," just as at Woburn Buildings.

They had tea in his study. Birds hopped at the sill to feed from the half-coconut. Canaries perched in the cage by the window; the dog lay by the gas fire. In his old age Willie had acquired some of Maud's patience with animals and had almost learned her ways with children. His chow dog resembled him, and the cat Pangur was affectionate, but Maud knew that Willie's young son and daughter found him quite intimidating. This afternoon he was in high spirits about his work. Not long before he had written Lady Dorothy Wellesley, "I thought my problem was to face death with gaiety, now I have learnt it is to face life."

How elegant he looked with his shock of white hair and brown skin and the fawn silk dressing gown to match—elegant and elated. Yet Maud had an overwhelming sense that she was seeing her oldest friend for the last time on earth. Somehow they managed to avoid arguing, and their tête-à-tête was harmonious. "As we said goodbye," she wrote, "he sitting in his armchair from which he could rise only with great effort said, 'Maud, we should have gone on with our Castle of the Heroes, we might still do it.' I was so surprised that he remembered I could not reply . . . I stood speechless beside him with the song of Red Hanrahan echoing through my mind, 'Angers that are like noisy clouds have set our hearts abeat.' "

A few weeks later when Yeats read in the newspaper "that a letter, or a portion of a letter, signed Maud Gonne MacBride, had been found by the English police on one of their IRA captives," he exclaimed, "What a woman! What vitality! What energy!" He wrote Sir William Rothenstein, "I wish you could find some way of making a drawing of Maud Gonne. No artist has ever drawn her, and just now she looks magnificent. I cannot imagine anything but an air-raid that would bring her to London. She might come to see the spectacle . . ."

That winter Yeats left Ireland for the last time. He died on January 28, 1939, at Cap Martin and was buried high above the Mediterranean coast in the cemetery of the little town of Roquebrune, overlooking the Cap and the white walls of Monaco.

Iseult wrote George Yeats "a letter to be unanswered . . . To me it was a sudden shock and it is still to realize I would never see Willy again but—and I know you will understand what I will be explaining so badly—it was also a relief. . . . There was something tragic about him because he had grown old . . . He tried in turns to adapt himself to it (being older than the oldest) and in turns he denied it altogether. . . . How grand it is to think of 'the predestined dancing place' where there is no such thing for him."

That summer Maud received a parcel of her letters which Willie had saved over the years. She wrote George thanking her for her courtesy:

> I have not the courage to open it today. You must know, I think, what a strain it is looking over old papers which bring back so many things but I will try and do so before Mr. Hone comes to see me next Monday, he said you suggested his coming to see me to tell him about the early days of Willie, when I met him as a boy. He asked me if I had any letters of his. Alas in all the many raids in my house, most have been lost and destroyed and very many I did not keep, because I always feared keeping papers connected with material which might be got hold of by the enemy. I am so sorry to hear that Michael had the measles . . . I hope, we may have a chance of meeting sometime but I am so old, I always fear I bore my friends. When you are a little freer from the worry of house moving perhaps you will spare me one afternoon and we can have tea together.
>
> Your affectionate,
> Maud Gonne MacBride

# The Tower of Age

No dark tomb-haunter once; her form all full
As though with magnanimity of light,
Yet a most gentle woman; who can tell
Which of her forms has shown her substance right?

In *A Servant of the Queen*, Maud wrote of herself always in motion, never in depth, and she had no pretensions about having created a work of art. She had hoped to make some money, but her timing was wrong. Hitler's Wehrmacht, De Valera's neutrality, the IRA's ultimatum demanding withdrawal of British forces from all of Ireland, followed by Sean Russell's bombing campaign, death-dealing explosions in London and Coventry: in the year of Munich, a book by an Irish rebel was not apt to find many readers. Only fifteen hundred copies were sold. The outbreak of war finished its brief career and by 1943 it was out of print. The unbound pages went up in flames when Gollancz's warehouse was hit during the Blitz.

As an author Maud had small success, yet with the decline of her physical ability to pursue the active life that had been hers for so long, she spent more and more of her time writing. "I am working on a second book," she informed her publisher while the first was going to press, "bringing the story up to the present day, whether or not for publication I am not certain." To write the sequel to *A Servant of the Queen*, which ended with her marriage to MacBride, would require so much discretion, so much dissembling, that she hesitated. Her restless body, her impatient mind were unaccustomed to the solitary occupation of a writer and the self-examination of a memoirist, but as the end of her life loomed closer, she could no longer exist only in the constantly diminishing present.

One by one her old friends were dying, and she longed to tell their stories so that future generations would know them and learn what it had been like to be alive in a time of revolution. Maud wept when Charlotte Despard died in 1939, and when she spoke a few words to the friends assembled at the grave in Glasnevin, her voice broke, and she was unable to go on.

She missed Willie and was glad of the opportunity to talk about him, as once he had been to speak her name. Joseph Hone went out to Roebuck to interview Maud for his biography of Yeats and found her sympathetic and solicitous. "How reckless of you losing your way," she teased in her letter to him. "You should have waited for the Goatstown bus. You must have been very tired. I enjoyed our talk very much. Talking to you helps me to dig out of my memory old forgotten things, which made life interesting." Still insistent that her first meeting with Yeats had taken place in Dublin, she added, "Willie joined the I.R.B. *before* I did, *possibly* before we met for the first time at John O'Leary's tea party."

Stephen Gwynn asked her to write a piece for a collection of tributes to the poet, and she surprised people who had watched their stormy friendship by praising his tremendous contribution to the political growth of the Irish nation; but for his intractable belief and dogged labor, the Irish literary movement would never have been born, and without its spark the Rising from which she dated the creation of the Republic might not have taken place. Together they had been part of history. "He is gone," she wrote, "and I am a prisoner of old age, waiting for release. The Ireland I live in is very different from the Ireland of our dream, because our dream is not yet achieved. . . ."

Maud's son-in-law, whose cynicism was trying, found her an "incongruous mixture of obliviousness, childlike eagerness, generosity, lack of self-knowledge and the humorlessness that results." Francis Stuart thought she should be able to see that the peasant society of Ireland which had captured her compassionate imagination "had become one of the most tenacious roots of the sour conservatism that blossomed after our liberation, economically and in almost every other way." She blamed those in power and kept her faith in the powerless. She was generous to the sardonic young novelist—restless, difficult, unfaithful—who was breaking her daughter's heart. "Grim dear," she wrote when his *Great Squire* was published in 1939, "it's a great book. Iseult is right about your genius . . ."

In April Iseult's husband left her at Laragh and went to Germany to read and lecture, eventually accepting a position in modern English and Irish literature at the University of Berlin. After a brief visit home he returned to Germany in January 1940, four months after the outbreak of the Second World War. Although Stuart made some broadcasts for the Germans and was in touch with German intelligence, he initiated his own political adventures. He was not officially involved in the IRA's German connections, sponsored by Joseph McGarrity of the Clan na Gael, who had helped Casement in 1915. As an Irishman living in Germany, Stuart was approached by a Nazi agent, Hermann Goertz, who was to be parachuted into Ireland. Stuart told him how to find Iseult, who would be able to put him in touch with the proper IRA contacts. Goertz landed in Meath in May and arrived at Laragh on foot. Iseult carried out instructions, and the German spy was duly installed in a safe house in Dublin. On May 23 the Irish police raided the house, which belonged to a German-born citizen, Stephen Held. Goertz escaped out the back door, leaving behind his parachute, wireless, and a safe filled with twenty thousand American dollars. Held was arrested, and the spy scare prompted the internment of four hundred IRA suspects in the Curragh camp. A man's suit found in Held's house was traced by its label to Switzers department store, where it was identified as one that Iseult had recently purchased. She was arrested, and Ian, left alone in the stone castle with his young sister, called his grandmother to tell her that the Gardai had taken Iseult away. Maud, sick with flu, sent Helena Molony to Laragh. Tried *in camera* by the Special Criminal Court on July 1, Iseult managed in her guileless way to talk herself out of the charge of having abetted a foreign agent. She was found not guilty. The Irish government and the German Embassy both wanted to avoid as much embarrassment as possible.

While Iseult was on remand in Dublin, Helena Molony waited at Laragh for Goertz to make his way back through the Wicklow Mountains and sent him off again to another friendly shelter. His mission to set up a fifth column in North Ireland was futile; he could trust no one. Stuart, who had briefed Goertz in Germany, was unaware of the deadly intrigues in the IRA. Sean Russell had fled to America and then to Germany after the bombings in England, and his successor as chief of staff, Stephen Hayes, had been forced to sign a confession that he was a government agent. "I did not think immediately about the possibility of treachery," Goertz wrote, "but I considered that the organization was rotten at its roots."

Sean MacBride thought IRA violence was self-destructive. In England Irish suspects were rounded up and deported. The De Valera government interned Republicans just as it had interned aliens during the war, known in neutral Ireland as "the emergency." The Military Tribunal was in session again, and Mountjoy and Arbour Hill were filled with IRA members; many were sent on to the internment huts in the barbed-wire compound at the Curragh, the hard-core cases confined to the notorious "Glass House." There were escape attempts, mutinies, and hunger strikes by Republicans agitating to be treated as political prisoners. Shootings by guards, executions were again daily events.

Opposed to what he considered a suicide course by his old comrades, MacBride was busy defending them in court. He petitioned for reprieves and demanded inquests for dead prisoners. When six IRA men all under nineteen were sentenced to death for the shooting of a Belfast policeman during a wave of reprisals for terrorism in the North, MacBride set up a reprieve committee in Dublin; more than two hundred thousand signatures were collected and the agitation was felt in America. Secretary of State Cordell Hull put pressure on the British Ambassador in Washington, and international sentiment was effective. Five of the six boys were saved; one, Thomas Williams, was hanged.

"The brave young men who have decided to carry war into England are getting the same terrible sentences when captured that Tom Clarke and his comrades got last century," Maud wrote her friend Bairbre MacDonagh Redmond in America. Again she was organizing protest meetings on behalf of the condemned men in the North and the IRA prisoners in the South, whose treatment was only a shade less brutal. The hunger strikers and the "strip" strikers, following the example of William O'Brien the Land Leaguer, shivered in their nakedness or made togas of their blankets rather than put on the stripes of the common criminal. Maud's sympathy for the proud violent men never diminished.

Sean had been a terrorist himself, a member of the early IRA in a time when it seemed that freedom could be won only by the use of physical force. Now, seeing anarchic terrorism become futile against the organized use of terror by despotic governments, he was searching for some legal machinery, national and international, that might give the victims of intolerable injustice and degradation another recourse.

Many of Maud's ideals, her compassion for human suffering, her belief in individual liberty, were Sean's. Even her feminist views had been transmitted to her son. He had grown up among women of an unusually independent nature. He had often stayed with her friend Madame Cama, the Indian nationalist, when Maud was away from Paris. He had known Constance Markievicz and Mrs. Despard. In the twenties he had accompanied his mother to meetings of the Women's International League for Peace and Freedom. He knew the president of the Irish section, Hanna Sheehy-Skeffington, and Dorothy Macardle and the "Mothers" of the WPDL. His wife had been his comrade under fire in the Four Courts. "Sean was the lucky boy when he got her to marry him," Maud wrote her new friend Ethel Mannin, the novelist. "Try to spare time to share our family supper at 7—unless you are afraid of a crowd of children who are my joy—homework absorbs the lot of them immediately after supper, and I want you to meet my son Sean and his wife Kid, who took a fearless part in our fight for freedom."

Kid's admiration and affection for her mother-in-law grew over the years. If Maud was demanding, she asked of others only what she expected of herself: absolute devotion to Ireland's cause and to every friend of the cause. There was always a guest or a "boarder," paying or nonpaying, in an upstairs bedroom. The furniture grew shabby, trees needed pruning, but people and their needs came first. If she happened to forget to pick up Kid's particular brand of cigarettes in Dublin, Maud would go back to town on the Goatstown bus to get them.

When Iseult visited Roebuck she brought her private world with her, allowing no one to enter but Maud. Her unhappiness sometimes upset the household; she would complain that Kid was not providing proper care and food for her mother. She would spend the whole day in Maud's room, and the two heart patients would lie side by side on the bed, talking and smoking incessantly. Since childhood Iseult had called her mother Moura, and it was still her private pet name for the person she trusted most.

The children, busy with their schoolbooks, sometimes felt they were older than Iseult. At Laragh she made up games to test their mettle. Tiernan found it quite an ordeal to listen to her ghost stories and then be made to go out after tea in the gathering twilight. He was always the first to panic and run back to the stone castle to face his aunt's scorn. "You must never be afraid of anything, even of death." Maud repeated Tommy's command so many times that it became part of her children's code.

Iseult had not asked to be protected, but when Francis left her she was bereft. She wrote to Germany, and later to Paris, begging him to come home at least for a visit. She knew he had another woman, another life, but his children needed him. She was worried about Kay, who was unhappy and "could so easily miss her life." She arranged through Sean for money to be sent to Francis when he was penniless in Paris, but family funds were low. She sold the ivory tankard and the Jacobean cabinet. Francis would not come home.

Sean MacBride was now a Senior Counsel of the Irish Bar, respected for his brilliant defense of civil liberties. The last tragic act of one of the longest imprisonments under the war emergency laws took place in Portlaoise Prison in the spring of 1946. The Ministry of Justice had refused to give IRA prisoners political treatment, and those who refused to submit had spent years in solitary confinement. On April 19, Sean McCaughey, who had been held for five years, went on hunger and thirst strike. The cry of "Release the Prisoners" was a rallying point once more. Maud was writing letters to the press again:

To the editor of the *Irish Times*

Sir—

Those unable to serve can *demand* nothing; therefore, I, who am almost 80 and bedridden, make my last *request . . .* I make it to the people and to the Government: Let no more young lives be sacrificed to uphold an old British rule of Victorian origin; be speedier than death in releasing young McCaughey; please, with him, release the others from Portlaoghise Jail who have been fighting that old British rule with the same spirit of courage and endurance which liberated twenty-six of our counties and among whom is the son of our comrade Lord Mayor McCurtin, who, dying for Ireland, entrusted his own children to her care. Only when this is done can our Government and people unitedly, without hypocrisy, demand that the ill treatment of prisoners in our six occupied counties shall cease.

Death released McCaughey before the government acted. Maud wrote that at the inquest Sean made the prison doctor admit that he would not "treat a dog as the prisoners had been treated." McCaughey's fellow prisoners were not allowed to give evidence. "They could have refuted the government nonsense that the reason they had been deprived for years of all open-air exercise, was because naked men could not be allowed for the sake of decency to run around prison and that outside they might catch cold! They had made themselves smocks out of their blankets."

So long as she had strength to write and talk, prisoners' relief and prison reform would be Maud's work. "I have been struggling so hard with my sloth," she wrote Ethel Mannin, "to finish my prison book and get myself perhaps out of the prison—my obsession about prisoners of the defeated nations still being held in slavery—and the mountains and bogs of hate their captivity is piling up in the world."

Mounting agitation for the release of prisoners was only one sign that De Valera and Fianna Fail had lost popular support during the repressive years of the "emergency." Maud's WPDL had been a springboard for De Valera in 1932; now the Release the Prisoners Association provided the impetus for Sean MacBride's political campaign to unseat him. "England's difficulty" had brought Ireland no material gain, and Fianna Fail's program for self-sufficiency had made little headway. Only the high rate of emigration of workers to better-paying war industries in the United Kingdom prevented total economic disaster, and peacetime meant wide-scale unemployment. In 1945, when the Second World War ended, the Irish people were weary of privation, restriction, and isolation.

MacBride seized the moment. Against strong opposition from the minority of die-hard Republicans and IRA militants who still refused to recognize the legitimacy of the Dail, he gathered enough supporters to form the Clann na Poblachta (Republican Family). Mindful of the corrupting influence of parliamentary power, the IRA Council voted to expel members who joined the Clann, but MacBride's party, committed to radical reform and the abolishment of Partition, drew a large following during 1947. The fragmented opposition to De Valera's conservatism welcomed new leadership and a fresh direction in politics.

Early that winter Maud left Roebuck for the first time in many months and went out to vote. Clann na Poblachta defeated Fianna Fail in two important by-elections, and, leaning on her son's arm, Maud Gonne MacBride entered Leinster House to see him seated as a deputy.

In February 1948 she was apologizing to Ethel Mannin for taking so long to acknowledge her recent novel, *Late Have I Loved Thee*, "the greatest of all your books . . . it has taken me some time to read, because my sight is so bad I read slowly now." She had been terribly upset over Gandhi's assassination. "I looked on him as the wisest and best man on this earth, so I was in no state to write letters." Roebuck House had been full of turmoil. "Not only my grandchildren, but every young thing I know were working, talking and thinking of nothing but the elections, ever since the amazing and *inexplicable* rage of the Government over Sean's being made a T.D. at the by-election. It was their unseemly fury which has brought all the trouble on themselves so that Dev punished the whole country with a general election in winter, which has not added to his popularity." De Valera had hoped to gain a vote of confidence in the 1948 election, to halt the Clann's momentum and restore the Fianna Fail's balance of power. "Neither he nor anyone else is satisfied with the results . . ." wrote Maud, "but I never saw as much voluntary work given by young people since the early days of the Sinn Fein movement."

In fact the Clann exceeded expectations. Fianna Fail won only 68 seats out of 147; the Clann had ten. In a move which ousted De Valera, MacBride negotiated a coalition government with the right-wing Fine Gael, the Labour Party, the Small Farmers' Party, and the independents. The IRA benefited from the immediate cessation of police harassment, and the last political prisoners were released in March. But orthodox Republicans saw their worst suspicions confirmed in the Clann's political alliance with their archenemies, men like Richard Mulcahy, general of the Free State forces, who had sent so many of MacBride's comrades to their death. The coalition selected the lawyer John Costello of Fine Gael to be the new Prime Minister. The Clann was represented in the cabinet by MacBride, Minister of External Affairs, and the radical Socialist Dr. Noel Browne, Minister of Health.

In December 1948 the interparty government took the historic step of repealing the External Relations Act, severing the last tie to the Commonwealth. On Easter Monday 1949, at the General Post Office, the Republic was formally proclaimed with speeches recreating the spirit of the Rising. In the North there was renewed alarm at the threat of "Rome Rule." The British Parliament's response was to pass Prime Minister Clement Attlee's Ireland Bill, which provided that Northern Ireland would never be separated from England without the consent of the Stormont government. The IRA picked up members again in the unending battle against partition, and MacBride as Minister for External Affairs carried the battle into the international sphere by refusing to involve Ireland in the postwar North Atlantic Treaty Organization as long as England ruled the six northern counties.

The umbrella of the new interparty government Mac-Bride had masterminded sheltered heterogeneous and potentially explosive elements. He was working in alliance with power-hungry politicians against power-hungry rivals. His united front was doomed to failure, in the tense period of reconstruction. The interparty government received a severe setback early in 1951, when the Minister of Health's proposal for a mother and child health scheme without a means test waved the red flag of socialized medicine and called forth full-scale opposition from the medical profession and the Catholic hierarchy. Early in the century the Church had condemned Maud's school-meal project; now state interference in maternal care was attacked as being against prohibitions written into the 1937 constitution to protect the sanctity of the family. The Clan expelled Dr. Browne. The Party began to disintegrate, and MacBride faced accusations that he had "sold out" for nothing.

Maud and Sean had not always been in agreement. When Michael MacLiammoir asked her about her son, she answered, "Oh, he must go his own way. We all do in the end." Maud had seen many idealistic movements rise and fall, but for her the phoenix dream of Ireland's destiny bound them all; as it had bound her to Yeats, it gave her faith in her son. She was proud of him, and raged at the "futility of old age" which kept her from taking part in the life around them, still exciting, still full of promise. "In spite of Bank strikes, Rent strikes, etc., I think Ireland is not doing too badly ... *There has been tremendous progress,*" she wrote Ethel Mannin.

"Sean has great plans for . . . land reclamation to end emigration."

Confined to bed at eighty-five because of her weak heart, Maud still made her voice heard; in the age of wireless miracles she could reach a wide audience without leaving home. "Radio Eireann came and made 3 records of my talk on *Innisfail the Isle of Destiny—Innisfail and Her Golden Age—Innisfail and the Figure 3* and is broadcasting them. I think Ireland is going to produce a *3rd Golden Age*, which may possibly make her a leader of the *Peace* thought in this world of confused thinking." The Irish edition of *A Servant of the Queen* was republished in 1950 by Golden Eagle Books, in Dublin. Maud looked forward to giving Ethel a copy and wrote that she was still "struggling with a 2nd vol—" "The Tower of Age" was the title she had chosen, but she could not summon up the strength to deal with the ghosts of the past. The future was more interesting.

Ethel Mannin was attentive to Maud and all her family —a London studio for Ian, a holiday in her Connemara cottage for Eileen MacBride, gifts of books and flowers—but the family considered her a busybody. "I needn't tell you to mention no family affairs to Ethel Mannin," Iseult wrote Francis. "It could make the most terrible mischief, but I am sure you know that yourself." Young Tiernan was often at Roebuck when Ethel visited alone or with her husband Reginald Reynolds, and he disliked her intensely. Maud adored her, a woman little more than half her age, with fine blond hair, a Botticelli look. "Were I 50 years younger I would be in love with your Reginald, not that I was one to fall in love much being too taken up with winning freedom for Ireland— But I like looking at him nearly as much as I like looking at yourself beautiful lady, so bring him to Ireland with you—au revoir à bientôt—love and friendship, Maud Gonne MacBride."

Sometimes she would sign her letters "the Shan Van Vocht" or "old Maedhe," but just as she had used her full signature in her letters to Willie, she was always Maud Gonne MacBride to Ethel Mannin. It was Yeats who had brought them together; ten years earlier Ethel had begun a correspondence with the poet, and in 1946, when she came to stay in Ireland for a season, she went to see Maud.

Ethel disdained the idea of celebrities but spent a great deal of time seeking them out. She considered herself skeptical and scientific, yet was attracted by powerful personalities. She fell under Maud's spell, and Maud, captivated by Ethel's reverent attention, saw in the ambitious younger woman a re-creation of her youthful self, independent, unconventional and passionate. Here was a free spirit bringing news from the world outside, as refreshing to the lonely rooms of her old age as the freesias, cyclamens, and fragrant hyacinths Ethel sent her.

Love and friendship were as intensely romantic for Maud as they had been all her life, a binding spiritual force. "Ethel dear—Your letter pleases me so much for the moment I met you in the dusk at Roebuck I knew we both were in the same pattern . . . next day I wrote to Iseult who is a part of Willie's and my pattern, how strangely you had affected me . . . There is much I would like to hear about that last time you saw Willie . . ."

Hanna Sheehy-Skeffington died in April 1946. "She was almost the dearest friend I had," Maud wrote Ethel, "and certainly the woman I admired most on earth— Her loss to Ireland is terrible and Dublin won't be the same place without her." In letter after letter Maud poured out her visionary thoughts. She had been reading Swedenborg: "You and I, Hanna, Willie and Iseult and others we may never have met in this life are part of one Spiritual entity, more closely knit than political groups which are fleeting things . . . we have no need of signs or pass-words to recognize each other when we do, for we *belong*—for instance, it explains why you, whose life is full and active, feel at home and happy with an old woman . . . and time as we know it is nonexistent in regard to eternity—I find the thought consoling, when I feel lonely for Hanna—"

Later that year Richard Ellmann, working on his first literary biography, *The Man and the Masks*, spent two evenings at Roebuck House. Maud wrote Ethel that she should talk to him about the friends Willie had in England in "his later years and the trend of his thought . . . for I think his book will be worthwhile." The young American scholar appeared to be "pro-British *though he said nothing to make me think this* and therefore he may be inclined to underestimate Ireland's influence on Willie's thought and work." She had done her best to remove "a misconception many people have that Willie's real devotion to Ireland started with his love of me—it did not, he got that from his child days in Sligo and the influence of those mountains and lakes."

Her old need for the land came back with full intensity as, housebound, she envied Ethel when she was living and writing in a lonely cottage in Connemara. Years earlier Maud had experienced terror and despair on Ireland's wild seacoast in north Mayo. She had heard the earth sing and felt the ominous power of the wild waters breaking on the shore. "I think it helped me understand the soft apathy of the people living there . . . We two, how much we have in common and when I first saw you standing in the twilight in my big bare drawing room at Roebuck, which is not home but only a tent or shelter, I knew we would be friends . . . I too had an English mother. Though she died when I was 4, her blood in me makes me able to understand English people and appreciate the good qualities in them you write of, even while my Irish blood obliges me to fight their governments." Ethel's father, like Maud's, claimed Irish ancestry; there was Mannin's Bay in Galway near Sligo, and Maud's imaginative will made much of the racial heritage they shared.

In 1938, Yeats had written Ethel: "I am arranging my burial place. It will be in a little remote country churchyard in Sligo, where my great-grandfather was the clergyman a hundred years ago. Just my name and dates and these lines:

> Cast a cold eye
> On life, on death;
> Horseman pass by.

Ten years later his coffin was brought home from France to be buried in his beloved countryside "under bare Ben Bulben's head," with Queen Maeve's mountain, Knocknarea, looming to the west of Drumcliffe Churchyard. George Yeats and Michael and Anne and the poet's brother Jack gathered with friends and townspeople for a simple ceremony. Maud's son represented the government. Often when Maud railed

against the prison of old age, the "guilt" of her eighty-odd
years, she thought, "How lucky Willie Yeats was to escape
into the freer life of the spirit beyond the limitations of time
and space . . ."

She almost escaped when she fell and broke her hip in
the spring of 1949, but by Easter she had recovered and was
writing Ethel to praise her work against Partition. She wrote
again that winter complimenting Ethel's performance at a
debate on women's rights. She was pleased that the government had appointed Josephine MacNeill an ambassador, "for
I think that until we have more women taking a directive
share in public life we shall never get a *peaceful* world—not
that we are better than men, but being born fosterers of life
we have greater instinct to *protect* life—"

The next year she was making recordings for broadcast
about Inghinidhe na hEireann on the fiftieth anniversary of
its founding. "I want a similar organization of young girls
ready to do the job to hand," she wrote Ethel in a letter
commenting on the latest novel, *Bavarian Story*. "I think your
description of Rudolf Ritters' state of mind which turned him
into an arrogant Nazi is so natural. I am not sure had I been
a German after the treaty of Versailles that I would not have
become a Nazi, except for the Nazi exclusion of women from
a share in the direction of affairs."

For Maud humanitarianism was indivisible. She could
equate the devastation of Hiroshima and Nagasaki with the
annihilation of Jews in the Nazis' gas chambers and the genocide of the Famines. She wrote letters for a campaign to send
aid to starving German children, condemning the "self appointed apostles of Peace and liberalism who seemed determined that help shall not reach Germany in time" and protesting the embargo England had placed against "bringing
out any of the starving children." She wrote Ethel, "Were I
beginning my life instead of ending it—I would join you and
Reginald in working for Peace—for *Peace and Freedom* are the
only worthwhile things to strive for and they are *indivisible.*"

Now that she could no longer leave bed or chair, the
world came to her, its news filtered through her family, the
papers, the radio, voices of friends on the phone, a few visitors. "Michael, dear," she said once when the actor MacLiam-

moir came to call, "they talk about the beauty of old age, don't believe a word of it, it's *HELL!*" But she was patient with the people who took care of her. She was dependent on Kid and on the grandchildren. Ian felt at peace when he visited. There were always fresh flowers and growing plants in her bedroom, and there were still singing birds. Tiernan helped take care of her when she could no longer be brought down to the drawing room to sit in her long low chair by the fire, where Edith Gonne's copies of the Fra Angelico angels hung over the mantel and the oval portraits of herself and her mother looked down from the wall between the tall windows. The college boy admired her courage, laughing with her when she said, "They forgot my hot-water bottle again." He would ask who she thought "they" were, and go down to the deserted kitchen to get hot water.

Her old friend Seumas MacManus came every year from America to visit the grave of his first wife, Anna Johnston. "What a traveler you are—" Maud wrote, "one day in Ireland, next day in America—I envy you, for I dearly loved moving around when I was able to . . ." She told him how much she enjoyed his *Story of the Irish Race*, "a book like that was badly needed—if I may criticize, you don't give enough importance to the early Sinn Fein movement and the Irish Literary Renaissance of which Standish O'Grady was a precursor and John O'Leary the Father, and Willie Yeats and Douglas Hyde, the most illustrious of its many gifted children." His book was "a real achievement and how happy Ethan would be reading it." She remembered visiting Ethan in her father's house on the Antrim road, and their walking in the hills with Alice Milligan. They talked "of the legends of Wolfe Tone and sometimes Willie Yeats was with us. Your book brings all those memories back to me—now that I am a prisoner of old age, which you, my dear old friend, have so bravely refused to become."

When airplanes swooped low over Roebuck House, she cursed them for invading her privacy. And yet they brought her welcome visitors. Maud Gonne had become a monument, "the most beautiful ruin" in Ireland. Monk Gibbon, a protégé of George Russell, who criticized Yeats and scorned Maud's politics, brought the American literary critic Van Wyck Brooks and his wife to see her and ". . . it was I, her detractor, who raised her heavily-veined brown hand and kissed it."

Tiernan let them in at twilight. Maud was downstairs stretched out on her chaise longue, facing the fire, "smoking a cigarette and reading a French yellowback novel," Brooks wrote. " 'How kind you are,' she exclaims, 'to come and see a deaf old woman!' She has bold features and deep-set eyes, with a high-bred manner and charming gestures, her voice very distinguished and she herself full of humor. . . . If she had not had trouble with her heart, she would still be, at eighty-seven, as active as ever. She was evidently proud of her son who is doing just what she would like to be doing herself. She feels that the success of the republic 'is wonderful' and says that in Ireland now no one needs to 'starve.' "

Her last months were painful, and Maud despaired that she had become "selfish and materialistic," wrote Iseult. "As it is also my experience with this rotten heart illness, I could only wretchedly agree. Then the day before her death, after she got the last sacraments, she had some kind of mystical experience and looked radiant, happy and young." Iseult was with her at the end. "One of the last words she spoke was 'I feel now an ineffable joy.' Then she went to sleep breathing lightly like a child and died that way the next day. Nobody knew the exact moment she ceased to breathe."

Maud died on April 27, 1953. She was buried at Glasnevin on April 29:

> The last sad tribute was paid yesterday to a lady who had devoted her life unselfishly and bravely to her country, when thousands followed the remains of Madame Maud Gonne MacBride from the Church of the Sacred Heart, Donnybrook, to the Republican Plot in Glasnevin Cemetery, or stood in silence as the cortege passed through Dublin's streets.
>
> At the G.P.O., the guard of honour who walked beside the wreath-covered hearse bearing the coffin draped in the Tricolour, turned for a mo-

ment in response to the quietly-spoken command "eyes left."

It was a simple gesture of remembrance—recalling the final sacrifice of Major John MacBride in the cause of the Republic, and the long years spent by Madame in succouring a people hungry and homeless under alien rule, and pleading the cause of her country.

The President was represented by his A.D.C., Comdt. T. O'Carroll . . . The huge attendance included the Taoiseach, who was accompanied by his A.D.C., Comdt. Sean Brennan.

In the Church of the Sacred Heart, Donnybrook, Requiem Mass was celebrated by Very Rev. T. B. Condon, P.P. So large was the congregation that many were unable to gain admittance.

Members of the Standing Committee of Clann na Poblachta carried the coffin from the church to the hearse, and hundreds of cars followed the remains into the city.

At Westmoreland Street, the procession was joined by a large body of I.R.A. veterans, who walked behind the hearse, on each side of which the guard of honour walked. Representatives of many national organisations took their place in the cortege and traffic was suspended as it passed through O'Connell Street.

There were among the veterans of the War of Independence, the women of Inghinidhe na hEireann and Cumann na mBann, with whom Madame MacBride laboured.

. . . an oration was delivered by the O'Rahilly, who spoke first in Irish. . . . The O'Rahilly said that many people had made sacrifices for causes in the past, but few had had the courage, the love of justice and the persistence that Maud Gonne MacBride possessed.

It was over sixty years since she, with a minimum of association with Ireland, found herself amongst a people depressed, starved and treated with injustice. And injustice was one of the things which she could not tolerate.

She realised that only by freeing Ireland from English rule could the lot of the people be improved and she devoted the remainder of her life to the Irish people.

# NOTES

The words following the page numbers conclude the material to which reference is made. The following abbreviations are used:

*AU* W. B. Yeats, *The Autobiography of William Butler Yeats* (New York, Macmillan, 1916; Collier Books, 1974)

*CP* W. B. Yeats, *The Collected Poems of W. B. Yeats* (New York, Toronto, Macmillan, Definitive Edition, with the author's final revisions, 1956; Collier-Macmillan Canada Ltd., 1969)

*Hone* Joseph Hone, *W. B. Yeats, 1865–1939* (London, Macmillan, 1943; Harmondsworth, Middlesex, England, Penguin/Pelican, 1971)

*LE* *The Letters of W. B. Yeats* (New York, Macmillan, 1955), ed. Allan Wade

*ME* W. B. Yeats, *Memoirs* (New York, Macmillan, 1973), ed. Denis Donoghue

*SQ* Maud Gonne MacBride, *A Servant of the Queen* (London, Victor Gollancz, 1938; 1974)

*SY* *Seventy Years, Being The Autobiography of Lady Gregory* (New York, Macmillan, 1974), ed. Colin Smythe

ALS   a letter sent

n.d.   no date

NLI   National Library of Ireland

NYPL   New York Public Library

Epigraph

p. xi   and laughing. *CP*, p. 385; from "The Old Age of Queen Maeve."

Chapter One—An Overpowering Tumult

p. 1   my father." *ME*, p. 40.

p. 2   hopeful recruit." *SQ*, p. 92.

p. 2   Old Ireland." *J. B. Yeats,*

*Letters to His Son W. B. Yeats and Others, 1869–1922* (New York, Dutton, 1946), ed. Joseph Hone, p. 5; from the preface by Oliver Elton.

p. 3   secondary notes." *ME*, p. 40.

p. 3   carry home." *SQ*, p. 92.

p. 3   Maud Gonne." Maud Gonne MacBride, "Yeats and Ireland," *Scattering Branches, Tributes to the Memory of W. B. Yeats* (New York, Macmillan, 1940), ed. Stephen Gwynn, p. 17.

p. 3   from me . . ." Joseph Hone, *op. cit.*, p. 297.

p. 4   divine race." *ME*, p. 40

p. 5   many converts." *LE*, p. 108; ALS W. B. Yeats to John O'Leary, Feb. 1, 1889.

p. 6   flying wheel. *LE*, p. 110; ALS W. B. Yeats to Ellen O'Leary, Feb. 3, 1889.

p. 7   all that." Monk Gibbon, *The Masterpiece and the Man, Yeats As I Knew Him* (New York, Macmillan, 1959), p. 73.

p. 8   to since." *AU*, p. 67.

p. 8   of being." *ME*, pp. 41–42.

p. 8   much energy." *AU*, p. 82.

p. 9   without peace . . ." *ME*, p. 42.

p. 9   mournful pride," *CP*, p. 36; "The Rose of the World."

p. 9   a student?' " *ME*, pp. 42–43.

p. 9   must out. *LE*, pp. 116–117; ALS W. B. Yeats to Katherine Tynan, Mar. 21, 1889.

p. 10   I love. *CP*, p. 40; "The Pity of Love."

p. 10   black hair" Katherine Tynan, *Twenty-five Years: Reminiscences* (New York, Devin-Adair, 1913), p. 166.

p. 10   remained empty." *AU*, p. 82.

Chapter Two—The Air of Freedom

p. 12   in Tongham. The question has been raised whether Maud Gonne was born in 1865 or 1866. She herself was often vague about dates in her writings and interviews. Neither her nor her sister's birth was formally registered—this was not required at the time. Information from J. P. Brooke-Little, Esq., Richmond Herald College of Arms (March 18, 1976), indicates that Maud Gonne was born December 21, 1866, and baptized at Tongham. Elizabeth Coxhead in her book *Daughters of Erin* (London, Secker & Warburg, 1965) uses the date 1866. According to their marriage certificate Edith Cook and Thomas Gonne were married December 19, 1865, at East Peckham, in Kent.

p. 13   to see." *SQ*, p. 13.

p. 13   Fenian men." Contemporary Irish song.

p. 14   were Fenians. *Devoy's Post Bag, 1871–1928, Vol. II, 1880–1928* (Dublin, C. J. Fallon, 1953), eds. William O'Brien and Desmond Ryan, p. 1.

p. 14   political prisoners. The Treason-Felony Act, in force since 1848, "provided that anyone who should levy war against the Queen, or endeavour to deprive her of her title, or by open and advised speaking, printing, or publishing, incite others to the same, should be 'deemed guilty of felony' and transported," according to John Mitchel in his book *Jail Journal* (New York, *The Citizen*, 1854), p. 21. Mitchel goes on to say that the law was passed originally to suppress his newspaper, the first *United Irishman*, as well as to destroy him.

p. 14  no benefactor." Marcus Bourke, *John O'Leary* (Tralee, Republic of Ireland, Anvil Books, 1967), p. 106.

p. 15  the Curragh. The main English military base in Ireland, some thirty-five miles from Dublin.

p. 15  the Fenians. Robert Kee, *The Green Flag* (New York, Delacorte, 1972), p. 439.

p. 15  Anglo-Irish families. Terence de Vere White, *The Anglo-Irish* (London, Victor Gollancz, 1972), p. 17.

p. 16  and turquoises." *SQ*, p. 11.

p. 17  of death." *Ibid.*

p. 18  Cavalry in Ireland. All genealogical information about the Gonne and Cook families was obtained from J. P. Brooke-Little, Esq., Richmond Herald College of Arms, and from Maud Gonne, *Servant of the Queen.*

p. 19  Clerkenwell Jail, Kee, *op. cit.*, pp. 346–347.

p. 19  the IRB. Bourke, *op. cit.*, pp. 33, 128–29, 132.

p. 21  we pleased." *SQ*, p. 17.

p. 23  going away." *Ibid.*, p. 23.

Chapter Three—Mademoiselle

p. 26  human beings. . . ." *SQ*, p. 25.

p. 27  be independent." *Ibid.*, p. 26.

p. 28  incalculable force": *Ibid.*, p. 15.

Chapter Four—The Making of a Rebel

p. 32  kneeling throngs." *SQ*, p. 106.

p. 33  their homes F. S. L. Lyons, *Ireland Since the Famine* (London, Weidenfeld, 1971; Collins/Fontana, 1973), p. 168.

p. 33  our cattle." *Ibid.*, p. 169; quoting J. L. Hammond, *Gladstone and the Irish Nation* (London, new ed., 1964), p. 51.

p. 33  death threats. *Ibid.*, p. 168.

p. 33  Land League . . ." Robert Kee, *The Green Flag* (New York, Delacorte, 1972), p. 373.

p. 35  and despair. Katherine Tynan, *Twenty-five Years: Reminiscences* (New York, Devin-Adair, 1913), p. 108. Maud Gonne does not mention the Phoenix Park murders in her memoirs. Perhaps she felt by the time she wrote them that the murders were part of ancient history gone over too many times. Moreover, in supporting Irish revolutionaries down the years, she tended to overlook their most negative acts. There were always violent excesses on both sides of the struggle for independence. In the balance, she chose not to pass judgment. In later years she met some of the men who had been associated with the event, including their "No. 1 Man," James Carey, who had escaped the finger of the informer. She is not the only one to have remained silent. There is a tantalizing gap, from March to June of 1882, in the letters of James Devoy, leader of the Clan na Gael. Publicly the Fenian groups—the IRB, the socialist Davitt, the Land League—all denounced the terrorist action and disassociated themselves from the Invincibles.

p. 36 hermetic crowd," James Joyce, *Ulysses* (New York, Modern Library, 1934; Vintage, 1961), p. 140.

p. 36 old magnificent," Mrs. George Cornwallis-West (Lady Randolph Churchill), *The Reminiscences of Lady Randolph Churchill* (New York, The Century Co., 1908), p. 98.

p. 36 with it." Elizabeth Countess of Fingall, *Seventy Years Young, Memories Told to Pamela Hinkson* (New York, Dutton, 1939), p. 69.

p. 37 water lily." Conrad A. Balliet, "Michael MacLiammoir Recalls Maud Gonne MacBride," an interview in *Journal of Irish Literature* (Newark, Delaware, University of Delaware, Proscenium Press, 1977), p. 54.

p. 38 Crown Jewels." *SY*, p. 209.
p. 38 of politics," *Ibid.*, p. 203.
p. 38 poor people." *Ibid.*, p. 209.
p. 39 her toes," R. B. O'Brien, *The Life of Charles Stewart*

*Parnell, 1846–1891*, Vol. I (New York, Harper and Brothers, 1898), p. 130.

p. 41 bear it." Taped interview in the 1930s; NLI.

p. 41 "Mr. R," *SQ*, p. 41.

p. 41 a lesson." *Ibid.*, p. 42.

Chapter Five—Banishment

p. 45 Russian Embassy. Maud Gonne MacBride, "My Reminiscences," *An Phoblacht*, March 1, 1930.

p. 45 at all. Barbara W. Tuchman, *The Proud Tower* (New York, Macmillan, 1962), p. 54.

p. 45 to romance." *AU*, p. 104.

p. 46 for fuel." Ford Madox Ford, *Return to Yesterday* (New York, Liveright, 1932), p. 80.

p. 48 the child." *SQ*, p. 53.

p. 50 residual income. Information provided by J. P. Brooke-Little, Esq., Richmond Herald College of Arms, March 18, 1976.

Chapter Six—The Bold Boulangiste

p. 52 in Picardy Information on Millevoye and his family background provided by Mme. N. Millevoye-Puerari, April 1975. See also *L'Encyclopédie Contemporaine*, No. 61, 1889, p. 56.

p. 53 "*Il reviendra!*" Raymond Rudorff, *The Belle Epoque* (New York, Saturday Review Press, 1972), p. 23.

p. 53 middle-class origin." Mrs. George Cornwallis-West

(Lady Randolph Churchill), *The Reminiscences of Lady Randolph Churchill* (New York, The Century Co., 1908), p. 258.

p. 55    *être maitresse.*" Curtis Cate, *George Sand, A Biography* (New York, Avon Books, 1975), p. xxvii.

p. 55    *belle Irlandaise*" *SQ,* p. 212.

p. 56    great Ambassador." Stephen Gwynn and Gertrude M. Tuckwell, *The Life of the Rt. Hon. Sir Charles W. Dilke*, Vol. 1 (New York, Macmillan, 1917), p. 266.

p. 57    Alexander III. Princess Catherine Radziwill, *My Recollections* (New York, James Pott and Co., 1904), p. 286.

p. 58    of ridicule." Count Paul Vassili (pseud. of Ekaterina Radziwill), *France from Behind the Veil: Fifty Years of Social and Political Life* (New York, Funk and Wagnalls, 1914), p. 254.

p. 58    in Europe," W. T. Stead, *The Truth About Russia* (New York, Cassell & Co., 1888), p. 38.

p. 59    coup d'état." *Ibid.*, p. 12.

p. 59    by England." *SQ,* p. 82.

p. 60    whatever subject." *Ibid.*, p. 80.

p. 60    political situation. *SQ,* p. 84; quoting W. T. Stead in the *Review of Reviews*, June 7, 1892.

Chapter Seven—Looking for a Revolution

p. 61    and twenty" Conversation with Mrs. Sean MacBride, Dublin, 1973.

p. 62    that book." *ME*, p. 44.

p. 62    bad painter." *Ibid.*, p. 43.

p. 62    *l'aime beaucoup.*" Elizabeth Coxhead, *Daughters of Erin, Five Women of the Irish Renascence* (London, Secker and Warburg, 1965), p. 135.

p. 63    beside her. Stephen Gwynn, *Experiences of a Literary Man* (London, Thornton, Butterworth, 1926), p. 74.

p. 63    bulldog stayed. Katherine Tynan, *Twenty-five Years* (New York, Devin-Adair, 1913), p. 364.

p. 64    one handled adulterer," James Joyce, *Ulysses* (New York, Modern Library, 1934; Vintage Books, 1961), p. 148.

p. 64    will die.") *ME*, pp. 55–56.

p. 65    courteous diction James Joyce, *Ulysses, op. cit.*, p. 141.

p. 65    Maud Gonne." *SQ,* p. 89.

p. 66    of men . . . Marcus Bourke, *John O'Leary* (Tralee, Republic of Ireland, Anvil Books, 1967), p. 190.

p. 66    Ellen O'Leary. Ellen O'Leary and Rossa, the wife of the intrepid O'Donovan, worked in the 1860s as paymistresses for the organization, frequently visiting Paris to pick up funds for the payment of men and the purchase of arms. In 1866 the Viceroy, Lord Wodehouse, called naturally the Woodlouse by the Fenians, would have liked to arrest and detain the two women couriers but shrank from doing so; "It is a ticklish work to meddle with women," he stated. Leon O Broin, *Fenian Fever*

(London, Chatto and
Windus, 1971), pp. 50–51.

p. 67    a Nation." *AU*, p. 143.

p. 67    without nationality";
Horace Reynolds,
"Introduction," W. B. Yeats,
*Letters to the New Island*
(Cambridge, Mass., Harvard
University Press, 1934), ed.
Horace Reynolds, p. 12.

p. 67    "Dark Rosaleen." W. B.
Yeats, *Uncollected Prose*, Vol.
I, 1886–1896 (London,
Macmillan, 1970) ed. John P.
Frayne, p. 150.

p. 68    National Library." *SQ*, p.
98.

p. 68    real life." *Ibid.*

p. 68    Protestant rector. Religious
prejudice was not a prime
issue among the upper
middle classes or the
intelligentsia until much
later. In 1910, as president of
the Gaelic League, Hyde
made this statement to allay
the fears of Protestants
apprehensive about their
future as a minority under
Home Rule: "I have for the
last seventeen years taken
part in a great popular
organisation, spreading over
every county in Ireland, and
consisting of 600 or 700
branches, and perhaps some
50,000 members. I may say
with absolute truth that
during all this time none of
us who were working in the
organisation ever thought of
inquiring what was the
religion of his
fellow-worker. . . . I myself
am a Protestant, yet I have
been annually re-elected
President of the Gaelic

League for the last
seventeen years. . . . I have
often heard people talk of
religious bigotry, so I
suppose it exists. But if it
does exist, it is not in the
Gaelic League. And I thank
God that I have myself been
fortunate never to have
come across it to any extent,
even in private life."
Douglas Hyde, *The Religious
Songs of Connacht* (New
York, Barnes and Noble
Books, div. Harper & Row,
1906), p. viii. Introduction by
Dominic Daly, O.S.A.

p. 68    her beauty!!" Dominic
Daly, *The Young Douglas
Hyde* (Dublin, Irish
University Press, 1974), p. 95.

p. 69    of grief. . . . *Ibid.*, p. 129.

p. 69    little tapers." W. B. Yeats,
*Letters to the New Island, op.
cit.*, p. 158. First quoted in
"The Irish National
Literary Society," *Boston
Pilot*, Nov. 19, 1892.

p. 69    a lot. Daly, *The Young
Douglas Hyde, op. cit.*, p. 95.

p. 70    her portrait. *Ibid.*, pp.
96–97.

p. 70    a revolutionist." *SQ*, p. 99.

p. 71    of disaffection. Dorothy
Macardle, *The Irish Republic*
(London, Victor Gollancz,
1937; Transworld, Corgi
Books, 1968), p. 53. These
demonstrations were often
extravagantly described.
Michael Davitt in *The Fall of
Feudalism in Ireland*
(Totowa, New Jersey,
Roman and Littlefield, 1904;
1970), p. 526, told of a little
boy arrested for looking at a
policeman with a

"humbugging sort of a
smile."

p. 71   the Crown. *Ibid.*

p. 74   being organized." Maud
Gonne MacBride, "Yeats
and Ireland," *Scattering
Branches, Tributes to the
Memory of W. B. Yeats* (New
York, Macmillan, 1940), ed.
Stephen Gwynn, p. 19.

Chapter Eight—The Wild Hillside
—the Woman of the Sidhe

p. 77   116 estates F. S. L. Lyons,
*John Dillon* (London,
Routledge and Kegan Paul,
1968), p. 109.

p. 77   "free-lance," *SQ,* p. 117.

p. 77   the builder" *Ibid.,* p. 116.

p. 77   house warmings." *Ibid.*

p. 78   the Sidhe," *Ibid.,* p. 134.

p. 78   people's lives.' " *ME,* p. 43.

p. 78   new bonnets." *Ibid.*

p. 78   was just." F. S. L. Lyons,
*John Dillon, op. cit.,* pp. 73–74;
quoting *United Irishman,* Oct.
10, 1885.

p. 80   so young." *AU,* p. 82.

p. 80   the spot." W. R. Rodgers,
"W. B. Yeats: A Dublin
Portrait," *In Excited Reverie*
(New York, St. Martin's
Press, 1965), eds. A. Norman
Jeffares and K. G. W. Cross,
p. 6.

p. 80   Maud Gonne." Coner
Cruise O'Brien, "Passion
and Cunning: An Essay on
the Politics of W. B. Yeats,"
*In Excited Reverie, op. cit.,* p.
212.

p. 81   of tricks," James Joyce,
*Ulysses* (New York, Modern
Library, 1934; Vintage
Books, 1961), p. 140.

p. 81   illogical,
incomprehensible."
*ME,* p. 24.

p. 81   "antithetical self" W. B.
Yeats, "Per Amica Silentia
Lunae," *Mythologies* (New
York, Macmillan, 1959;
Collier Books, 1969), p. 337.

p. 81   fire balloon," AU, p. 135.

p. 82   a miracle.' " *SQ,* p. 257.

p. 82   with Theosophy." *Ibid.*

p. 82   of nitroglycerin, *Devoy's
Post Bag, 1871–1928, Vol. II,
1880–1928* (Dublin, C. J.
Fallon, 1953), eds. William
O'Brien and Desmond Ryan,
p. 188n.

p. 82   Living Death" *Ibid.,* p. 242.

p. 83   feet wide." *SQ,* p. 127.

p. 84   the letter. *ME,* pp. 107–108.

Chapter Nine—A Double Life

p. 85   his country. Dominic Daly,
*The Young Douglas Hyde*
(Dublin, Irish University
Press, 1924), p. 99.

p. 87   I hope!" *SQ,* p. 133.

p. 89   the priests." *SY,* p. 248.
ALS Lady Gregory to W. B.
Yeats, Aug. 25, 1891.

Chapter Ten—The New
"Speranza"

p. 90   "Shoot him!" *ME,* p. 44.

p. 90   six months.' " *Ibid.*

p. 91   mournful breeze. *National
Observer,* 1899; see also *CP,*
p. 42.

p. 91   his temples. *Paris and the
Arts, 1851–1896: from the
Goncourt Journal* (Ithaca, N.
Y., Cornell University Press,
1971), eds. and trans. George
J. Becker and Edith Philips,
p. 143.

p. 93    a nation. W. B. Yeats, "The New 'Speranza,'" *United Ireland,* Jan. 16, 1892, *Uncollected Prose,* Vol. I (London, Macmillan, 1970), ed. John P. Frayne, pp. 213–214.

p. 93    first child, It is difficult to ascertain just when Maud Gonne's first child was born. She does not mention him at all, and other sources are confusing. On p. 48 of his *Memoirs,* Yeats refers to the child as her "Georgette," which might lead to the assumption that the child was a girl. But on p. 47 he says that Maud told him of the child she had "adopted" three years earlier, a little boy. Three years seems unlikely, and a member of the MacBride family told the author that he had seen a photograph of an infant a little over a year old and thought Iseult's little brother only lived to be one and a half, which would mean he was born in 1890.

p. 94    Irish affairs. Elizabeth Coxhead, *Daughters of Erin, Five Women of the Irish Renascence* (London, Secker and Warburg, 1965), p. 35.

p. 94    black skirt." *United Irishman,* Feb. 7, 1903, Maud Gonne, "In Memoriam Augusta Holmes."

p. 95    of God. W. B. Yeats, "Maud Gonne," *Letters to the New Island* (Cambridge, Mass., Harvard University Press, 1970), ed. Horace Reynolds, pp. 151–152. First published in *Boston Pilot,* July 30, 1892.

p. 95    of flame." W. B. Yeats, "The New 'Speranza,'" *Uncollected Prose,* Vol. I, *op. cit.,* p. 213.

p. 96    her pen." *Ibid.*

p. 96    the Gods." *SQ,* p. 163.

Chapter Eleven—Life out of Death

p. 97    and indolent." *ME,* p. 45.

p. 97    a virgin. *Ibid.,* p. 72.

p. 98    the world." *Ibid.*

p. 98    speaking vehemently." *Ibid.,* p. 46.

p. 98    above all." A. Norman Jeffares, *W. B. Yeats: Man and Poet* (London, Routledge and Kegan Paul, 1949), p. 68; quoting from an interview with Maud Gonne.

p. 99    not die. *CP,* p. 41; first pub., *National Observer,* 7, 1892.

p. 99    own share." *LE,* p. 186. ALS W. B. Yeats to John O'Leary, Dec. 1891.

p. 99    of rest," *ME,* p. 47.

p. 99    all resistance." *Ibid.,* p. 46.

p. 100   after doctor." *Ibid.,* p. 47.

p. 100   a second lieutenant." Barbara W. Tuchman, *The Proud Tower* (New York, Macmillan, 1962), p. 213.

p. 101   home forever. Sean O'Casey, *Pictures in the Hallway* (New York, Macmillan, 1960), pp. 19–20.

p. 101   and flames." *Hone,* p. 90.

p. 101   death eternally." *SQ,* p. 175.

p. 102   as AE, AE was a printer's error for aeon, which

Russell had taken for his pen name.

p. 102 seeking reunion. *ME,* p. 49.

p. 102 Mathers's wife. *LE,* pp. 182–183. ALS W. B. Yeats to George Russell, Nov. 15, 1891.

p. 102 of children. *ME,* p. 62.

p. 102 wild creature." *Ibid.,* p. 49.

p. 102 Deus Inversus." George Mills Harper, *Yeats's Golden Dawn* (London, Macmillan, 1974), pp. 228 and n, 316.

p. 103 et Recte," *Ibid.,* pp. 314–316.

p. 104 to guard." *SQ,* p. 252.

p. 104 to Dublin." *LE,* p. 181. ALS W. B. Yeats to John O'Leary, Nov. 1891.

p. 104 old passion"; E. Dowson, "non sum qualis eram bonae sub regno cynarae," *Oxford Book of English Verse* (London, Oxford University Press, 1939), p. 1086.

p. 105 to speak." *ME,* p. 95.

p. 105 to her, Jeffares, *W. B. Yeats: Man and Poet, op. cit.,* p. 75. Conversation with Maud Gonne.

p. 105 *vous esmerveillant . . .* D. B. Wyndham Lewis, *Ronsard* (New York, Coward-McCann and Sheed and Ward, 1944), p. 259.

p. 105 mystical love. Virginia Moore, *The Unicorn* (New York, Octagon Books, 1973), p. 425. Conversation with Maud Gonne.

p. 105 not where . . . W. B. Yeats, "The Countess Cathleen," *The Collected Plays of W. B. Yeats* (New York, Macmillan, 1934; 1952), p. 22.

Chapter Twelve—Revival and Discord

p. 106 double agent. *Devoy's Post Bag, 1871–1928, Vol. II, 1880–1928* (Dublin, C. J. Fallon, 1953), eds. William O'Brien and Desmond Ryan, pp. 242–243n.

p. 106 John Redmond, Leon O Broin, *The Prime Informer* (London, Sidgwick and Jackson, 1971), p. 128.

p. 106 in power, The Liberal Party was returned in 1892, but despite mounting pressure from both wings of the Irish Party, the Home Secretary, Asquith, refused to review the cases of political prisoners. The anti-Parnellite Justin McCarthy complained that he "shut the gates of mercy with a clang." Roy Jenkins, *Asquith* (New York, Chilmark, 1964), p. 66. Lacking the support of a united Irish Party, Gladstone's second Home Rule Bill, which aroused the threats of violence and bloodshed from Ulstermen, was defeated in 1893 by the combined opposition of Tories and Unionists. It was a final defeat for the "Grand Old Man," who stepped down in 1894. The Liberals were not to regain power until 1905, so for the next ten years the issue of Home Rule was dormant in the British Parliament.

p. 107 visible rival." *ME,* p. 63.

p. 107 been returned." *Ibid.*

p. 107   seeking excitement"; *Ibid.*, pp. 60–61.

p. 107   brood mare." *Ibid.*, p. 61.

p. 107   to lecture." *LE*, pp. 181–182. ALS W. B. Yeats to John O'Leary, Nov. 1891.

p. 107   and occultism." *LE*, p. 183. ALS W. B. Yeats to George Marshall, Nov. 15, 1891.

p. 108   her hands." *ME*, p. 60.

p. 109   and Pepperpots." *AU*, p. 147.

p. 109   Owen Roe! Thomas Davis, "The Lament for the Death of Owen Roe O'Neill," *Irish Renaissance* (Dublin, Dolmen Press, 1965), eds. Robin Skelton and David R. Clark, p. 91.

p. 110   a society." *AU*, p. 155.

p. 110   perplexed wooing." *ME*, p. 65.

p. 110   from "backwoodsmen," Richard P. Davis, *Arthur Griffith* (Dublin, Anvil Books, 1974), p. 6.

p. 111   Separatist movement." *SQ*, p. 178.

p. 112   the operation." *ME*, p. 67.

p. 112   inner confusion." Maud Gonne MacBride, "Yeats and Ireland," *Scattering Branches, Tributes to the Memory of W. B. Yeats* (New York, Macmillan, 1940), ed. Stephen Gwynn, p. 19.

Chapter Thirteen—La Sale Epoque

p. 114   and triumphant." Winston Churchill, *Great Contemporaries* (London, Collins/Fontana, 1959), p. 249.

p. 114   "*L'homme sinistre,*" Barbara W. Tuchman, *The Proud Tower* (New York, Macmillan, 1966), p. 188.

p. 114   "Venetian Republic," *Le Figaro*, March 4, 1894, p. 1. Letter from Millevoye to M. Develle. Collection of Mme. Puerari Millevoye.

p. 114   the other." *SQ*, p. 164.

p. 114   "G men," Plainclothes political constabulary.

p. 115   of adders " Karl Baedeker, *Paris and Its Environs* (New York, Charles Scribner's Sons, 1924), p. 424.

p. 115   *belle Irlandaise.*" *SQ*, p. 212.

p. 116   the temple," *LE*, p. 671. ALS W. B. Yeats to George Russell, July 1, 1921.

p. 117   dead roses." W. B. Yeats, *Uncollected Prose*, Vol. I (London, Macmillan, 1970), ed. John P. Frayne, p. 324. First quoted in "A Symbolical Drama in Paris," *Bookman*, April 1894.

p. 117   opera glass . . ." *Ibid.*, p. 323.

p. 117   for us . . ." Epigraph, W. B. Yeats, *The Secret Rose* (London, Lawrence and Bullens, 1897), p. vi.

p. 117   her lover, *ME*, p. 133.

p. 117   named Iseult, *Ibid.* In *Servant of the Queen*, written when Maud Gonne was in her seventies, she gives an account of her first lecture tour in America and says it occurred in November 1894. According to all available documentation, this trip did not take place at that time. Yeats, who was keeping a strict account of Maud's whereabouts, never mentions any voyage in 1894. The error may have been typographical, like many others in her book, but the events of her three visits in America—which actually took place in 1897, 1900, and 1901—are so mixed up that it is hard not to suspect deliberate obfuscation. Maud had a reason to be secretive about her activities at the end of 1894, the period of her confinement. Iseult, who was born early in 1895, was still alive in 1938 and had never been publicly described as Maud's daughter, but was known as "adopted" or as a "kinswoman."

Chapter Fourteen—"In Dreams Begins Responsibility"

p. 119  Begins Responsibility" *CP*, p. 98; quoting an Old Play in the dedication to *Responsibilities*, 1914.

p. 120  prison gates. *SQ*, p. 164.

p. 120  her more." Curtis Cate, *George Sand* (New York, Avon Books, 1975), p. xvi.

p. 121  were asleep." *ME*, p. 87.

p. 121  to me," *ME*, p. 87n.

p. 121  the mirror." *AU*, p. 242.

p. 121  they are." Jean Giraudoux, *Lying Woman* (New York, Winter House, 1972), trans. Richard Howard, p. 50.

p. 122  inner being." *ME*, p. 124.

p. 122  strange places." Maud Gonne MacBride, "Yeats and Ireland," *Scattering Branches, Tributes to the Memory of W. B. Yeats* (New York, Macmillan, 1940), ed. Stephen Gwynn, pp. 22–23.

p. 123  of intimacy." *ME*, p. 125.

p. 123  race itself." *Ibid.*

p. 124  him back." E. R. Dodds, *Journal and Letters of Stephen MacKenna* (New York, William Morrow and Co., 1937), p. 12.

p. 124  "inestimable value." *My Uncle John, Edward Stevens's Life of J. M. Synge* (London, Oxford University Press, 1974), ed. Andrew Carpenter, p. 150n.

p. 124  or tolerated." Dodds, *Journal MacKenna, op. cit.*, p. 39.

p. 125  uncompromising silence. David H. Greene and Edward M. Stephens, *J. M. Synge 1871–1909* (New York, Macmillan, 1959), pp. 62–63.

p. 126  by results.' " *AU*, p. 241.

p. 126  doing anything." *SQ*, p. 196.

Chapter Fifteen—Jubilees and Conspiracies

p. 127  the Empire." *SQ*, p. 272.

p. 128  I knew," *Ibid.*, p. 233.

p. 128  you betrayed. Samuel Levenson, *James Connolly* (London, Martin Brian and O'Keefe, 1973), pp. 49–50.

p. 129  her heart" *ME*, p. 112.

p. 129  be afraid." Nora Connolly (O'Brien), conversation with author in 1973.

p. 129  her Jubilee?" *AU*, p. 244.

p. 130  funeral procession. *SQ*, pp. 273–274.

p. 130  of power." *ME*, pp. 112–113 and n.

p. 130  from friends!" Levenson, *James Connolly, op. cit.*, p. 53.

p. 131  and freedom." *AU*, p. 242.

p. 131  the door. *LE*, pp. 287–288.

ALS W. B. Yeats to Lady Gregory, Oct. 3, 1897.

p. 131  years before, *ME*, p. 82.

p. 131  of "Dynamitards." Sullivan was accused of the murder of Dr. Patrick Cronin, a Devoy follower, in May 1889. His sensational trial in Chicago won him an acquittal, but the incident intensified the Clan's internal divisions.

p. 132  "No. 1" Tynan in fact was not No. 1 of the Invincibles. Captain John McCafferty was in charge of the Invincibles in Dublin in 1882. *Devoy's Post Bag, 1871–1928, Vol. II, 1880–1928* (Dublin, C. J. Fallon, 1953), eds. William O'Brien and Desmond Ryan, p. 177. Tynan remained a grateful friend of Maud's until his death in 1936.

p. 132  Irish Brotherhood. *Ibid.*, pp. 342–343.

p. 132  the case. *Ibid.*, p. 342.

p. 133  infamous way. *LE*, p. 282. ALS W. B. Yeats to John O'Leary, Mar. 31, 1897.

p. 134  in America." *LE*, p. 289. ALS W. B. Yeats to Lady Gregory, Nov. 1, 1897.

p. 134  luck's sake." *AU*, p. 242.

Chapter Sixteen—The Land of the Clan

p. 136  get money." *SQ*, p. 195.

p. 137  Sounds mount," *Ibid.*, p. 194.

p. 137  of Ireland. "Maud Gonne Here," *Irish World*, Oct. 30, 1897. NYPL.

p. 138  a half." *Ibid.* Quoting Maud Gonne's speech at the Grand Opera House, New York, Oct. 27, 1897.

p. 138  in America The Irish-born population in America reached an all-time high of 1,872,000 in the 1890s. See Sean Cronin, *The McGarrity Papers* (Tralee, Republic of Ireland, Anvil Books, 1972), p. 16. Between 1841 and 1925 Irish emigration sent 4,750,000 people to America, 370,000 to Australia, 70,000 to Canada. See F. S. L. Lyons, *Ireland Since the Famine* (London, Weidenfeld, 1971; Collins/Fontana, 1973), p. 45; quoting "Report of the commission on emigration and other population problems, 1948–1954 (Dublin, 1954), pr. 2541.

p. 138  the work," Cronin, *The McGarrity Papers, op. cit.*, p. 16.

p. 139  and perfect" *SQ*, p. 198. Cockran had a love affair with the widowed Jennie Churchill in 1895 and served briefly in an avuncular role for her son. With "the tongue of gentleness whose words ripple as flowing water" Cockran could also sound two octaves of thunder, and young Winston Churchill took his oratory as a model. But as for his mentor's advocacy of Home Rule, he wrote, "your views on Ireland could never coincide with mine . . . " ALS Winston Churchill to Bourke Cockran, April 12, 1896.

p. 139  been attained." *Ibid.*

p. 140  the ego." B. L. Reid, *The Man from New York, John Quinn and His Friends* (New York, Oxford University Press, 1968), p. 19.

p. 140  from Ireland. *SQ*, p. 202.

p. 141  with us." *Ibid.*, p. 203.

p. 141  his teeth." Robert Kee, *The Green Flag* (New York, Delacorte, 1972), p. 358.

Chapter Seventeen—The Spirit of '98

p. 142  in shame? Traditional Irish Song.

p. 143  for students?" *SQ*, p. 282.

p. 143  Mr. T. B. Kelly." *Ballina Herald*, March 17, 1898. Clipping provided through the kindness of H. J. P. Dillon-Malone, whose father, J. P. Malone, was on the Ballina Reception Committee on that occasion.

p. 143  almost electrical." *Ibid.*

p. 143  French Army," *SQ*, p. 283.

p. 143  thousand demonstrators Marcus Bourke, *John O'Leary* (Tralee, Republic of Ireland, Anvil Books, 1967), p. 220.

p. 144  of humanity . . ."? Barbara W. Tuchman, *The Proud Tower* (New York, Macmillan, 1962), p. 182.

p. 144  Thomas Pile, Later Sir Thomas Pile. As mayor he had earlier refused the use of the Mansion House (the mayor's residence used also for public meetings) in Dublin to the Wolfe Tone Centenary Executive Committee.

p. 144  made it.' " *ME*, p. 114.

p. 144  turning point *Ibid.*

p. 145  not present *SQ*, p. 280.

p. 145  Daniel O'Connell,

O'Connell was a popular leader and a great orator; he organized the people in "monster" demonstrations, the first mass political movement in Ireland. He obtained "Catholic Emancipation" in 1829, and some reductions in tithes, but his movement failed in its efforts for Irish independence.

p. 146  or secretly . . ." *SQ*, pp. 227–228. Pamphlet is in the William O'Brien Archives, NLI.

p. 147  and best." Traditional Irish song.

p. 147  "heart failure." *SQ*, p. 230.

p. 148  their will." *United Irishman*, Feb. 22, 1902. NLI.

p. 148  the starving." *Ibid.*

p. 149  sacred rage." F. S. L. Lyons, *John Dillon* (London, Routledge and Kegan Paul, 1968), p. 180; quoting William O'Brien, *An Olive Branch in Ireland* (1910), p. 86.

p. 149  876 creameries F. S. L. Lyons, *Ireland Since the Famine* (London, Weidenfeld, 1971; Collins/Fontana, 1973), pp. 210–211.

p. 150  is born." *SQ*, p. 217.

p. 150  Irish landlord?" *SY*, p. 231.

p. 151  the country." F. S. L. Lyons, *John Dillon, op. cit.*, p. 225.

p. 152  against civilization." *SQ*, p. 225.

Chapter Eighteen—A Spiritual Marriage

p. 153  raging abstraction" *AU*, p. 242.

p. 154  people's rights. *SQ*, p. 264.

p. 155  my youth . . ." *CP*, p. 149;
"His Phoenix."

p. 155  literary movement." *LE*, p.
295. ALS W. B. Yeats to
George Russell, Jan. 22, 1898.

p. 155  hard up, "Until I was
nearly fifty, my writing
never brought me more than
two hundred a year, and
most often less, and I am
not by nature economical."
*AU*, p. 273.

p. 155  deeper self." *LE*, p. 297.
ALS W. B. Yeats to George
Russell, March 27, 1898.

p. 156  Celtic gathering." *LE*, p.
298. ALS W. B. Yeats to
Lady Gregory, April 25, 1898.

p. 156  discreet vice . . ." John
Masefield, *Some Memories of
W. B. Yeats* (New York,
Macmillan, 1940), p. 15.

p. 157  the morning." Virginia
Moore, *The Unicorn* (New
York, Octagon Books, 1973),
p. 65.

p. 157  "skrying" *Ibid.*, p. 63.

p. 157  of itself" *Ibid.*, p. 62.

p. 157  green fire." *Ibid.*, p. 71.

p. 157  memoried self." *AU*, p. 182.

p. 158  on them," Maud Gonne
MacBride, "Yeats and
Ireland," *Scattering Branches,
Tributes to the Memory of W.
B. Yeats* (New York,
Macmillan, 1940), ed.
Stephen Gwynn, p. 19.

p. 158  who was." *ME*, p. 131.

p. 158  compromise her," *Ibid.*

p. 158  the beech." *Lady Gregory's
Journals, 1916–1930* (New
York, Macmillan, 1947), ed.
Lennox Robinson, p. 22.

p. 158  exceeding long.' " *ME*, p.
125.

p. 159  of enthusiasms," *Lady
Gregory's Journals, op. cit.*, p.
340.

p. 159  a reality. Forerunner of
the Abbey, the Irish
Literary Theatre had its
inception at Coole Park,
when Lady Gregory and
Edward Martyn met there
with Yeats in 1898. Edward
Martyn was a playwright
and the Catholic landlord of
Tulira Castle in County
Galway. He was the first
president of Sinn Fein. Even
less tolerant of popular
drama than Yeats, he later
broke with the Abbey
Theatre to form his own.

p. 159  and brother." *ME*, pp.
160–161.

p. 159  us more . . ." *Ibid.*

p. 159  to Ireland," *AU*, p. 306.

p. 159  Literary Theatre In 1899
three hundred pounds a year
for the Irish Literary
Theatre was guaranteed by a
list of about fifty sponsors
representing all shades of
Dublin political affiliation:
Hyde, O'Leary, and
Redmond, as well as Lord
and Lady Ardslaun and Miss
Constance Gore-Booth.

p. 159  not reverent." Maud
Gonne MacBride, *Scattering
Branches, op. cit.*, pp. 28–29.

p. 160  of money." *SQ*, p. 332.

p. 161  for him. Maud Gonne
MacBride, *Scattering Branches,
op. cit.*, pp. 27–28.

p. 162  Maud Gonne Two ALS
fragments from Maud
Gonne to W. B. Yeats, date
and address unknown, found
among Lady Gregory's
papers. Collection, NYPL.

p. 162  wild birds . . . *CP*, p. 70.
"He Wishes His Beloved
Were Dead," *The Wind
Among the Reeds.* First

published in *The Sketch*, Feb. 1898.

p. 163  ungratified passion?" George Moore, *Hail and Farewell, Vale* (New York, D. Appleton and Co., 1919), p. 176.

p. 163  merely conjectural." *Ibid.*, p. 178.

p. 163  ". . . to me often enough." George Moore, *Hail and Farewell, op. cit.*, p. 290.

p. 163  he tells." *Irish Literary Portraits* (New York, Taplinger, 1973), ed. W. R. Rodgers, p. 78.

p. 163  London reckoning." *Shaw, An Autobiography 1856–1898* (New York, Weybright and Talley, 1969), selected from his writings by Stanley Weintraub, p. 14.

p. 164  remember nothing." *ME*, p. 132.

p. 164  for two." *Ibid.*, p. 132.

p. 164  stone Minerva." *Ibid.*, p. 134.

p. 164  spiritual marriage." W. B. Yeats, unpublished material from white calf notebook given to W. B. Yeats by Maud Gonne in 1908. Collection of Senator Michael Yeats.

p. 165  physical love.'" *ME*, p. 134.

p. 165  became repellent. *Ibid.*, p. 133.

p. 165  not there.'" Ibid.

p. 165  her conscience." *Ibid.*

p. 166  highest heaven. *LE*, pp. 311–312. ALS W. B. Yeats to Lady Gregory, Feb. 4, 1899.

p. 167  evicted tenants. *LE*, pp. 312–313. ALS W. B. Yeats to Lady Gregory, Feb. 19, 1899.

Chapter Nineteen—The Crowded Years

p. 168  to hand." *SQ*, pp. 308–309.

p. 169  for England." Barbara W. Tuchman, *The Proud Tower* (New York, Macmillan, 1962), p. 215.

p. 169  polite reply." Arthur Lynch, *My Life Story* (London, J. Long, 1924), p. 146.

p. 170  to see." *Ibid.*, p. 145.

p. 170  his mercy." Henry W. Nevinson, *Changes and Chances* (New York, Harcourt, Brace and Co., 1923), p. 210.

p. 171  Boer freedom." Michael Davitt, *The Boer Fight for Freedom* (New York, Funk and Wagnalls, 1902), p. 318.

p. 171  Irish Brigade The brigade was formed by men of Irish origin in the Transvaal, mainly Americans, pledged to fight for the Boers, under the command of Colonel Blake, a former American army officer, who was first in command until he was wounded and his place taken by John MacBride. The Brigade fought against the British at Colenso, Spion Kop, Ladysmith, etc., from Sept. 1899 to Sept. 1900. According to Robert Kee, *The Green Flag* (New York, Delacorte, 1972), pp. 443–444 notes, 1,000 men in the Irish Brigade was an exaggeration.

p. 171  "under-dogs" Henry W. Nevinson, *More Changes, More Chances* (New York, Harcourt, Brace and Co., 1925), pp. vii–ix.

p. 171  good will. Few nationalists of the time identified with the nonwhite subjects of the British Empire, at least until the movement for independence was well under way in India. Even Michael Davitt, who was exceptional in his lack of race prejudice, overlooked the Boers' exploitation of black Africans in the need to make common cause against England. There were a few exceptions to the prevailing attitudes. Alice Stopford Green, the Irish historian, saw parallels in the exploited populations of all of England's dominions and influenced Roger Casement, whose report on conditions in the Belgian Congo and in South America gained him a knighthood in 1911.

p. 171  against me." *J. B. Yeats, Letters to His Son W. B. Yeats and Others* (New York, Dutton, 1946), ed. Joseph Hone, p. 66.

p. 171  never succeed." F. S. L. Lyons, *John Dillon* (London, Routledge and Kegan Paul, 1968), p. 216.

p. 171  South Africa." F. Sheehy Skeffington, *Michael Davitt* (London, T. Fisher Unwin, 1908), p. 208.

p. 172  Ireland's Opportunity." *SQ,* p. 291.

p. 172  come heavily . . . Douglas Hyde's translation of old Irish verse in his essay "The Return of the Fenians," Robert Kee, *The Green Flag, op. cit.,* p. 438.

p. 173  Irish people." F. S. L. Lyons, *Ireland Since the Famine* (London, Weidenfeld, 1971; Collins/Fontana, 1973), p. 249; quoting William Rooney, *Prose Writings* (Dublin, 1909), pp. 73–75.

p. 173  dozen organizers. *Devoy's Post Bag, 1871–1928, Vol. II, 1880–1928* (Dublin, C. J. Fallon, 1953), eds. William O'Brien and Desmond Ryan, p. 350. ALS John MacBride to John Devoy, June 10, 1902.

p. 173  contributed articles, W. K. Magee was a school friend of W. B. Yeats and later a friend of AE and George Moore. A journalist and critic, he was associated with the National Library. James S. Starkey, a poet, founded and edited *Dublin Magazine.* Oliver St. John Gogarty, poet, physician and wit, was Buck Mulligan in *Ulysses;* Joyce once shared his Martello Tower. His best-known exploit was his escape from IRA gunmen during the Civil War— "pleading a natural necessity he got into the garden" of his house beside the Liffey and, in Yeats's version of the tale, "plunged under a shower of revolver bullets and as he swam the ice-cold December stream promised it, should it land him in safety, two swans." *Oxford Book of Literary Anecdotes* (London, Oxford University Press, 1975), ed. James Sutherland, pp. 330–331.

Padraic Colum was one of the first Abbey playwrights. Poet, folklorist, and lecturer, he wrote a biography of Arthur Griffith and, with his wife, Mary Colum, *Our Friend, James Joyce.*

p. 173   in Ireland." Richard Ellmann, *Selected Joyce Letters* (New York, Viking, 1966; 1975), p. 102. ALS James Joyce to Stanislaus Joyce, Sept. 6, 1906.

p. 173   himself second. Winston Churchill described Griffith as "that rare phenomenon, a silent Irishman," and after dealing with him in the 1921 treaty negotiations added that he was "a man of high integrity." Ulick O'Connor, *The Troubles* (Indianapolis/New York, Bobbs-Merrill, 1975), p. 25.

p. 174   balancing eyes." Anne Marreco, *The Rebel Countess* (London, Weidenfeld and Nicolson, 1967; Corgi Books, 1969), p. 100; quoting P. S. O'Hegarty, *Victory of Sinn Fein.*

*p. 174*   English people." C. Desmond Greaves, *The Life and Times of James Connolly* (New York, International Publishers, 1971), p. 114.

p. 175   the stars." Sean O'Casey, *Drums Under the Window* (New York, Macmillan, 1955), p. 17.

p. 175   "Joe's War," Tuchman, *The Proud Tower, op. cit.,* p. 55.

p. 175   Beresford Place. Marcus Bourke, *John O'Leary* (Tralee, Republic of Ireland, Anvil Books, 1967), pp. 225–226. See also Greaves, *The Life and*

*Times of James Connolly, op. cit.,* pp. 117–18.

p. 176   first excursion." Sean O'Casey, *Pictures in the Hallway* (New York, Macmillan, 1960), p. 311.

p. 176   the Castle?" *SQ*, p. 302.

p. 177   of warfare." *SQ*, p. 304.

p. 178   *en meer,*" ALS Dr. Leyds to Montagu White, Jan. 21, 1900. Leyds Archives, Pretoria, S.A. Information supplied by Professor Arthur Davey, University of Capetown.

p. 178   Man's burden" Tuchman, *The Proud Tower, op. cit.,* p. 159.

p. 179   at hand." *Irish World,* Feb. 10, 1900. NYPL.

p. 179   than forty Davitt, *The Boer Fight for Freedom, op. cit.,* p. 325.

Chapter Twenty—Daughters of Erin

p. 181   a grave! *SY,* p. 375.

p. 181   the Boers." *Ibid.*

p. 182   grievous sin." Father P. F. Kavanagh, leaflet issued for distribution and also published in *United Irishman,* Dec. 23, 1899; *Bean na hEireann,* No. 25, 1910, pp. 10–11; NLI.

p. 182   five hundred." *SY,* p. 372.

p. 183   bandages with." *Ibid.,* p. 355.

p. 183   extraordinary energy." *LE,* p. 326. ALS W. B. Yeats to Lily Yeats, Nov. 1, 1899.

p. 183   no more. . . . "The Beginning of the Anti-Enlistment Movement," article dated Oct. 12, 1899. *Bean na hEireann*, No. 25, 1910, pp. 10–11. Maud Gonne had drafted this. It was published for many weeks in *United Irishman* and circulated widely as a leaflet. NLI.

p. 184 young men." *SQ*, p. 292.

p. 184 on it" *SY*, p. 375. Reported to her by an old miller.

p. 184 in Ireland." W. B. Yeats, "Noble and Ignoble Loyalties," *United Irishman*, April 21, 1900; *Uncollected Prose by W. B. Yeats*, Vol. II (New York, Columbia University Press, 1926), eds. John P. Frayne and Colton Johnson, p. 212.

p. 184 the platform. *LE*, p. 336. Letter in *Freeman's Journal*, Mar. 20, 1900. The Rotunda was a Dublin public meeting hall.

p. 184 Irish Brigade." *LE*, p. 338. ALS W. B. Yeats to Lady Gregory, April 10, 1900.

p. 185 the gutter." *Ibid.*, p. 339.

p. 185 the crowds." *LE*, p. 337. ALS W. B. Yeats to Lady Gregory, Mar. 29, 1900.

p. 185 silent people." James Joyce, no source; Frank Tuohy, *Yeats* (New York, Macmillan, 1976), p. 107.

p. 185 of kings." *LE*, p. 338. ALS W. B. Yeats to *Daily Express*, Dublin, April 3, 1900.

p. 186 and honour. Maud Gonne, "The Famine Queen," Elizabeth Coxhead, *Daughters of Erin, Five Women of the Irish Renascence* (London, Secker and Warburg, 1963), p. 46. "Reine de la Disette," trans. from *l'Ireland Libre*, April 7, 1900.

p. 186 very loyal . . ." *LE*, pp. 338–339. ALS W. B. Yeats to Lady Gregory, April 10, 1900.

p. 187 and apology." *United Irishman*, May 30, 1903. NLI.

p. 187 working girls. "Inghinidhe na hEireann, The Story of the First Meeting," *Bean na hEireann*, 1910(?). NLI.

p. 187 National Organisations." *SQ*, p. 290.

p. 188 the men." Brian Farrell, "Markievicz and the Women of the Revolution," *Leaders and Men of the Easter Rising, Dublin: 1916* (Ithaca, N.Y., Cornell University Press, 1967), ed. F. X. Martin, p. 228.

p. 188 a woman." Maud Gonne, "The Famine Queen," Coxhead, *Daughters of Erin, op. cit.*, p. 45.

p. 188 Maire nic Shiubhlaigh. First Annual Report of Inghinidhe na hEireann, 1900–1901 (Dublin, O'Brien and Ards, 1901). NLI.

p. 188 Irish Independence. *Ibid.*, pp. 1–2.

p. 189 over thirty?" *AU*, p. 245.

p. 189 was over." *SQ*, p. 295.

p. 189 Maud Gonne." Coxhead, *Daughters of Erin, op. cit.*, p. 47.

p. 190 evil? England." Hone, p. 175.

p. 190 womanly feeling . . ." Brian Farrell, "Markievicz and the Women of the Revolution," *Leaders and Men of the Easter Rising, op. cit.*, p. 227.

p. 190 a nightmare . . ." *Ibid.* pp. 227–228; quoting Katherine

Tynan in *A Trumpet Call to Irish Women.*

p. 190  a cart," *Hone,* p. 213.

p. 190  inspired Yeats." Oliver St. John Gogarty, *As I Was Going Down Sackville Street* (New York, Reynal and Hitchcock, 1937), p. 300.

p. 191  and women." Proclamation of the Provisional Government of the Irish Republic, Easter 1916.

p. 191  a change." *Leaders and Men of the Easter Rising, op. cit.,* p. 230; quoting *United Irishman.*

p. 192  unite all . . ." *SQ,* p. 266.

p. 193  the candle-flames." Ella Young, *Flowering Dusk* (New York, Longmans, Green and Co., 1945), pp. 57–58.

Chapter Twenty-One—Broken Alliances

p. 194  years ago." *Irish-American,* Aug. 4, 1900. NYPL.

p. 195  Maud chérie." *SQ,* p. 288.

p. 196  love Ireland." *Ibid.,* p. 289.

p. 196  "Irish revolutionaries," *Ibid.,* p. 289.

p. 197  of life," *Ibid.*

p. 197  a career . . ." Colette, *Break of Day* (New York, Farrar, Straus and Cudahy, 1961), trans., Enid McLeod, p. 30.

p. 197  vaguely threatening. Author's conversation with Ian Stuart, sculptor, son of Iseult, 1975.

p. 198  in disgrace. *ME,* p. 116 and n.

p. 198  Irish again." *SQ,* p. 311.

p. 198  of *farceurs,*" *Ibid.,* p. 310.

p. 199  Transvaal Committee. *Hone,* p. 172.

p. 199  a man" *SQ,* p. 314.

p. 199  this man." *Ibid.,* p. 313.

p. 199  use them." *Ibid.,* p. 293.

p. 199  revolutionary activity. From the Oath of the Irish Republican Brotherhood (Constitution of 1894):
". . . I will do my utmost to establish the national independence of Ireland, and that I will bear true allegiance to the Supreme Council of the Irish Republican Brotherhood and Government of the Irish Republic and implicitly obey the Constitution of the Irish Republican Brotherhood and all my superior officers and that I will preserve inviolable the secrets of the organization."

Chapter Twenty-Two—Major MacBride

p. 201  concentration camps. Marcus Bourke, *John O'Leary* (Tralee, Republic of Ireland, Anvil Books, 1967), p. 221.

p. 201  20,000 died J. B. Priestley, *The Edwardians* (New York and Evanston, Harper and Row, 1970), p. 41.

p. 201  valuable service" *Irish-American,* Dec. 1, 1900. NYPL.

p. 202  many friends." *SQ,* p. 319.

p. 202  its folds." *Ibid.,* p. 321.

p. 203  the nation." F. S. L. Lyons, *Ireland Since the Famine* (London, Weidenfeld, 1971; Collins/Fontana, 1973), quoting R. M. Henry, *The Evolution of Sinn Fein* (Dublin, 1920), p. 63.

p. 203   me, then." *SQ,* p. 320.

p. 203   vice-president Richard Davis, *Arthur Griffith* (Dublin, Anvil Books, 1974), p. 18.

p. 204   great strengths." Lyons, *Ireland Since the Famine, op., cit.,* p. 250; quoting P. S. O'Hegarty, *A History of Ireland Under the Union* (London, 1952), p. 639.

p. 204   important indeed." *A U,* p. 284.

p. 204   stagger humanity." *Irish-American,* Dec. 9, 1900. NYPL.

p. 204   of Hell.' " *Irish-American,* Dec. 1, 1900. NYPL.

p. 205   young Irishman." *Devoy's Post Bag, 1871–1928, Vol. II, 1880–1928* (Dublin, C. J. Fallon, 1953), eds. William O'Brien and Desmond Ryan, pp. 346–347. ALS from John O'Leary in Paris to John Devoy in New York, Nov. 30, 1900.

p. 205   Major MacBride." *Irish-American,* Feb. 1901. NYPL.

p. 205   unsatisfactory interview." *SQ,* p. 322.

p. 206   to Paris. *Irish World,* Feb. 23, 1901. NYPL.

p. 206   of mine." ALS John MacBride to his mother from McCoy's Hotel, Chicago, Ill., Mar. 7, 1901. NLI.

p. 206   the same." ALS John MacBride to his mother from Janesville, Wisconsin, Mar. 13, 1901. NLI.

p. 207   is wonderful." ALS John MacBride to his mother from Marquette, Michigan, Mar. 20, 1901. NLI.

p. 207   Forceful Utterances." San Francisco *Chronicle,* June 23, 1901. NYPL.

p. 207   war on." *SQ,* p. 342.

p. 208   Ourselves Alone! Padraic Colum, *Ourselves Alone* (New York, Crown Publishers, 1959), p. 32.

p. 208   May 13. *Irish-American,* May 18, 1901. NYPL.

p. 208   to know," Davis, *Arthur Griffith, op. cit.,* p. 4; quoting Arthur Griffith, preface to W. Rooney, *Poems and Ballads* (Nov. 1910), p. ix.

p. 208   affect him." *LE,* p. 352. ALS W. B. Yeats to Lady Gregory, May 21, 1901.

p. 208   the flow." *LE,* p. 352. ALS W. B. Yeats to Lady Gregory, May 25, 1901.

p. 209   Maud Gonne. ALS Maud Gonne to W. B. Yeats, n.d. prob. June 1901. Berg Collection, NYPL.

Chapter Twenty-Three—Cathleen ni Houlihan

p. 210   "Bridge," *SQ,* p. 325.

p. 210   Colonel T. D. Pilcher His book on the army, *Some Lessons from the Boer War,* 1899–1902, was published in London by Isbister & Co., 1904.

p. 211   dowdy. Conrad A. Balliet, "Michael MacLiammoir Recalls Maud Gonne MacBride," an interview in *Journal of Irish Literature* (Newark, Delaware, University of Delaware, Proscenium Press, May 1977), p. 47.

p. 211   youthful appearance *SQ,* p. 328.

p. 212   hollow moon. *CP*, pp. 78–79; "Adam's Curse," first published in *Monthly Review*, Dec. 1901.

p. 212   peaceful life." *SQ*, pp. 329–330.

p. 213   in speech." *Hone*, p. 180; quoting Dorothy Richardson.

p. 213   the brains." *SQ*, p. 333.

p. 214   street lamp." *Hone*, p. 157 n.

p. 214   Indian Princess," *SQ*, p. 331.

p. 214   of England. *Ibid.*

p. 215   the room. J. M. Synge, *The Aran Islands and Other Writings* (New York, Vintage Books, 1962), ed. Robert Tracy, pp. 364–365; quoting *L'Européen* (Paris, May 31, 1902).

p. 215   a people," *Uncollected Prose by W. B. Yeats*, Vol. II (New York, Columbia University Press, 1976), eds. John P. Frayne and Colton Johnson, p. 286.

p. 215   heavy feet . . ." George Moore, *Hail and Farewell*, *Ave* (New York and London, D. Appleton and Co., 1917), p. 46.

p. 216   demonstrations, refused." *AU*, p. 297.

p. 216   Ireland herself." *Hone*, p. 176.

p. 216   them for ever. W. B. Yeats, "Cathleen ni Hoolihan," *W. B. Yeats Selected Plays* (London, Macmillan, 1952), ed. A. Norman Jeffares, pp. 254–255.

p. 217   fine house—" *LE*, p. 365. ALS W. B. Yeats to Lady Gregory, Jan. 20, 1902.

p. 217   Maud Gonne ALS Maud

Gonne to W. B. Yeats, postmarked Feb. 3, 1902, Paris. Berg Collection, NYPL.

p. 218   standing ovation. *United Irishman*, Feb. 22, 1902. NLI.

p. 218   *Vive Les Boers!*" *United Irishman*, March 1, 1902. NLI.

p. 218   little play." *Hone*, p. 176.

p. 218   to dominate." *LE*, p. 367. ALS W. B. Yeats to Lady Gregory, Mar. 22, 1902.

p. 218   the rehearsals." *J. B. Yeats, Letters to His Son W. B. Yeats and Others, 1869–1922* (New York, E. P. Dutton, 1946), ed. Joseph Hone, p. 70. ALS J. B. Yeats to W. B. Yeats, Sunday 1902.

p. 219   a reflection. . . ." *United Irishman*, Apr. 12, 1902. NLI.

p. 219   standing patrons." Maire nic Shiubhlaigh and Edward Kenny, *The Splendid Years* (Dublin, James Duffy, 1955), p. 17.

p. 219   the bough." William George Fay and Catherine Carswell, *The Fays of the Abbey Theatre* (New York, Harcourt, Brace and Co., 1935), p. 119.

p. 220   the stage." Maire nic Shiubhlaigh and Edward Kenny, *The Splendid Years, op. cit.*, p. 19.

p. 220   weird power." *LE*, p. 368. ALS W. B. Yeats to Lady Gregory, April 3, 1902.

p. 220   evict us . . ." Maud Gonne MacBride, "Yeats and Ireland," *Scattering Branches, Tributes to the Memory of W. B. Yeats* (New York, Macmillan, 1940), ed. Stephen Gwynn, pp. 29–30.

p. 220   final curtain . . ." Seumas

O'Sullivan, "The Irish National Theatre," *The Rose and the Bottle and Other Essays* (Dublin, Talbot Press, 1946), pp. 120–121.

p. 220 English shot?" *CP*, p. 337; "The Man and the Echo," *Last Poems*.

p. 220 audience stirred." Stephen Gwynn, *Irish Literature and Drama*, p. 158; A. Norman Jeffares, *W. B. Yeats, Man and Poet* (London, Routledge and Kegan Paul, 1949), p. 138.

p. 220 a queen." W. B. Yeats, "Cathleen ni Hoolihan," *Selected Plays, op. cit.*, p. 256.

Chapter Twenty-Four—The Great Storm

p. 222 drawings exquisite. John Quinn, diary of trip to Ireland, 1904. Quinn Papers, NYPL.

p. 223 pastel sketch Now in the possession of the author; purchased from the Oriel Gallery, Dublin, 1975.

p. 223 expect anything." John Quinn, diary of a trip to Ireland, 1904. Quinn Papers, NYPL.

p. 223 of genius" *Ibid.*

p. 223 active members. Robert Kee, *The Green Flag* (New York, Delacorte, 1972), p. 436.

p. 224 landlord greed." *United Irishman*, Oct. 11, 1902. NLI.

p. 224 helpless destitution. Between 1903 and 1920 nine million acres changed ownership. F. S. L. Lyons, *Ireland Since the Famine* (London, Weidenfeld, 1971; Collins/Fontana, 1973), p. 219.

p. 224 checking emigration."

*United Irishman*, Oct. 11, 1902. NLI.

p. 224 come true." *United Irishman*, Aug. 23, 1902. NLI.

p. 224 "their Intensities," *Selected Joyce Letters* (New York, Viking, 1966; 1975), ed. Richard Ellmann, p. 21. ALS Joyce to Gogarty, June 3, 1904.

p. 225 not desired . . ." *United Irishman*, Mar. 29, 1902. NLI.

p. 225 Irish movement . . ." W. B. Yeats, "The Cutting of an Agate," *Essays and Introductions* (New York, Macmillan, 1961; Collier Books, 1968), p. 259.

p. 225 Kathleen ni Houlihan." *Florence Farr, Bernard Shaw, W. B. Yeats, Letters* (New York, Dodd, Mead, 1942), ed. Clifford Bax, p. 74. ALS W. B. Yeats to Florence Farr.

p. 226 Lascivious people." James Joyce, *Ulysses* (New York, Modern Library, 1934; Vintage Books, 1961), pp. 42–43.

p. 227 Maud Gonne Stanislaus Joyce, *My Brother's Keeper* (New York, Viking, 1958), pp. 198–199.

p. 227 shabby appearance" *Ibid.*, p. 198.

p. 227 with her,' " *Ibid.*, p. 128.

p. 227 to go." Richard Ellmann, *James Joyce* (New York, Oxford University Press, 1959), p. 127.

p. 228 the month." *United Irishman*, February 14, 1903. NLI.

p. 228 song about . . ." *CP*, p. 89; "Reconciliation," *In the Seven Woods*.

p. 229 for long." *SQ*, p. 349.

p. 229  for you." *Ibid.*
p. 229  his wife . . ." *Ibid.*
p. 229  get married." *Ibid.*, p. 348.
p. 230  electric blue." *United Irishman*, Feb. 28, 1903. NLI.
p. 230  of Ireland." *Ibid.*
p. 230  further trouble. ALS Maud Gonne to Lady Gregory from Bayeux, Calvados, Feb. 28, 1903. Berg Collection, NYPL.
p. 231  has gone!" Ella Young, *Flowering Dusk* (New York, Longmans, Green and Co., 1945), p. 76.
p. 231  larch down." *SY*, p. 427.
p. 231  of things . . ." W. B. Yeats, Preface to "In the Seven Woods," *The Variorum Edition of the Poems of W. B. Yeats* (New York, Macmillan, 1973), eds. Peter Allt and Russell K. Alspach, p. 814 n.
p. 231  her husband. Conversation between author and Helen Roeloffs, Dublin, 1973.
p. 232  of Mr. McB. *Letters from AE* (New York, Abelard-Schumann, 1961), ed. Alan Denson, pp. 45–46. ALS George Russell to W. B. Yeats, April 28, 1903.
p. 232  has wept!" *CP*, p. 388; "The Old Age of Queen Maeve."
p. 233  the feet." *SY* p. 424. In August 1906 Joyce, his ear for Dublin gossip tuned in from Rome, wrote his brother: "W. B. Yeats ought to hurry up and marry Lady Gregory—to kill talk." *Selected Letters of James Joyce* (New York, Viking, 1957), p. 96. ALS James Joyce to Stanislaus Joyce, Aug. 19, 1906.

p. 233  Maud Gonne." Seumas MacManus, unpublished ms. Collection of Patricia MacManus.
p. 233  a politician." *Ibid.*
p. 234  stormy petrel." *Ibid.*
p. 234  a Nationalist . . ." *United Irishman*, May 30, 1903. NLI.
p. 234  Redmondite revolt!" Seumas MacManus, *op. cit.*
p. 234  are incapacitated." *Letters from AE, op. cit.*, p. 47; ALS George Russell to W. B. Yeats, May 1903.
p. 235  tangible thing." *United Irishman*, July 11, 1903. NLI.
p. 235  the country. *United Irishman*, July 16, 1903. NLI.
p. 235  own people." W. B. Yeats, *Freeman's Journal*, July 13, 1903, W. B. Yeats, *Uncollected Prose*, Vol. II (New York, Columbia University Press, 1976), eds. John P. Frayne and Colton Johnson, p. 304.
p. 235  was lifted." *United Irishman*, July 25, 1903. NLI.
p. 236  in Ireland. Maud Gonne taped interview from Radio Telifis Eireann Archives.
p. 236  first quarrel." Maud Gonne MacBride, "Yeats and Ireland," *Scattering Branches, Tributes to the Memory of W. B. Yeats* (New York, Macmillan, 1940), ed. Stephen Gwynn, p. 30.
p. 237  peasant woman" *The Story of the Abbey Theatre* (London, New English Library/Four Square Books, 1967), ed. Sean McCann, p. 131.
p. 237  their work." *Ibid.*, p. 130.
p. 237  the glass.' " William George Fay and Catherine Carswell, *The Fays of the Abbey Theatre* (New York,

Harcourt, Brace and Co., 1935), p. 140.

p. 237   Boccaccio story" *Ibid.*, p. 141.

p. 237   the world." *United Irishman*, Oct. 24, 1903. NLI.

p. 238   of Ireland. *Ibid.*

p. 238   all summer." *LE*, p. 414. ALS W. B. Yeats to Lady Gregory, Nov. 16, 1903.

Chapter Twenty-Five—The Red-Haired Man's Wife

p. 239   to you. James Stevens, "The Red-Haired Man's Wife," *Collected Poems* (New York, Macmillan, 1909; 1954), pp. 69–70.

p. 240   golden-haired boy." Ella Young, *Flowering Dusk* (New York, Longmans, Green and Co., 1945), pp. 101–102.

p. 240   in Ireland." Donald T. Torchiana, " 'Among School Children,' and the Education of the Irish Spirit," *In Excited Reverie* (New York, St. Martin's Press, 1965), eds. A. Norman Jeffares and K. G. W. Cross, p. 169.

p. 240   the classes." ALS Maud Gonne to Lady Gregory, Nov. 30, 1903. Berg Collection, NYPL. See also *In Excited Reverie*, p. 138.

p. 241   MacBride family. Information about the baptism given to the author by Sean MacBride and Leon O Broin, 1973.

p. 241   than before. Henry W. Nevinson, *More Changes, More Chances* (New York, Harcourt, Brace and Co., 1925), p. 30.

p. 241   as ever." ALS W. B. Yeats

to John Quinn, early July 1904. Quinn Papers, NYPL.

p. 242   I can . . . )" *Ibid.*

p. 242   of friends." *LE*, p. 427. ALS W. B. Yeats to Lady Gregory, Jan. 21, 1904.

p. 242   over you." James Joyce, *Ulysses* (New York, Modern Library, 1934; Vintage Books, 1961), p. 217.

p. 243   for Yeats." Richard Ellmann, *James Joyce* (New York, Oxford University Press, 1959), p. 296.

p. 243   great delicacy. Ella Young, *Flowering Dusk, op. cit.*, p. 199.

p. 244   handsome woman." John Quinn, diary of a trip to Ireland, Oct. 1904. Quinn Papers, NYPL.

p. 244   unspellable name" Anne Marreco, *The Rebel Countess* (London, Weidenfeld and Nicolson, 1967; Corgi Books, 1969), p. 86.

p. 244   "very charming," John Quinn, diary of a trip to Ireland, Oct. 1904. Quinn Papers, NYPL.

p. 244   never satisfied." *Devoy's Post Bag, 1871–1928, Vol. II, 1880–1928* (Dublin, C. J. Fallon, 1953), eds. William O'Brien and Desmond Ryan, pp. 351–352. ALS John MacBride to John Devoy, Nov. 15, 1904.

p. 245   very far." *Ibid.*, p. 352.

p. 245   faery world" Ella Young, *Flowering Dusk, op. cit.*, p. 102.

p. 245   our luck." Maud Gonne MacBride, "Dawn," *Lost Plays of the Irish Renaissance* (Gerrards Cross, Bucks, England, Proscenium Press,

1970), eds. Robert Hogan and James Kilroy, p. 84.

p. 246   for separation. ALS W. B. Yeats to John Quinn, March 11, 1905. Quinn Papers, NYPL.

p. 247   help her." *Hone*, p. 212.

p. 247   movement itself. ALS W. B. Yeats to John Quinn, Jan. 14, 1905. Quinn Papers, NYPL.

p. 247   unfortunate sister. ALS W. B. Yeats to John Quinn, March 11, 1905. Quinn Papers, NYPL.

p. 247   unconventional life. *Ibid.*

p. 248   the matter." ALS John Quinn to W. B. Yeats, May 6, 1905. Quinn Papers, NYPL.

p. 248   accounts even." ALS John Quinn to W. B. Yeats, June 17, 1905. Quinn Papers, NYPL.

p. 248   of this," Elizabeth Coxhead, *Daughters of Erin, Five Women of the Irish Renascence* (London, Secker and Warburg, 1965), p. 59.

p. 249   public life." ALS Annie Elizabeth Fredericka Horniman to Lady Gregory, April 10, 1905, Railway Hotel, Westport. Berg Collection, NYPL.

p. 249   public house," *Ibid.*

p. 249   *sauft nicht.*" ALS A. Horniman to Lady Gregory, April 11, 1905. Berg Collection, NYPL.

p. 249   she did." *Ibid.*

p. 249   considered important." ALS A. Horniman to Lady Gregory, April 10, 1905. Berg Collection, NYPL.

p. 249   very much?" *Devoy's Post Bag, 1871–1928, Vol. II, 1880–1928*

*op. cit.*, p. 354. ALS P. T. Daly to John Devoy, April 18, 1905.

p. 249   little chap." *Selected Joyce Letters* (New York, Viking, 1966; 1975), ed. Richard Ellmann, p. 57. ALS James Joyce to Stanislaus Joyce, March 15, 1905.

p. 250   in kind. *Irish Independent,* Feb. 28, 1905. NYPL.

p. 250   denied it." ALS John Quinn to Maud Gonne, Paris, May 24, 1906. Quinn Collection, NYPL.

p. 251   most wearisome . . . Fragment ALS Maud Gonne to W. B. Yeats, date uncertain, March or April 1905. Berg Collection, NYPL.

p. 253   marry him." *New York World,* August 13, 1905.

p. 254   had done." *James Joyce, The Critical Writings* (New York, Viking, 1959), eds. Ellsworth Mason and Richard Ellmann, p. 191.

p. 254   called teetotallers," Marcus Bourke, *John O'Leary* (Tralee, Republic of Ireland, Anvil Books, 1967), p. 230.

p. 255   like her. Fragment ALS Maud Gonne to W. B. Yeats, Dec. 16, 1905(?), 13 Rue de Passy. Berg Collection, NYPL. Lady Gregory's *White Cockade*, a historical drama about Sarsfield and King James's escape after the battle of the Boyne, was first produced on December 9, 1905. The little "drawing" of Iseult is now in the possession of Yeats's daughter, Anne.

p. 256   John MacBride!" Mary

Colum, *Life and the Dream*
(Garden City, N.Y.,
Doubleday, 1947), p. 142.
p. 256  of shock." *Ibid.*
p. 256  being drowned." *Ibid.*
p. 256  the people." CP, p. 149;
"The People."

Chapter Twenty-Six—
    Reconciliations

p. 257  are brave." *SQ*, p. 15.
p. 257  in France." ALS Maud
    Gonne to John Quinn, June
    22, 1909. Quinn Papers,
    NYPL.
p. 258  last consummated.
    Information supplied by
    Professor Richard Ellmann
    in a letter to the author,
    Oct. 17, 1974. Until all
    correspondence between
    Maud Gonne and W. B.
    Yeats becomes available, it
    remains uncertain just when
    they became lovers.
    Ellmann, biographer and
    perceptive critic, found
    evidence in one of the poet's
    cryptic diaries that "at least
    once" at the time of the
    reconciliation in Paris in
    1907, Yeats's love for Maud
    was "requited." His opinion
    was confirmed by Mrs. W.
    B. Yeats, the poet's widow.
    Ellmann, in *Golden Codgers*,
    also points to a shift of
    emphasis in Yeats's work
    dealing with love and sex
    after 1907 as further proof.
    "In a journal of Yeats's
    which has not been
    published, it is made clear
    that at least once, about 1907,
    his unrequited love for
    Maud Gonne found requital.

'The first of all the tribe lay
there,' as he was afterwards
to boast in a poem." The
poem referred to is "A Man
Young and Old" Verse VI,
"His Memories from the
Tower," 1928. Richard
Ellmann, *Golden Codgers*
(New York and London,
Oxford University Press,
1973), pp. 107n–108n.
p. 258  her children." W. B. Yeats,
    white calf notebook, 1908,
    collection of Senator
    Michael Yeats. Transcrip-
    tion corroborated by G. M.
    Harper, *Yeats's Golden Dawn*,
    n. 3, p. 168. (Yeats corrected
    the date in this passage from
    1899 to 1898.)
p. 258  blue toads." Colette, *The
    Pure and the Impure* (New
    York, Farrar, Straus and
    Giroux, 1975), trans. Herma
    Briffault, p. 76.
p. 258  should be." Philippe
    Jullian, *Dreamers of Decadence*
    (New York, Praeger, 1971),
    trans. Robert Baldick, p. 22;
    quoting Oscar Wilde.
p. 259  touches lip . . ." *LE*, p.
    480. ALS W. B. Yeats to
    Florence Farr, Sept. 30,
    1906.
p. 259  it all . . . ALS Maud
    Gonne to W. B. Yeats from
    Passy, June 26, 1908. White
    calf notebook, *op. cit.*
p. 259  mystic marriage." W. B.
    Yeats, white calf notebook,
    *op. cit.*
p. 259  was arrested." Virginia
    Moore, *The Unicorn* (New
    York, Macmillan, 1952;
    Octagon Books, 1973), pp.
    198–199.
p. 260  with it. ALS Maud Gonne

to W. B. Yeats, July 26, 1908. White calf notebook, *op. cit.*

p. 261 been crossed. *CP,* p. 90, "King and No King," from *The Green Helmet* (whose first eight poems deal with Yeats's and Maud Gonne's reunion in 1908–1909. Draft of "King and No King" appears in white calf notebook, dated Dec. 1909.

p. 261 religious mystery . . . ALS W. B. Yeats to Mabel Dickinson, Paris, June 20, 1908. Bancroft Collection, University of California, Berkeley, CA.

p. 262 happy marriage . . ." *Letters to W. B. Yeats,* Vol. I (London, Macmillan, 1977), eds. Richard J. Finneran, George Mills Harper, William M. Murphy, p. 204. Yeats consulted James Richard Wallace of Manchester about Maud Gonne's horoscope and received a letter from him dated July 31, 1908. It verifies the date of her birth. "The '1866 case' refers to Maud Gonne (b. 21 December, 1866). 'Wallace says that he is rectifying by Saturn ("soul at the nadir of matter") in opposition to . . . midheaven . . . In such a case there could be no happy marriage even if Jupiter . . . should be in the Seventh House (for which the key word is 'partnership'). In this astrological position the native at its best is the perfect partner in a real reciprocity of interest.' Her loss of popularity is due to

the Sun being in opposition to the Moon."

p. 263 can destroy." Maud Gonne entry in white calf notebook, *op. cit.,* Oct. 20, 1908. Yeats later crossed out "Aileel" in the notebook and wrote in its place his initials from the Golden Dawn, D E D I. Aileel is the name of Queen Maeve's husband; of the bard who loves the Countess Cathleen in the revised version of Yeats's play; and also of the poet lover of Dectora in *The Shadowy Waters.*

p. 263 will pray." Yeats's unpublished journal, Jan. 21, 1909; Moore, *The Unicorn, op. cit.,* p. 202.

p. 264 well-paid." ALS Maud Gonne to John Quinn, 1911 (?). Quinn Papers, NYPL.

p. 265 was speaking. ALS Maud Gonne to W. B. Yeats, June 26, 1908, white calf notebook, *op. cit.*

p. 266 own work . . ." ALS Maud Gonne to John Quinn, July 11, 1908. Quinn Papers, NYPL.

p. 266 terrible theatre." ALS Maud Gonne to John Quinn, Jan. 7, 1909. Quinn Papers, NYPL.

p. 266 the kitchen!' " *LE,* p. 532. ALS W. B. Yeats to J. B. Yeats, July 17, 1909 (?).

p. 266 as complete." Moore, *The Unicorn, op. cit.,* p. 202; quoting Yeats's notebook.

p. 266 a clown. *ME,* p. 145 and n. This poem was never published.

p. 266 till midnight ALS Maud
Gonne to John Quinn, Jan.
19, 1910. Quinn Papers,
NYPL.

p. 267 he said." *Lady Gregory's
Journals* (New York,
Macmillan, 1947), p. 330.

p. 267 always mourn. *The Letters
of Oscar Wilde* (New York,
Harcourt, Brace and World,
1962), p. 863.

p. 267 long windows. Ella
Young, *Flowering Dusk* (New
York, Longmans, Green and
Co., 1945), pp. 206–207.

p. 267 other book," *Hone*, p. 240.

p. 268 fairy book," ALS Maud
Gonne to John Quinn
enclosing note from Iseult
Gonne, Jan. 26, 1910. Quinn
Papers, NYPL.

p. 268 wrecked city," ALS Maud
Gonne to John Quinn, Jan.
19, 1910. Quinn Papers,
NYPL.

p. 268 most exciting." ALS Iseult
Gonne to John Quinn, Jan.
26, 1910. Quinn Papers,
NYPL.

p. 268 making mischief." ALS
Maud Gonne to John
Quinn, Aug. 5, 1909. Quinn
Papers, NYPL.

p. 268 keep quiet." ALS Maud
Gonne to John Quinn, Sept.
12, 1909. Quinn Papers,
NYPL.

p. 269 my thoughts . . ." ALS
Maud Gonne to John
Quinn, Aug. 16, 1909. Quinn
Papers, NYPL.

p. 269 be told." Brian Inglis,
*Roger Casement* (New York,
Harcourt, Brace, Jovanovich,
1973), p. 287; quoting from
letter to Alice Green.

p. 269 mystic victim." W. B.

Yeats, "Modern Ireland,"
*Irish Renaissance* (Dublin,
Dolmen Press, 1965;
Brattleboro, Vt., Vermont
Printing Co.), p. 23.

p. 270 law again." ALS Maud
Gonne to John Quinn, Mar.
25, 1908. Quinn Papers,
NYPL.

p. 271 her heart. Anne Marreco,
*The Rebel Countess* (London,
Weidenfeld and Nicolson,
1967; Corgi Books, 1969), pp.
128 and 303n. ALS Maud
Gonne to Count
Markiewicz, May 14, 1931.

p. 272 lunatic asylums." ALS
Maud Gonne to John
Quinn, Oct. 29, 1910. Quinn
Papers, NYPL.

p. 272 in London. Tim Pat
Coogan, *The IRA* (London,
Fontana/Collins, 1970), p. 32.
The poor were crowded into
foul dwellings in incredible
numbers. Nearly 26,000
families lived in 5,000
tenements; of the tenements,
more than 1,500 were
condemned as not only unfit
for human habitation, but
incapable of ever being
rendered fit for habitation.
See Emmet Larkin, *James
Larkin* (London, New
English Library/Mentor,
1968), p. 36.

p. 272 childish systems." Maud
Gonne, "Responsibility,"
*Irish Review*, Dec. 1911, pp.
483–484. NLI.

p. 272 sapping it—" ALS Maud
Gonne to John Quinn, Dec.
31, 1910. Quinn Papers,
NYPL.

p. 273 the matter. Public Records

Office, Dec. 20, 1910
(#CO904/12 X/K3735);
Chancery Lane, London,
WCZ.

p. 273  strode past. Information
from Bairbre MacDonagh
Redmond given to author,
Dublin, 1973.

p. 273  prime importance," *Leaders
and Men of the Easter Rising,
Dublin: 1916* (Ithaca, N. Y.,
Cornell University Press,
1967), ed. F. X. Martin, p.
154.

p. 274  the ages." Young,
*Flowering Dusk, op. cit.*, p.
80.

Chapter Twenty-Seven—A
Separate Peace

p. 275  at peace *ME*, p. 246. From
draft of "Against Unworthy
Praise," in journal, May 11,
1910; see also *CP*, p. 91.

p. 275  Les Mouettes According to
Francis Stuart in his
autobiographical novel,
*Black-List, Section H*
(Carbondale and
Edwardsville, Ill., Southern
Illinois University Press,
1971), p. 147, Les Mouettes
was a gift to Iseult from her
father. Denis Donoghue
writes in the Yeats *Memoirs*
(p. 247) that Maud Gonne
and her cousin May Gonne
Clay shared the house in
Normandy.

p. 276  of beauty . . ." ALS Maud
Gonne to John Quinn, Sept.
12, 1909. Quinn Papers,
NYPL.

p. 276  and understanding." *J. B.
Yeats Letters to His Son W. B.
Yeats and Others* (New York,

E.P. Dutton, 1946), ed.
Joseph Hone, p. 37.

p. 276  and friendship. "The
American Girl, an Irish
View," *Harper's Weekly*,
April 23, 1910.

p. 277  the Yeatssssss's," B. L.
Reid, *The Man from New
York, John Quinn and His
Friends* (New York, Oxford
University Press, 1968), p.
308.

p. 277  ink bottle." *Ibid.*, p. 81.

p. 277  "London monstrosity,"
ALS Maud Gonne to John
Quinn, Sept. 12, 1909. Quinn
Papers, NYPL.

p. 278  her form. *CP*, p. 90;
"Peace."

p. 278  re-create it." *ME*, p. 247.

p. 278  or proportion." W. B.
Yeats, *Essays and Introductions*
(New York, Macmillan, 1961;
Collier Books, 1968), p. 340.

p. 278  the Saint," William Butler
Yeats, "If I Were Four and
Twenty," *Explorations* (New
York, Macmillan, 1962;
Collier Books, 1973), p. 264.

p. 279  Irish have!" *Ibid.*

p. 279  of youth." *ME*, p. 246.
Journal (May 1910) Colleville,
Calvados.

p. 279  in Ireland." ALS Maud
Gonne to John Quinn, Dec.
31, 1910. Quinn Papers,
NYPL.

p. 279  "wonderfully peaceful,"
*Ibid.*

p. 280  the government." *Ibid.*

p. 280  the past." *Ibid.*

p. 280  and Hughes John Hughes,
a Franco-Irish sculptor, had
been at art school with
Yeats and George Russell.
His statue of Queen
Victoria, which stood for

many years on Kildare Street in front of Leinster House, was often referred to as "the hippopotamus," but Yeats preferred his brother Jack's description: "I like it because she looks so old and so dull and so brave." Yeats met Hughes again in Paris in 1909 through Maud, who studied painting with him and the French artist Joseph Granié. See *LE*, pp. 524n., 525. ALS W. B. Yeats to J. B. Yeats, Jan. 17, 1909.

p. 280   outside art." ALS Maud Gonne to John Quinn, Feb. 13, 1911. Quinn Papers, NYPL.

p. 281   Chinese painting." ALS Maud Gonne to John Quinn, June 17, 1911. Quinn Papers, NYPL.

p. 281   starving children." ALS Maud Gonne to John Quinn, March 16, 1914. Quinn Papers, NYPL.

p. 282   the meeting. ALS Maud Gonne to John Quinn, Aug. 28, 1911. Quinn Papers, NYPL.

p. 283   the least." ALS Maud Gonne to John Quinn, Nov. 3, 1911. Quinn Papers, NYPL.

p. 283   smuggled arms. Ella Young, *Flowering Dusk* (New York, Longmans, Green and Co., 1945), p. 115.

p. 283   not stealing," Taped interview with Maud Gonne, Radio Telifis Eireann, 1947 (?).

p. 283   supine indifference." Maud Gonne, "Responsibility," *Irish Review*, Dec. 1911, p. 484. NLI.

p. 284   things here." ALS Maud

Gonne to John Quinn, Nov. 3, 1911. Quinn Papers, NYPL.

p. 284   in Ireland." Dorothy Macardle, *The Irish Republic* (London, Victor Gollancz, 1937; London, Corgi Books, 1968), p. 78.

p. 285   helped her." ALS Maud Gonne to John Quinn, April 11, 1912. Quinn Papers, NYPL.

p. 285   her hat . . ." James and Margaret Cousins, *We Two Together* (London, Luzac, 1951), pp. 158–159.

p. 286   canvas tunnel," *Ibid.*, pp. 161–162.

p. 286   the wind? *CP*, p. 120; "To a Child Dancing in the Wind."

p. 287   its authority." Ulick O'Connor, *The Troubles* (Indianapolis/New York, Bobbs-Merrill, 1975), p. 40.

p. 287   be withstood," *Leaders and Men of the Easter Rising: Dublin, 1916* (Ithaca, N.Y., Cornell University Press, 1967), ed. F.X. Martin, p. 168.

p. 287   into bloom." *Ibid.*

p. 288   to England." ALS Maud Gonne to John Quinn, Nov. 20, 1913. Quinn Papers, NYPL.

p. 288   govern ourselves." ALS Maud Gonne to John Quinn, Dec. 29, 1913. Quinn Papers, NYPL.

p. 288   Real Criminals." *Irish Worker*, Nov. 1913; Elizabeth Coxhead, *Daughters of Erin, Five Women of the Irish Renascence* (London, Secker and Warburg, 1965), p. 62.

p. 288   children alive." ALS Maud Gonne to John Quinn, Nov.

20, 1913. Quinn Papers, NYPL.

p. 289  found it—" ALS Maud Gonne to W. B. Yeats, n.d., first p. missing; circa fall 1913. Collection of Senator Michael Yeats.

p. 289  isn't it?" ALS Maud Gonne to John Quinn, Nov. 20, 1913. Quinn Papers, NYPL.

p. 290  British Law . . ." O'Connor, *The Troubles, op. cit.,* p. 60.

p. 290  Home Rule bluffers." *Devoy's Post Bag, 1871–1928, Vol. II, 1880–1928* (Dublin, C. J. Fallon, 1953), eds. William O'Brien and Desmond Ryan, p. 447. ALS John MacBride to John Devoy, May 16, 1914.

p. 290  and women." *Leaders and Men of the Easter Rising, Dublin: 1916, op. cit.* p. 233.

p. 290  the situation. ALS Maud Gonne to John Quinn, Dec. 29, 1913. Quinn Papers, NYPL.

p. 290  the snow. Reid, *The Man from New York, op. cit.,* p. 123.

p. 291  today, disappear . . ." ALS Maud Gonne to John Quinn, Dec. 29, 1913. Quinn Papers, NYPL.

p. 291  Parnell did." ALS Maud Gonne to John Quinn, March 8, 1914. Quinn Papers, NYPL.

p. 292  charming creature," *SY,* p. 494. ALS W. B. Yeats to Lady Gregory, May 13, 1914.

p. 292  est l'intelligence.' " Maud Gonne from W. B. Yeats, 1912. Brown leather notebook. Collection of Senator Michael Yeats.

p. 292  Northern countries.' " *Ibid.*

p. 292  to do." ALS Maud Gonne to W. B. Yeats, July 9, 1914. Collection of Senator Michael Yeats.

p. 293  the future." ALS Maud Gonne to John Quinn, n.d.; received May 12, 1914. Quinn Papers, NYPL.

p. 294  Maud Gonne ALS Maud Gonne to W. B. Yeats, July 30, 1914. Arrens, Haute Pyrénées. Collection of Senator Michael Yeats.

p. 295  National Volunteers." *SY,* p. 512.

p. 295  Armageddon." O'Connor, *The Troubles, op. cit.* p. 61.

p. 296  the vanquished. ALS Maud Gonne to W. B. Yeats, Arrens, Aug. 26, 1914. Collection of Senator Michael Yeats.

p. 296  Irish paper." *Ibid.*

p. 296  are left . . ." *Ibid.*

p. 296  swept away—" *Ibid.*

Chapter Twenty-Eight—The Terrible Sacrifice

p. 297  is preparing . . . quoting Clemenceau in Barbara W. Tuchman, *The Proud Tower* (New York, Macmillan, 1966), p. 409.

p. 297  at peace. Padraic Pearse, *Collected Works* (Dublin, 1924), p. 137; William Irvin Thompson, *The Imagination of an Insurrection* (New York, Oxford University Press, 1967; Harper Colophon, 1972), p. 89.

p. 297  watch suffering." ALS Maud Gonne to W. B. Yeats, Sept. 25, 1914.

Collection of Senator
Michael Yeats.

p. 297 real life." *Ibid.*

p. 298 this war." ALS Maud
Gonne to W. B. Yeats, Aug.
26, 1914. Collection of
Senator Michael Yeats.

p. 298 by it—" ALS Maud
Gonne to W. B. Yeats, Sept.
25, 1914. Collection of
Senator Michael Yeats.

p. 298 English footballers . . ."
*Hone*, p. 292.

p. 298 seized Ireland. Upwards of
250,000 Irishmen enlisted in
the British Army. Irish
NCOs and men killed in
Europe numbered 27,405;
and, including those who
died in hospitals in England
and Ireland, the war dead
totaled some 40,000. The
number of Irish officers lost
is not known. See Dorothy
Macardle, *The Irish Republic*
(London, Victor Gollancz,
1937; Corgi Books, 1968), p.
114n.

p. 298 National Anthem" *SY*, p.
514.

p. 299 joining it . . ." C.
Desmond Greaves, *The Life
and Times of James Connolly*
(New York, International
Publishers, 1971), p. 352.

p. 299 the same— ALS Maud
Gonne to W. B. Yeats, Nov.
7, 1914. Collection of Senator
Michael Yeats.

p. 300 some generations—" *Ibid.*

p. 300 defy both." ALS Maud
Gonne to John Quinn, Jan.
7, 1915. Quinn Papers,
NYPL.

p. 300 but Ireland." Macardle,
*The Irish Republic, op. cit.*, p.
123.

p. 301 and chilled" B. L. Reid,

*The Man from New York, John
Quinn and His Friends* (New
York, Oxford University
Press, 1968), p. 206.

p. 301 and sincerity, ALS Maud
Gonne to John Quinn, July
15, 1915. Quinn Papers,
NYPL.

p. 301 "seeking refuge." *SQ*, p.
260.

p. 301 "generous cheque"; ALS
Maud Gonne to John
Quinn, July 15, 1915. Quinn
Papers, NYPL.

p. 302 not know." *Ibid.*

p. 302 and cheated." *Ibid.*

p. 302 love her." *Ibid.*

p. 302 the trenches." Reid, *John
Quinn, op. cit.*, p. 217.

p. 302 I can." *Ibid.*, p. 216.

p. 303 winter's night. *LE*, p. 600.
ALS W. B. Yeats to Henry
James, Aug. 20, 1915. See also
*CP*, p. 153; "On Being Asked
for a War Poem."

p. 303 shall die. Pearse, *Collected
Works, op. cit.*, p. 25;
Thompson, *Imagination of an
Insurrection, op. cit.*, p. 123.

p. 303 Fenian faith." F. S. L.
Lyons, *Ireland Since the
Famine* (London,
Weidenfeld, 1971;
Collins/Fontana,
1973), p. 337.

p. 303 Spring fighting." ALS
Maud Gonne to John
Quinn, Feb. 4, 1916. Quinn
Papers, NYPL.

p. 304 same way!" *Ibid.*

p. 304 the war! *Ibid.*

p. 304 redeem Ireland." Pearse,
*Collected Works, op. cit.*, p. 98;
Thompson, *Imagination of an
Insurrection, op. cit.*, p. 89.

p. 304 by force." Thompson,
*Imagination of an Insurrection,
op. cit.*, p. 89.

p. 304   of ammunition, George Dangerfield, *The Damnable Question* (Boston, Toronto, Little-Brown, 1976); p. 166.

p. 305   Fairyhouse races. On April 24 there were only III officers and 2,316 troops stationed in Dublin itself. See J. Bowyer Bell, *The Secret Army, The IRA 1916–1970* (New York, John Day, 1971), p. 10.

p. 305   her freedom." Desmond Ryan, *The Rising* (Dublin, Golden Eagle Books, 1949; 1966), p. 127.

p. 305   perfunctory cheers" *Ibid.*, p. 125.

p. 305   "At last!" *Ibid.*, p. 126.

p. 306   "terrible slaughter," *SY*, pp. 532–533.

p. 306   Irish Republic." Henry Summerfield, *That Myriad Minded Man* (Totowa, New Jersey, Rowman and Littlefield, 1975), p. 177.

p. 306   twenty to one Lyons, *Ireland Since the Famine, op. cit.*, p. 372.

p. 306   there glaring . . ." Ulick O'Connor, *The Troubles* (Indianapolis/New York, Bobbs-Merrill, 1975), p. 84.

p. 307   my men," *Ibid.*, p. 86.

p. 307   of it." Maire nic Shiubhlaigh and Edward Kenny, *The Splendid Years* (Dublin, James Duffy and Co., 1955), p. 185.

p. 307   in Ireland," ALS Maud Gonne to John Quinn, April 30, 1916. Quinn Papers, NYPL.

p. 307   get over." *Ibid.*

p. 308   O'Connell Street The name of Sackville Street was changed May 5, 1924, to O'Connell Street. Information obtained from Dublin Corporation, Engineering Department.

p. 308   and dying . . ." *LE*, p. 613. ALS W. B. Yeats to Lady Gregory, May 11, 1916.

p. 308   born again.' " *Ibid.*

p. 308   the tragedy—" ALS Maud Gonne to John Quinn, May 11, 1916. Quinn Papers, NYPL.

p. 308   to me." *Ibid.*

p. 309   nothing else." *Ibid.*

p. 309   English paper." *Ibid.*

p. 309   always desired—" ALS Maud Gonne to John Quinn, Aug. 16, 1916. Quinn Papers, NYPL. Father Augustine, the Franciscan who was with MacBride at the time of his execution in Kilmainham jail, not only wrote to Maud and to MacBride's mother, but later set down a full account of the death of a hero. ". . . He asked quietly not to have his hands bound and promised to remain perfectly still. 'Sorry, sir,' the soldier answered, 'but these are the orders.' Then he requested not to be blindfolded, and a similar answer was given. Turning slightly aside, he said to me, quite naturally in a soft voice: 'You know, Father Augustine, I've often looked down their guns before.' Later a piece of white paper is pinned above his heart, and, inspired by the Holy spirit, I whisper into his ear: 'We are all sinners. Offer up your life for any faults or sins of the past.' And this brave man, fearless of death, responds like a child, yet firmly: 'I'm glad you told me that, Father. I will.'

"Then two soldiers and myself now move along the corridor, turn to the left and enter a yard where the firing squad of twelve is already waiting with loaded rifles. Six now kneel on one knee and behind them six stand. He faces them about fifty feet from the guns, two or three feet from the wall.

"The two soldiers withdraw to the left near the Governor and the Doctor, and I, oblivious of all but him, stand close at his right, in prayer.

"The officer approaches, takes me gently by the arm and leads me to a position below himself at the right.

"He speaks a word. The prisoner stiffens and expands his chest. Then quickly, a silent signal, a loud volley, and the body collapses in a heap." ALS Father Augustine to Maud Gonne, June 22, 1916.

In 1917 Maud Gonne sent John Quinn a copy of Father Augustine's letter of June 22, 1916. She added a postscript: "Through my solicitor, Mr. Feury, I found out that after the execution at Kilmainham the body was interred along with the rest at Arbour Hill. . . . Mr. Feury said the English authorities would not allow any of the leaders of the executed men to be exhumed and interred in Glasnevin as I wished Major MacBride to have been. I do not mind, for he is with his comrades and England is powerless to dishonour their memories." ALS Maud Gonne to John Quinn, June 4, 1917. Quinn Papers, NYPL.

p. 309    national loss." *Ibid.*

p. 310    a complexion." *Hone*, p. 307.

p. 310    get old." *Ibid.*

Chapter Twenty-Nine— Transformations

p. 311    is born. *CP*, pp. 179–180; "Easter 1916," Sept. 25, 1916.

p. 312    casual comedy; *Ibid.*

p. 312    is born. . . . *CP*, pp. 179–180; "Easter 1916," published 1920.

p. 312    political prisoners." *Hone*, pp. 307–308.

p. 312    of life . . ." Maud Gonne MacBride, "Yeats and Ireland," *Scattering Branches, Tributes to the Memory of W. B. Yeats* (New York, Macmillan, 1940), pp. 31–32.

p. 312    his mind." *Ibid.*

p. 312    more intense . . ." *SY*, p. 548.

p. 313    the dishes." *W. B. Yeats and T. T. Sturge Moore, Their Correspondence, 1901–1937* (London, Routledge and Kegan Paul, 1953), ed. Ursala Bridge, p. 28.

p. 313    her memory. B. L. Reid, *The Man from New York, John Quinn and His Friends* (New

York, Oxford University Press, 1968), p. 243.

p. 313 into English." ALS Maud Gonne to John Quinn, Aug. 16, 1916. Quinn Papers, NYPL.

p. 313 Jeanne d'Arc.' " William Butler Yeats, "Per Amica Silentia Lunae," *Mythologies* (New York, Macmillan, 1959; Collier Books, 1969), p. 368.

p. 313 Dublin Catholics" *Hone*, p. 308.

p. 313 a spoon." ALS Ezra Pound to John Quinn, Aug. 15, 1916. Quinn Papers, NYPL.

p. 314 great success." *Hone*, p. 308.

p. 314 barbarous tongue. *CP*, p. 120; "Two Years Later."

p. 314 looks wonderful." ALS Maud Gonne to John Quinn, Oct. 8, 1916. Quinn Papers, NYPL.

p. 315 a squint." *Ibid.*

p. 315 live in!" ALS Maud Gonne to John Quinn, Nov. 24, 1916. Quinn Papers, NYPL.

p. 315 of tyranny . . ." *Ibid.*

p. 315 not gay!" ALS Maud Gonne to John Quinn, March 11, 1917. Quinn Papers, NYPL.

p. 316 prison yard. Unsigned letter in the National Library, Dublin

p. 317 been better . . ." ALS Maud Gonne to John Quinn, March 11, 1917. Quinn Papers, NYPL.

p. 317 other characters . . ." ALS Maud Gonne to John Quinn, May 12, 1917. Quinn Papers, NYPL.

p. 317 by Joyce," *Ibid.*

p. 318 in Normandy." ALS Maud Gonne to John Quinn, July 30, 1917. Quinn Papers, NYPL.

p. 318 wood, etc." *Ibid.*

p. 318 peace advocate— *Ibid.*

p. 318 the impulse.' " *LE*, p. 628. ALS W. B. Yeats to Lady Gregory, Aug. 12, 1917.

p. 319 yet encountered." *Ibid.*, p. 631.

p. 319 with me.' " *Ibid.*, p. 632.

p. 319 tranquil life." ALS Ezra Pound to John Quinn, Sept. 20, 1917. Quinn Papers, NYPL.

p. 319 something wild," *LE*, p. 632. ALS W. B. Yeats to Lady Gregory, Aug. 12, 1917.

p. 320 art school." *Hone*, p. 310.

p. 320 of time!" ALS Arthur Symons to John Quinn, Nov. 11, 1917. Quinn Papers, NYPL.

p. 320 Willie's verse . . ." Reid, *John Quinn, op. cit.*, p. 308. ALS Lily Yeats to John Quinn, Dec. 10, 1917.

p. 320 with Pound. Years later, in answer to questions about the perfection of his writing and speaking style in English, Sean MacBride explained that he had been fortunate in having as his tutors the two foremost writers of his time, Yeats and Pound.

p. 320 "strangely exotic," ALS Arthur Symons to John Quinn, Oct. 13, 1918. Quinn Papers, NYPL.

p. 321 Iseult Gonne." *Ibid.*

p. 321 red-bearded egotist. Information from author's conversation with Francis Stuart, Dublin, 1972. See also

Francis Stuart, *Black-List, Section H*, p. 25.

p. 321 paint soldiers." ALS Maud Gonne to John Quinn, Dec. 8, 1917. Quinn Papers, NYPL.

p. 321 and Verlaine." Reid, *John Quinn, op. cit.*, p. 304.

p. 321 for France.' " *Ibid.*

p. 321 *will* be." ALS Maud Gonne to John Quinn, Oct. 24, 1917. Quinn Papers, NYPL.

p. 321 as bad." ALS Maud Gonne to John Quinn, n.d. (received Sept. 14, 1917). Quinn Papers, NYPL. Sir Bryan T. Mahon replaced General Maxwell as Commander of Forces in Ireland.

p. 322 the country. F. S. L. Lyons, *Ireland Since the Famine* (London, Weidenfeld, 1971; Collins/Fontana, 1973), p. 390.

p. 322 the Volunteers. Among them were Griffith, De Valera, Count Plunkett, William Cosgrave, Con Markievicz, Mrs. Tom Clarke. Michael Collins of the Volunteers had evaded arrest. Except for Dr. McCartan, who was in America, every Sinn Fein M.P. was now in jail.

p. 322 to live." Dorothy Macardle, *The Irish Republic* (London, Victor Gollancz, 1937; Corgi Books, 1968), p. 213.

p. 322 thought otherwise . . ." Vera Ryder, *The Little Victims Play* (London, Robert Hale, 1974), p. 33.

p. 323 country, Ireland." ALS Maud Gonne to John Quinn, Dec. 8, 1917. Quinn Papers, NYPL.

p. 323 least—significant." *Irish Nation*, Feb. 16, 1918. NLI.

p. 323 comes Mother," Taped interview, 1934 (?). NLI.

p. 323 recognize me." *Ibid.*

p. 324 of death. *CP*, p. 151; "Broken Dreams."

p. 324 Sean O'Casey G. B. Shaw wrote O'Casey on Dec. 3, 1919: "I am afraid the National question will insist on getting settled before the Labour question. That is why the National question is a nuisance and a bore: but it can't be helped." D. Krause (ed.), *Letters of Sean O'Casey*, Vol. 1, p. 88.

p. 325 her condolences. Susan and Thomas Cahill, *A Literary Guide to Ireland* (New York, Charles Scribner's Sons, 1973), p. 113. In an interview at Coole Park in the 1970s the gardener, Tom O'Loughlin, then in his eighties, told how in his youth when he worked for Lady Gregory he had played football with Sean while at Coole. No other record of Maud's visiting Coole is available. If she did go, it was probably before 1919.

p. 325 greatest intensity." *LE*, p. 649. ALS W. B. Yeats to Clement Shorter, May 17, 1918.

p. 325 "German plot" Macardle, *The Irish Republic, op. cit.*, p. 236.

p. 326 indefinite time" *Ibid.*

p. 326   wild Irishwomen."
Elizabeth Coxhead, *Daughters
of Erin, Five Women of the
Irish Renascence* (London,
Secker and Warburg, 1965),
p. 65.

p. 326   politics today." Anne
Marreco, *The Rebel Countess*
(London, Weidenfeld and
Nicolson, 1967; Corgi Books,
1969), p. 237n.

p. 327   application up." *Ibid.*, pp.
66–67.

p. 327   in prison . . ." A. Norman
Jeffares, *W. B. Yeats, Man and
Poet* (London, Routledge and
Kegan Paul, 1949; 1966), p.
188.

p. 328   they lie? *CP*, p. 181; "On a
Political Prisoner."

p. 328   without delay." Medical
Report, Oct. 22, 1918. Copy
sent to John Quinn by Ezra
Pound, Oct. 24, 1918. Quinn
Papers, NYPL.

p. 328   this country." ALS John
Quinn to Iseult Gonne,
Nov. 7, 1918. Quinn Papers,
NYPL.

p. 328   been released. Kathleen
Clarke, who also became
seriously ill in Holloway,
was not released until
March 1919. Constance
Markievicz was freed on
Feb. 20, 1919. By then she
had become the first woman
elected to the British
Parliament, but as a Sinn
Fein M.P. She naturally
refused to take her seat at
Westminster.

p. 328   time being." ALS John
Quinn to Iseult Gonne,
Nov. 7, 1918. Quinn Papers,
NYPL.

p. 328   and ill," ALS Ezra Pound

to John Quinn, Dec. 28, 1918.
Quinn Papers, NYPL.

p. 328   solitary boy." ALS W. B.
Yeats to John Quinn, July
23, 1918. Quinn Papers,
NYPL.

p. 328   Irish "monomania." ALS
Ezra Pound to John Quinn,
Nov. 15, 1918. Quinn Papers,
NYPL.

p. 328   feeling there . . . *Ibid.*

p. 328   his career." ALS Ezra
Pound to John Quinn, Nov.
20, 1918. Quinn Papers,
NYPL.

p. 328   "unsuitable" climate. *Ibid.*

p. 329   were flunkies. ALS Ezra
Pound to John Quinn, Nov.
15, 1918. Quinn Papers.
NYPL.

p. 329   Forty-nine thousand
Macardle, *The Irish Republic,
op. cit.*, p. 242.

p. 329   by name?" ALS Maud
Gonne to John Quinn, n.d.,
received Sept. 14, 1917. Quinn
Papers, NYPL.

p. 329   of Ulster." Macardle, *The
Irish Republic, op. cit.*, p. 243.
ALS Lloyd George to Bonar
Law, Oct.–Nov. 1918.

p. 329   87,500 troops George
Dangerfield, *The Damnable
Question* (Boston,
Atlantic–Little, Brown,
1976), p. 298; quoting Alan J.
Ward, *Ireland and
Anglo-American Relations,
1899–1911* (London, 1967).

p. 330   to take . . ." ALS Ezra
Pound to John Quinn, Dec.
28, 1918. Quinn Papers,
NYPL.

p. 330   Red Cross Nurse.
Interview, Radio Telifis
Eireann, NLI.

p. 330   in peace." ALS Ezra
Pound to John Quinn, Dec.

2, 1918. Quinn Papers, NYPL.

p. 330   of mischief." ALS Ezra Pound to John Quinn, Dec. 28, 1918. Quinn Papers, NYPL.

p. 330   of keepers." ALS Ezra Pound to John Quinn, Dec. 2, 1918. Quinn Papers, NYPL.

p. 330   her house. *Hone,* pp. 318–319.

p. 331   public building.'" *SY,* p. 350.

p. 331   angry wind? *CP,* pp. 186–187. "A Prayer for My Daughter."

Chapter Thirty—The Terrible Necessity

p. 332   against injustice. Albert Camus, *The Rebel (L'Homme Révolté)* (Paris, Gallimard, 1951; New York, Vintage Books, 1956), trans. Anthony Bower, p. 169.

p. 333   Madame Gonne MacBride. *Hone,* p. 319.

p. 333   tragic sight." B. L. Reid, *The Man from New York, John Quinn and His Friends* (New York, Oxford University Press, 1968), p. 388. ALS W. B. Yeats to John Quinn, Jan. 21, 1919.

p. 334   much better." *Lady Gregory's Journals* (New York, Macmillan, 1947), ed. Lennox Robinson, p. 57.

p. 334   more picturesque," *LE,* p. 658. ALS W. B. Yeats to John Quinn, July 11, 1919.

p. 335   Sinn Fein is.'" George Dangerfield, *The Damnable Question* (Boston, Atlantic–Little, Brown, 1976), p. 304.

p. 335   going back," Maire Comerford, *The First Dail* (Dublin, Joe Clarke, 1969), p. 51.

p. 335   and welfare." *Ibid.,* p. 115.

p. 336   Irish people." Dorothy Macardle, *The Irish Republic* (London, Victor Gollancz, 1937; Corgi Books, 1968), p. 271.

p. 337   the Bench." *Ibid.*

p. 338   never accepted." *Ibid.,* p. 296.

p. 339   a "dunce," *CP,* p. 333; "Why Should Not Old Men Be Mad?" "A girl that knew all Dante once/Live to bear children to a dunce . . ."

p. 339   the young." *SY,* p. 300. The quotation, which is printed under illustration following p. 300, is from Lady Gregory's play, *Devorgilla.*

p. 339   so skeptical," W. B. Yeats, "Modern Ireland," *The Irish Renaissance* (Dublin, Dolmen Press, 1965), eds. Robin Skelton and David R. Clark, p. 23.

p. 339   strong hand." Macardle, *The Irish Republic, op. cit.,* p. 314.

p. 340   their rank. *Ibid.,* p. 315. Black and Tans were paid ten shillings per day, the Auxiliaries a pound. By 1921 the armed police forces totaled 14,174. In addition there were about 50,000 British troops in Ireland under General Macready. See Dangerfield, *The Damnable Question, op. cit.,* pp. 322–323. The full strength of the IRA may have been as much as 15,000, but the largest number on active duty at any time was probably about 5,000, or by Collins's estimate, 3,000. See F. S. L. Lyons, *Ireland Since the Famine* (London, Weidenfeld, 1971; Collins/Fontana, 1973), pp. 416–417.

p. 340  doing it" *Lady Gregory's Journals, op. cit.*, p. 152.

p. 340  of them." *Ibid.*, pp. 152–153.

p. 341  "water-filled silences" *Hone*, p. 330.

p. 341  the glen," *Ibid.*

p. 341  tweed trousers." *Ibid.*

p. 341  writing something. . . .' " *Ibid.*

p. 341  my words . . ." *CP*, p. 212; "On a Picture of a Black Centaur by Edmund Dulac."

p. 342  Croke Park, Bloody Sunday, Nov. 21, 1919.

p. 342  was hanged. ALS Maud Gonne to Ethel Mannin, Jan. 8, 1946. NLI. Maud Gonne remembered the year of Whelan's execution as 1918, instead of March 14, 1921, a day of public mourning in Dublin.

p. 342  a 'Parabellum,' " Ernie O'Malley, *Army Without Banners* (Boston, Houghton Mifflin, 1937), pp. 248–249. A parabellum is an automatic pistol.

p. 342  "brain waves." Conversation with author, Dublin, 1973.

p. 343  each other.' " *Ibid.*

p. 343  our spirit." ALS Maud Gonne to John Quinn, Feb. 21, 1921. Quinn Papers. NYPL.

p. 343  Viceroy's sister." *Ibid.*

p. 344  Black and Tans. *Ibid.*

p. 344  three months. Francis

Stuart, *Black-List, Section H* (Carbondale and Edwardsville, Illinois, Southern Illinois Press, 1971), p. 46.

p. 345  became unassailable." Macardle, *The Irish Republic, op. cit.*, p. 418.

p. 345  utmost patience." Sean Cronin, *The McGarrity Papers* (Tralee, Republic of Ireland, Anvil Books, 1972), p. 104.

p. 345  was signed. Total Irish casualties in the Black and Tan war are difficult to estimate; not all civilian dead and wounded were listed. From Jan. 1, 1919, to July 12, 1921, there were at least 752 IRA and civilian dead, 866 wounded. See Lyons, *Ireland Since the Famine, op. cit.*, p. 417.

p. 345  hear music." ALS Maud Gonne to Ethel Mannin, 1949, 1950(?). NLI.

p. 345  out everything." *Ibid.*

p. 345  Opera house." *Ibid.*

p. 346  terrible war," Lyons, *Ireland Since the Famine, op. cit.*, p. 447 n.

p. 346  death warrant." *Ibid.*, p. 439.

p. 346  changing life." Maud Gonne MacBride, "Yeats and Ireland," *Scattering Branches, Tributes to the Memory of W. B. Yeats* (New York, Macmillan, 1940), ed. Stephen Gwynn.

p. 346  speakers against The other women deputies were Mary McSwiney, T. D., widow of Cork's Lord Mayor; Mrs. Callaghan, widow of Limerick's Lord Mayor;

Mrs. Pearse, mother of Padraic and William Pearse; Mrs. Tom Clarke, widow of the Easter 1916 martyr; and Dr. Ada English. All were accused of having a personal view.

p. 346    for chaos." Lyons, *Ireland Since the Famine, op. cit.*, p. 564.

p. 347    inherit bitterness." *LE*, p. 675. ALS W. B. Yeats to Olivia Shakespear, Dec. 22, 1921.

p. 347    the fox." *Ibid.*

p. 348    of intrigue," Robert Brennan, *Allegiance* (Dublin, Brown and Nolan, 1950), p. 335.

p. 348    in London. *SQ*, p. 173.

p. 348    wild-eyed refugees." Maud Gonne MacBride, "The Real Case Against Partition," *Capuchin Annual*, 1943, p. 321. NLI.

p. 348    with terror" *Ibid.*

p. 349    the government.'" *Ibid.*

p. 349    *has promised . . .*" *Ibid.*

p. 349    Four Courts In an article in 1923, Maud Gonne MacBride quoted from debates in the House of Commons (*Hansard*, June 26, 1922, vol. 155, no. 84) to explain her conviction that the Provisional Government acted under pressure from Churchill, who feared a concerted action by Republicans against Ulster: Mr. Churchill: "If it (the occupation of the Four Courts) does not come to an end, either from weakness, from want of courage, or some other even less creditable reasons it is not

brought to an end, then it is my duty to say, on behalf of His Majesty's Government, that we shall regard the Treaty as having been formerly violated." Later in the same debate, Mr. Lloyd George: "We have communicated our views to the Provisional Government on this matter."
Mr. Lyle Samuel: "Are you giving them a time limit?"
Mr. Lloyd George: "I do not want at the present moment to give any details of the communication which we have sent to the Provisional Government. I would rather they acted on their own initiative rather than with the appearance that they are doing it under compulsion from the British Government."
Maud Gonne MacBride, "How the Free State Persisted in Making Civil War," *Eire*, Sept 22, 1923. NLI.

p. 350    of peace," *Ibid.*

p. 351    keep order." Elizabeth Coxhead, *Daughters of Erin, Five Women of the Irish Renascence* (London, Secker and Warburg, 1965), p. 69.

p. 352    "renegade" Englishman, Macardle, *The Irish Republic, op. cit.*, p. 740.

p. 352    toward Ireland." *Ibid.*, p. 743.

p. 353    Civil War. Lyons, *Ireland Since the Famine, op. cit.*, p. 467. In the year of the Civil War the Free State government executed seventy-seven prisoners, more than three times the number executed by the British in 1920–21 during the Black and Tan War. See Macardle, *The Irish Republic, op. cit.,* pp. 912–914.

p. 353   been arrested." Maud Gonne MacBride, "Prisoners in the Free State," *An Phoblacht,* March 12, 1932. NLI.

p. 353   Terry did." *Freeman's Journal,* Nov. 11, 1922. NLI.

p. 353   of men." *Irish Times,* Nov. 9, 1922. NLI.

p. 353   the crush. Eoin Neeson, *The Civil War in Ireland 1922–1923* (Dublin, Mercier Press, 1969), p. 326.

p. 354   our work." *An Phoblacht, op. cit.*

p. 354   not given." *SQ,* p. 15.

p. 354   MacBride's House." *Freeman's Journal,* Nov. 13, 1922. NLI.

p. 354   them ablaze." *Ibid.*

p. 355   future generations. Reid, *The Man from New York, John Quinn and His Friends, op. cit.,* p. 243.

p. 355   my papers." ALS Maud Gonne to J. B. Hone, Feb. 17, 1940. NLI. After Yeats's death, in 1939, Mrs. Yeats returned to Maud many of the letters she had written to Yeats. They are in the possession of the MacBride family and are not available for research.

Chapter Thirty-One—The Fanatic Heart

p. 356   Sean MacBride Today MacBride spells his name Sean. His mother used that spelling in her later years instead of Seagan.

p. 356   "option out." Northern Ireland included a fifth of the total area of the country, 40 percent of its taxable capacity, the bulk of its industry, and what had been in the 1911 census nearly a third of the population. See D. R. O'Connor Lysaght, *The Republic of Ireland* (Cork, Ireland, Mercier Press, 1970), p. 73.

p. 357   British Empire." Maud Gonne MacBride, "Yeats and Ireland," *Scattering Branches, Tributes to the Memory of W. B. Yeats* (New York, Macmillan, 1940), ed. Stephen Gwynn, p. 25.

p. 357   the government. *LE,* p. 697. ALS W. B. Yeats to Olivia Shakespear, Jan. 5, 1923.

p. 357   left us." *LE,* p. 604. ALS W. B. Yeats to Lily Yeats, Dec. 10, 1915.

p. 357   being shot," *LE,* p. 694. ALS W. B. Yeats to Edmund Dulac, Dec. 1, 1922.

p. 357   their profession." *LE,* p. 698. ALS W. B. Yeats to Olivia Shakespear, March 22, 1923.

p. 358   of nothing." *Ibid.*

p. 358   the paying." *Seventy Years Young, Memories of Elizabeth, Countess of Fingall* (New York, Dutton, 1939), told to Pamela Hinkson, p. 414.

p. 358   at Killarney. Sean Cronin, *The McGarrity Papers* (Tralee, Republic of Ireland, Anvil Books, 1972), p. 136.

p. 358  be terrifying." B. L. Reid, *The Man from New York, John Quinn and His Friends* (New York, Oxford University Press, 1968), p. 583. ALS Susan Mitchell to John Quinn, Feb. 22, 1923.

p. 359  the sick." *Hone*, p. 357.

p. 359  witches' hats." *LE*, p. 697. ALS W. B. Yeats to Olivia Shakespear, Jan. 5, 1923.

p. 359  either way?" ALS Maud Gonne MacBride to Ethel Mannin, May 15, 1946. NLI.

p. 359  dump arms. Tim Pat Coogan, *The IRA* (London, Collins/Fontana, 1971), p. 56.

p. 360  for him) . . ." *Sinn Fein*, Aug. 25, 1923. NLI.

p. 360  College Green. Conversation with Terence de Vere White, Dublin, 1973.

p. 360  by enemies," Conversation with Maire Comerford, Dublin, 1973.

p. 360  the ground." *Ibid.*

p. 361  their lips" Monk Gibbon, *The Masterpiece and the Man* (New York, Macmillan, 1959), p. 72.

p. 361  the south." *Sinn Fein*, Aug. 17, 1923. NLI.

p. 361  "insincere" *Lady Gregory's Journals* (New York, Macmillan, 1947), ed. Lennox Robinson, p. 189.

p. 361  Free State." *Sinn Fein*, Aug. 25, 1923. NLI.

p. 362  us all." *Sinn Fein*, July 5, 1924. NLI.

p. 363  "tame hare." *CP*, p. 166; "Two Songs of a Fool."

p. 363  public man" *CP*, p. 213; "Among School Children."

p. 363  the wind" *Ibid.*

p. 363  million pounds. F.S.L. Lyons, *Ireland Since the Famine* (London, Weidenfeld, 1971; Collins/Fontana, 1973), p. 468n.

p. 364  of Ireland." Emmet Larkin, *James Larkin* (London, New English Library, 1968), p. 252; quoting *Freeman's Journal*, Aug. 26, 1924.

p. 364  *opium dream.*" *Hone*, p. 369.

p. 365  of capitalism . . ." *Eire*, Sept. 20, 1921. NLI.

p. 365  that order." *Ibid.*

p. 365  Republican ideal . . ." *Ibid.*

p. 365  7 children!" *Sinn Fein*, May 9, 1925. NLI.

p. 366  the sea," *Ibid.*

p. 366  heart out." *Ibid.*

p. 366  next station." *Ibid.*

p. 367  the Mass." *Sinn Fein*, April 18, 1925. NLI.

p. 367  yourselves again." Donal Dorcey, "The Big Occasions," *The Story of the Abbey Theatre* (London, Four Square Books, 1967), ed. Sean McCann, pp. 150–151.

p. 367  then O'Casey?" *Ibid.*

p. 367  the play," *The Letters of Sean O'Casey, 1910–1941*, Vol. I (New York, Macmillan, 1975), ed. David Krause, pp. 167–168. ALS Mrs. Hanna Sheehy-Skeffington to *Irish Independent*, Feb. 15, 1926.

p. 368  popular opinion." *Ibid.*

p. 368  about heroes," Ibid., p. 180. *Irish Independent*, March 2, 1926, report concerning debate between O'Casey and Mrs. Sheehy-Skeffington.

p. 368  live in." Ibid., p. 175. ALS Sean O'Casey to *Irish Independent*, Feb. 26, 1926.

p. 368  over him." William Irvin Thompson, *The Imagination of an Insurrection* (New York, Harper Colophon, 1972), p. 204; quoting Sean O'Casey, *Autobiographies II* (London, 1963), p. 149.

p. 368    daughter still." Sean O'Casey, *Inishfallen Fare Thee Well* (New York, Macmillan, 1949), p. 244.

p. 368    the message. *Hone*, p. 393.

p. 369    great hope." Francis MacManus, "The Delicate High Head," *Capuchin Annual*, 1960, pp. 128–129. NLI.

p. 369    I have." Conor Cruise O'Brien, "Passion and Cunning: An Essay on the Politics of W. B. Yeats," *In Excited Reverie* (New York, St. Martin's Press, 1965), eds. A. Norman Jeffares and K. G. W. Cross, p. 247 and n. ALS W. B. Yeats to Olivia Shakespear, April 1933.

p. 369    of jurors." *LE*, p. 727. ALS W. B. Yeats to Olivia Shakespear, July or Aug. 1927.

p. 370    jealous meddler" *Lady Gregory's Journals, op. cit.*, pp. 166 and 238.

p. 370    drawn up"; . . . *CP*, p. 300; "Beautiful Lofty Things."

p. 371    trod unflinchingly." Jacqueline Van Voris, *Constance de Markievicz* (Amherst, Mass., University of Massachusetts Press, 1967), p. 349.

p. 371    ease and station" *CP*, p. 229; "In Memory of Eva Gore-Booth and Con Markievicz."

p. 371    both Beautiful . . . *Ibid.*

p. 371    her manner. Conversation with Bairbre MacDonagh Redmond, Dublin, 1973.

p. 371    her hopes." Mary Colum, *Life and the Dream* (Garden City, N.Y., Doubleday, 1947), pp. 278, 280.

p. 372    oppressed races." *LE*, p. 739. ALS W. B. Yeats to Lady Gregory, April 1, 1928.

p. 372    your shoulder." Conversation with Bairbre MacDonagh Redmond, Dublin, 1973.

Chapter Thirty-Two—La Grande Patriote

p. 373    Grande Patriote." Conversation with Mrs. Sean MacBride, Dublin, 1973.

p. 373    from Millevoye. Francis Stuart, *Black-List, Section H* (Carbondale and Edwardsville, Illinois, Southern Illinois University Press, 1971), p. 147.

p. 374    her favorite. Conversations with Maud Gonne's grandchildren, Anna MacBride White, Tiernan MacBride, and Ian Stuart; Dublin and Laragh, 1973.

p. 374    special treat. Letter to author from the Reverend Mother of Holy Faith Convent, Trinidad, B.W.I., daughter of Eileen MacBride, Sept. 7, 1976.

p. 375    a governess. Jonathan Gathorne-Hardy, *The Unnatural History of the Nanny* (New York, Dial, 1973), pp. 126–129.

p. 375    for Maud. Conversations with family. Dublin, 1975.

p. 375    Great War ALS Maud

Gonne to W. B. Yeats, July 25, 1914. Collection of Senator Michael Yeats.

p. 376   a tyranny." *Uncollected Prose by W. B. Yeats,* Vol. II (New York, Columbia University Press, 1976), eds. John P. Frayne and Colton Johnson, pp. 487–488.

p. 376   badly written." *Ibid.,* p. 480n.

p. 376   small ambitions.' " W. B. Yeats, *A Vision* (New York, Macmillan, 1937; Collier Books, 1975), p. 6.

p. 377   of arms." J. Bowyer Bell, *The Secret Army, The IRA, 1916–1970* (New York, John Day, 1971), p. 77.

p. 378   to be." *Ibid.,* pp. 80, 95n.; quoting Irish Free State, Department of Justice, Memorandum on Revolutionary Organizations (S5864), April 5, 1930.

p. 378   informers beware. *Ibid.,* p. 86.

p. 378   the house." *An Phoblacht,* July 25, 1931. NLI.

p. 379   Sunday mornings." *An Phoblacht,* March 12, 1932. NLI.

p. 379   living memory." *An Phoblacht,* March 19, 1932. NLI.

p. 379   of Ireland." *Ibid.*

p. 380   necessity remains." *An Phoblacht,* July 16, 1932. NLI.

p. 380   public life." *Ibid.*

p. 380   Mrs. Desparate." Conrad A. Balliet, "Michael MacLiammoir Recalls Maud Gonne MacBride," an interview in *Journal of Irish Literature* (Proscenium Press, University of Delaware, May 1977), p. 49.

p. 381   black orchid," *Ibid.,* p. 45.

p. 381   deserted her Conversation with Professor Roger McHugh, University College, Dublin, 1973.

p. 381   a fan. Conversation with Liam Redmond, Dublin, 1973.

p. 381   to suggest." Conrad A. Balliet, interview in *Journal of Irish Literature, op. cit.,* p. 54.

p. 382   be practical.' " *Ibid.,* p. 48.

p. 382   into power." *LE,* p. 805. ALS W. B. Yeats to Olivia Shakespear, Feb. 2 (perhaps), 1933.

p. 383   turned amicable." *Ibid.,* p. 811. ALS W. B. Yeats to Olivia Shakespear, July 13, 1933. The assumption seems legitimate that the name not supplied is that of Maud Gonne. In other letters to Olivia Shakespear Yeats used the initials M. G. Maud Gonne was still alive when Wade's collection was published.

p. 383   Northern worker." Brendan Behan, *Brendan Behan's Island* (London, Bernard Geis, dist. by Random House, 1962), p. 29.

p. 383   of going. Francis Stuart, "The Thomas Davis Lectures," Radio Eireann, *The Yeats We Knew* (Cork, Ireland, Mercier Press, 1969), ed. Francis MacManus, pp. 39–40.

p. 384   educated classes . . ." *LE,* pp. 811–812. ALS W. B. Yeats to Olivia Shakespear, July 13, 1933.

p. 384   bullet wounds." ALS

Maud Gonne to Ethel
Mannin, Feb. 15, 1947. NLI.
p. 384   return ticket. Interview.
p. 385   of Ireland." *Hone,* p. 473.
p. 388   to Freedom. *SQ,* p. vii.
p. 388   "scandalous" Conversation
with Bairbre MacDonagh
Redmond, Dublin, 1973.
p. 388   libel action. ALS
Maud Gonne MacBride to
Victor Gollancz, Sept. 6,
193?(8). Files of Victor
Gollancz Ltd.
p. 388   a refusal. ALS Maud
Gonne MacBride to Victor
Gollancz, July 10, 1938. Files
of Victor Gollancz Ltd.
p. 388   misprint quotations." *LE,*
pp. 909–910. ALS W. B.
Yeats to Maud Gonne
MacBride, June 16, 1938.
p. 389   in full. ALS Maud
Gonne MacBride to Victor
Gollancz, August n.d., 1938.
Files of Victor Gollancz
Ltd.
p. 389   British Empire. ALS
Maud Gonne MacBride to
Victor Gollancz, Sept. 6,
1938. Files of Victor Gollancz
Ltd.
p. 389   may spring." *John
O'London's Weekly,* Nov. 18,
1938. NLI.
p. 389   amuse you." *LE,* p. 910.
ALS W. B. Yeats to Maud
Gonne MacBride, June 16,
1938.
p. 390   of slaves" W. B. Yeats,
"From 'On the Boiler,'
1939," writings selected by
Mrs. W. B. Yeats, *W. B.
Yeats, Explorations* (New
York, Macmillan, 1962;
Collier Books, 1973), p.
424.
p. 390   armoured horses." *Ibid.,* p.
425.

p. 390   the nation"— *LE,* p. 915.
ALS W. B. Yeats to Edith
Shackleton Heald, Sept. 4,
1938.
p. 390   bed-hot harlot." W. B.
Yeats, *Explorations, op. cit.,* p.
443.
p. 390   and Morris," *LE,* p. 872.
ALS W. B. Yeats to Ethel
Mannin, Dec. 11, 1936.
p. 390   Wicked Man," *CP,* p. 307;
"The Wild Old Wicked
Man."
p. 391   social systems." Maud
Gonne MacBride, "Fascism,
Communism and Ireland,"
*Ireland Today,* Vol. 3, 1938, p.
241. NLI.
p. 391   fomenting war." *Ibid.*
p. 391   systems agree." *Ibid.,* p.
243.
p. 391   a nation." *Ibid.,* pp.
242–243.
p. 391   "Yeats," Oliver St. John
Gogarty, *As I Was Going
Down Sackville Street* (New
York, Reynal and Hitchcock,
1937), p. 105.
p. 392   face life." *Letters on Poetry
from W. B. Yeats to Dorothy
Wellesley* (London, Oxford
University Press, 1940; 1964),
p. 149. ALS W. B. Yeats to
Dorothy Wellesley, Nov. 20,
1937.
p. 392   hearts abeat.' " Maud
Gonne MacBride, "Yeats
and Ireland," *Scattering
Branches, Tributes to the
Memory of W. B. Yeats* (New
York, Macmillan, 1940), ed.
Stephen Gwynn, p. 25.
p. 392   What energy!" *Hone,* p.
474.
p. 392   the spectacle . . ." Sir
William Rothenstein, "Yeats
as a Painter Saw Him,"
*Scattering Branches, Tributes to*

*the Memory of W. B. Yeats, op. cit.*, ed. Stephen Gwynn, pp. 51–52.

p. 393    for him." ALS Iseult Stuart to George Yeats, n.d. Collection of Senator Michael Yeats.

p. 393    Maud Gonne MacBride ALS Maud Gonne MacBride to George Yeats, June 21, 1939. Collection of Senator Michael Yeats.

Chapter Thirty-Three—The Tower of Age

p. 394    substance right? *CP*, pp. 328–329; "A Bronze Head."

p. 395    not certain." ALS Maud Gonne MacBride to Victor Gollancz, July 21, 1938. Files of Victor Gollancz Ltd.

p. 395    go on. *Irish Press*, April 28, 1953. NLI.

p. 395    tea party." ALS Maud Gonne to Joseph Hone, July 20, 1939. NLI.

p. 395    yet achieved . . ." Maud Gonne MacBride, "Yeats and Ireland," *Scattering Branches, Tributes to the Memory of W. B. Yeats* (New York, Macmillan, 1940), ed. Stephen Gwynn, pp. 25–26.

p. 396    that results." Francis Stuart, review of new edition of SQ, *Hibernia*, April 12, 1974.

p. 396    other way." *Ibid.*

p. 396    your genius . . ." ALS Maud Gonne MacBride to Francis Stuart, n.d. Southern Illinois University Special Collections, Morris Library.

p. 397    as possible. Enno Stephan, *Spies in Ireland* (London, New English Library, Four Square Books, 1965), pp. 83–85, 100–117.

p. 397    its roots." *Ibid.*, p. 117. A year later Goertz was arrested by the Irish Government and detained in various prison camps. After the war at his request he was given asylum in Ireland, got a job in Dublin and became secretary of a relief organization, the Save the German Children Fund. In April 1947, De Valera acquiesced to the Western Allies' demand that all former agents be extradited for interrogation. Rather than return to Germany, Goertz committed suicide by swallowing poison.

p. 398    was hanged. Tim Pat Coogan, *The IRA* (London, Fontana/Collins, 1971), p. 233.

p. 398    last century," ALS Maud Gonne to Bairbre MacDonagh Redmond, March 25, 1939. Collection of Bairbre Redmond.

p. 398    another recourse. Henry B. Burnett, Jr., "Sean MacBride," *Skeptic* (New York, 1977), p. 54. *Skeptic:* "Do you think terrorism is justified today? Do you think it's necessary in order to deal with oppression?" MacBride: It's very hard to say. I think it's a question of degree. If injustice is so unbearable, so damaging, people probably have a right to react against it and defend themselves from it. If oppression amounts to genocide, for instance, people are entitled to fight back. The framers of the Universal Declaration of Human Rights recognized that; in the declaration they point out that unless human rights are protected under the rule of law, people will be driven to the use of violence." (Sean MacBride was one of the promoters of the European Convention for the Protection of Human Rights in 1948 and signatory of the Geneva [Red Cross] Conventions for the Protection of War Victims [1949]. When he was awarded the Nobel Peace Prize in 1974 for founding Amnesty International and for his work for Namibia, South West Africa, as UN Commissioner and Assistant Secretary-General of the U.N., MacBride stated in his acceptance speech: "If those vested with authority and power practice injustice, resort to torture and killing, is it not inevitable that those who are victims will react with similar methods?")

p. 399  for freedom." ALS Maud Gonne MacBride to Ethel Mannin, Nov. 20, 1945. NLI.

p. 399  aunt's scorn. Conversation with Tiernan MacBride, Dublin, 1973.

p. 399  of death." *SQ*, p. 1.

p. 399  her life." ALS Iseult Stuart to Francis Stuart, date unclear, May (?), 19(?). Southern Illinois University Special Collections, Morris Library.

p. 400  Jacobean cabinet. ALS Iseult Stuart to Francis

Stuart, date unclear, Oct. 17, 19(?). Southern Illinois University Special Collections, Morris Library.

p. 400  shall cease. *Irish Times*, May 10, 1946. NLI.

p. 400  been treated." ALS Maud Gonne MacBride to Ethel Mannin, May 15, 1946.

p. 401  their blankets." *Ibid.*

p. 401  the world." ALS Maud Gonne MacBride to Ethel Mannin, Sept. 21, 1946. NLI.

p. 402  write letters." ALS Maud Gonne MacBride to Ethel Mannin, Feb. 10, 1947 [1948]. NLI.

p. 402  a T.D. T.D. is the abbreviation for Teachta Dala, a member of the Dail.

p. 402  his popularity." ALS Maud Gonne MacBride to Ethel Mannin, Feb. 10, 1947 [1948]. NLI.

p. 402  Sinn Fein movement." *Ibid.*

p. 403  the end." Conrad A. Balliet, "Michael MacLiammoir Recalls Maud Gonne MacBride," an interview in *Journal of Irish Literature* (Newark, Delaware, University of Delaware, Proscenium Press, May 1977), p. 56.

p. 403  old age" ALS Maud Gonne MacBride to Ethel Mannin, Jan. 23, 1951. NLI.

p. 404  end emigration." *Ibid.*

p. 404  confused thinking." *Ibid.*

p. 404  2nd vol—" *Ibid.*

p. 404  of Age" Roy Foster, review of *Maud Gonne*, by Samuel Levenson, *Times Literary Supplement*, Sept. 30, 1977.

p. 404   that yourself." ALS Iseult Stuart to Francis Stuart, Aug. 24, 1949(?). Southern Illinois University Special Collections, Morris Library.

p. 404   Maud Gonne MacBride." ALS Maud Gonne MacBride to Ethel Mannin, Oct. 29, 1946. NLI.

p. 405   saw Willie . . ." ALS Maud Gonne MacBride to Ethel Mannin, Nov. 14, 1945. NLI.

p. 405   without her." ALS Maud Gonne MacBride to Ethel Mannin, April 21, 1946. NLI.

p. 405   for Hanna—" ALS Maud Gonne MacBride to Ethel Mannin, July 2, 1946. NLI.

p. 405   be worthwhile." ALS Maud Gonne MacBride to Ethel Mannin, Oct. 29, 1946. NLI.

p. 406   and lakes." *Ibid.*

p. 406   their governments." ALS Maud Gonne MacBride to Ethel Mannin, May 3, 1948. NLI.

p. 406   pass by. ALS W. B. Yeats to Ethel Mannin, August 22, 1938. NLI. See also *CP*, pp. 343–344; "Under Ben Bulben."

p. 406   Ben Bulben's head," *CP*, pp. 343–344; "Under Ben Bulben."

p. 407   and space . . ." ALS Maud Gonne MacBride to Ethel Mannin, Jan. 23, 1951. NLI.

p. 407   *protect* life—" ALS Maud Gonne MacBride to Ethel Mannin, Nov. 21, 1949. NLI.

p. 407   of affairs." ALS Maud Gonne MacBride to Ethel Mannin, n.d., possibly 1949. NLI.

p. 407   in time" ALS Maud Gonne MacBride to Ethel Mannin, n.d. NLI.

p. 407   are *indivisible.* " ALS Maud Gonne MacBride to Ethel Mannin, Oct. 9, 1951. NLI.

p. 408   it's *HELL!*" Conrad A. Balliet, an interview in *Journal of Irish Literature, op. cit.,* p. 59.

p. 408   bottle again." Conversation with Tiernan MacBride, Dublin, 1973.

p. 408   able to . . ." ALS Maud Gonne MacBride to Seumas MacManus, June 1949, Collection of Patricia MacManus.

p. 408   gifted children." ALS Maud Gonne MacBride to Seumas MacManus, July 25, 1951. Collection of Patricia MacManus.

p. 408   to become." *Ibid.*

p. 408   beautiful ruin" Mary Colum, *The Life and the Dreams* (Garden City, N.Y., Doubleday, 1947), p. 151.

p. 409   kissed it." Monk Gibbon, *The Masterpiece and the Man* (New York, Macmillan, 1959), p. 73.

p. 409   to 'starve.' " Van Wyck Brooks, *From the Shadow of the Mountain* (New York, Dutton, 1961), pp. 157–158.

p. 409   to breathe." ALS Iseult Stuart to Francis Stuart, May 2, 1953. Southern Illinois University Special Collections, Morris Library.

p. 411   Irish people. . . . *Irish Press,* April 30, 1953. NLI.